International Trade, Economic Development and National Welfare

This book presents a comprehensive analysis of contemporary issues in international trade and economic development. Emphasising the significance of economic development within policymaking, the book covers important issues like the provisioning of public goods, its implication in a liberalised regime, crime and corruption, skilled–unskilled wage inequality, income distribution and unemployment, environmental regulation and role of educational capital and informal sector. The volume deals with the impact that different aspects of international trade and investment are likely to have on the above-mentioned areas. The essays, written to honour the memory of Professor Sarbajit Chaudhuri, also examine topics that focus on public policy related to immigration of skilled workforce, political resistance and political compulsions that a democratic government might face in keeping with its commitment to tariff reforms, gender wage gap and issues related to globalisation, income distribution and unemployment.

The book will be of invaluable interest to postgraduate students, scholars and researchers of development economics, international economics and labour economics and to those working on theoretical research on applications of general equilibrium trade models in developing countries.

Kausik Gupta is Professor of Economics at the University of Calcutta, Kolkata, India. He was also former Vice-Chancellor of West Bengal State University, Barasat, West Bengal, India. He did his PhD in Economics from Jadavpur University, Kolkata, India, and his Post-Doctoral Research as a World Bank Fellow from the University of York, UK. Professor Gupta was one of the closest friends of Professor Sarbajit Chaudhuri since their Master's Level when they were classmates, did their PhD under the same supervisor, Professor Manash Ranjan Gupta, and had similarities in their research interests like Trade and Development, Labour Economics and Environmental Economics. Professor Gupta also published a large number of research papers in reputed international and national journals and has supervised a large number of PhD students. Professor Gupta's current research interest is in the field of theoretical modelling related to trade and development.

Jayanta Kumar Dwibedi is Associate Professor of Economics at Brahmananda Keshab Chandra College, Kolkata, India. He did his PhD from the University of Calcutta, India, in 2008, working under the supervision of Professor Sarbajit Chaudhuri. With his specialisation in Trade and Development and Labour Economics, Dwibedi has published a number of research articles in many renowned international and national journals such as *The Manchester School*, *International Journal of Economic Theory*, *International Review of Economics and Finance*, *Bulletin of Economic Research*, *Research in Economics*, *Review of Development Economics* and *Economic and Political Weekly*. His current research interests include Development Economics, Labour Economics and issues related to Public Finance and Public Policy.

International Trade, Economic Development and National Welfare

Essays in Memory of Sarbajit Chaudhuri

Edited by Kausik Gupta and Jayanta Kumar Dwibedi

Routledge
Taylor & Francis Group
LONDON AND NEW YORK

First published 2023
by Routledge
4 Park Square, Milton Park, Abingdon, Oxon OX14 4RN

and by Routledge
605 Third Avenue, New York, NY 10158

Routledge is an imprint of the Taylor & Francis Group, an informa business

British Library Cataloguing-in-Publication Data
A catalogue record for this book is available from the British Library

Library of Congress Cataloging-in-Publication Data
A catalog record has been requested for this book

ISBN: 978-1-032-30950-7 (hbk)
ISBN: 978-1-032-45024-7 (pbk)
ISBN: 978-1-003-37505-0 (ebk)

DOI: 10.4324/9781003375050

Typeset in Sabon
by Deanta Global Publishing Services, Chennai, India

A Tribute in Memory of Professor Sarbajit Chaudhuri

(1965–2021)

Contents

Figures

Preface

This volume is written in honour of Professor Sarbajit Chaudhuri who sadly passed away suddenly on April 25, 2021. Professor Chaudhuri was an excellent teacher and a renowned researcher in the field of trade and development. He wrote numerous research articles in renowned international journals. His ability to use the general equilibrium framework to analyse issues which are relevant to a developing economy makes him an expert in this area. To his students, he was more than a teacher and a guide; he was a motivator and continuous inspiration for many of his students. His research works, particularly works with important policy implications, have inspired and will inspire many researchers across the globe.

General equilibrium modelling is a type of framework which can address inter-linkages among sectors on the one hand and can examine the impact of different types of policies on the economy as a whole on the other hand. Professor Chaudhuri has been a pioneer in this field with more than 100 published papers on general equilibrium trade models and economic development in reputed international journals along with some books published by prestigious publishers (including Routledge). Professor Chaudhuri is a well-known figure in the academic world, especially among those who work on international trade models in the general equilibrium framework. He was associated with the Department of Economics, University of Calcutta, West Bengal, India, as a Professor of Economics for a long time till his death.

This edited volume is published to honour his intellect and his contribution to the field of trade and development. It is not possible to write in detail about the different areas of Prof. Chaudhuri's contribution to the field of general equilibrium in this preface. However, we can briefly mention that it includes the political economy of trade theory, immigration of workforce, skilled–unskilled wage inequality, gender wage inequality, corruption and trade, efficiency of labour, role of informal sector in developing economy, trade and environment etc. All these issues are covered in the present book.

Professor Kausik Gupta was one of the closest friends of Professor Sarbajit Chaudhuri. They were classmates at the Master's level at the University of Calcutta, did their PhD under the same supervisor, Professor

Manash Ranjan Gupta, from Jadavpur University and were colleagues at the Department of Economics, University of Calcutta. Their areas of research interests are also similar. Dr. Jayanta Kumar Dwibedi was a PhD student of Professor Sarbajit Chaudhuri at the Department of Economics, University of Calcutta. Dr. Dwibedi also shared the paper "Labour Economics" as a Guest Teacher at the Department of Economics, University of Calcutta, at the Master's level with Professor Chaudhuri for a long period. The editors in no way can compensate for the loss and the suffering of Professor Sarbajit Chaudhuri's wife, Pampa Chaudhuri, and daughter, Salonkara Chaudhuri, due to his sad demise. The present book is just a small tribute in memory of Professor Chaudhuri on part of the editors.

Kausik Gupta
Jayanta Kumar Dwibedi

July 28, 2022
Kolkata, West Bengal, India

Contributors

Rajat Acharyya is Professor of Economics at Jadavpur University, Kolkata, and former Dean of the Faculty Council of Arts, Jadavpur University. Professor Acharyya received his M.Sc. (Economics) degree from Calcutta University in 1990 and his PhD (Economics) degree from Jadavpur University in 1996. He was a Ford Foundation Postdoctoral Fellow at Rochester University, New York, during 1997–1998. He was awarded the EXIM Bank International Trade Research Award in 1997, the Global Development Network (Washington DC) Research Medal in 2003, the Mahalanobis Memorial Medal in 2006 and the Best University Teacher Award by the Government of West Bengal in 2016.

Dibyendu Banerjee is currently Associate Professor of Economics at Serampore College, West Bengal, India, with 20 years of teaching and research experience in various fields of the subject. He obtained his doctorate degree from the University of Calcutta. Dr. Banerjee, with his specialisation in advanced economic theory, has contributed several research papers to many renowned national and international journals.

Sarmistha Banerjee is Research Scholar at Jadavpur University, Kolkata.

Hamid Beladi is Professor of Economics and Associate Dean of Research at the University of Texas at San Antonio, College of Business. He served as Editor of the *International Review of Economics and Finance* (1992–2018), Series Editor of *Frontiers of Economics and Globalization*, Associate Editor of the *Review of International Economics* (since 1992) and Managing Editor of the *North American Journal of Economics and Finance* (since 2009). He also serves as an Advisory Editor of the *International Review of Financial Analysis* and is a member of the editorial boards of several other journals. He is Co-founder of the International Economics and Finance Society (IEFS). Beladi has published more than 260 papers in a wide spectrum of scholarly journals.

Purbasha Bhattacharyya completed her M.Sc. from the University of Calcutta (2017) and is pursuing a PhD from the same university. She is currently working as a State Aided College Teacher at Basanti Devi College at the University of Calcutta.

Avik Chakrabarti, Associate Professor of Economics at the University of Wisconsin-Milwaukee, conducts theoretical and empirical research related to the fields of international economics and industrial organisation. He has taken a lead in laying the foundation of co-creation thinking in economics. *European Economic Review*, *Journal of International Economics* and *Journal of Mathematical Economics* are among the journals publishing his research. His writings also include an entry in the Princeton Encyclopedia of the World Economy and a chapter in *India and the Global Economy* that contains the inaugural speech by the Prime Minister of India and a valedictory address by the President of India.

Salonkara Chaudhuri is currently pursuing her doctoral degree in Economics from the School of Economics, The University of Queensland (Australia). Her research interests are in labour economics, development economics and environmental economics. Her research methodologies include applied partial and general equilibrium models and micro-theoretic models.

Sarbajit Chaudhuri was Professor of Economics at the University of Calcutta since the late 1990s. His area of research was mainly in the field of general equilibrium theoretical models of trade and development. He wrote numerous research articles in renowned international journals and is well known as a specialist in this area. This book itself is dedicated to the memory of Professor Chaudhuri.

Asmita Das has completed her Master's in Economics from the University of Calcutta.

Swaraj Das is working as Assistant Professor in Economics at Bangabasi Evening College, Kolkata, under the University of Calcutta. Before joining Bangabasi Evening College, Kolkata, he obtained his MPhil degree in Economics from Jadavpur University. His current research areas include the competitive general equilibrium model, applied econometrics and trade theory. His teaching interests are Mathematical Economics, Macroeconomics and Econometrics.

Priya Brata Dutta is working as Assistant Professor in Economics at Visva-Bharati University, Shantiniketan. Before joining Visva-Bharati, he obtained his PhD degree in Quantitative Economics from Indian Statistical Institute, Kolkata. His current research areas include growth theory, competitive general equilibrium models and trade theory.

Kausik Gupta is Professor of Economics at the University of Calcutta, Kolkata, India. He was also former Vice-Chancellor of West Bengal State

University, Barasat, West Bengal, India. His main areas of research interest are international trade theory and environmental economics. He has published quite a large number of papers in reputed national and international journals. He is one of the editors of this book.

Manash Ranjan Gupta is retired Professor at Indian Statistical Institute, Kolkata. He has also taught at Jadavpur University, the University of Burdwan and the Indian School of Mines, Dhanbad. He is currently affiliated with the School of Economics and Business at Adamas University. His current research areas include growth theory, competitive general equilibrium models and trade theory. He is also awarded Panchanan Chakraborty Memorial Award. He has published numerous research papers in reputed national and international journals.

Daniel Hollas is Professor Emeritus of Economics at the University of Texas at San Antonio. He received his PhD degree in economics from the University of Illinois at Urbana Champaign. His research interests include topics in industrial organisation and the global economy.

Saibal Kar is Reserve Bank of India Chair Professor of Economics at the Centre for Studies in Social Sciences, Calcutta (CSSSC), India, and a Research Fellow of the Institute of Labor Economics (IZA), Bonn. He has been Fellow of the prestigious Alexander von Humboldt Foundation during 2008–2009. He held visiting positions at the Amsterdam School of Economics, Santa Fe Institute, Hamburg University, United Nations University etc. in recent years. He is the Managing Editor of the *South Asian Journal of Macroeconomics and Public Finance* (Sage). He also serves as the Director of the Eastern Regional Centre of Indian Council of Social Science Research (ICSSR).

Rohan Kanti Khan is Assistant Professor of Applied Economics at the Maulana Abul Kalam Azad University of Technology, India, and PhD Scholar at the Department of Economics, University of Calcutta, India. His main research interests are labour economics, corruption and crime, with a special interest in household modelling and child labour. His research methodology includes applied general equilibrium models and micro-theoretical models.

Sajal Lahiri has been Academic Economist since 1978, specialising in international trade, development economics and environmental economics. He obtained his PhD degree from the Indian Statistical Institute, Kolkata. He worked at the University of Essex, UK, during 1978–2002, and since 2002, he holds the endowed Vandeveer Chair in Economics at the Southern Illinois University Carbondale, where he is also a Distinguished Scholar. He has worked and published extensively in the areas of international trade, development economics and environmental economics.

Sushobhan Mahata holds a position as a Junior Research Fellow (University Grants Commission (UGC), New Delhi) at the Department of Economics, University of Calcutta, India. His main research interests are in corruption, crime, labour economics and political economics, with a special interest in household modelling and development economics. His research methodology includes applied game-theoretic models, applied general equilibrium models and micro-theoretic models.

Biswajit Mandal is Associate Professor at the Department of Economics and Politics, Visva-Bharati, Shantiniketan, India. His current research interests include international trade theory and policy, development economics and health economics. Dr. Mandal has published a number of research articles in renowned national and international journals.

Soumyajit Mandal is Assistant Professor at the Department of Economics, St. Xavier's College (Autonomous), Kolkata, India, and PhD Scholar at the Department of Economics, University of Calcutta, India. His main research interests are agriculture economics, labour economics, education and environmental economics. His research methodology includes applied general equilibrium models, applied game theory and micro-theoretical models.

Sugata Marjit is currently the First Distinguished Professor of the Indian Institute of Foreign Trade. He was the former Director of the Centre for Studies in Social Sciences, Calcutta, former Vice-Chancellor of the University of Calcutta and former Chairman of the West Bengal State Council of Higher Education. He has taught at different renowned institutes and universities all over the world. Professor Marjit is not only considered a leading economist in India but also one of the top researchers in the world. His research interests include international trade theory, international finance, industrial organisation and development economics. He has published a large number of research articles in different leading national and international journals.

Sudeshna Mitra is Assistant Professor of Economics at St. Paul's Cathedral Mission College, Kolkata, and Visiting Faculty at the Department of Economics at the University of Calcutta. She has authored/co-authored quite a few research articles in international/national journals and books. Her research areas are international economics and labour economics and has a keen interest in domains like microeconomics, development economics and environmental economics.

Shyani Mukherjee is a student at St. Xavier's College, Kolkata.

Ranjanendra Narayan Nag is Associate Professor at the Department of Economics, St. Xavier's College (Autonomous), Kolkata, India. His main research interests include open economy macroeconomics, general equilibrium and international trade.

Sangita Roy is Research Scholar at the Department of Economics and Politics, Visva-Bharati, Shantiniketan, India.

Tavishi Rupani is a student at St. Xavier's College, Kolkata.

Damayanti Sau has completed her Master's in Economics from the University of Calcutta.

1 Introduction

The issue of international trade and economic development is a well-discussed area among economists, policymakers and common persons. However, when we are interested to examine the true impact of different policies on different sectors of an economy, this issue is not confined to a discussion at the popular level. In fact, to chalk out the impact of different policies and their effects on the economy's welfare, we need a well-framed model for a developing economy taking into account interactions among different sectors. General equilibrium modelling is a type of framework which can address inter-linkages among sectors on the one hand and can examine the impact of different types of policies on the economy as a whole on the other hand. In particular, it covers issues that are related to the impact of policies on variables like income, employment, inequality and welfare, and for this a multi-sector general equilibrium model is more appropriate to handle the policy impacts compared to a partial equilibrium model. The linkages between international trade and economic development in the era of globalisation can be best captured by theoretical frameworks that are based on general equilibrium trade models which are not only multi-sector in nature but also have features which have a close resemblance with that of real life so far as developing economies are concerned. The linkage between international trade and economic development in the majority of the works ultimately boils down to an analysis of different domestic and trade policies on welfare. These multi-sector models usually consider the economy as a small open one so that the economy is a price taker in the world market, production function in each sector exhibits constant returns to scale, the competitive equilibrium conditions explain the price system and the endowment allocation conditions explain the factor market equilibrium conditions. The existence of non-traded final goods and intermediate goods implies the price of the product of this sector is determined endogenously. The common way to capture different policies is to consider small shocks (also known as infinitesimal changes) in the general equilibrium system to examine the impact on sectoral output levels, employment, welfare and unemployment. Welfare in all these models is captured either in terms of a quasi-concave

DOI: 10.4324/9781003375050-1

social welfare function or in terms of national income measured at domestic prices as a proxy for welfare.

The multi-sector general equilibrium trade models are actually stylised theoretical versions of different contemporary issues in the era of globalisation related to international trade and economic development and they are constructed on the basis of some empirical facts and figures that are available for different developing economies. These models are basically hybrid of Heckscher–Ohlin–Samuelson and sector-specific structures which are able to capture the diversified trade basket of a developing economy.[1] Once the model is specified, different contemporary issues are analysed in terms of these models. For example, the immiserising effects of foreign capital inflow in a developing economy on welfare, in the presence of full repatriation of foreign capital income, are known as the Brecher–Alejandro (1977) proposition and it is an old issue well known in the literature on international trade and economic development. In spite of the fact that the proposition is an old one, it has been examined by different authors over years by capturing different features of a developing economy like the presence of urban unemployment and migration of the workforce from the rural sector to urban area, existence of informal sector and skilled–unskilled division of the workforce. Such features of a developing economy require a tight trade-theoretic general equilibrium framework which can be best captured in terms of the hybrid structure as mentioned above. All these are treated as essential components of economic development and hence international trade can easily be linked with economic development where trade policies and also domestic policies play an important role. Quite a large number of recent works that examine the linkages between international trade and economic development have focused on finite changes instead of infinitesimal changes in policy variables to capture the issue of a vanishing sector in a developing economy. These finite changes are referred to as large shocks which can be captured either in the form of a change in regime from no capital mobility to a regime of perfect capital mobility or it can be captured in the form of protectionism to a regime of free trade in terms of reduction in tariff rate in all the protected sectors. If as a result of such regime change some of the sectors were shut down (unless there is any government support), we have a different regime in the model and we refer to it as a finite change.

The issue of economic development covers a wide area, but there are some specific areas that deserve special attention. In this volume we have focused on those specific areas to make it lucid for the readers to understand the importance of these trade models to analyse the impact of various domestic and trade policies on some major variables that explain the level of development of the economy. These areas include broadly political-economic issues, crime and corruption, gender inequality, skilled–unskilled wage inequality, income distribution and unemployment, environmental regulation, role of educational capital, informal sector, international fragmentation, exportable quality etc. Though there are scattered research papers on the above-mentioned aspects, a single edited volume covering all these issues in a trade-theoretic general equilibrium framework by eminent researchers is missing. This lacuna has inspired us to edit this particular volume. The proposed volume deals with the impact of different facets of globalisation, trade and investment liberalisation in particular, on the above-mentioned aspects. It is mainly targeted towards postgraduate students of development economics, international economics and labour economics and also the researchers who are pursuing theoretical research on applications of general equilibrium trade models in developing countries. This volume is also aimed at suggesting alternative policies to policymakers in developing economies to tackle various hindrances to economic development and hence to achieve improvement in the level of welfare.

1.1 Plan of the Present Book

The current volume provides a fairly comprehensive analysis of contemporary issues in international trade and development. It covers issues like the provisioning of the public good and its implication in a liberalised regime, crime and corruption, skilled–unskilled wage inequality, income distribution and unemployment, environmental regulation, role of educational capital, informal sector, international fragmentation and exportable quality etc. Researchers from around the world have written on these contemporary and extremely relevant issues and they are presented in 12 chapters in this volume. It is not possible for us to include all emerging aspects of a developing economy which one can cover in the context of trade and development in this volume. We could not include aspects like global E-Commerce firms in the home market and the potential implications for the retail sector, the role of time zone in international trade and development, poverty and inequality in the context of trade liberalisation etc. in this volume, and such an omission can be considered as a limitation of the present book. However, the aspects that we have covered are all areas of major research that are not only relevant for a developing economy but are also closely linked with the areas in which Professor Sarbajit Chaudhuri had his major research interest. The topics that are omitted in this volume will definitely be a part of our future research agenda. We now briefly state the contents of the 12 chapters (Chapters 2–13) of this volume.

Chapter 2 develops a competitive model for a small open economy with a restricted public good to show how income distribution and political-economic considerations have implications for the optimal provision of a restricted public good. The chapter also examines the effect of a change in the international terms of trade on the optimal provision of the public good.

It characterises the optimal level of the public good under different scenarios. In the benchmark scenario there are no lobbying and no distributional considerations in the government's objective function. Here the optimal level of public good provision is given by the Samuelsonian golden rule. The chapter then allowed for lobbying by skilled workers and the capitalists for public good provision but did not allow for distributional considerations by the government. It derives a necessary and sufficient condition for the optimal level of public good provision to be bigger than the one in the benchmark case.

Chapter 3 deals with issues that focus on public policy related to the immigration of skilled workforce from developing to developed countries in terms of a general equilibrium framework that explicitly models the political considerations of the policymaker. The model shows how the media image of the political ruler can be linked with the restriction of skilled immigration of the workforce. An important result that comes out of the model is that the outflow of investment as a response to higher skilled wage rate might make the policymaker even more aggressive and might further restrict immigration and raise the skilled wage rate. One can easily relate the results of the model with the recent policy regulations in the USA regarding tougher restrictions on skilled immigration. The model also explains the fact that why the US economy is strict about the immigration of the workforce even in the presence of wide-scale investment by the US economy in various countries. It explains why the politics in power in the USA might not care much about the threat of capital flight to other countries when the cost of skilled labour rises as a consequence of the immigration policy.

Chapter 4 delves into the issue of political resistance and political compulsions that a democratic government might face in keeping with its commitment to tariff reforms. The chapter also relates to a parallel literature that studies political motives for choosing the level of government consumption or size of the government sector in open economies. Using a simple general equilibrium model of politically optimum tariff, where tariff revenue finances the government's economic programmes and thus the size of the government, the chapter shows that the government chooses a tariff rate higher than the revenue-maximising tariff to maximise political support from the domestic income earners. Thus, if the government pre-commits itself to a tariff reform, then it might face political resistance and lose political support due to the distributional consequences of the tariff reform. At the same time, the politically optimum high tariff rate leads to a less than the largest size that a revenue-maximising tariff can support.

Chapter 5 develops an efficiency wage macro-static model where the efficiency of labour not only varies directly with the wage rate and unemployment rate but also varies inversely with the size of the criminal sector. In this sense, the efficiency wage model of the present chapter is more general than the conventional one. A fraction of the working population is involved in criminal activities, and this allocation of labour between employment and crime is determined by the rational behaviour of the representative criminal. These criminals snatch a fraction of the income of factory owners to finance their consumption and take the risk of being punished. The punishment is made in terms of a fine to be paid to the government. So the size of the criminal sector is determined endogenously in the general equilibrium, and this determination is not independent of the determination of factor prices and of employment and output of the economy. The chapter then examines how changes in factor endowments affect the unemployment rate, the size of the criminal sector and the level of national income of the country. It also analyses how strengthening of punishment policies for criminals affects the unemployment rate, the size of the criminal sector and the level of national income.

Chapter 6 of the book also deals with the issue of crime and corruption. The chapter aims to explore the nexus between organised crime and corruption in the backdrop of liberalised foreign investment policy. Using a four-stage game-theoretic model to determine endogenously the bribe rate and the effective enforcement of law and order from the strategic interaction among the political party currently in power, an incumbent firm and a potential entrant firm, the chapter investigates whether foreign capital inflow acts as a panacea to curb corruption and crime endogenously or rather help augment this nexus. It is shown that the existence of the organised crime sector becomes necessary to sustain corruption that leads to the formation of the nexus between these two illegal activities. The results of the chapter show that foreign capital is detrimental to the law-and-order situation and augments the incidence of corruption; however, it may lead to decriminalisation in terms of a fall in the number of criminals. This reflects the internal contradictions of a democratic state in a developing economy distorted with political cronyism and corruption with the existence of the criminal sector.

Chapter 7 focuses on asymmetric adjustment costs and the gender wage gap with fragmentation in a simple general equilibrium model. It presents a tractable general equilibrium model that can capture the effects of fragmentation on the wedge between male and female workers when costs of adjustment differ. The chapter identifies formal conditions under which fragmentation widens the gender gap in wages in the presence of a higher cost of adjustment in the import-competing sector(s). In effect, it demonstrates the sensitivity of the effects of fragmentation, on the gap between male and female workers, to asymmetries in costs of adjustment. The findings have non-trivial implications to the extent that gender inequality in wages can exacerbate income inequality for economies engaged in offshore outsourcing.

Chapter 8 of the book focuses on a general equilibrium trade model on skilled–unskilled wage inequality, unemployment and tourism development. Using a static competitive general equilibrium model of a small open economy with skilled labour, unskilled labour and physical capital being three primary factors of production, the chapter captures the phenomenon of both rural and urban tourism development. The chapter derives interesting results to show how tourism development affects unemployment and wage inequality conditional on assumptions of factor intensity.

Chapter 9 of the book deals with the issues related to globalisation, income distribution and unemployment in a general equilibrium framework. The chapter makes an attempt to explain how different interconnected measures of globalisation, land augmenting technological progress and adverse supply shocks arising due to COVID-19 play a major role not only in determining skilled–unskilled wage disparity and unemployment of skilled labour but also in income distribution in general. The findings in this chapter have a specific accent on policymaking for a developing country like India. There is no gainsaying that the pandemic crisis is an eye opener, and it warrants a relook at policymaking. The chapter makes an attempt to address issues pertaining to the pandemic crisis as well.

Chapter 10 of the book focuses on environmental regulation in a general equilibrium setting. Using a static three-sector, specific factor competitive general equilibrium model of a small open developing economy, it highlights the role of environmental pollution in the determination of the skilled–unskilled wage inequality and the extent of urban unemployment as a result of different economic policies. It shows how the inflow of foreign direct investment (FDI) exerts a favourable impact on average low-skilled wage as well as on the relative wage inequality although the unemployment situation of urban unskilled workers may worsen. Trade liberalisation, on the other hand, aggravates wage inequality but improves the urban unemployment problem unconditionally. However, *Stringent* environmental regulation is likely to produce an adverse impact on skilled–unskilled wage inequality though the impact on urban unemployment is ambiguous. These results do not hinge on the nature of capital mobility between different sectors and, therefore, are robust.

The issue of the environment is discussed in more detail in Chapter 11 of the book. The chapter argues that participation in multilateral and multi-country pollution abatement treaties is often a contentious matter, owing to the gaps between domestic and international gains associated with it. The present chapter shows that the welfare implications of cross-country carbon trade could vary considerably across participating and non-participating countries and that it is a function of gains from trade. It shows that through direct trade-related impacts, non-participating countries suffer welfare loss when they choose to ignore environmental consequences, and the justification to be a party to multilateral negotiations can independently be motivated by selfish benefits associated with standard gains from trade. Using a standard three-country model of trade in commodities and emissions, it captures the effects of non-participation in environmental treaties for some countries. The present effort is a step towards coupling trade and environmental concerns for countries engaging in multilateral negotiations.

The informal sector comprising unrecorded, unregistered activities in developing economies of the world is a common feature in the present scenario. The existence of such sectors in an economy clearly reflects the weakness of the government to provide employment opportunities for all.

Such informal activities are again facilitated through the extortionists who are bribed by the informal producers. Chapter 12 of the book focuses on this particular issue. Under such an economic structure, the chapter examines the effect of inflow of educational capital on endogenously determined factor prices and output of formal and informal sectors of an economy. Though there is no change in the factor earnings, an inflow of educational capital gives a boost to the output of skilled sector irrespective of the factor intensity assumption, whereas the output of formal sector depends on the factor intensity assumption. But quite interestingly no change is seen in the output of informal sector. On the other hand, inflow of educational capital leads to the dampening of intermediation activities which is a positive result, and hence this can help the policymakers to choose the right path of development.

Chapter 13 deals with the issue of product quality in the context of developing countries. The issue becomes more important when it is linked with international fragmentation. The chapter develops a model without international fragmentation and then develops a model in the presence of international fragmentation. A four-sector four-factor model of a small open developing economy has been considered for this purpose. The chapter examines how tariff cut, FDI and an increase in the endowment of skilled labour force affect exportable product quality both in the presence and in the absence of international fragmentation.

Note

1 Actually they are a hybrid of Jones (1965) and Jones (1971) models.

References

Brecher, R. and Alejandro, C.F.D. (1977): "Tariffs, Foreign Capital and Immiserizing Growth", *Journal of International Economics*, 7(4): 317–322.

Jones, R.W. (1965): "The Structure of Simple General Equilibrium Models", *Journal of Political Economy*, 73(6): 557–572.

Jones, R.W. (1971): "A Three Factor Model in Trade, Theory and History", in J.N. Bhagwati et al. (Eds.): *Trade, Balance of Payments and Growth*. North Holland, Amsterdam, pp. 3–21.

2 Optimal Provision of a Restricted Public Good under Lobbying and Income Inequality

Sarbajit Chaudhuri and Sajal Lahiri

2.1 Preface from Sajal Lahiri

This volume is in honour of my co-author of this chapter, Sarbajit Chaudhuri, who sadly passed away on April 25, 2021. In this preface I shall very briefly say a few words about my relationship with him, and I do not want to repeat what the editors of this volume write about him in the introduction. About 20 years or so ago when I was still at the University of Essex in England, Sarbajit wrote to me. This was the start of our long professional and personal relationship. I think he was at an early stage of his academic year. Since then he used to write to me at regular intervals asking my advice on the papers that he was working on at that time. It was clear to me then that he was a very bright young man full of very interesting ideas, and I was very happy to help him resolve some of the difficulties that he used to face in his research. This went on for over ten years without us meeting face to face. Then once when I told him that I was going to visit Kolkata, he requested that I visit him at his department in Kantakol, which I did. By then, he had become one of the most prolific academic economists in India. Then I became a regular visitor at Kantakol and we became personal friends even though he was much younger than me. During one of my visits to Kantakol, we started talking about public goods and some of the open issues in that literature. That was how the work for this chapter began. Most of the work was done jointly, but we could not complete it because of his administrative duties as the Head of the Department. I am very happy to be able to complete it for a volume in his honour.

2.2 Introduction

The presence of public goods is a well-known reality in most economies, and various aspects of it have been analysed extensively in the literature (see Oakland, 1987; Sandmo, 2017). Two properties that distinguish a *pure public good* from a private one are that public goods are (1) non-rivalrous in the sense that they should be accessible by all and one person's consumption does not affect their availability for others or by the same person later and (2) non-excludable in the sense that they are available for consumption at zero price to each and every member of the society; that is, it is impossible

DOI: 10.4324/9781003375050-2

to exclude any individual from consuming the good. Public goods can be impure if they satisfy one or both conditions only to a limited extent. A private park with an entry fee, or a road with toll charges, does not satisfy the non-excludability assumption and that is called a *club good*. A crowded highway, or a congested national park, without any toll charges or an entry fee, is a *mixed good*, and it does not satisfy the non-rivalrous property.

In this chapter, we introduce a new type of public good which we call a *restricted public good*. For this concept, it is necessary to have heterogeneity among the population in terms of their preferences. Some good may be *potentially* accessible to the entire population and it satisfies the non-excludability assumptions. However, some sections of the population may not *voluntarily* consume that good for a host of reasons. One reason could be the non-availability of time needed to consume the good, and therefore the existence of opportunity costs of consumption. The reason that we consider in this chapter is the lack of interest in that good on the part of a section of the population. That is, the consumption of that good provides no utility to a section of the population. Some people do not get any utility from modern or any art work and do not visit art galleries even though there is no entry fee. One can provide many more examples of restricted public goods.

We develop a competitive model for a small open economy with three groups of people: Capitalists, skilled workers and unskilled workers. The public good is endogenously produced by the government and it is paid for by lump-sum taxation of the capitalists. The public good does not give any utility to the unskilled workers, but it does to the other two groups who lobby the government for the provision of the public good. As we shall see, income distribution and political-economic considerations have implications for the optimal provision of a restricted public good. We also examine the effect of a change in the international terms of trade on the optimal provision of the public good. We describe the model in detail in Section 2.3. Section 2.4 then examines the optimal provision of the public good under different scenarios. The effect of international terms of trade on the optimal provision of the public good is analysed in Section 2.5. We conclude with some remarks in Section 2.6.

2.3 The Model

We consider a small open economy which produces and trades N private goods and produces one local public good. Let p denote the vector of given international prices and g the amount of the public good produced. There are many factors of production, but two are considered explicitly and those are unskilled labour and skilled labour; the inelastically supplied endowments of these factors are $\bar{L}_u$ and $\bar{L}_s$, respectively. The production of g requires all the factors other than the two types of labour. Without loss of generality, we assume that each labourer works for one unit of time and that there is one capitalist who owns all other factors of production. All goods and factor markets are perfectly competitive, and there is no unemployment of any factor. With these notations and definitions, the production side of the economy can be described by a restricted revenue function $R\left(p, g, \bar{L}_u, \bar{L}_s\right)$, which is the total value of production in the private sector. As is well known, R_1 is the vector of outputs, R_i (i = 3, 4) are the two-factor prices and $-R_2$ is the unit cost of producing the public good (see, for example, Dixit and Norman (1980) for the properties of revenue functions, and Abe (1992) for that of restricted revenue functions[1]).

As for the government budget constraint, we assume that the production of the public good is paid for a lump-sum tax T on the capitalists. Thus, the government budget constraint is given by:

$$-gR_2 = T, \tag{2.1}$$

and the two-factor prices w_u and w_s are given by:

$$w_u = R_3, w_s = R_4. \tag{2.2}$$

Turning to the preferences of the three groups – unskilled workers, skilled workers and capitalists – these are represented by the indirect utility functions:

$$v^u = V^u\left(p, Y_u\right), v^s = V^s\left(p, g, Y_s\right), \text{and } v^c = V^c\left(p, g, Y_c\right), \tag{2.3}$$

where Y_u, Y_s and Y_c are the incomes of the three groups and are given by:

$$\begin{aligned} Y_u = R_3\bar{L}_u, Y_s = R_4\bar{L}_s, \textit{ and } Y_c &= R(\cdot) - gR_2 - Y_u - Y_s - T \\ &= R(\cdot) - Y_u - Y_s. \end{aligned} \tag{2.4}$$

In the above formulation we have made the implicit assumption that unskilled workers do not voluntarily consume or benefit from the public good which we call a restricted public good. This completes the description of our model for a given g level of the restricted public good. We shall now turn to the determination of the amount of the public good provided.

2.4 Optimal Provision of Restricted Public Good

The government decides on the level of public good provision by choosing the amount of lump-sum taxation that maximises its objective function:

$$W = v^u + \theta_s v^s + \theta_c v^c, \tag{2.5}$$

where $\theta_s \geq 1$ and $\theta_c \geq 1$ are the subjective weights that the government puts on the utility of the skilled workers and capitalists, respectively. These may reflect the lobbying that the government receives from these two groups. This is best described as a political support function (see Long and Vousden (1991)). It can also be seen as a reduced form of campaign contribution model *a la* Grossman and Helpman (1994).

As shown by Varian (1992, chapter 22), the levels of marginal utilities of different groups play an important role in the determination of optimal policies. In our case, the marginal utilities of unskilled labour, unskilled labour and the capitalists are V_2^u, V_3^s and V_3^c, respectively, and the magnitudes of the marginal utilities have distributional implications.

To start with, differentiating (2.1), we get

$$\frac{dg}{dT} = -\frac{1}{r_2 + gR_{22}} > 0, \tag{2.6}$$

since $R_{22} \leq 0$ (see Abe (1992)).

This is as one would expect. An increase in the lump-sum tax T increases funds for the public good production and therefore increases public good provision.

Then from (2.3) we obtain

$$\frac{dW}{dT} = \left(\frac{dg}{dT}\right)\Big[\left(V_2^u - \theta_c V_3^c\right)R_{32}\bar{L}_u + \left(\theta_s V_3^s - \theta_c V_3^c\right)R_{42}\bar{L}_s + \theta_s V_2^s + \theta_c V_2^c + \theta_c V_3^c R_2\Big]. \tag{2.7}$$

An increase in T increases g and this increase in g induces a number of changes which are reflected in the terms within the square bracket. An increase in g changes the wage rates of both the unskilled and the skilled workers. If they increase (decrease), the welfare of the worker will increase (decrease) and that of the capitalists will decrease (increase). These effects are given by the first two terms inside the square brackets. It will increase the welfare of the skilled workers and the capitalists as they benefit from the public good directly, and these are given in the next two terms. Finally, an increase in g will shrink the private sector and this will hurt the capitalists. This effect is captured by the last term.

From (2.7), and using (2.6), we obtain the first-order condition for the optimality of T (i.e., of public good provision) as

$$\left(V_2^u - \theta_c V_3^c\right)R_{32}\bar{L}_u + \left(\theta_s V_3^s - \theta_c V_3^c\right)R_{42}\bar{L}_s + \theta_s V_2^s + \theta_c V_2^c + \theta_c V_3^c R_2 = 0. \tag{2.8}$$

The various terms in (2.8) have already been explained. Equation (2.8) simply equates the marginal social cost and marginal social benefit of providing the public good. Having obtained a general expression of the first-order condition for the optimal provision of the public good, we shall now characterise the optimal level of T under different scenarios.

First of all, we shall consider a benchmark case where distributional issues are absent in the sense that the marginal utilities are the same at the optimal level of T, i.e., $V_2^u = V_3^s = V_3^c = V_3$ (say), and where there is no lobbying, i.e., $\theta_s = \theta_c = 1$. In this case (2.8) reduces to

$$\frac{V_2^s + V_2^c}{V_3} = \left(-R_2\right). \tag{2.9}$$

That is, the marginal willingness to pay for the public good by the skilled workers and the capitalists is equal to the marginal cost of producing the public good. The marginal cost is equal to $(-R_2)V_3$ and includes costs to the capitalists since they are taxed to pay for it. This is the so-called Samuelsonian golden rule for the provision of a public good. It is to be noted that because of the restricted nature of the public good, marginal benefits do not include the willingness to pay by the unskilled workers, and therefore the optimal provision of public good is lower than what it would have been if the unskilled workers also benefited from it. We shall denote this level of lump-sum tax by T_{GR}.

Before proceeding further, let us define two elasticities:

$$\varepsilon^u = -\frac{\partial(-R_2)}{\partial \bar{L}_u}\cdot\frac{\bar{L}_u}{(-R_2)} = \frac{R_{23}\bar{L}_u}{(-R_2)}, \text{ and } \varepsilon^s = -\frac{\partial(-R_2)}{\partial \bar{L}_s}\cdot\frac{\bar{L}_s}{(-R_2)} = \frac{R_{24}\bar{L}_s}{(-R_2)}, \tag{2.10}$$

and these tell us how responsive is the unit cost of public good production to changes in the two labour endowments. We shall call these labour supply elasticities of public good.

With these definitions, (2.8) can be rewritten as

$$\begin{aligned}&\left(V_2^u - \theta_c V_3^c\right)\left(-R_2\right)\varepsilon^u + \left(\theta_s V_3^s - \theta_c V_3^c\right)\left(-R_2\right)\varepsilon^s \\ &\quad + \theta_s V_2^s + \theta_c V_2^c + \theta_c V_3^c R_2 = 0.\end{aligned} \tag{2.11}$$

Now, let us move away from the benchmark case, by relaxing the assumption that $\theta_s = \theta_c = 1$, by considering the situation where $\theta_s = \theta_c > 1$. That is, we continue to disregard distributional considerations but assume that both the skilled labour and capitalists lobby the government. In this case (2.11) reduces to

$$\frac{V_3(1-\theta_c)(-R_2)\varepsilon^u}{\Theta_c} + V_2^s + V_2^c + V_3^c R_2 = 0. \tag{2.12}$$

Comparing (2.9) and (2.16), we see that there is an extra term in (2.16), which is the first term, and this extra term is positive if and only if $\varepsilon^u < 0$ since $\theta_c > 1$. From (2.10), we know that $\varepsilon^u < 0$ if and only if $R_{23} = R_{32} < 0$, i.e., if an increase in public good production reduces the unskilled workers' wage rate. We denote by T_L the level of T satisfying (2.16), and we have

$$T_L \underset{>}{\overset{<}{-}} T_{GR} \quad \Leftrightarrow \quad \varepsilon^u \underset{<}{\overset{>}{-}} 0.$$

This result is stated as a proposition.

> **Proposition 2.1** When the skilled workers and the capitalists lobby the government, the optimal provision of the restricted public good will be smaller than that in the absence of lobbying if and only if an increase in public good provision increases the wage rate of the workers who do not receive any utility from the public good.

If an increase in the provision of public good increases unskilled wages, it would reduce the income and therefore the utility of the capitalists. Since the capitalists lobby and the unskilled workers do not, the marginal value of the political support function will go down. The effect of an increased wage for the skilled workers and the induced decrease in the income of capitalists will cancel each other out as both groups lobby. Therefore whether public good provision goes down under lobbying depends crucially on the wage rate of unskilled workers.

Finally, let us assume the marginal utilities to be different but assume away any lobbying, i.e., $\theta_s = \theta_c = 1$. Also, it is reasonable to assume that $V_2^u > V_3^s > V_3^c$. Here (2.11) simplifies to

$$\left(V_2^u - V_3^c\right)\left(-R_2\right)\varepsilon^u + \left(V_3^s - V_3^c\right)\left(-R_2\right)\varepsilon^s + V_2^s + V_2^c + V_3^c R_2 = 0. \tag{2.13}$$

We denote the optimal value of T satisfying (2.13) by T_D. Comparing (2.13) with (2.9), we note that the marginal benefit of public good provision is positive (negative) here if both ε^u and ε^s are positive (negative). That is, $T_D > T_{GR}$ if $\varepsilon^u > 0$ and $\varepsilon^s > 0$, and $T_D < T_{GR}$ if $\varepsilon^u < 0$ and $\varepsilon^s < 0$. This result is stated formally below.

> **Proposition 2.2** When the skilled workers and the capitalists do not lobby the government, the optimal provision of the restricted public good will be (i) smaller than that in the absence of differential marginal utilities if an increase in public good provision reduces the wage rate of both types of workers, and (ii) larger than in the absence of differential marginal utilities if an increase in public good provision increases the wage rate of both types of workers

Once again, the result depends on how public good provision affects the wage rates. In this case, however, the effect of skilled wages and the induced effect on capitalist income do not cancel out as both groups have different values for marginal utilities.

2.5 Terms of Trade and Public Good Provision

In this section we shall examine the effect of a change in the international terms of trade vector p on the level of public good provision g. Since there is a strictly increasing relationship between g and T (see (2.6)), we shall examine how p affects the optimal value of T. In carrying out this exercise we shall abstract away from distributional concerns and follow Varian (1992, chapter 22) and rewrite the expression for welfare (2.5) by the following:

$$W = \frac{1}{V_2^u} \cdot v^u + \frac{1}{V_3^s} \cdot \theta_s v^s + \frac{1}{V_3^c} \cdot \theta_c v^c. \tag{2.14}$$

Furthermore, we shall assume marginal utilities of income to be constant by considering a specific form of the preferences given in (2.3):

$$v^u = \bar{V}^u(p) + a^u Y_u,\ v^s = \bar{V}^s(p,g) + a^s Y_s, \text{ and } v^c = \bar{V}^c(p,g) + a^c Y_c, \tag{2.15}$$

where $a^u = V_2^u$, $a^s = V_3^s$ and $a^c = V_3^c$.

With this simplification, the first-order condition for the optimality of T becomes

$$F(T,p) = (1-\theta_c)(-R_2)\varepsilon^u + (\theta_s - \theta_c)(-R_2)\varepsilon^s + \frac{\theta_s V_2^s}{V_3^s} + \frac{\theta_c V_2^c}{V_3^c} + \theta_c R_2 = 0. \tag{2.16}$$

Differentiating (2.16), we find

$$\frac{dT}{dp_i} = -\frac{F_{p_i}}{F_1}, \tag{2.17}$$

where

$$F_1 = \frac{dg}{dT}\left[\left\{\theta_c\left(1+\varepsilon^u+\varepsilon^s\right) - \left(\varepsilon^u + \theta_s\varepsilon^s\right)\right\} R_{22}\right],$$

$$F_{p_i} = \left[\left\{\theta_c\left(1+\varepsilon^u+\varepsilon^s\right) - \left(\varepsilon^u + \theta_s\varepsilon^s\right)\right\}\left(R_{2p_i} + R_{22}\cdot\frac{\partial g}{\partial p_i}\right)\right]$$

$$\frac{\partial g}{\partial p_i} = -\frac{gR_{2P_i}}{R_2 + gR_{22}},$$

where $F_1 < 0$ from the second-order condition for the optimality of T.[2]

Using the expression for $\partial g/\partial p$ and (2.16) into the expression for $F_p i$, we rewrite $F_p i$ as

$$F_{p_i} = -\frac{R_{2p_i}}{R_2 + gR_{22}}\left[\frac{\theta_s V_2^s}{V_3^s} + \frac{\theta_c V_2^c}{V_3^c}\right] \tag{2.18}$$

From (2.17) and (2.18), we see that an increase in p_i will increase T and therefore g if and only if $R_{2p}i$ is positive, that is, if and only if an increase in p_i reduces $(-R_2)$, the unit cost of producing the public good. Since $R_{2p}i = (\partial R_p i/\partial g)$ and $R_p i$ is the output of the *i*th good, it would be normal to assume that $R_{2p}i < 0$. This is because an increase in g means more resources will be needed for the production of the public good at the expense of the private good. Formally,

> **Proposition 2.3** An increase in the price of a private good will, under normal circumstances, reduce the optimal provision of the restricted public good.

Another way of looking at the above result is that an increase in the price of a private good will take resources away from the production of the public good, reducing its provision.

2.6 Conclusion

In this chapter we constructed a perfectly competitive, general equilibrium model of a small open economy in which there are three groups of agents or factors of production: Unskilled labour, skilled labour and capitalists. The capitalists own all the factors of production other than skilled and unskilled labour. The government which is susceptible to lobbying uses a lump-sum tax on the skilled labour force and capitalists to produce a public good which is restricted in the sense that unskilled labourers do not consume it and therefore do not receive any utility from it. We modelled the production side of the economy using the revenue function, and therefore the structure of the production side is very general. The skilled workers and the capitalists, who receive positive utility from the public good, lobby the government for the provision of the public good.

We characterised the optimal level of the public good under different scenarios. In the benchmark scenario there is no lobbying and no distributional considerations in the government's objective function. Here the optimal level of public good provision is given by the Samuelsonian golden rule. We then allowed for lobbying by skilled workers and the capitalists for public good provision but did not allow for distributional considerations by the government. Here we derived a necessary and sufficient condition for the optimal level of public good provision to be bigger than the one in the benchmark case. The (necessary and sufficient) condition depends on the sign of the elasticity of the unit cost of production for the public good with respect to the endowment of unskilled labour. In the third scenario, we rule out lobbying but allow for income distributional considerations in the government's objective function. Here we found sufficient conditions (but not necessary conditions) for the optimal level of public good provision to be higher or lower than that under the benchmark case. We also examined how the optimal provision of public good reacts when there is an appreciation of the country's international terms of trade and derived a necessary and sufficient condition for an appreciation of the terms of trade to decrease the optimal level of public good provision. We argue that this condition is a normal condition.

Notes

1 For a function f, we denote by f_i the partial derivative of it with respect to the ith argument.

2 Substituting (2.16) into the expression for F_1, we in fact get

$$F_1 = \frac{dg}{dT}\left[-\frac{R_{22}}{R_2}\left(\frac{\theta_s V_2^s}{V_3^s} + \frac{\theta_c V_2^c}{V_3^c}\right)\right] < 0.$$

References and Notes

Abe, K. (1992) Tariff reform in a small open economy with public production, *International Economic Review* 33(1), 209–222.

Dixit, A. and V. Norman (1980) *Theory of International Trade*, Cambridge University Press.

Grossman, G. M. and E. Helpman (1994) Protection for sale, *American Economic Review* 84, 833–854.

Oakland, W. H. (1987) Theory of public goods, in: *Handbook of Public Economics*, eds. Alan J. Auerbach and Martin Feldstein (Vol. 2, pp. 485–535), Elsevier.

Sandmo, A. (2017) Public goods, *The New Palgrave Dictionary of Economics*, pp. 1097310984, Springer Link.

Van Long, N. and N. Vousden (1991) Protectionist responses and declining industries, *Journal of International Economics* 30(1–2), 87–103.

Varian, H. R. (1992) *Microeconomic Analysis*, 3rd edition, W. W. Norton & Co.

3 New Protectionism and Political Economy of Immigration of Skilled Labour[1]

Sarbajit Chaudhuri, Kausik Gupta and Sugata Marjit

3.1 Introduction and Motivation

The purpose of this chapter is to analyse the public policy regarding the immigration of skilled workers from developing to developed countries within a framework that explicitly models the political considerations of the policymaker. Subsequently we generalise the results with international capital flows triggered by wage movements of the skilled workers. The topic seems to lie at the core of policy concerns in the USA.

In the context of the restriction of skilled immigrants, we find that there are similarities in the ideas of US President Donald Trump and underlying BREXIT in the case of the UK. In the USA when Trump came to power, the slogan was "make America great again" instead of the then-existing slogan like "stronger together". Similarly the UK at the time of its exit from the European Union (EU), interpreted as BREXIT, raised the slogan of "take back control" instead of the basic idea of the EU like "stronger in".[2] Donald Trump's Presidential campaign was based on restricting immigration (especially illegal immigration). A major part of this campaign was based on the promise to build a substantial wall on the US–Mexico border. Though the focus of the restrictive immigration policy of Trump was on the unskilled workforce (especially at the US–Mexico border), after becoming US President his focus shifted to the restriction of skilled immigration along with illegal immigration (mainly of unskilled workers from Mexico). In sharp contrast to his predecessor, Mr. Barack Obama, he has imposed restrictions on the issuance of H1B visas for skilled immigrants to the USA.[3] The US economy is usually on average the home to 19 percent of the world's migrant stock while accounting for only 4 percent of the world's population.[4] In fact, the USA is the top destination for migrants from most of the developing countries. So restriction of immigrants to the USA (both skilled and unskilled) has wide implications for the global economy. Along with this restriction on the immigration of skilled workforce in the USA, we find that a series of tariffs have been imposed in recent years as a part of "New Protectionism". In January 2018, Trump has imposed tariffs on solar panels and washing machines of 30–50 percent. Later in the same year

DOI: 10.4324/9781003375050-3

he imposed tariffs on steel (25 percent) and aluminium (10 percent) from most countries.[5] Most strikingly Mr. Trump set a tariff of 25 percent on 818 categories of goods imported from China worth $50 billion.[6] Things were more accommodative since January 2021 when Joe Biden became the President of the USA. Visa rules were more relaxed though the trade war with China is still ongoing. However, the expectation is always there under Biden's regime that the trade-related conflicts with China would be resolved in near future.

In this backdrop we now focus on the literature that takes into account the economics of immigration. The literature is quite vast and we start from the seminal work in this line by Borjas (1994). It deals with an excellent survey covering both the empirical and the theoretical aspects of the economics of immigration. It starts with a brief history of immigration to the USA and then focuses on the performance of the immigrants in the host country in terms of empirical facts and figures along with the application of econometric techniques. It also focuses on a survey of works on wage convergence between immigrants and ethnically similar nations. Theoretical models of self-selection immigrant flow have also been discussed in the paper. On the other hand, there is a vast theoretical literature that relates international migration of labour to skilled–unskilled wage inequality. Some of the notable works are those by Gupta (1994), Chaudhuri (2004), Marjit and Kar (2005), Yabuuchi and Chaudhuri (2007), Beladi, Chaudhuri and Yabuuchi (2008) etc.[7] While Gupta (1994), Chaudhuri (2004) and Beladi, Chaudhuri and Yabuuchi (2008) used Harris-Todaro (1970) framework, Marjit and Kar (2005) and Chaudhuri and Yabuuchi (2007) have used full-employment structures for dealing with those aspects.

If we focus on the immigration of workforce in the US economy, we find a very important contribution in this regard, which is the survey paper by Borjas (2013). The paper concludes, by reviewing various works on the immigration of workforce in the US economy, that though immigration makes the aggregate economy larger, the actual net benefit that accrues to the natives of the American economy is quite small. Borjas (2013) has argued that even though the overall net impact on natives is small, this does not mean that the wage losses that have been suffered by some natives or the income gains that have accrued to other natives are insignificant. In fact some groups of workers face a great deal of competition from immigrants. These workers are mainly the poorer sections of society. The biggest winners from immigration are owners of businesses that employ a lot of immigrant labour. The immigrants themselves also gain by working in the American economy.

From the empirical and the theoretical literature, we find that though there are a large number of works on the immigration of workforce in general and also on the US economy in particular, work on the restriction of the immigration of skilled workforce keeping the US economy in mind along with the political economy associated with this immigration restriction has not been captured yet in the context of the literature on trade theory.

The motivation behind this study has been generated not only because there is a dearth of literature on the political economy of skilled immigration in general and the US economy in particular but also because it provides a structure which can analyse the implications of immigration policies related to the skilled workforce in a developed economy. Our model considers the payoff function of a politician in an otherwise general equilibrium set up to analyse various issues of new protectionism in terms of a stylised theoretical model.[8] To the best of our knowledge, this is the first attempt to integrate the general equilibrium trade model, skilled immigration and the political economy of such immigration in terms of a single structure. Our chapter thus can be considered an important value addition in the context of the immigration of skilled workforce and the political economy associated with it.

In the present chapter, we have deliberately chosen a very simple general equilibrium structure with the intention of focusing more on the political economy of immigration policy related to skilled workforce for a developed economy. Though the model has been designed on the basis of the US economy's immigration policy, our stylised model can be applied to skilled immigration for any developed economy. To make matters simple, we have assumed that the economy in which we are interested is a small open (developed) economy and it is a price taker in the international market. Though questions may be raised about this oversimplification, it can easily be argued that the purpose of the model is to examine the implications of US skilled immigration policy and the political economy associated with it when international "terms of trade" are given in terms of a very simple framework.[9] One can assume that demand curves facing the traded products are perfectly elastic. For this purpose, we have considered Jones's (1971) specific factor model to develop the general equilibrium structure before linking it with the behaviour of the politician.[10]

Restricted immigration increases equilibrium skilled wage but that has a natural impact on the competitive strength of local capital in the global economy. A question that seems reasonable in this context is that what will happen if there is capital outflow from the USA along with immigration of skilled labour force. Does it make the policymaker less aggressive in terms of restrictive policy? Countering such conventional wisdom, our chapter shows that there is a case where policymaker becomes even more aggressive and restricts immigration further. One innovation of our construction is to include "media image" of the politician. Our work is thus related in spirit to Long and Tuuli (2018) which focuses on offshoring and reverse offshoring.

The chapter is organised in the following manner. Section 3.2 deals with the general equilibrium model. The behaviour of the politician is analysed in Section 3.3. In this section we combine the behaviour of the politician with that of the general equilibrium structure. The comparative static results are analysed in Section 3.4. Finally the concluding remarks are summarised in Section 3.5.

3.2 The Model

We consider a two-sector, specific factor full-employment model (à la Jones (1971)) for an open developed economy like the USA with three factors of production, namely unskilled labour, skilled labour and capital. The returns to the three factors of production are w, w_s and r, respectively. In this model, the intersectorally mobile factor of production is capital, while unskilled labour and skilled labour are specific to sector y (low-skill sector) and sector x (high-skill sector), respectively. The other standard assumptions of a competitive general equilibrium model like constant-returns-to-scale technologies of production with positive but diminishing marginal productivity to each factor etc. hold. Sector x and sector y are the exportable sector and the import-competing sector of the economy, respectively. We assume that the relative price of the exportable good that the country faces in the world market is given at p^*, which implies that the international terms of trade are given for the country. The domestic returns to the three factors of production, unskilled labour, skilled labour and capital, are w, w_s and r, respectively. We assume that at the initial situation $w_S > w_S^*$, where w_s^* denotes exogenously given skilled the wage rate prevailing at the international market.

The equational structure of the model is as follows:

The usual zero-profit conditions for the two sectors are given by the following two equations:

$$w_S a_{SX} + r a_{KX} = p^* \tag{3.1}$$

$$w\, a_{LY} + r a_{KY} = 1 \tag{3.2}$$

Here a_{ji} is the amount of the jth factor required to produce one unit of output of the ith commodity with $j = K, L, S$ and $i = x, y$.

All three factors of production are fully employed. The full-employment conditions are as follows:

$$a_{SX} X = (S + S_0) \tag{3.3}$$

$$a_{LY} Y = L_0 \tag{3.4}$$

$$a_{KX} X + a_{KY} Y = K \tag{3.5}$$

In Equation (3.3) S is the size of the immigrant skilled labour force, whereas S_o is the domestically endowed skilled labour force. L is the domestic endowment of unskilled labour. It is assumed that there is a complete ban on the immigration of unskilled labour. Hence, the unskilled Labour force throughout remains fixed at L. A country's capital stock is K which is assumed to be given. The output levels of sectors x and y are given by X and Y, respectively.

The expression for the national income valued at world prices (or domestic prices) is given by the following equation:[11]

$$\psi = p^{*}X + Y \tag{3.6}$$

Immigration of skilled labour to the country takes place because at the beginning $(w_s - w_s^{*}) > 0$. If there were perfect/unrestricted international mobility of skilled labour, the domestic endowment inclusive of immigrants, $(S_0 + S)$, would have gone increasing, thereby leading to a continuous reduction in the domestic skilled wage, w_s. International migration of skilled labour would have come to an end only when the two skilled wages were equalised, i.e. when $w_s = w_s^{*}$. However, in reality, international labour mobility is never unrestricted. Hence, keeping an eye on reality, we begin with the situation where $w_s > w_s^{*}$ and the international mobility of skilled labour is restricted and is a decision variable of the policymaker of the economy. There is a politician in the scene who decides on the optimal magnitude of immigration in the economy through his/her maximising behaviour.[12] Here the term "politician" refers to the representative leader of a political party in a democratic setup who is already in power. We would study the behaviour of the politician in detail in Section 3.3.

Differentiating Equation (3.6) and using Equations (3.3)–(3.5), we get

$$d\psi = (p^{*}dX + dY) = [p^{*}\frac{\partial X}{\partial(S_o + S)}(dS + dS_o) + p^{*}\frac{\partial X}{\partial K_X}dK_X] + [\frac{\partial Y}{\partial L_o}dL_o + \frac{\partial Y}{\partial K_Y}dK_Y]$$

Or, $d\psi = w_s dS + r(dK_X + dK_Y) + w dL_o$

$$(d\Psi/dS) = w_s \qquad \text{or (3.7)}$$

It is to be noted that $\partial X/\partial j$ is the marginal productivity of jth factor in sector x and $\partial Y/\partial j$ is the marginal productivity of jth factor in sector y $(\forall j = S, K, L)$.

We also have $dS_o = dL_o = dK = 0$, though $dS > 0$.

From Equation (3.7), it is clear that additional immigration of skilled labour by one physical unit raises national income by the amount of skilled wage, w_s, which is equal to the marginal product of skilled labour, i.e. MP_S. It is extremely important to mention now that the assumption behind Equation (3.7) is that no part of the income of the immigrant high-skill workers is remitted to their source countries. On the contrary, if the entire income earned by the high-skill immigrants is sent back to their source countries, then $(d\Psi/dS) = 0$.

3.3 The Behaviour of the Politician[13]

The payoff function of a representative politician is given by:

$$\Omega = aq(w_s, I)V + (1-a)\Psi \tag{3.8}$$

where Ω is the payoff function of the politician which is the weighted average of the politician's expected payoff from winning the next election and the level of national income.[14] The expected payoff from winning the next election is given by $q(w_s, I)V$, where V is the payoff from rewinning the election and $q(w_s, I)$ is the probability of winning the vote which is a positive function of both the skilled wage rate and a proxy parameter, I, that captures the "media image" or "media-created image" of the politician.[15] The sign restrictions of the $q(.)$ function are as follows: $0 < q(.) < 1$, $q_1(.) > 0$; $q_{11}(.) < 0$; $q_2(.) > 0$. An increase in the skilled wage rate increases the probability of winning the next election by the politician so that $q_1 > 0$.[16] Again a good media image of the politician increases his/her probability of winning the vote so that $q_2 > 0$. The sign $q_{11} < 0$ implies that an increase in the skilled wage rate increases the probability of winning the vote by the politician at a diminishing rate. The sign of q_{12} cannot be easily predicted. For example $q_{12} < 0$ it implies that if the media image of the politician is substantially positive, it is less necessary to use w_s as a political strategy (like winning the vote) so that the marginal increase in the probability of winning the election due to a rise in the skilled wage rate falls, the loftier the media image of the political leader. Again $q_{12} > 0$ implies that the marginal increase in the probability of winning the election due to an increase in the skilled wage rate increases, the lower the media image of the political leader. Apart from this, ψ is the level of national income of the economy and the weights are a and $(1-a)$ where $0 < a < 1$. The parameter "a" can be interpreted as the degree of preference of the politician towards winning the election and remaining in power rather than his/her concern for the economy's welfare, measured in terms of national income. In other words, the higher the value of "a", the higher the politician's political ambition to remain in power.

The politician wants to maximise the payoff with respect to the stock of immigrant skilled labour. Thus using Equation (3.7), the first-order condition of maximisation is written as follows:

$$\frac{d\Omega}{dS} = aq_1(.)V\frac{dw_s}{dS} + (1-a)w_s = 0 \tag{3.9}$$

One can rewrite Equation (3.9) as

$$aq_1(.)V(-\frac{dw_s}{dS}) - (1-a)w_s = 0 \tag{3.9.1}$$

One can thus interpret Equation (3.9.1) as the equality of marginal benefit, $aq_1(.)V(-\frac{dw_s}{dS})$, with that of marginal cost, w_S. The marginal benefit arises from the fact that a fall in S raises w_S and hence raises the probability of winning the vote. As a consequence the expected payoff associated with winning the vote increases. We interpret it as the marginal benefit of payoff. The marginal cost arises from the fact that a reduction in S reduces national income by w_S, given the weightage attached to national income on part of the politician as a part of its payoff is $(1-a)$. This reduction in national income due to one unit reduction in immigrant skilled labour is interpreted as the marginal cost which is positive and is actually given by the marginal cost of payoff which is $(1-a)w_S$. The optimum level of immigration of skilled labour force is achieved when the marginal benefit of payoff is equal to the marginal cost of payoff.

Using the production relations of the specific factor model, we get $w_S = f(S_o + S)$ where $f'(S_o + S) < 0$. Using this relation, we can again rewrite Equation (3.9) as

$$\Omega'(S) = aq_1[f(S_o + S), I]Vf'(S_o + S) + (1-a)f(S_o + S) = 0 \tag{3.9.2}$$

The second-order condition is given by:

$$\Omega''(S) = aq_{11}V[f'(S_o + S)]^2 + aq_1Vf''(S_o + S) + (1-a)f'(S_o + S) \tag{3.10}$$

Maximisation of payoff on part of the politician requires that the second-order condition, given by $\Omega''(S) < 0$, is satisfied and a sufficient condition for the fulfilment of the second-order condition is given by $f''(S_o + S) \le 0$. We will assume that this restriction holds in the subsequent portions of our analysis.[17] We can represent $\Omega'(S)$ (as shown by Equation (9.1)) and also the relation $w_S = f(S_o + S)$, with $f'(S_o + S) < 0$ in terms of Figure 3.1.

In Figure 3.1 the $\Omega'(S)$ curve, as shown by the *PP* curve, is negatively sloped as $\Omega''(S) < 0$. The inverse relation between w_s and S follows from the fact that in the specific factor model the two are inversely related and it is depicted by a negatively sloped curve *MM* in Figure 3.1 which is the marginal productivity of skilled Labour, MP_S curve. The level of S that maximises the payoff to the politician is shown by point S^e in Figure 3.1. It shows the level of S^e where $\Omega'(S) = 0$. The corresponding level of the skilled wage rate is w_s^e, where $w_s^e > w_s^*$ showing that some immigration of skilled labour is allowed in the economy by setting the equilibrium skilled wage rate above the international level.

The general equilibrium is a mix of the sector-specific model (Equations (3.1)–(3.6) and Equations (3.8) and (3.9). Thus there are eight equations with exactly the same number of endogenous variables like $w, r, w_s, X, Y, \psi, \Omega$ and S. The sector-specific part of the model implies as usual that the structure is indecomposable.

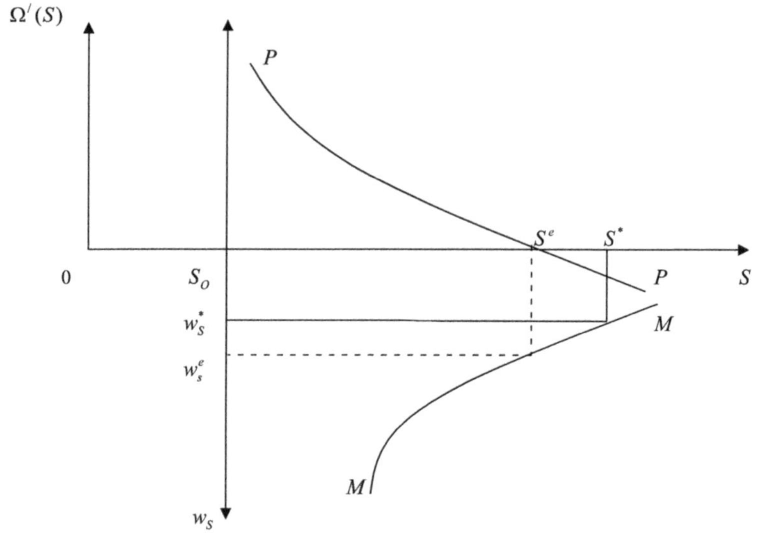

Figure 3.1 Optimal skilled workforce and maximisation of the payoff of the politician

3.4 Comparative Statics

In this section of the chapter, we would like to see how changes in shift parameters/exogenous variables like I, a and K would affect the optimal level of immigration, S, and the skilled wage, w_s. In a static model like this, the analysis of changes in all the shift parameters cannot be carried out simultaneously. Hence, to fix ideas we examine their effects one by one.

3.4.1 Effects of an Increase in Media-Created Image of the Politician

The impact of the change in media-created image of the politician can be analysed from two angles. Though a good media image of the politician increases his/her probability of winning the vote, it is to be noted that if the media image of the politician is high, it is less necessary to use w_s as a political strategy (like winning the vote) so that the marginal increase in the probability of winning the election falls and we have $q_{12} < 0$. In other words, the loftier image created by the media is not positively related to the protectionist strategy of raising the skilled wage rate and thus reducing immigration. Hence, in this case the *PP* curve shifts to the right and that causes an increase in the level of skilled immigrants and a reduction in the skilled wage rate.

The results will be the opposite when the media-created image is not so positive. So higher w_s is more effective for political success, i.e. $q_{12} > 0$. In this case, from Figure 3.1, we find a rise in the equilibrium level of the skilled wage rate. This leads us to the following proposition.

Proposition 3.1: Better media-created image reduces the need for political success through a rise in w_s, and hence the level of skilled immigration is greater. Negative media image does the opposite.

Proof: We can rewrite Equation (3.8) as

$$\Omega(S,I,a,K) = aq(w_S,I)V + (1-a)\psi \tag{3.8.1}$$

Hence from Equation (3.8.1) we get the first-order condition which is similar to that of Equation (3.9), i.e.

$$\frac{\partial\Omega(S,I,a,K)}{\partial S} = \Omega'(S,I,a,K) = aq_1(w_S,I)V\frac{\partial w_S}{\partial S} + (1-a)w_S = 0 \tag{3.9*}$$

From Equation (3.9*), i.e., $\Omega'(S,I,a,K) = 0$, for $da = dK = 0, dI > 0$ we get[18]

$$d\Omega'(S,I,a,K) = \frac{\partial\Omega'}{\partial S}dS + aq_{12}V\frac{\partial w_S}{\partial S}dI = 0$$

Thus, $\dfrac{dS}{dI} = \dfrac{-aq_{12}V\dfrac{\partial w_S}{\partial S}}{\Omega''}$, where $\Omega'' = \dfrac{\partial\Omega'}{\partial S} < 0$.

Hence we have $dS/dI \;>\; =\; <\; 0$ iff $q_{12} \;<\; =\; >\; 0$ QED.

3.4.2 *Effects of an Increase in Desire to Remain in Power by the Politician*

An increase in the desire to remain in power by the politician can be captured in terms of an increase in "a". It shows an increase in the weightage given by the politician on the expected payoff from winning the vote. An increase in the value of a implies an increase in the weight attached to the expected payoff from winning the next election, and hence the politician increases the level of w_S as it increases the probability of winning the vote. An increase in w_S implies a protectionist strategy as it reduces the level of skilled immigration (the level of S) in this specific factor model. It implies that the $\Omega'(S)$ locus or the *PP* curve, as shown in Figure 3.1, shifts in the downward direction. Hence the equilibrium immigration of skilled labour falls and the equilibrium skilled wage rate increases. The following proposition is thus immediate.

Proposition 3.2: The higher the politician's political ambition, measured by a, the lower would be the equilibrium magnitude of skilled immigration and the higher will be the skilled wage.

Proof: From Equation (3.9*), we get

$$d\Omega'(S,I,a,K) = \Omega'' dS + [q_1 V \frac{\partial w_S}{\partial S} - w_S] da = 0$$

It implies $\frac{dS}{da} = \frac{[q_1 V(-\frac{\partial w_S}{\partial S}) + w_S]}{\Omega''}$

Hence we have $dS/da < 0$ as $q_1(.) > 0$, $\partial w_S / \partial S < 0$ and $\Omega'' < 0$ QED.

The intuition behind Proposition 3.2 is simple. The higher the aim of the politician to remain in power, the higher will be the weight on the expected payoff from winning the next election and it depends mainly on the probability of winning the vote. Given the level of media image, the probability of winning the vote depends crucially on the skilled wage rate and the level of skilled outmigration. So if the level of skilled immigration falls and the skilled wage rate within the economy increases, that will definitely lead to an increase in the probability of winning the vote. Hence the politician will definitely want to increase the skilled wage rate as an increase in the skilled wage rate reduces the level of skilled immigration which helps the politician to get his/her vote. As a comment to Proposition 3.2, we can say that the politician to remain in power may follow a stringent immigration policy by citing the reason to preserve more white-collar jobs for domestic high-skill workers.[19] This restrictive policy not only adversely affects the job prospects of high-skill workers from developing countries in developed countries like the USA but also the profitability of the developing country-based multinational companies that are used to send many of their employees to the USA for deputation vacancies and/or further skill formation.

3.4.3 Effects of Outward Foreign Direct Investment (FDI)

The usual impact of raising domestic skilled wages by restricting the immigration of skilled labour is to drive away capital as the rate of return on capital falls relative to the existing global level. Apparently this makes the effort to raise w_S less worthwhile and puts a check on restrictive immigration policy. As we show below, this may not be the case.

Here by outward FDI, we mean the outflow of capital from the US economy to the rest of the world. If the interest rate in the USA falls due to a rise in w_S, it results in the outflow of capital from the US economy to the rest of the world. This causes the domestic (here US) skilled wage to fall following the decrease in its marginal productivity even at the same endowment of high-skill workforce (domestic plus immigrants) $(S_0 + S)$.

For the analytical purpose, we capture outward FDI in terms of the outflow of capital[20] and hence we rewrite marginal productivity of skilled labour[21] as $w_S = f(S_o + S, K)$. We thus write $\partial w_S / \partial S = \partial MP_S / \partial S = f_1(S_o + S, K)$.

As already mentioned earlier, we assume $\partial^2 w_s / \partial S^2 = \partial^2 MP_S / \partial S^2 = f_{11} \leq 0$.[22] We also assume that $\partial^2 w_s / \partial K \partial S = \partial^2 MP_S / \partial K \partial S = f_{21} \leq 0$. In fact $f_{21} < 0$ is a standard assumption that follows from a Cobb–Douglas production function.[23] However, if the stock of skilled labour force or the stock of capital is very high, the value of f_{21} can be approximated to be equal to zero in the case of the Cobb–Douglas production function as well.

From Equation (3.9.1), we get

$$d\Omega'(S,I,a,K) = \Omega'' dS + [aq_{11}f_2Vf_1(.) + aq_1(.)Vf_{21} + (1-a)f_2]dK = 0.$$

We can rewrite it as

$$\frac{d\Omega'(S)}{dK} = \Omega'' \frac{dS}{dK} + A = 0 \text{ where } A = [aq_{11}f_2Vf_1(.) + aq_1(.)Vf_{21} + (1-a)f_2].$$

The sign of A cannot be predicted definitely. The impact of capital outflow on the expected payoff from winning the vote on part of the politician, as shown by the first two terms of A, is ambiguous. The first term shows a fall in the expected payoff due to a fall in the skilled wage rate as a result of the downward shift of the marginal productivity of the skilled labour curve, given by $f_2 > 0$. As $q_{11} < 0$ and $f_1 < 0$, the first term in the expression A is positive which implies a decrease in the expected payoff from winning the vote on part of the politician as a result of outward FDI when the level of the marginal productivity of skilled labour force curve is given as a negatively sloped curve. The second term of A includes a term f_{21} which shows the change in the slope of the marginal productivity of skilled labour curve when there is an outflow of capital stock. Thus a reduction in capital stock not only shifts the marginal productivity schedule in the downward direction but also raises its slope (captured by the term $f_{21} < 0$) implying a downward rotation. It implies the second term of expression A is negative, and hence the net impact on the expected payoff cannot be predicted. The third term of the expression A, however, is positive. From a welfare point of view, a fall in national income due to a reduction in the stock of skilled immigrants is measured by the skilled wage rate. Capital outflow reduces the skilled wage rate and definitely reduces the value of A.

We thus have downward shifts of both *PP* and *MM* locus (the *MM* locus also becomes more steep), implying a fall in the stock of the immigrant workforce. The impact on the skilled wage rate, however, remains ambiguous and it depends on the downward rotation of the *MM* curve. In fact, when we have $f_{21} = 0$ (though $f_2 > 0$), we find only a downward shift and *not a downward rotation* of the marginal productivity of skilled Labour curve. In this case expression A becomes positive which again implies a leftward shift of the *PP* curve along with a downward shift of the *MM* curve. It is only when $f_{21} < 0$ and the absolute value of f_{21} is sufficiently high, we find

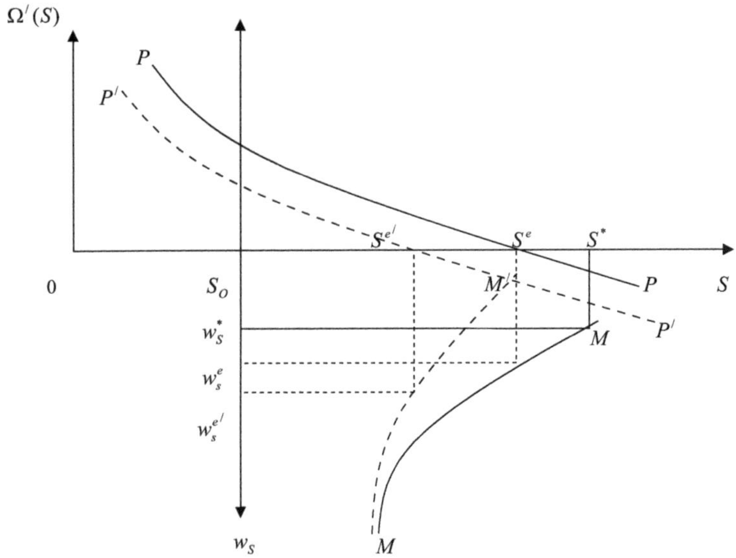

Figure 3.2 Effects of outward FDI on skilled immigration

that A can be negative and we have a rightward shift of the PP locus along with a downward rotation of the MM locus. The conventional result in case of capital outflow shows that there is an increase in r and hence there is a reduction in w_s. It causes an increase in the immigration of skilled workforce. Our model shows that we can have a different result and the conventional result is just a special case. The possibility of such an unconventional result is shown in Figure 3.2.

Figure 3.2 shows that as a result of capital outflow there is a reduction in the stock of immigrants and also an increase in the skilled wage rate. It increases the probability of winning the vote on part of the politician as well as an increase in the expected payoff from winning the vote. In fact when there is outward FDI under reasonable conditions, the case of rising skilled wage rate and strict immigration is more likely to occur than the conventional case.

We have thus the following proposition.

Proposition 3.3: Outflow of FDI from the US economy, contrary to the conventional wisdom, may reduce the stock of skilled immigrants and raise the skilled wage rate under reasonable conditions.

Proof: It follows from the discussion above.

We have $dS/dK = -A/\Omega'' > 0$ iff $A > 0$

Hence under reasonable conditions a fall in K reduces S. It opens up the possibility that there is an increase in the skilled wage rate. QED.

The interesting part of this analysis is that without the rotation issue of the MP_S curve, skilled immigration must fall since A will be positive. Whether the skilled wage rate will increase depends on the rotation factor. Initially as K flows out and skilled wage drops, it increases marginal revenue from lower S and reduces marginal cost again due to lower S, and thus on both counts S will fall. But an increase in skilled wage will depend on the rotation factor as A can be negative. But the main point is that the political ruler will not necessarily increase S.

The possibility of an increase in the skilled wage rate increases the expected payoff from winning the vote on part of the politician. This proposition shows why the US economy is strict about the immigration of workforce (starting from the era of Donald Trump to the era of Joe Biden) even in the presence of wide-scale investment by the US economy in various countries. Our analysis shows that outward FDI from the USA to any developing economy may cause the skilled immigrants from that developing economy to return back to their own economy.[24]

3.5 Concluding Remarks

In this chapter we have analysed the issues that focus on public policy related to the immigration of skilled workforce from developing to developed countries in terms of a general equilibrium framework that explicitly models the political considerations of the policymaker. The model starts with the traditional sector-specific Jones's (1971) structure, and then it introduces the payoff function of a politician. It has been shown that a good media image of the politician reduces his/her need for political success in terms of a rise in the skilled wage rate. Such a good media image causes no restriction on the immigration of skilled workforce. However, negative media image does the opposite. It has also been shown that the magnitude of skilled immigration depends on the political ambition of the politician in the sense that higher ambition restricts the equilibrium magnitude of skilled immigration. The most striking result of our analysis is that the outflow of FDI from a developed economy restricts skilled immigration of workforce and contrary to the conventional wisdom raises skilled wage rate and reduces skilled immigration under reasonable conditions. This result is striking in the sense that outward FDI from developed countries by raising the skilled wage rate increases the expected payoff of winning the vote on part of the politician on the one hand and makes the economy follow a much stricter immigration policy on the other hand.

One can analyse the behaviour of the economy as well as that of the politician as a result of an increase in the tariff rate on importables. An increase in the tariff rate on importables raises the domestic price of importables and hence reduces the domestic price ratio. It causes the skilled wage rate to fall at a given level of skilled workforce (domestic plus immigrants) in terms of a downward shift of the marginal productivity of skilled labour curve.[25] This fall in the skilled wage rate reduces the expected payoff of the politician at a given level of skilled labour. Hence the marginal payoff function shifts in the downward direction which causes a reduction in the immigration of skilled labour force. It ultimately causes the possibility of an increase in the skilled wage rate and hence raises the expected payoff of the politician from winning the vote. An increase in the tariff rate on importables on part of a developed country is related to the issue of new protectionism that has been followed by various economies in recent years. The US economy has also adopted this type of policy in the name of new protectionism recently. In the US economy where we find that there has been an increase in the tariff rate in recent years on imported products from China along with a restriction on the immigration of skilled workforce in terms of H1B visas. The present model helps to explain such a situation.

Our results are very much relevant for the US economy, especially under the recent new protectionism era. Our model also explains the fact that why the US economy is strict about the immigration of workforce even in the presence of wide-scale investment by the US economy in various countries. In fact there is an underlying bargaining game between Indian corporates and the US hiring firms in the transaction of skilled workforce more popularly known as body shopping. Increasing the skilled wage in the USA implies that local firms are forced to pay more to the Indian skilled workers. Previously the return to skilled labour supplying companies from India was generated by the surplus between the market wage of the skilled workers in the USA and the wage the US firms were paying to Indian partners. If US firms have to pay more now, the Indian firms will face higher costs of sending their workers to work for US companies. This could be modelled differently but will confirm lower labour flows to the USA. Future research in this line needs to explore this issue in more detail.

Notes

1 The chapter is a tribute to the late Sarbajit Chaudhuri. The earlier draft of the chapter was prepared when he was alive. After his sad demise, the other two authors completed the present version of the chapter. A preliminary version of this chapter was presented in the Annual "Arthabisleshon" Workshop of the Society for Economic Research in Bengali at GMSM Mahavidyalaya, South 24 Parganas, West Bengal, India, in January 2018. The insightful comments of Baishakhi Marjit on that version in that workshop are highly acknowledged as those comments have motivated the authors to develop the chapter in its present form. The authors are also indebted to an anonymous referee of the book on an earlier draft of the chapter for some insightful comments, and the present version of the chapter has been revised on the basis of those comments. However, the usual disclaimer applies.

2 In the case of the UK's exit from the EU, London voted in favour of the policy of free trade in goods, services and factors to remain within the EU, whereas other parts of the UK voted against it.

3 In India the major companies in the Information Technology sector like Wipro, Infosys, Tata Consultancy Services are adversely affected due to restrictions in the grant of H1B visas. Even if they are granted in a large number of cases, they are not granted for three years. The shorter durations of H1B visas make conversion of H1B visa to Green Card next to impossible. Voice against outsourcing was being heard in the USA much earlier than the Trump regime. Problems related to outsourcing tax and unemployment have been discussed by Bandyopadhyay, Marjit and Yang (2014).

4 Source: Lane and Milesi-Ferretti (2014), United Nations (2015) and World Bank (2016).

5 On June 1, 2018, this was extended to the European Union, Canada and Mexico. See Heather (2018). The only countries which remain exempted from the steel and aluminium tariffs are Australia and Argentina.

6 China retaliated to the aggressive trade policies of the USA by cancelling contracts with US suppliers and also by imposing tariffs on US imports. Apart from this, China imposed a limit on the number of Chinese students who are willing to study in American Universities. Source: Lawder and Blanchard (2018). Also available at http://www.reuters.com (June 15, 2018).

7 Other works which are not based on a general equilibrium framework but are relevant in this context are the works by Docquier and Rapoort (2003), Epstein and Nitzan (2006), Quibria (2010) etc. Docquier and Rapoort (2003) have focused on a theoretical model of interdependency between emigration, education, investment and discrimination in the context of an ethnically divided developing economy. The work of Epstein and Nitzan (2006) is related more to the political economy aspects of migration rather than to immigration which determines endogenously migration quota in terms of a model. The application of the model has also been considered in the context of immigration of workers in European Union countries and also in the USA. The work of Quibria (2010) is something new in the context of the literature on immigration. It focuses on a growth model that assumes imperfect substitutability between immigrants and native workforce and has shown that long-run impact of immigration may not be adverse for the host country. One can consider in this context work of Stark and Byra (2012). It deals with the issue of the back-door brain drain. In this paper the impact of the international migration of unskilled workers on skill formation and the average skill level in the home country have been studied. The paper shows that even without the departure of skilled workers, the home country suffers from reduced aggregate skill formation so that there is a decrease in the average level of human capital in the home country. Recent empirical works on international migration also deal with interpretations of mobility, neo-liberal models of the migration state in the global south and various social issues related to international migration during the COVID-era are of importance, and in this context the works of Adamson and Tsourapas (2020) and Adamson (2019) deserve special mention. In the Indian context the issue of reverse migration (national and international) in the post-COVID economy has been taken care of by Khan and Arokkiaraj (2021). Also in the context of general equilibrium see Anwar (2006) for an extension of Marjit and Kar (2005). One can also refer to Marjit and Kar (2013) and also Beladi, Kar and Marjit (2013).

8 See Note 12 in this context.

9 It is just a simplifying assumption as our purpose is to analyse the implications of US immigration policy for skilled workforce with the intention to obtain some striking results for the US economy in the context of its immigration policy. In fact under the World Trade Organisation (WTO) regime it is quite plausible that the developed economies are not in a position to dictate the terms of trade and act just as a player in the world market like that of the developing economies. In

fact endogenous terms of trade, as we find in the case of a large country, will not also change the essence of our basic problem as analysed in the present chapter. Another argument in favour of given international prices can be that the recent tariff war between trading giants, the USA and the rest of the world (China for example), is nothing but a no-win outcome for the two countries. So both the countries in their own interests might not ultimately be engaged in such type of tariff war and let the international terms of trade remain unchanged.

10 This is also related to the general approach of Jones (2018a, 2018b).

11 In the absence of tariffs national income valued at world prices is the same as that of national income valued at international prices.

12 Here the word/term "politician" has been used in a very broad sense. It refers to a political party which is in power in a democratic set-up with a very comfortable majority at the parliament/congress. Hence, the government is very strong and stable such that it can take bold decisions that it thinks would be good for the national interest.

13 See Note 12 in this context.

14 This type of payoff function is borrowed from the literature on political economy models. See the works of Shleifer and Vishny (1994), Besley (2004), Ashworth and Bueno de Mesquita (2008) etc. It is to be noted that a more practical payoff function of the politician would have been to include skilled and/or unskilled unemployment. As the present chapter does not take into account any unemployment, we have not considered it in our payoff function. But the model can easily be extended by introducing unemployment. We just want to mention that large-scale unemployment reduces the level of GDP or national income, and as the politician gives some weight to national income in the payoff function, lower unemployment implies higher economic activities and hence a high level of national income. So unemployment is implicit in the payoff function.

15 It, apparently, appears that the probability of winning the next election, $q(.)$, depends solely on the skilled wage apart from the "media image" and that the electorates include only skilled workers. However, a close scrutiny of the general equilibrium structure of our model reveals that given the commodity prices, both skilled and unskilled wages move in the same direction. In other words, because capital is the intersectorally mobile factor, two wages must move symmetrically. Hence, if the interest of the skilled workers is protected, unskilled workers are automatically taken care of.

16 See Note 15.

17 Suppose we consider the Cobb–Douglas production, $X = (S_o + S)^{\alpha}(K_X)^{1-\alpha}$ for sector X with $1 > \alpha > 0$. Here α is the output elasticity of skilled labour. From this specific algebraic form of the production function, it follows that $dX/dS = \alpha(S_o + S)^{\alpha-1}(K_X)^{1-\alpha} = w_s = f(S_o + S)$. Besides, given that $\left(dw_s/dS\right) = f'(S_o + S)$ and $\left(d^2w_s/dS^2\right) = f''(S_o + S)$, we find $f''(S_o + S) = [\frac{\alpha(\alpha-1)(\alpha-2)(K_X)^{(1-\alpha)}}{(S_o + S)^{(2-\alpha)}}]$.

Now, if α is small and/or S is high, the magnitude of $f''(S_o + S)$ is very small and therefore can be ignored.

18 Given that $d\Omega'(S,I,a,K) = [\partial\Omega'/\partial S \, dS + \partial\Omega'/\partial I \, dI + \partial\Omega'/\partial a \, da + \partial\Omega'/\partial K \, dK] = 0$.

19 In the present model, there is no unemployment of either type of labour. However, an increase in the number of high-skill immigrants lowers the skilled wage, w_s, thereby lowering the income of each domestic high-skill worker. In other words, the interests of the domestic high-skill workforce get adversely affected due to immigration, which in turn would affect the political prospects

of the politician negatively. However, it is to be noted that the national income raises with an increase in the magnitude of immigration because $\left(\frac{d\Psi}{dS}\right) = w_s > 0$. See Equation (3.7).

20 To avoid algebraic complications and for analytical convenience, the increase in the international rate of return on capital is analysed here in terms of a fall in K.

21 Instead of stating $f' < 0$, we write $f_1 < 0$.

22 The assumption $f'' \leq 0$ is replaced here by the assumption $f_{11} \leq 0$.

23 Consider the Cobb–Douglas production, $X = (S_o + S)^{\alpha}(K_X)^{1-\alpha}$ for sector X with $1 > \alpha > 0$. Here α is the output elasticity of skilled labour. From this specific algebraic form of the production function, it follows that $MP_S = w_s = f(S_o + S, K_X)$. We thus find $f_1 = \left(\partial MP_S / \partial S\right) = -[\alpha(1-\alpha)(S_o + S)^{-(2-\alpha)} K_X^{(1-\alpha)}] < 0$;

$$f_2 = \left(\partial MP_S / \partial K_X\right) = [\alpha(1-\alpha)(S_o + S)^{\alpha-1} K_X^{-\alpha}] > 0; \text{ and } \left(\partial^2 w_s / \partial K \partial S\right) = \left(\partial^2 MP_S / \partial K \partial S\right)$$

$$= f_{21} = -[\alpha(1-\alpha)^2 (S_o + S)^{-(2-\alpha)} K_X^{-\alpha}] < 0 \cdot$$

24 In 2017, the US investments made abroad amounted to approximately US$6.01 trillion. Along with this we find that the US President has followed a policy of strict immigration of skilled workers in the form of restrictions on the issuance of H1B visas to the USA. So our results match with empirical facts and figures.

25 It can also be explained in terms of the price magnification effect in the sector-specific model.

References

Adamson, F.B. (2019): "Sending States and the Making of Intra-diasporic Politics: Turkey and Its Diaspora(s)", *International Migration Review*, 53(1): 210–236.

Adamson, F.B. and Tsourapas, G. (2020): "The Migration State in the Global South: Nationalizing, Developmental and Neoliberal Models of Migration Management", *International Migration Review*, 54(3): 853–882.

Anwar, S. (2006): "Factor Mobility and Wage Inequality in the Presence of Specialisation-Based External Economies", *Economics Letters*, 93(1): 88–93.

Ashworth, S. and Bueno de Mesquita, E. (2008): "Informative Party Labels with Institutional and Electoral Variation", *Journal of Theoretical Politics*, 20(3): 251–273.

Bandyopadhyay, S., Marjit, S. and Yang, L. (2014): "International Oligopoly, Barriers to Outsourcing and Domestic Employment", *Canadian Journal of Economics/Revue Canadienne d'Économique*, 47(4): 1372–1386.

Beladi, H., Chaudhuri, S. and Yabuuchi, S. (2008): "Can International Factor Mobility Reduce Wage Inequality in a Dual Economy?", *Review of International Economics*, 16(5): 893–903.

Beladi, H., Kar, S. and Marjit, S. (2013): "Emigration, Finite Changes and Wage Inequality", *Economics and Politics*, 25(1): 61–71.

Besley, T. (2004): "Paying Politicians: Theory and Evidence", *Journal of the European Economic Association*, 2(2–3): 193–215.

Borjas, G.J. (1994): "The Economics of Immigration", *Journal of Economic Literature*, 32: 1667–1771.

Borjas, G.J. (2013): "Immigration and the American Worker: A Review of Academic Literature", Center for Immigration Studies, Mimeo, Harvard Kennedy School, Harvard University, Cambridge, Massachusetts, USA.

Chaudhuri, S. (2004): "International Migration of Skilled and Unskilled Labour, Welfare and Skilled-Unskilled Wage Inequality: A Simple Model", *Journal of Economic Integration*, 19(4): 726–741.

Docquier, F. and Rapoort, H. (2003): "Ethnic Discrimination and Migration of Skilled Labour", *Journal of Development Economics*, 70(1): 159–172.

Epstein, G.S. and Nitzan, S. (2006): "The Struggle over Migration Policy", *Journal of Population Economics*, 19(4): 703–723.

Gupta, M.R. (1994): "Immigration in Less Developed Countries: A Theoretical Note", *Journal of Economic Integration*, 9(3): 410–416.

Harris, J.R. and Todaro, M.P. (1970): "Migration, Unemployment and Development: A Two-Sector Analysis", *The American Economic Review*, 60(1): 126–142.

Heather, L. (2018): "Trump Has Officially Put More Tariffs on U.S. Allies than on China", *The Washington Post*, May 31, 2018.

Jones, R.W. (1971): "A Three Factor Model in Theory, Trade and History", in J. Bhagwati et al. (eds), *Trade, Balance of Payments and Growth*, North Holland, Amsterdam: 3–21.

Jones, R.W. (2018a): "International Trade Theory and Competitive Models: Features, Values and Criticisms", *World Scientific Studies in International Economics*, World Scientific Publishing Co.Pvt. Ltd., USA: 65.

Jones, R.W. (2018b): "Thoughts and Remarks after 50 Years of Simple General Equilibrium Models", in S. Marjit and S. Kar (eds), *International Trade, Welfare and the Theory of General Equilibrium*, Cambridge University Press, Cambridge, UK: 1–17.

Khan, A. and Arokkiaraj, H. (2021): "Challenges of Reverse Migration in India: A Comparative Study of Internal and International Migrant Workers in the Post-COVID Economy", *Comparative Migration Studies*, 9(1): 49. https://doc.org/10.1186/s40878-021-00260-2.

Lane, P.R. and Milesi-Ferretti, G. (2014): "Global Imbalances and External Adjustment after the Crisis", *IMF Working Paper*, No. WP/14/151.

Lawder, D. and Blanchard, B. (2018): *Trump Sets Tariffs on $50 Billion in Chinese Goods: Beijing Strikes Back*, 15th June 2018. http://www.reuters.com.

Long, N.V. and Tuuli, M. (2018): "Offshoring and Reshoring: The Roles of Incomplete Contracts and Relative Bargaining Power", *Frontiers of Economics in China*, 13(1): 32–51.

Marjit, S. and Kar, S. (2005): "Emigration and Wage Inequality", *Economics Letters*, 88(1): 141–145.

Marjit, S. and Kar, S. (2013): "International Capital Flow, Vanishing Industries and Two-Sided Wage Inequality", *Pacific Economic Review*, 18(5): 574–583.

Quibria, M.G. (2010): "Immigration and Long Run Economic Outcomes", *Economics Bulletin*, 30(4): 2567–2575.

Schewel, K. (2010): "Understanding Immobility: Moving Beyond the Mobility Bias in Migration Studies", *International Migration Review*, 54(2): 328–355.

Shleifer, A. and Vishny, R.W. (1994): "Politicians and Firms", *The Quarterly Journal of Economics*, 109(4): 995–1025.

Stark, O. and Byra, L. (2012): "A Back Door Brain Drain", *Economics Letters*, 116(3): 273–276.

United Nations (2015): *The Millennium Development Goals Report*, United Nations Report, New York.

World Bank (2014): *World Bank Annual Report*, World Bank Group, New York.

World Bank (2016): *World Bank Annual Report*, World Bank Group, New York.

Yabuuchi, S. and Chaudhuri, S. (2007): "International Migration of Labour and Skilled-Unskilled Wage Inequality in a Developing Economy", *Economic Modelling*, 24(1): 128–137.

4 Discontent and Political Resistance to Tariff Reform

Rajat Acharyya[1]

4.1 Introduction

Since the 1980s, there has been a general resurgence of export promotion and trade liberalisation in the developing world, ushering in a new era of globalisation. An increasingly large number of developing countries started adopting liberal trade policies unilaterally. In some cases, such unilateral trade reforms, integration of domestic economies with the globalising world and adoption of export-led growth strategies were conscious choices of national governments of the developing countries as part of their development strategies. Such had been the case particularly for China, Korea and many East Asian countries. But in many other cases, liberal trade policies and economic reforms were initiated under the influences of international funding agencies like the World Bank and the IMF as pre-conditions for bailout packages in periods of crises faced by countries such as the Latin American and South Asian countries. Unilateral trade reforms have also been the outcome of commitment to accession to the WTO membership. However, whether as part of the development strategy or due to compulsions and commitments, unilateral trade reforms have not always delivered the good as was expected.

On the other hand, discontents about such trade reforms and globalisation have been rising in recent times due to the quite large adverse effects in terms of redistribution of incomes in favour of capital owners and skilled workers; large-scale destruction of jobs in import-competing sectors without a commensurate increase in employment in other sectors; and displacement of unskilled workers from formal-sector employment to informal-sector (Bogliaccini, 2013; Brady, Kaya, and Gereffi, 2011; Cornia and Kiskii, 2001; IMF, 2014; Pickety, 2014; Francese and Mulas-Granados, 2015; Acemoglu and Robinson, 2015). The IMF (2014) study, for example, reveals that inequality measured by the Gini coefficient for disposable incomes – market incomes minus direct taxes plus cash transfers – has increased by more than 3 percentage points in one-third of the advanced economies and half of the emerging economies in Europe during 1980–2010. Inequality also rose in most economies in Asia and the Pacific and the Middle East and North

DOI: 10.4324/9781003375050-4

Africa. On the other hand, the Latin American experience reveals growing wage inequality through the large-scale destruction of formal-sector employment due to import competition. For example, Bogliaccini (2013) observed that in the more industrially advanced Latin American countries, formal industrial employment was dismantled as a consequence of trade liberalisation and no alternative sources of formal employment were put in place. The destruction of formal-sector jobs reduced the income of displaced workers who were pushed into survival strategies in the informal sector.

The emerging discontents about globalisation and trade liberalisation as a development strategy as a consequence of all these distributional impacts have a larger political ramification. Choice of trade policies, and policy reforms, in democratic developing countries is often constrained by political resistance and apprehension of loss of political support (Baldwin, 2006; Cassing and Hilman, 1985]; Francois and Nelson, 2014; Nelson, 2009). Adverse distributional consequences of policy reforms for the larger number of interest groups are the primary sources of such political resistance. On the other hand, consumers, producers and income earners all value their *relative* positions more than their absolute positions. So even a Pareto superior tariff reform through compensation to the losers may generate political resistance. Thus, distributional consequences of tariff reforms will lower political support and raise the political risk for a democratic government if reforms create more losers than winners, and/or their lobbying power is larger relative to the winning classes. Consequently, for a democratic *incumbent* government which is concerned with the maximisation of political support and minimisation of political risks, trade policy as a development strategy may be difficult to sustain if it worsens income inequality. Latin American experiences provide some support for this political-support maximising hypothesis. Destruction of formal employment was more severe in those Latin American countries where trade reforms were backed by authoritarian regimes or by recently democratised regimes with weak civil societies. Thus, there was very little political backlash for trade reforms-induced wage and income inequality (Harvey, 2005; Portes and Roberts, 2005; Brady, Kaya, and Gereffi, 2011).[2] In developing countries, tariff reforms have an additional implication for the political support for a democratic government, which constitutes another source of political resistance for tariff reforms. Tariff revenues, being a significant proportion of total tax revenue in many instances, finance government's employment-generating projects as well as the employment of a large contingent of bureaucratic and administrative staff. Under a balanced budget, tariff reforms thus may adversely affect such employment in the public sector (or in government projects) and correspondingly lead to political resistance and loss of political support from workers employed in such sectors.

In this chapter these political resistances and political compulsions that a democratic government might face in keeping with its commitment to tariff reforms are analysed in a general equilibrium setting of a small open economy. The chapter also relates to a parallel literature that studies political motives for choosing the level of government consumption or size of the government sector in open economies (Annett, 2001; Blomberg, 1996; Kim and Lee, 2021, Musau, 2019; Ram, 2009; Rodrik, 1995, 1998; Velasco, 1997; Wu and Lin, 2012). In developing countries public sector production is often viewed as means of employment generation and economic security for the poor. There are thus both political and social resistances to the successful and unsuccessful attempts of downsizing this sector to achieve economic efficiency. Privatisation efforts in India in the last decade and a half have not been smooth either, sharing similar experiences in many other developing countries with multi-party democracy.

We consider a small open economy with a private sub-economy and a government sector. The private sub-economy has the specific-factor structure a la Jones (1971), whereas the government sector is modelled partly following Findlay and Weillisz (1982). The wage bill in the government sector, which constitutes the entire cost in this sector, is paid out of the tariff proceeds collected from imports by the private sub-economy. The government has no other sources of revenue to finance the wage bill. It chooses the rate of tariff by maximising its political support from the domestic economic agents.[3]

Given such a perspective, we show that the political support for maximising tariffs is larger than both revenue-maximising and welfare-maximising tariff rates. This is similar to the result shown by Baldwin (2006) that a politically optimum tariff is larger than an economic optimum tariff. The political-support motive, therefore, provides an alternative explanation of why the tariff rates in many developing countries are quite high, at least higher than what the pure economic motives would have dictated. We also demonstrate that when the local government pre-commits itself to a tariff reform, the size of the government sector, which is constrained by the tariff revenue, need not decline as is often apprehended for a revenue-constrained government. However, aggregate employment may still decline depending on the value of elasticity of factor substitution in the import-competing private sector. This, together with the distributional consequences of the tariff reform, determines the political support for carrying out such a tariff reform. However, if initially the political-support maximising tariff rate was chosen, then a tariff reform must reduce the overall political support. Accordingly, it may be difficult for a democratic government to sustain and remain committed to the reform policy. A policy reversal may follow sooner or later depending on the intensity of internal political conflict and threat to the incumbent government.[4]

On the other hand, if we focus on the size of the government, a political-support maximising government will *not* choose its largest possible size under the balanced-budget constraint. That is, the political support is maximised for a smaller size of the government than that the maximum tariff revenue can finance.

The rest of the chapter is organised as follows. In Section 4.2 we describe the basic model of the private sector sub-economy and the aggregate employment generated in the entire economy for any given tariff rate and the corresponding size of the government sector. Section 4.3 derives the political-support maximising tariff rate and discusses political resistance to a tariff reform committed by the government. A simple example is provided in Section 4.4 for the behaviour of the balanced-budget constraint to illustrate the conditions under which the results hold. Section 4.5 discusses the size of the government that the political-support maximising tariff generates under the balanced-budget rule and its implications for aggregate employment. Finally, concluding remarks are made in Section 4.6.

4.2 The Framework of the Economy

Consider a small open economy with private competitive sectors, which produce two traded goods X and Y, and a government sector producing an output G. Good X is exported and good Y is imported at the given world prices. Imports are subject to an ad valorem tariff at the rate $0 < t < 1$. Good X serves as the numeraire. The two traded goods are produced by sectorally mobile labour (L) and sector-specific capital K_X and K_Y by the constant-returns-to-scale production technology. The output of the government sector is produced only by labour. We can conceive this government sector simply as a service sector hiring people to provide the citizens with basic civic amenities, maintain law and order and run the administration. To keep things simple, we do not distinguish between the skills of people who work in the government sector to provide these services or run the administration and of workers who are engaged in the production of traded private goods. The government does not charge the users for the services it provides. The wage bill incurred by the government is financed entirely out of the tariff proceeds collected by the government from the imports of good Y by the private sub-economy.[5] Throughout the economy, the real wage (measured in terms of good X) is assumed to be fixed at a pre-determined level $\overline{W}$ higher than the level that can maintain full employment of the labour force. But the (real) rates of return to the two types of capital adjust fully and instantaneously to equate the demand for and supply of capital.

We assume a balanced budget so that for any $\overline{W}$, the rate of ad valorem tariff determines the number of workers L_g who can be employed in the government sector to provide the services:

$$\overline{W}L_g = tP_Y^*M \tag{4.1}$$

and correspondingly determines the amount of government services, G, which is also the size of the government sector:

$$G = \frac{L_g}{a_{Lg}} \tag{4.2}$$

where a_{Lg} is the number of workers to produce one unit of the government service. Note, in (4.1), P_Y^* is the exogenously given world price of the import-competing good Y (in terms of good X), and M is the volume of imports, which is basically the excess demand for good Y in the domestic market.

Denoting local production of the imported good by Y, the domestic demand for it by D_Y and the national income (again measured in terms of good X) by I, the import volume is given by:

$$M = D_Y\left(\left(1+t\right)P_Y^*, I\right) - Y \tag{4.3}$$

Here we assume the usual demand function: Domestic demand for Y is decreasing in the tariff-inclusive (relative) price and increasing in the national income. The national income, on the other hand, equals the sum of factor incomes or, equivalently, the aggregate value of production of the traded private goods at the domestic prices plus the tariff revenue:

$$\begin{aligned} I &= \overline{W}L_e + r_X\overline{K}_X + r_Y\overline{K}_Y \\ &= X + p_dY + tP_Y^*M \end{aligned} \tag{4.4}$$

where $p_d = \left(1+t\right)P_Y^*$ is the tariff-inclusive domestic relative price of the import-competing good.

Perfect competition prevails in all sectors of this economy so that the following zero-profit conditions describe equilibrium in the domestic markets for the traded goods:

$$1 = a_{LX}\overline{W} + a_{KX}r_X \tag{4.5}$$

$$\left(1+t\right)P_Y^* = a_{LY}\overline{W} + a_{KY}r_Y \tag{4.6}$$

where r_X and r_Y are the (real) rates of return to capital specific in the two sectors, and a_{ij} ($i = L,K$; $j = X,Y$) is the per unit requirement of factor, i, in the production of good, j.

Under the constant-returns-to-scale production technology, the optimum input combinations depend only on the relevant factor prices:

$$a_{iX} = a_{iX}\left(\overline{W}, r_X\right),\ a_{iY} = a_{iY}\left(\overline{W}, r_Y\right),\ i = L,K \tag{4.7}$$

The model is closed by the factor market conditions. Whereas flexibility of rates of return to the sector-specific capital guarantees their full utilisation:

$$\overline{K}_X = a_{KX}X \tag{4.8}$$

$$\overline{K}_Y = a_{KY}Y \tag{4.9}$$

full employment of labour cannot be ensured a priori because of the rigid wage:

$$L_e = a_{Lg}G + a_{LX}X + a_{LY}Y \tag{4.10}$$

Note, the aggregate employment depends on the size of the government sector (G), which by (4.1) and (4.2) is determined by the rate of tariff. For any given size of G thus determined, a rigid money wage above the level corresponding to the full employment level would lead to unemployment of labour through the factor-substitution effects regardless of how large the endowments of the sector-specific capital are.

For any given ad valorem tariff rate, t, the exogenously given world prices of the traded private goods determine the rates of return to the two sector-specific capital and consequently the optimal input combinations. The output levels and the national income are then determined by the endowments of the sector-specific capital. The tariff rate, given Y and I, then determines the import volume and correspondingly the number of workers who can be employed in the government sector. The aggregate level of employment thus is determined from (4.10).

4.3 Political-Support Maximising Tariff

Political support for the government depends on how government actions benefit or hurt the different sections of the population. Here we focus on political support to the government extended by different earning classes of the population. Both the employment generation through government production and the imposition of tariffs – the two economic actions of the government in this model – benefit, differently though, the wage earners and the capitalists and therefore generate political support for the government. First consider employment generation through larger governance, G. With the money wage fixed at a pre-determined level, the larger size of the government, ceteris paribus, means higher aggregate employment. Thus, the larger is the G, the higher the political support from the workers. Note that for any given rate of tariff and the world prices of the two private goods, the rates of return to the two types of capital remain invariant. Thus the workers who are already employed and the capitalists have no reason to withdraw their support when the government expands in size.

A higher import tariff, on the other hand, benefits owners of the type of capital used in the import-competing sector, as is evident from the zero-profit condition (4.6):

$$\hat{r}_Y = \frac{\gamma}{\theta_{KY}}\hat{t} > 0 \tag{4.11}$$

where "hat" over a variable denotes proportional change (e.g., $\hat{t} \equiv {dt}/{t}$); $\gamma \equiv {t}/{1+t}$ and θ_{KY} is the capital-cost share in the production of good Y.

Employment in this sector increases as well through factor substitution and scale effects. A higher capital cost induces the producers of the import-competing good to substitute capital with labour to minimise the cost of production. The capital released through such a change in the technique of production, however, allows the physical production to expand:

$$\hat{Y} = \sigma_Y \gamma \frac{\theta_{LY}}{\theta_{KY}} \hat{t} > 0 \tag{4.12}$$

where σ_Y is the elasticity of factor substitution. With the output of the export good X not changing, aggregate employment, therefore, increases, for any given size of the government sector by these technique and scale effects in sector Y:

$$\begin{aligned} \hat{L}_e &= \lambda_{LY}\left(\hat{a}_{LY} + \hat{Y}\right) \\ &= \lambda_{LY}\left(\sigma_Y \gamma \hat{t} + \sigma_Y \gamma \frac{\theta_{LY}}{\theta_{KY}} \hat{t}\right) = \sigma_Y \gamma \frac{\lambda_{LY}}{\theta_{KY}} \hat{t} > 0 \end{aligned} \tag{4.13}$$

where λ_{LY} is the share of the import-competing sector in aggregate employment of labour.

Thus, a higher tariff on imports gathers higher political support as well, from both owners of capital specific to the import-competing sector Y and the workers as a whole.

If S denotes the political support, from the above discussions it follows that:

$$S = S(G, t),\ S_G > 0,\ S_t > 0 \tag{4.14}$$

where S_j, $j = G, t$, denotes the partial derivative with respect to argument, j.

The iso-political support loci are, therefore, negatively sloped in the (t, G) space and we assume strict convexity. It is easy to check that a higher iso-political support curve means higher *total* political support. These curves are shown in Figure 4.1.

But under the balanced-budget rule, the government cannot choose G independent of the tariff rate. From (4.1) and (4.2), the size of the government is constrained by the revenue that a tariff rate generates to finance the wage bill in the government sector. Thus, the problem of the government boils down to choosing a tariff rate to maximise political support S subject to the balanced-budget rule (4.1). The relation between the size of the government and the tariff rate under the balanced-budget rule depends on the behaviour of the tariff-revenue function. It is straightforward to check that:

$$\begin{aligned} \hat{R} &= \hat{t} + \hat{M} \\ &= \frac{\left[1 + \psi\eta\gamma\theta_Y\left(1 + \sigma_Y \frac{\theta_{LY}}{\theta_{KY}}\right) - \left(\psi\varepsilon + \sigma_Y \chi \frac{\theta_{LY}}{\theta_{KY}}\right)\gamma\right]\hat{t}}{1 - \eta\psi\theta_R} \end{aligned} \tag{4.15}$$

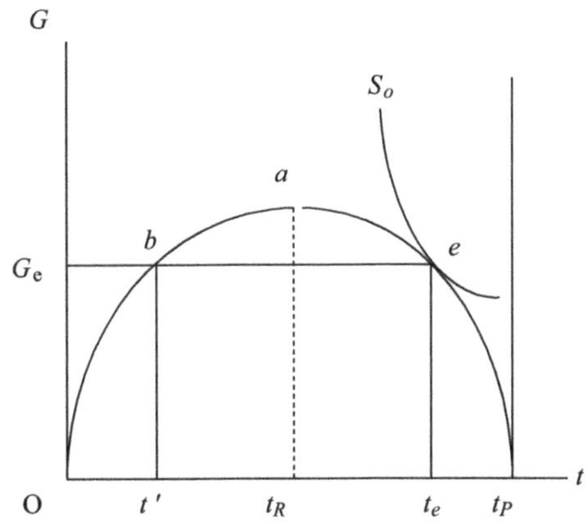

Figure 4.1 The political–support maximising. Size of the government

where R denotes tariff revenue; ε and η are, respectively, price elasticity and income elasticity of the import-competing good Y; θ_Y and θ_R are the shares of the import-competing sector and tariff revenue, respectively, in the national income evaluated at the tariff-inclusive domestic price; $\psi \equiv \frac{D_Y}{M} > 1$ and $\chi \equiv \frac{Y}{M}$.

Note first that $\eta\psi\theta_R < 1$ by stability as shown in Appendix A. Second, the value of χ varies positively with the tariff rate by definition. The value of the price elasticity of demand for imports, ε, also varies positively with the tariff rate (for a given world price of imports) for a large class import demand function including the linear one. Thus, for a very small initial value of the tariff, both ε and χ are close to zero, and consequently the tariff revenue increases with the tariff rate. But with successive increases in the tariff rate, as these values get larger, the rate of increase in the tariff revenue falls. Beyond a threshold value of the tariff rate, the tariff revenue falls, $\hat{R} < 0$, with further increase in the tariff rate. Thus, the tariff-revenue curve is inverted-U shaped as shown in Figure 4.1. Note, t_R is the tariff rate that maximises tariff revenue, and t_p prohibitive tariff rate that chokes off all imports. With the fixed input coefficient in the government sector and pre-determined money wage, the balanced-budget size of the government sector thus expands with the tariff rate till t_R and thereafter contracts since successively larger tariff rates than this generate successively smaller tariff revenues.

Given this balanced-budget constraint, the political support is maximised for the tariff rate t_e corresponding to the point of tangency e between the iso-political support curve S_o and the balanced-budget constraint curve Oat_P. The size of the government that this political-support maximising tariff rate can sustain is given by G_e. The assumed strict convexity of the iso-political support loci and the concavity of the tariff-revenue function ensure that the political-support maximising tariff rate is unique.

It should also be noted that the tariff rate t_e required to finance the political-support maximising government size (or expenditure) exceeds the revenue-maximising tariff rate. Essentially, the distributional consequence of a higher tariff rate and the associated higher political support induce the government to choose a higher tariff rate t_e. This result is similar to what Baldwin (2006) had shown in a different context. Thus,

Proposition 4.1:

Under the balanced-budget requirement, the political-support maximising tariff rate is larger than the revenue-maximising tariff rate.

Proof: Follows from the above discussion and Figure 4.1.

From the above analysis of political-support maximisation, it is immediate that there will be political resistance to the tariff reform. That is, when the government is committed to tariff reform, it is going to lose some political support. It may be of some interest, however, to know which income classes would be opposing such tariff reforms.

First of all note that starting from an initial tariff level of t_e that maximised the political support for the government, any tariff reduction due to such commitment in the range (t', t_e) will in fact increase the size of the government sector and consequently generate additional employment. Clearly, these people who find employment in the government sector will in fact favour the tariff reform. The owners of capital specifically in the import-competing sector will, of course, be the one income class who will be opposing such a tariff reform since their income will fall.

There will be a fall in employment as well in this sector for reasons spelt out above. However, if the elasticity of factor substitution in this sector is small, aggregate employment will still rise so that the workers on the whole will favour the tariff reform and the political resistance will come only from the capitalists. But if the elasticity of factor substitution is sufficiently large, aggregate employment will fall. In such a case, workers will also join hands with the capitalists to put political resistance to the tariff reform. But in any case, as long as the tariff cut is in the range (t', t_e), the government employees will not be opposing the tariff reform.[6] It is the private sector that will be hurt by foreign competition and, therefore, will not support the reform.

4.4 An Example

All the results derived above depend critically on the shape of the balanced-budget curve, or the tariff-revenue curve. It is, therefore, worthwhile to give an example where such a shape of the curve will hold well. We consider the simplest case of Cobb–Douglas utility and production functions:

$$U = D_X^{\alpha} D_Y^{1-\alpha} \tag{4.16}$$

$$X = L_X^{\delta} K_X^{1-\delta} \tag{4.17}$$

$$Y = L_Y^{\beta} K_Y^{1-\beta} \tag{4.18}$$

It is straightforward to check that the aggregate demand for the import-competing good is

$$D_Y = \frac{(1-\alpha)I}{(1+\alpha t)P_Y^*} \tag{4.19}$$

where I is the national income as defined in (4.4).

The cost-minimising capital-output ratios, on the other hand, are obtained from the equality of the marginal rate of technical substitution and the wage-rental ratio for each sector:

$$a_{KY} \equiv \frac{K_Y}{Y} = \varphi\left(\frac{\overline{W}}{r_Y}\right)^{\beta} \tag{4.20}$$

$$a_{KX} \equiv \frac{K_X}{X} = \phi\left(\frac{\overline{W}}{r_X}\right)^{\delta} \tag{4.21}$$

where $\varphi \equiv \left[\frac{\beta}{1-\beta}\right]^{-\beta}$ and $\phi \equiv \left[\frac{\delta}{1-\delta}\right]^{-\delta}$.

Therefore, using (4.8) and (4.9), we obtain the output levels which fully utilise the capital endowments as

$$Y = \frac{\overline{K}_Y}{\varphi}\left(\frac{\overline{W}}{r_Y}\right)^{-\beta} \tag{4.22}$$

$$X = \frac{\overline{K}_X}{\phi}\left(\frac{\overline{W}}{r_X}\right)^{-\delta} \tag{4.23}$$

Given these output levels, from the first-order conditions for cost minimisation, the labour coefficients can be obtained as:

$$a_{LX} = \frac{1}{\mu}\left(\frac{r_X}{\overline{W}}\right)^{1-\delta} \tag{4.24}$$

$$a_{LY} = \frac{1}{\rho}\left(\frac{r_Y}{\overline{W}}\right)^{1-\beta} \tag{4.25}$$

where $\mu \equiv \left[\frac{1-\delta}{\delta}\right]^{1-\delta}$ and $\rho \equiv \left[\frac{1-\beta}{\beta}\right]^{1-\beta}$.

Substitution of (4.20), (4.21), (4.24) and (4.25) in the zero-profit conditions yields the rates of return to the two sector-specific capital as

$$r_X = \left[\frac{1}{\left(\frac{1}{\mu}+\phi\right)\overline{W}^{\delta}}\right]^{\frac{1}{1-\delta}} \tag{4.26}$$

$$r_Y = \left[\frac{(1+t)P_Y^*}{\left(\frac{1}{\rho}+\varphi\right)\overline{W}^{\beta}}\right]^{\frac{1}{1-\beta}} \tag{4.27}$$

Finally, combining (4.4), (4.22), (4.23), (4.26) and (4.27), and using (4.19) we arrive at the import demand function as (see Appendix A):

$$M = \frac{(1-\alpha)A - \alpha B(1+t)^{\frac{\beta}{1-\beta}}}{2\alpha t P_Y^*} \tag{4.28}$$

where

$$A \equiv \left[\frac{\overline{K}_X}{\phi\overline{W}^{\delta}}\right]\left[\frac{1}{\left(\frac{1}{\mu}+\phi\right)\overline{W}^{\delta}}\right]^{\frac{\delta}{1-\delta}} > 0 \text{ and } B \equiv \left[\frac{P_Y^*\overline{K}_Y}{\varphi\overline{W}^{\beta}}\right]\left[\frac{P_Y^*}{\left(\frac{1}{\rho}+\varphi\right)\overline{W}^{\beta}}\right]^{\frac{\beta}{1-\beta}} > 0.$$

First of all note that $\frac{\partial M}{\partial t} < 0$ and $M = 0$ for the prohibitive tariff rate:

$$t_P = \left[\frac{(1-\alpha)A}{\alpha B}\right]^{\frac{1-\beta}{\beta}} - 1$$

It is also straightforward to check the (total) tariff elasticity of import demand:

$$e \equiv \frac{t}{M}\frac{\partial M}{\partial t}$$

is an increasing function of the tariff rate with values of e at $t = 0$ and at $t = t_P$ equal to zero and infinity, respectively. Therefore, the tariff revenue should increase with the tariff rate for all tariff rates for which the elasticity has less than the unity value and then fall with the tariff rate as the value of the total elasticity exceeds unity.

4.5 Size of the Government Sector and Aggregate Employment

The interesting feature of the political-support maximising equilibrium depicted in Figure 4.1 is that the size of the government sector that the politically optimum tariff rate can finance is smaller than the largest government sector G_{max} that the revenue-maximising tariff t_R could finance. This result follows simply from the fact that the iso-political support loci are downward sloping.

A larger G than G_e, for example, means higher employment and, therefore, larger political support measured by $S_g dG$. But under the balanced-budget requirement, the tariff revenue must also be greater than that generated by the tariff rate t_e. Given the shape of the tariff-revenue curve, and the higher equilibrium value of the tariff rate t_e than the tariff-revenue maximising rate, it is immediate that the tariff rate must be lowered to finance such a larger size of government. The balanced-budget rule (4.1) requires that such a reduction in the tariff rate must equal

$$dt = \frac{a_{Lg}\overline{W}}{(1-e)P_Y^* M}dG \tag{4.29}$$

where e is the *total* tariff elasticity of the import demand function.[7]

But a lower tariff rate means a fall in political support because the rate of return to capital used in the import-competing sector falls. The extent of tariff reduction which leaves the government with exactly the same level of total political support S_o as for the optimum pair (G_e, t_e) equals

$$dt\big|_{S_0} = -\frac{S_g}{S_t}dG \tag{4.30}$$

The convexity of the iso-political support loci, however, implies that $dt\big|_{S_0}$ is smaller than dt. That is, a larger tariff reduction is required to generate the additional tariff revenue to finance the additional wage bill in a larger government sector than the tariff reduction which maintains the same level of political support. Consequently, under the balanced-budget rule, the gain of political support for the larger government (than G_e) from the wage earners cannot compensate for the loss of political support from the capitalists due to the corresponding reduction in the tariff rate.[8]

Clearly, the political-support maximising size of the government will generate smaller employment in the public sector than in the largest government sector, under the balanced-budget rule. Does the aggregate employment fall? Interestingly, quite on the contrary, aggregate employment may increase. In other words, the largest government sector, under the balanced-budget rule, may lower the aggregate employment. This is because, though the largest government sector G_{max} generates higher employment than the political-support maximising size G_e, the corresponding lower tariff required to generate additional fund to finance the wage bill has a contractionary effect. Using (4.1) and (4.10), it is easy to check that the aggregate employment falls if the elasticity of factor substitution in the import-competing sector, σ_Y, is sufficiently large:

$$\hat{L}_e = \left[\lambda_{Lg}(1-e) + \lambda_{LY}\frac{\theta_{LY}}{\theta_{KY}}\sigma_Y\gamma\right]\hat{t} \qquad (4.31)$$

Thus,

Proposition 4.2:

A larger government sector than the one that the political-support maximising tariff can finance lowers the aggregate employment under the balanced-budget rule, if the elasticity of factor substitution in the import-competing sector exceeds the critical value defined in (4.31a).

Proof:

Given the property of the balanced-budget constraint (4.1), a larger G than G_e requires a lower tariff to generate higher revenue. Thus, $\hat{t} < 0$ in (4.31). Since around G_e, the value of e exceeds unity, the first term in the parentheses on the right-hand side in (4.18) is negative. Therefore, the aggregate employment falls ($\hat{L} < 0$) if

$$\sigma_Y > \sigma_Y^* \equiv \gamma(e-1)\frac{\lambda_{Lg}}{\lambda_{LY}}\frac{\theta_{KY}}{\theta_{LY}} \qquad (4.31a)$$

The intuition is simple. The required tariff reduction lowers the rate of return to capital used in the import-competing sector. Given the fixed money wage, this induces producers to substitute labour with capital. For a given output level, employment in this sector contracts. But the intensive use of capital which is specific in this sector and already fully used causes the physical output to contract as well and thereby lowers employment further. If the elasticity of factor substitution is very large in the sense defined in (4.31a), these adverse technique and scale effects on employment are large too, causing the aggregate employment to fall despite the expansion of employment in the larger government sector.

4.6 Conclusion

This chapter shows that under a balanced-budget rule, the political-support maximising tariff is larger than the revenue-maximising tariff. From the above analysis of political-support maximisation, it is immediate that there will be political resistance to tariff reform. That is, when the government is committed to tariff reform, it is going to lose some political support. Workers and capitalists in the import-competing sector will both lose from a tariff reform – capitalists lose because of a lower rate of return they now earn, whereas some workers lose their jobs. There will be, however, employment gain in the government sector, provided the tariff reform is moderate. Consequently, if the elasticity of factor substitution in the import-competing sector is small, then the aggregate employment may still rise. Thus, the workers on the whole are expected to favour the tariff reform and the political resistance will come primarily from the capitalists.

On the other hand, we have shown that the largest government sector in a small open economy does not get the maximum political support from the income earners. Moreover, even though employment generated in the government sector is maximum for such a largest size, the aggregate employment in fact may fall depending on the elasticity of factor substitution in the import-competing sector.

Appendix A

A.1 Change in Tariff Revenue

Total differentiation of the revenue function, $R = tP_Y^*M$, and standard operations yield

$$\hat{R} = \hat{t} + \hat{M} \tag{A.4.1}$$

Note, by the small country assumption, $\hat{P}_Y^* = 0$. Recalling $M = D_Y(p_d, I) - Y$ from (4.3) in the text, where $p_d = (1 + t)P_Y^*$, the change in import volume can be worked out as:

$$dM = \frac{\partial D_Y}{\partial p_d} dp_d + \frac{\partial D_Y}{\partial I} dI - dY$$

$$= D_Y[-\varepsilon p_d + \eta I] - Y(Y)$$

where $\varepsilon \equiv -\frac{p_d}{D_Y}\frac{\partial D_Y}{\partial p_d}$ is the absolute price elasticity of demand for good Y

and $\eta \equiv \frac{I}{D_Y}\frac{\partial D_Y}{\partial I}$ is the income elasticity of demand for good Y.

Using $\hat{p}_d = \gamma\hat{t}$, the above expression boils down to

$$\hat{M} = -\psi\varepsilon\gamma\hat{t} + \eta\psi\hat{I} - \chi\hat{Y} \tag{A.4.2}$$

where $\psi \equiv \frac{D_Y}{M}$ and $\chi \equiv \frac{Y}{M}$.

From (4.8) and (4.9) in the text, and using the least-cost conditions $\theta_{KX}\hat{a}_{KX} + \theta_{LX}\hat{a}_{LX} = 0$ and $\theta_{KY}\hat{a}_{KY} + \theta_{LY}\hat{a}_{LY} = 0$, we obtain changes in the output levels as:

$$\begin{aligned}\hat{X} &= -\hat{a}_{KX}\\ &= -\hat{a}_{KX} + \theta_{KX}\hat{a}_{KX} + \theta_{LX}\hat{a}_{LX}\\ &= -\theta_{LX}(\hat{a}_{KX} - \hat{a}_{LX})\end{aligned}$$

Defining elasticity of factor substitution in sector X as $\sigma_X = \frac{\hat{a}_{KX} - \hat{a}_{LX}}{\hat{\bar{W}} - \hat{r}_X}$, the above expression boils down to

$$\hat{X} = -\sigma_X\theta_{LX}\left(\hat{\bar{W}} - \hat{r}_X\right) \tag{A.4.3}$$

Similarly,

$$\hat{Y} = -\sigma_Y\theta_{LY}\left(\hat{\bar{W}} - \hat{r}_Y\right) \tag{A.4.4}$$

Given the wage rigidity, from the zero-profit conditions (4.5) and (4.6), we obtain the changes in the rates of returns to the two types of capital as

$$\hat{r}_X = 0, \hat{r}_Y = \frac{\gamma\hat{t}}{\theta_{KY}} \tag{A.4.5}$$

Substitution of (A.4.5) in (A.4.3) and (A.4.4) yields

$$\hat{X} = 0,\ \hat{Y} = \sigma_Y\gamma\frac{\theta_{LY}}{\theta_{KY}}\hat{t} \tag{A.4.6}$$

Now, from (4.4), the proportionate change in national income can be derived as

$$\hat{I} = \theta_X \hat{X} + \theta_Y \left(\hat{Y} + \hat{p}_d \right) + \theta_R \left(\hat{M} + \hat{t} \right) \tag{A.4.7}$$

where $\theta_X \equiv \frac{X}{I}$ is the share of sector X in national income, $\theta_Y \equiv \frac{p_d Y}{I}$ is the share of sector Y in national income evaluated at the domestic (relative) price of Y, and $\theta_R \equiv \frac{tP_Y^* M}{I}$ is the share of tariff revenue in national income (which by (4.1) is essentially the share of the government-sector wage bill in national income).

Substitution of (A.4.6) in (A.4.2) yields

$$\hat{M} = -\psi\varepsilon\gamma\hat{t} + \eta\psi\hat{I} - \chi\sigma_Y\gamma\frac{\theta_{LY}}{\theta_{KY}}\hat{t} = -\gamma\left(-\psi\varepsilon + \chi\sigma_Y \frac{\theta_{LY}}{\theta_{KY}} \right)\hat{t} + \eta\psi\hat{I} \tag{A.4.2a}$$

On the other hand, the substitution of (A.4.6) and $\hat{p}_d = \gamma\hat{t}$ in (A.4.7) yields

$$\hat{I} = \left[\theta_Y \gamma \left(1 + \sigma_Y \frac{\theta_{LY}}{\theta_{KY}} \right) + \theta_R \right] \hat{t} + \theta_R \hat{M} \tag{A.4.7a}$$

By Cramer's Rule, we can solve for $\hat{M}$ and $\hat{I}$ simultaneously:

$$\begin{bmatrix} -\eta\psi & 1 \\ 1 & -\theta_R \end{bmatrix} \begin{bmatrix} \hat{I} \\ \hat{M} \end{bmatrix} = \begin{bmatrix} -C\hat{t} \\ D\hat{t} \end{bmatrix}$$

where $C \equiv \gamma\left(-\psi\varepsilon + \chi\sigma_Y \frac{\theta_{LY}}{\theta_{KY}} \right)$, $D \equiv \theta_Y\gamma\left(1 + \sigma_Y \frac{\theta_{LY}}{\theta_{KY}} \right) + \theta_R$ and $\Delta \equiv \eta\psi\theta_R - 1$.

Note that $\Delta < 0$ by stability. This follows from the fact that the (positively sloped) locus of combinations of $\hat{M}$ and $\hat{I}$ satisfying (A.4.2a) must be steeper than the (positively sloped) locus representing (A.4.7a) in the $\left(\hat{M}, \hat{I} \right)$ space.

Hence,

$$\hat{M} = \frac{\left[\eta\psi\left[\theta_R + \theta_Y\gamma\left(1 + \sigma_Y \frac{\theta_{LY}}{\theta_{KY}} \right) \right] - \gamma\left(\psi\varepsilon + \sigma_Y\chi\frac{\theta_{LY}}{\theta_{KY}} \right) \right]}{\left[1 - \eta\psi\theta_R \right]} \hat{t}$$

Now, given $\hat{R} = \hat{t} + \hat{M}$, we have

$$\hat{R} = \frac{\left[1 + \psi\eta\gamma\theta_Y\left(1 + \sigma_Y \frac{\theta_{LY}}{\theta_{KY}} \right) - \left(\psi\varepsilon + \sigma_Y\chi\frac{\theta_{LY}}{\theta_{KY}} \right)\gamma \right]\hat{t}}{1 - \eta\psi\theta_R}$$

as in the text.

A.1.1 Import Demand Function

Substitution of (4.22) and (4.23) in (4.4) in the text yields the national income as:

$$I = \frac{\overline{K}_X}{\phi \overline{W}^{\delta}}(r_X)^{\delta} + \frac{(1+t)P_Y^* \overline{K}_Y}{\varphi \overline{W}^{\beta}}(r_Y)^{\beta} + tP_Y^* M \tag{A.4.8}$$

which using (4.26) and (4.27) in the text boils down to

$$I = A + B(1+t)^{\frac{\beta}{1-\beta}} \tag{A.4.9}$$

where A and B are as defined in the text.

Thus, national income is an increasing function of the tariff rate. The income gain from a higher tariff despite no terms-of-trade gain arises due to the higher employment generated by such a tariff.

Then combining (4.3), (4.19) and (A.4.9) we arrive at the import demand function as defined in (4.28) in the text.

Notes

1 I would like to thank Ngo Van Long for his helpful comments on an earlier draft. The usual disclaimer applies, however.
2 See Przeworski et al (2000) and Varshney (2002) for similar arguments that an authoritarian regime being free from political compulsions can implement policies even if that hurts a few interest groups in the short term.
3 We focus solely on the supply side of the political market abstracting from the lobbying decisions of the private agents as in, for example, Grossman and Helpman (1994). Our approach resembles more to the political-support function approach of Cassing and Hillman (1985).
4 Policy reversals in many Latin American countries during the 1980s are cases in point.
5 The government can also collect revenues through domestic taxes. However, to focus on the political resistance to tariff reforms, we simplify our analysis by abstracting from such additional sources of revenue to finance government services.
6 Of course, government employees will support the tariff reform if they have a separatist attitude towards the workers in the private sector.
7 This total elasticity takes into account both the price and the (national) income effect of the tariff on import demand and is greater than one in value along the declining part of the tariff-revenue (or the balanced-budget) curve.
8 Note that this result *may* hold even when the iso-political support loci are concave.

References and Notes

Acemoglu, D. and J. A. Robinson (2015). The Rise and Decline of General Laws of Capitalism. *Journal of Economic Perspectives*, 29(1): 3–28, Winter. http://dx.doi.org/10.1257/jep.29.1.3 doi=10.1257/jep.29.1.3

Annett, A., 2001, "Social Fractionalization, Political Instability, and the Size of the Government", *IMF Staff Papers* 48: 561–592.

Baldwin, R., 2006, "Multilateralizing Regionalism: Spaghetti Bowls as Building Blocs on the Path to Global Free Trade", *The World Economy* 29(11): 1451–1518.

Blomberg, S.B., 1996, "Growth, Political Instability and the Defense Burden", *Economica* 63(252): 649–672.

Bogliaccini, J.A., 2013, "Trade Liberalization, De-industrialisation, and Inequality: Evidence from Middle-Income Latin American Countries", *Latin American Research Review* 48(2): 79–105.

Brady, D., Y. Kaya, and G. Gereffi (2011). Stagnating Industrial Employment in Latin America. *Work and Occupations*, 38(2). https://doi.org/10.1177/0730888410387987

Cassing, J.H. and A.L. Hillman, 1985, "Political Influence Motives and the Choice Between Tariffs and Quotas", *Journal of International Economics* 19(3–4): 279–290.

Cornia, G., and S. Kiiski, (2001). Trends in Income Distribution in the Post-World War II Period Evidence and Interpretation, Working Paper # 89, World Institute for Development Economic Research (UNU-WIDER).

Findlay, R. and S. Wellisz, 1982, "Endogenous Tariffs, the Political Economy of Trade Restrictions, and Welfare", in J.N. Bhagwati, ed., *Import Competition and Response*, Chicago, IL: University of Chicago Press, 223–243.

Francese, M. and C. Mulas-Granados (2015). Functional Income Distribution and Its Role in Explaining Inequality. IMF Working Paper, WP/15/244.

Francois, J. and D.R. Nelson, 2014, "Political Support for Trade Policy in the European Union", *European Journal of Political Economy* 36: 243–253.

Grossman, G.M., and E. Helpman (1994). Protection for sale. *American Economic Review*.84: 833–850.

Harvey, D. (2005). *A brief history of neoliberalism*. New York, NY: Oxford University Press.

IMF Policy Paper, (2014), Fiscal Policy and Income Inequality, IMF (January).

Jones, R.W., 1971, "A Three Factor Model in Trade, Theory and History", in J.N. Bhagwati et al., eds., *Trade, Balance of Payments and Growth*, Amsterdam: North Holland, 3–21.

Kim, D. and C.-I. Lee, 2021, "Government Size, Trade Openness, and Intersectoral Income Fluctuation: An International Panel Analysis", *Public Finance Review* 49(2): 294–332.

Musau, A., 2019, "A Replication Study of "Openness, Country Size, and Government Size, *Public Finance Review* 47(4): 775–792.

Nelson, D.R., 2009, "The Political Economy of Protection", in K.A. Reinert, R. Rajan, A.J. Glass, and L.S. Davis, eds., *Princeton Encyclopedia of International Economics*, Princeton, NJ: Princeton University Press, pp. 916–924.

Piketty, T. (2014), *Capital in the Twenty-First Century*. Cambridge: Harvard University Press.

Portes, A. and B.R. Roberts (2005). The free-market city: Latin American urbanization in the years of the neoliberal experiment. *Studies in Comparative International Development*. 40: 43–82.

Przeworski, A., M. E. Alvarez, J. A. Cheibub, and F. Limongi, 2000, *Democracy and Development*, Cambridge University Press.

Ram, Rati, 2009, "Openness, Country Size, and Government Size: Additional Evidence from a Large Cross-Country Panel", *Journal of Public Economics* 93(1–2): 213–218.

Rodrik, D., 1995, "Political Economy of Trade Policy", in Gene Grossman and Kenneth Rogoff, eds., *Handbook of International Economics*, vol. III, Amsterdam: Elsevier Science B.V., 1457–1494.

Rodrik, D., 1998, "Why Do More Open Economies Have Bigger Governments?", *Journal of Political Economy* 106(5): 997–1032.

Varshney, A., 2002, "Poverty Eradication and Democracy in the Developing World", Background Paper, *Human Development Report*, United Nations: New York.

Velasco, A., 1997, "A Model of Endogenous Fiscal Deficits and Delayed Fiscal Reforms", *NBER Working Paper* # 6336.

Wu, A. and M. Lin, 2012, "Determinants of Government Size: Evidence from China", *Public Choice* 151(1–2): 255–270.

5 Crime, Efficiency of Labour and Economic Development

A Theoretical Analysis

Manash Ranjan Gupta and Priya Brata Dutta

5.1 Introduction

There exist substantial works on unemployment in labour markets, and a subset of this literature deals with the efficiency wage hypothesis.[1] According to this hypothesis, the labour efficiency of a worker varies positively with the wage rate and the unemployment rate. An increase in the unemployment rate lowers the expected income in the outside labour market and thus lowers the marginal benefit of shirking. Hence the worker shirks less and his efficiency is improved. Since unemployment generates a favourable effect on the efficiency of labour, profit-maximising firms keep the employment level below the market clearing level.

However, these efficiency wage models do not analyse the interaction between the unemployment problem and criminal activities, and this interaction is important when labour efficiency receives a negative feedback from the development of criminal activities. Workers are always threatened to lose their income and life from those criminal activities, and this fear generates a strong disutility from criminal activities. This demotivates a worker to earn more and to work hard in an unprotected place. The larger the volume of criminal activities, the higher the level of the marginal disutility of working hard.

In reality, a significant share of the population in different countries is involved in various criminal activities including thefts, robberies, snatching etc. Many empirical works support this, and the works of Carmichal and Ward (2000), Bukenya (2005), Nilsson (2004), Sachsida et al. (2010), Witt et al. (1998), Papps and Winkelmann (2000) and Wu and Wu (2012) may be mentioned as examples. These studies show that low income of the people along with unemployment and underemployment induces them to be involved in criminal activities. These studies also point out that this problem of crime exists not only in low-income countries but also in different regions of various economically advanced countries like the USA, the UK, Sweden, Brazil, New Zealand and Russia.[2] So the existence of criminal activities implies the loss of a part of the labour endowment from its productive use. A fraction of open unemployed people join the criminal sector.

DOI: 10.4324/9781003375050-5

While unemployment causes a favourable effect by raising the efficiency of labour, criminal activities generate adverse effects by lowering the efficiency of labour.

Many theoretical works[3] analyse the economics of crime and punishment where crime is treated as a high-return risky activity. These models determine equilibrium values of the size of the criminal sector and the rate of punishment and then analyse the effectiveness of different anti-crime policies. A few of these models show multiple equilibria with a stable crime trap equilibrium as well as with a stable crime-less society equilibrium. Some of these models introduce job search mechanisms to focus on the interaction among crime, income inequality and unemployment. However, these models do not take care of the production side of the economy. So these models fail to analyse how criminal activities affect national income and economic growth.

We develop an efficiency wage macro-static model in this chapter. The efficiency of labour not only varies directly with the wage rate and unemployment rate but also varies inversely with the size of the criminal sector. In this sense, our efficiency wage model is more general than the conventional one. A fraction of the working population is involved in criminal activities, and this allocation of labour between employment and crime is determined by the rational behaviour of the representative criminal. These criminals snatch a fraction of the income of factor owners to finance their consumption and take the risk of being punished.[4] The punishment is made in terms of a fine to be paid to the government. So the size of the criminal sector is determined endogenously in the general equilibrium, and this determination is not independent of the determination of factor prices and of employment and output of the economy.

The size of the criminal sector generates a negative effect on the efficiency of labour. The larger the number of criminals in society, the greater the threat of crime to be faced by factor owners. So the criminal sector generates a social bad. It enhances the marginal disutility of the effort of the worker when the worker works in an unprotected social environment. So when the efficiency of labour varies positively with the unemployment rate and inversely with the size of the criminal sector, profit-maximising firms reduce the employment rate to fight against the negative effect of crime. Hence the relative size of the criminal sector and the unemployment rate in the labour market are determined simultaneously in the general equilibrium.

Many interesting comparative static results can be derived from this model. An exogenous increase in capital endowment raises the intensity of crime in society as well as the rate of unemployment. So economic growth through capital accumulation may fail to solve the unemployment problem in the presence of crime. On the other hand, it aggravates the unemployment problem through the development of criminal activities when the anti-crime policies of the government are very weak. The increase in capital stock may also reduce the level of national income in such cases. The increase in the rate of criminalisation as well as the increase in the rate of unemployment takes place following capital accumulation, and these may lower the rate of productive utilisation of worker endowment. This indirect negative effect on worker endowment may outweigh the direct positive effect of capital accumulation when the expected cost of punishment is negligible. Existing literature on growth and development does not focus on this negative effect of capital accumulation which is generated in a crime-affected society.

In Section 5.2, we derive the efficiency function of labour, and, in Section 5.3, we develop the macro-static model. Various comparative static properties are analysed in Section 5.4. Final remarks are made in Section 5.5.

5.2 Efficiency Function of Labour

This section provides the micro-foundation of the labour efficiency function of the worker who takes the risk of shirking since shirking lowers his disutility of effort. This efficiency function is derived from the utility-maximising behaviour of the worker who derives utility from consumption but derives disutility from effort as well as from a public bad called criminal activity. The size of the criminal activity may be measured by the number of individuals involved in the criminal activity.

Let Y_e be the expected income (consumption) of the worker and $\pi(Y_e)$ be the utility function, and $V(e,Z)$ be the disutility function where e is the effort level and Z is the size of the criminal sector. We assume the following conditions to be satisfied: (i) $V_1 > 0$, $V_2 > 0$, $V_{11} < 0$, $V_{22} < 0$, $V_{12} > 0$ and (ii) $\pi'(.) > 0$, $\pi''(.) \leq 0$. Here, $V_{12} > 0$ implies that the marginal disutility of labour varies positively with the size of the criminal activity. This is valid when leisure and public bad are complementary. $\pi''(.) = (<)0$ implies that the worker is risk neutral (averter).

The worker attempts to maximise the net utility given by:

$$J = \pi(Y_e) - V(e,Z)$$

with respect to the choice of effort, e. A higher level of effort, e, implies a lower rate of shirking. Here

$$Y_e = pw + (1-p)w^a$$

where $(1-p)$ is the probability of the worker being fired due to shirking and w is the wage rate earned in the work place. The intensity of the threat of firing is measured by this probability of firing. Here w^a represents the alternative expected income that the worker can earn after being fired. This probability is assumed to vary inversely with the effort level. Mathematically,

$$p = p(e) \text{ with } p'(e) > 0.$$

$p''(e) < 0$ is assumed for the sake of simplicity.

$$w^a = (1-u)w^*.$$

Here u denotes the probability of remaining unemployed after being fired. This probability is measured by the unemployment rate defined as the ratio of the number of unemployed workers to the total number of workers. w^* stands for the actual wage rate in the alternative job.

Using all these equations, we have

$$Y_e = p(e)w + (1-p(e))(1-u)w^*.$$

This is the expected income of the worker, and it is a function of e. However, the actual wage income, w, does not depend on the level of effort, e.

Using all these equations, we have

$$J = \pi\left(\left\{p(e)w + (1-p(e))\left\{(1-u)w^*\right\}\right\}\right) - V(e,Z),$$

or

$$J = \pi\left(\left\{p(e)\left(w - w^* + uw^*\right) + (1-u)w^*\right\}\right) - V(e,Z).$$

This, net utility, J, is to be maximised with respect to e, and the first-order condition of maximisation is given by:

$$\pi'(.)p'(e)\left\{\left(w - w^*\right) + uw^*\right\} = V_1.$$

Here the right-hand side of this equation stands for the marginal disutility of labour and its left-hand side denotes the marginal utility of effort through consumption. $\pi'(.)$ stands for the marginal utility of expected income (consumption) and $p'(e)\left\{\left(w - w^*\right) + uw^*\right\}$ stands for the marginal contribution of effort on expected income.

The second-order condition of maximisation is given by:

$$D = \left[\left(\pi''(.)\, p'(e) + \pi'(.)\, p''(e)\right)\left\{\left(w - w^*\right) + uw^*\right\} - V_{11}\right] < 0.$$

This is satisfied because $w \geq w^* > 0$, by assumption. Also, by assumption, $p''(e) < 0$, $V_{11} > 0$ and $\pi''(.) \leq 0$.

For a risk-neutral worker, $\pi''(.) = 0$, and $D < 0$ because $p''(e) < 0$ and $V_{11} > 0$. Utility defined over expected income makes sense when we assume risk neutrality, i.e., $\pi''(.) = 0$.

From the first-order condition of maximisation and with $\pi''(.) = 0$, we have

$$\mathrm{Dde} = -p'(e)\left\{dw + w^{*}du\right\} + V_{12}dZ.$$

Hence

$$\frac{de}{dw} = -\frac{p'(e)}{D} > 0,$$

$$\frac{de}{du} = -\frac{p'(e)w^{*}}{D} > 0,$$

and

$$\frac{de}{dZ} = \frac{V_{12}(.)}{D} \langle 0 \,\text{if}\, V_{12} \rangle 0.$$

If e^{*} is the utility-maximising level of effort of the worker, then

$$e^{*} = e^{*}(w, Z, u)$$

is the optimum effort function, and this is the labour efficiency function in this model. Now, we can easily establish the following proposition.

Proposition 5.1: Labour efficiency of the worker varies positively with the wage rate and with the unemployment rate. It also varies inversely with the size of the criminal sector if the marginal disutility of labour varies positively with the size of the criminal sector.

We provide intuitive explanations behind the proposition. An exogenous increase in the wage rate means a rise in the marginal return on her effort, and this indirectly implies a rise in the opportunity cost of her shirking. So she must shirk less following an increase in the wage rate. Similarly a rise in the unemployment rate means a fall in her expected income from an alternative source which, in turn, implies a rise in the cost of shirking. So she works harder in her present workplace when there is a higher unemployment rate in the outside labour market. An exogenous increase in the size of the criminal sector raises the marginal disutility of labour of the worker when leisure and this public bad are complementary in worker's preference. So the worker works hard to earn more due a reduction in the size of the criminal sector.

One may note that the efficiency of labour varies directly with the size of the criminal sector when $V_{12} < 0$, i.e., when leisure and this public bad are substitutes in her preference. We get back to the conventional efficiency wage hypothesis in the special case, where $V_{12} = 0$. However we go ahead with the assumption that $V_{12} > 0$.

5.3 The Model

We consider a macro-static model with only one production sector and with two factors of production called labour and capital where all exchanges take place in competitive markets. The production function satisfies all standard neo-classical properties including constant returns to scale. Labour is measured in efficiency units, and the number of workers is exogenously given. The wage rate is perfectly flexible. However, unemployment exists in the labour market, and this unemployment equilibrium is explained by the efficiency wage hypothesis. According to the conventional version of the efficiency wage hypothesis, the efficiency of a worker varies positively with the wage rate and the unemployment rate. The special feature of this model is that the efficiency of labour also varies inversely with the size of the criminal sector. The rental rate on capital is perfectly flexible and this flexibility ensures full utilisation of capital stock. The representative firm maximises profit, and so all profit-maximising input–output coefficients depend on the wage-rental ratio. The representative consumer maximises utility subject to the budget constraint.

There exists a self-employed criminal sector formed by some workers. Those who do not work in the production sector remain either unemployed or join the criminal sector. Criminals snatch a fraction of factor income and the fraction of snatched income varies directly with the relative size of the criminal sector. The relative size is defined as the number of criminals divided by the number of workers available in the economy. Joining the criminal sector involves risk. Every criminal faces a positive probability of being caught and punished. Punishment is made in terms of a fine to be paid to the government, and this fine revenue is redistributed equally among all individuals. When the government strengthens punishment policies, criminals face a higher probability of punishment and are forced to pay a higher fine after punishment.

The representative risk-neutral criminal enters (quits) the criminal sector when the gain from crime exceeds (falls short of) the opportunity cost of joining the criminal sector. The gain is the per-capita snatched income, and the expected value of the fine, defined as the amount of fine multiplied by the probability of being punished, plus the expected wage rate, defined as the actual wage rate multiplied by the rate of employment, is the opportunity cost of doing crime. In migration equilibrium, the average snatched income is equal to the opportunity cost of being a criminal.

The following notations describe variables and parameters:

z = Number of criminals (absolute size of the criminal sector).
λ = Relative size of the criminal sector.
$1-\phi$ = Fraction of income snatched by criminals.
p = Exogenously given probability of punishment to be faced by a criminal.
T = Fine to be paid by a criminal after punishment.
u = The rate of unemployment.
L = Number of workers.

K = Capital stock.
X = Level of output.
h = Efficiency of labour.
w = Wage rate.
a_L = Labour-output coefficient.
a_K = Capital-output coefficient.
θ_L = Labour share of output.
θ_K = Capital share of output.
ε_w = Elasticity of labour efficiency with respect to the wage rate.
ε_u = Elasticity of labour efficiency with respect to the rate of unemployment.
ε_z = Elasticity of labour efficiency with respect to the size of the criminal sector.
r = Rental rate on capital.
Y = Total factor income.

The following equations describe the model:

$$z = \lambda L \tag{5.1}$$

$$\phi = \phi(\lambda) = (1-\lambda) \text{ with } \phi'(\lambda) < 0 \tag{5.2}$$

$$\frac{(1-\phi(\lambda))Y}{z} = pT + w(1-u) \tag{5.3}$$

$$1 = a_L\left(\frac{w}{h}\right) + a_K r; \tag{5.4}$$

$$h = h(w,u,z) \textit{ with } h_j > 0 \textit{ for } j = w,u \textit{ and } h_j < 0 \textit{ for } j = z; \tag{5.5}$$

$$\varepsilon_w = h_w . \frac{w}{h} = 1; \tag{5.6}$$

$$a_L X = Lh(1-u)(1-\lambda); \tag{5.7}$$

$$a_K X = K; \tag{5.8}$$

and

$$Y = wL(1-\lambda)(1-u) + rK. \tag{5.9}$$

Here Equation (5.1) is a definitional identity. The relative size of the criminal sector denoted by λ is measured by the fraction of workers involved in criminal activities. Equation (5.2) implies that the fraction of income snatched by criminals varies positively with the relative size of the criminal sector. As the fraction of criminals in society increases, individuals face a larger number of criminal activities and thus lose a higher fraction of their income. Equation (5.3) is the equilibrium condition allocating workers between the production sector and the criminal sector. $(1-\varphi(\lambda))$ fraction of total factor income is snatched. So the left-hand side of Equation

(5.3) represents the average snatched income (consumption) of criminals. pT stands for the expected value of the fine to be paid by the criminal after punishment. It is defined as the actual amount of fine multiplied by the probability of punishment. $w(1-u)$ is the expected wage rate to be sacrificed while joining the criminal sector because a criminal cannot work in the production sector. This expected wage rate is defined as the actual wage rate multiplied by the rate of employment. So $(pT+w(1-u))$ represents the opportunity cost of joining the criminal sector. The average snatched income of the representative criminal is the gain of joining the criminal sector and it is equal to the opportunity cost of joining the criminal sector in equilibrium. Equation (5.4) represents the profit-maximising condition of the representative competitive firm. The price of the product is normalised to unity in one commodity model. Price is equal to marginal cost in competitive equilibrium, and marginal cost is equal to average cost when production technology satisfies constant returns to scale (CRS). a_L and a_K are functions of $\left(\frac{w}{h}\right)$ and r because they stand for profit-maximising factor-output coefficients in a variable coefficient production technology. Equation (5.5) stands for the efficiency function of labour. The efficiency of labour varies positively with the wage rate and with the unemployment rate but varies inversely with the size of the criminal sector. The efficiency of labour is a concave function in terms of its every argument. It is the optimum effort function of a utility-maximising worker derived in the presence of threat of firing when the worker shirks. The effective unit cost of employing labour is $\left(\frac{w}{h}\right)$, and this unit cost is minimised with respect to the wage rate, w. Equation (5.6) shows the first-order condition of minimisation. It is similar to Solow (1979) condition which implies that wage elasticity of labour efficiency is equal to unity. Equation (5.7) represents how labour is utilised in production. $Lh(1-u)(1-\lambda)$ is the availability of an effective labour force to be used in production and a_LX shows the requirement of labour in the production sector. Equation (5.8) stands for capital market equilibrium, and this equilibrium is automatically attained by the flexibility of the rental rate on capital. Equation (5.9) shows that national income at factor cost is equal to the sum of wage income and rental income.

Using Equations (5.4), (5.7)–(5.9), we have

$$wL(1-\lambda)(1-u)+rK=\left(\frac{w}{h}\right)a_LX+ra_KX$$

$$\Rightarrow Y=X$$

So national income at factor cost is equal to national income at product price (total output). The price of the product is normalised to unity in the one-sector model.

Here we have nine equations with nine unknowns given by: z, λ, ϕ, w, h, r, X, u and Y. Their equilibrium values are to be obtained in terms of four parameters: K, L, T and p. Equations (5.4)–(5.6) solve w, r and h. Their values are independent of parameters – K, L, T and p. Hence values of a_L and a_K are also independent of these parameters. Equation (5.8) solves X in terms of K, and X = Y. Equations (5.1)–(5.3) and (5.7) solve z, λ, ϕ and u.

From Equations (5.1)–(5.3) and (5.9), we have[5]

$$-w\lambda(1-u)+r\frac{K}{L}=pT. \tag{5.10}$$

So Equation (5.10) represents the labour mobility condition between the production sector and the criminal sector.

5.4 Working of the Model

5.4.1 Factor Prices

From Equation (5.4), we have

$$0=\theta_{LU}\left(\hat{w}-\hat{h}\right)+\theta_{KU}\hat{r}. \tag{5.11}$$

From Equation (5.5), we have

$$\hat{h}=\hat{w}+\varepsilon_u\hat{u}+\varepsilon_z\left(\hat{\lambda}+\hat{L}\right). \tag{5.12}$$

From Equation (5.6), we have

$$\hat{h}=\hat{w}. \tag{5.13}$$

Hence Equations (5.11) and (5.13) imply that

$$\hat{r}=0.$$

Differentiating Equation (5.6), we have

$$h_{ww}\frac{(w)^2}{h}\hat{w}-\varepsilon_u\hat{u}-\varepsilon_z\hat{z}=0; \tag{5.14}$$

where

$$\hat{z}=\hat{\lambda}+\hat{L}.$$

Equations (5.12) and (5.13) imply

$$\varepsilon_u \hat{u} + \varepsilon_z \left(\hat{\lambda} + \hat{L}\right) = 0. \tag{5.15}$$

Equations (5.13)–(5.15) imply

$$\hat{w} = \hat{h} = 0. \tag{5.16}$$

So w, h and r are independent of changes in parameters: K, L, T and p. An exogenous increase in the amount of fine, T, and/or in the rate of punishment, p, takes place due to strengthening of punishment policies of the government.

This leads to the following proposition.

Proposition 5.2: Strengthening of punishment policies designed to control criminal activities and the change in factor endowments have no effect on factor prices and the efficiency of labour when workers are paid efficiency wages.

We provide the intuition behind this proposition. Workers are paid an efficiency wage. So, in the competitive equilibrium, labour cost per efficiency unit is minimised, and this minimum value is independent of the strengthening of punishment policy parameters. Since the price of the product is normalised to unity, the rental rate on capital becomes a function of efficiency wage in the competitive equilibrium and thus remains unaffected by changes in these parameters.

Equation (5.15) shows how the rate of unemployment is changed in response to the change in the size of the criminal sector. Employers make this adjustment of employment in order to protect labour efficiency at the profit-maximising level, i.e., to ensure the payment of efficiency wage to employed workers. The interesting implication obtained from this equation is that the change in the unemployment rate is not directly sensitive to capital accumulation and punishment policies. However, it may be indirectly sensitive to those parameters through the change in the size of the criminal sector.

In the conventional efficiency wage model, $\varepsilon_z = 0$, and hence Equation (5.15) implies that $\hat{u} = 0$. So the equilibrium unemployment rate is also independent of changes in these parameters – K, T and p – in the conventional efficiency wage model.

From Equation (5.10),[6] we have

$$\frac{w\lambda u}{pT}\hat{u} - \frac{w\lambda(1-u)}{pT}\hat{\lambda} = -\frac{r\frac{K}{L}}{pT}\left(\hat{K} - \hat{L}\right) + \hat{T} + \hat{p}. \tag{5.17}$$

This Equation (5.17) shows how the relative size of the criminal sector is changed due to changes in the parameters which affect the labour mobility condition between the production sector and the criminal sector. In the conventional efficiency wage model, $\varepsilon_z = 0$, and so Equation (5.15) implies that $\hat{u} = 0$.

Hence Equation (5.17) alone solves $\hat{\lambda}$ in that model. However, in the present model, $\hat{\lambda}$ and $\hat{u}$ are simultaneously determined by Equations (5.15) and (5.17).

5.4.2 Unemployment and Crime

Using Equations (5.15) and (5.17), we have

$$\begin{bmatrix} \dfrac{w\lambda u}{pT} & -\dfrac{w\lambda(1-u)}{pT} \\ \varepsilon_u & \varepsilon_z \end{bmatrix} \begin{bmatrix} \hat{u} \\ \hat{\lambda} \end{bmatrix} = \begin{bmatrix} -\dfrac{r\frac{K}{L}}{pT}(\hat{K}-\hat{L})+\hat{T}+\hat{p} \\ -\varepsilon_z\hat{L} \end{bmatrix}$$

These two Equations (5.15) and (5.17) solve for two unknowns – $\hat{\lambda}$ and $\hat{u}$ – in terms of parameters. So these two equations together show how the unemployment rate and the rate of criminalisation of the society interact with each other.

Now the determinant of the coefficient matrix of the LHS side is given by:

$$|D| = \begin{vmatrix} \dfrac{w\lambda u}{pT} & -\dfrac{w\lambda(1-u)}{pT} \\ \varepsilon_u & \varepsilon_z \end{vmatrix},$$

$$\Rightarrow |D| = \varepsilon_z\frac{w\lambda u}{pT} + \varepsilon_u\frac{w\lambda(1-u)}{pT} = \frac{w\lambda}{pT}\left[\varepsilon_z u + \varepsilon_u(1-u)\right].$$

In the conventional efficiency wage model, $\varepsilon_z = 0$, and hence $|D| > 0$. However, in the present model,

$$|D| > 0 \text{ if and only if} \left[\varepsilon_u\frac{(1-u)}{u} + \varepsilon_z\right] > 0.$$

We assume this to be true because this assumption ensures the stability of equilibrium[7]. Now, we derive the expressions of $\hat{u}$ and $\hat{\lambda}$.

$$\hat{u} = \frac{1}{|D|}\left[\varepsilon_z\hat{T} + \varepsilon_z\hat{p} - \frac{r\frac{K}{L}}{pT}\varepsilon_z\hat{K} + \varepsilon_z\left(-\frac{w\lambda(1-u)}{pT} + \frac{r\frac{K}{L}}{pT}\right)\hat{L}\right]. \tag{5.18}$$

From Equation (5.11), we have

$$-\frac{w\lambda(1-u)}{pT} + \frac{r\frac{K}{L}}{pT} = 1.$$

Hence, using Equations (5.11) and (5.18), we have

$$\hat{u} = \frac{1}{|D|}\left[\varepsilon_z\hat{T} + \varepsilon_z\hat{p} - \frac{r\frac{K}{L}}{pT}\varepsilon_z\hat{K} + \varepsilon_z\hat{L}\right]. \tag{5.19}$$

Here, $\varepsilon_z < 0$ and $|D| > 0$ ensure that

$$\frac{\hat{u}}{\hat{T}} = \frac{\varepsilon_z}{|D|} < 0;$$

$$\frac{\hat{u}}{\hat{p}} = \frac{\varepsilon_z}{|D|} < 0;$$

$$\frac{\hat{u}}{\hat{K}} = -\frac{r\frac{K}{L}\varepsilon_z}{pT|D|} > 0;$$

and

$$\frac{\hat{u}}{\hat{L}} = \frac{\varepsilon_z}{|D|} < 0.$$

So, in the present model, the unemployment rate varies (i) negatively with the amount of fine as well as with the rate of punishment, (ii) positively with the capital stock and (iii) negatively with the worker endowment. However, in the conventional efficiency wage model, $\varepsilon_z = 0$. So the unemployment rate is independent of changes in parameters related to punishment policies, capital accumulation and the growth of the working population in a conventional efficiency wage model.

We also have[8]

$$\hat{\lambda} = \frac{1}{|D|}\left[-\varepsilon_u\hat{T} - \varepsilon_u\hat{p} + \varepsilon_u\frac{r\frac{K}{L}}{pT}\hat{K} - \frac{1}{pT}\left(w\lambda u\varepsilon_z + \varepsilon_u r\frac{K}{L}\right)\hat{L}\right]. \tag{5.20}$$

Here, $\varepsilon_u > 0$ and $|D| > 0$ ensure that

$$\frac{\hat{\lambda}}{\hat{T}} = -\frac{\varepsilon_u}{|D|} < 0;$$

$$\frac{\hat{\lambda}}{\hat{p}} = -\frac{\varepsilon_u}{|D|} < 0;$$

and

$$\frac{\hat{\lambda}}{\hat{K}} = \frac{r\frac{K}{L}\varepsilon_u}{pT|D|} > 0.$$

So the relative size of the criminal sector denoted by λ varies (i) inversely with the amount of fine as well as with the probability of punishment and (ii) directly with the capital stock. In the conventional efficiency wage model, $\varepsilon_z = 0$. Hence

$$|D| = \frac{w\lambda}{pT}\varepsilon_u(1-u).$$

Hence, $\frac{\hat{\lambda}}{\hat{T}}$, $\frac{\hat{\lambda}}{\hat{p}}$ and $\frac{\hat{\lambda}}{\hat{K}}$ are independent of the magnitude of ε_u even though they have the same signs.

However,

$$\frac{\hat{\lambda}}{\hat{L}} = -\frac{w\lambda u\varepsilon_z + \varepsilon_u r\frac{K}{L}}{pT|D|}$$

is ambiguous in sign.

$$\text{If } -\varepsilon_z \lesseqgtr \frac{\varepsilon_u r\frac{K}{L}}{w\lambda u}, \text{ then } \frac{\hat{\lambda}}{L} \lesseqgtr 0.$$

So how λ would vary with worker endowment should depend on $\frac{K}{L}$, ε_u and ε_z. We assume that

$$-\varepsilon_z < \frac{\varepsilon_u r\frac{K}{L}}{w\lambda u}.$$

Hence λ varies inversely with L in this case. In the conventional efficiency wage model, $\varepsilon_z = 0$. Hence this assumption is always satisfied.

In the present model,

$$|D| > 0 \Rightarrow -\varepsilon_z < \varepsilon_u \frac{1-u}{u};$$

and hence we need the restriction on the equilibrium unemployment rate given by:

$$1-u \geq \frac{rK}{wL\lambda}.$$

We can establish the following proposition.

Proposition 3: (i) Strengthening of anti-crime policies of the government lowers the unemployment rate as well as the relative size of the criminal sector. (ii) An increase in capital stock raises the unemployment rate as well as the relative size of the criminal sector. (iii) An increase in the size of the working population lowers both the unemployment rate and the relative size of the criminal sector.

We provide an intuitive explanation behind this proposition. An increase in the amount of fine and/or in the probability of punishment raises the expected cost of punishment of criminals, and so this lowers the relative size of the criminal sector. So the efficiency of labour goes up, and employers raise the rate of employment to lower the efficiency back to the profit-maximising level. This lowers the rate of unemployment in the labour market.

An increase in capital endowment raises the average snatched income of criminals. So this raises the size of the criminal sector. Hence the efficiency of labour is reduced, and employers lower the rate of employment to prevent efficiency from that decline. On the other hand, an increase in the number of workers lowers the average snatched income of criminals and thus produces exactly opposite effects on the relative size of the criminal sector as well as on the unemployment rate.

5.4.3 National Income

We define a new notation, g, given by:

$$g = (1-u)(1-\lambda).$$

Here g represents the rate of productive utilisation of worker endowment.

It can be easily shown that

$$\hat{g} = -\left(\frac{u}{1-u}\hat{u} + \frac{\lambda}{1-\lambda}\hat{\lambda}\right). \tag{5.21}$$

So using Equations (5.19)–(5.21), we have

$$\frac{\hat{g}}{\hat{K}} = -\left(\frac{u}{1-u}\frac{\hat{u}}{\hat{K}} + \frac{\lambda}{1-\lambda}\frac{\hat{\lambda}}{\hat{K}}\right) < 0;$$

$$\frac{\hat{g}}{\hat{L}} = -\left(\frac{u}{1-u}\frac{\hat{u}}{\hat{L}} + \frac{\lambda}{1-\lambda}\frac{\hat{\lambda}}{\hat{L}}\right) > 0 \text{ if } -\varepsilon_z < \frac{\varepsilon_u r \dfrac{K}{L}}{w\lambda u};$$

$$\frac{\hat{g}}{\hat{T}} = -\left(\frac{u}{1-u}\frac{\hat{u}}{\hat{T}} + \frac{\lambda}{1-\lambda}\frac{\hat{\lambda}}{\hat{T}}\right) > 0;$$

and

$$\frac{\hat{g}}{\hat{p}} = -\left(\frac{u}{1-u}\frac{\hat{u}}{\hat{p}} + \frac{\lambda}{1-\lambda}\frac{\hat{\lambda}}{\hat{p}}\right) > 0.$$

We have already assumed that

$$-\varepsilon_z < \frac{\varepsilon_u r \frac{K}{L}}{w\lambda u}.$$

Hence, in the present model, the rate of productive utilisation of worker endowment varies (i) positively with the amount of fine as well as with the probability of punishment, (ii) inversely with the stock of capital and (iii) directly with the labour (worker) endowment. This rate of utilisation, g, by definition, varies inversely with the unemployment rate, u, as well as with the relative size of the criminal sector, λ. So the intuition behind this result can be easily understood by looking at the intuitions behind proposition 5.2.

From Equations (5.9), (5.19) and (5.20), we have[9]

$$\hat{Y} = -\frac{wL}{Y|D|}\{\varepsilon_z(1-\lambda)u - \varepsilon_u\lambda(1-u)\}(\hat{T}+\hat{P})$$
$$+\frac{wL}{Y}\left[(1-\lambda)(1-u) - \frac{1}{|D|}\left\{\varepsilon_z(1-\lambda)u - \lambda(1-u)\frac{1}{pT}\left(w\lambda u\varepsilon_z + \varepsilon_u r\frac{K}{L}\right)\right\}\right]\hat{L}$$
$$+\frac{rK}{Y}\left[1+\frac{w}{pT}\frac{1}{|D|}\{\varepsilon_z(1-\lambda)u - \varepsilon_u\lambda(1-u)\}\right]\hat{K}. \tag{5.22}$$

In the one-sector full employment neo-classical model, $\lambda = u = 0$. Hence

$$\hat{Y} = \frac{wL}{Y}\hat{L} + \frac{rK}{Y}\hat{K}.$$

From Equation (5.22), we have

$$\frac{\hat{Y}}{\hat{T}} = \frac{\hat{Y}}{\hat{p}} = -\frac{wL}{Y|D|}\{\varepsilon_z(1-\lambda)u - \varepsilon_u\lambda(1-u)\} > 0;$$

and

$$\frac{\hat{Y}}{\hat{L}} = \frac{wL}{Y}\left[(1-\lambda)(1-u) - \frac{1}{|D|}\left\{\varepsilon_z(1-\lambda)u - \lambda(1-u)\frac{1}{pT}\left(w\lambda u\varepsilon_z + \varepsilon_u r\frac{K}{L}\right)\right\}\right]$$

$$> 0 \text{ if} - \varepsilon_z < \frac{\varepsilon_u r \frac{K}{L}}{w\lambda u}.$$

In that case,

$$\frac{\hat{Y}}{\hat{L}} > \frac{wL(1-\lambda)(1-u)}{Y}.$$

However,

$$\frac{\hat{Y}}{\hat{K}} = \frac{rK}{Y}\left[1 + \frac{w}{pT}\frac{1}{|D|}\left\{\varepsilon_z(1-\lambda)u - \varepsilon_u\lambda(1-u)\right\}\right]$$

is ambiguous in sign. Here $\frac{\hat{Y}}{\hat{K}} > 0$ if the absolute value of $\left\{\varepsilon_z(1-\lambda)u - \varepsilon_u\lambda(1-u)\right\}\frac{w}{pT}\frac{1}{|D|}$ is less than unity. In that case, $0 < \frac{\hat{Y}}{\hat{K}} < \frac{rK}{Y}$.

Otherwise, $\frac{\hat{Y}}{\hat{K}} < 0$, and this possibility is strengthened when pT is very low.

So the level of national income varies (i) positively with the amount of fine as well as with the rate of punishment and (ii) positively with the worker endowment. However, the effect of capital accumulation on national income is not unambiguous. The nature of the effect depends on the expected cost of punishment. If the expected cost of punishment is very high (low), then capital accumulation leads to the growth (decline) of national income.

We find that

$$\left(\frac{\hat{Y}}{\hat{K}}\right) < \frac{rK}{Y} \text{ and } \left(\frac{\hat{Y}}{\hat{L}}\right) > \frac{wL(1-\lambda)(1-u)}{Y}.$$

Hence, in the present model, the labour (capital) elasticity of output is higher (lower) than that in the full employment model. The capital elasticity of output is less than the competitive output share of capital, but the labour elasticity of output exceeds the competitive output share of labour. The increase in the worker (capital) endowment in this model leads to a higher (lower) rate of growth of national income than that in the neo-classical full employment model.

The aggregate supply curve has a rightward shift when the government strengthens punishment policies to stop criminal activities. The initial equilibrium is characterised by a loss of productive utilisation of the entire worker endowment. So the punishment policies lead to better utilisation of that worker endowment. This curve also shifts rightward due to the increase in the worker endowment. However, it may shift leftward due to capital accumulation.

We now establish the following proposition.

Proposition 4: (i) Strengthening of punishment policies raises the level of national income. (ii) An exogenous increase in capital stock either raises the national income at a lower rate or lowers it when the expected cost of punishment is very low. (iii) An exogenous increase in the worker endowment always raises the level of national income at a higher rate.

We now provide the intuition behind the proposition. Strengthening of punishment policies implies an increase in the expected cost of punishment. This discourages the workers to join the criminal sector, and thus the relative size of the criminal sector is reduced. This raises the efficiency level of the worker above the profit-maximising level, and so employers create more employment opportunities to bring back the efficiency at the profit-maximising level. Thus the rate of unemployment is reduced. So this reduction in the relative size of the criminal sector accompanied by the fall in the unemployment rate leads to an increase in the productive utilisation of the existing worker endowment. Since the marginal productivity of labour is always positive, this causes an increase in the level of output.

The effect of capital accumulation in this model is really interesting because, in any standard development model, this creates more employment opportunities and raises the level of output. We obtain a non-conventional result in this model due to the properties of the labour efficiency function and due to the existence of the criminal sector that creates a distortion. The increase in capital stock raises the average income of criminals who snatch a fraction of national income. So this encourages many workers to join this criminal sector when the expected cost of punishment is very low. This leads to an increase in the size of the criminal sector and thus produces a negative effect on the efficiency of labour. Firms lower the level of employment to bring back the efficiency to the profit-maximising level. Thus the level of unemployment is increased. Here unemployment is created to improve the efficiency of the worker. So the expansion of employment does not accompany capital accumulation. On the other hand, this increase in the rate of unemployment, accompanied by the increase in the relative size of the criminal sector, lowers the productive utilisation of the worker endowment. This decline in productive utilisation of worker endowment is very high when the expected cost of punishment of criminals is very low, and this indirect negative effect on output may outweigh the direct positive effect of capital accumulation in this special case.

An exogenous increase in the size of the working population lowers the average income of criminals and thus the general equilibrium system now moves along the opposite path leading to an increase in the national income.

5.5 Conclusion

We develop an efficiency wage macroeconomic model where a part of the working population is involved in criminal activities and where the efficiency of the worker not only varies positively with the wage rate as well as with the unemployment rate but also varies inversely with the size of the criminal sector. We analyse the effect of strengthening anti-crime policies as well as the effects of changes in capital endowments and worker endowments on the rate of criminalisation of society, unemployment rate and national income.

Many interesting results are derived from this model. An exogenous increase in the worker endowment lowers the relative size of the criminal sector as well as the unemployment rate but raises the level of national income. An exogenous increase in the capital stock raises the unemployment rate as well as the relative size of the criminal sector but may lower the national income if the expected cost of punishment of criminals is negligible. Globalisation leads to foreign capital inflow to and outmigration of domestic labour from less developed countries, and these, in turn, lead to an increase (decrease) in capital (worker) endowment. So globalisation may not have any favourable effect on the economic development of a backward economy in the presence of crime when anti-crime policies are poorly implemented and when criminal activities generate adverse effects on the efficiency of labour. So our findings are in line with the sceptic view of Rodrik (1997), Deardorf (2002), Wolf (2004) etc. who think that the economic benefits of globalisation may be outweighed by the negative effects of criminal activities.

However, our analysis is based on many restrictive assumptions. We assume that criminals snatch a fraction of factor income, and this generates a negative effect only on the efficiency of labour. We use a static one-period model and so fail to analyse the different intertemporal effects of crime. For example, criminal activities may generate illegal income transfer from the low consumption propensity group of individuals to the high consumption propensity group of individuals because criminals generally do not save their illegal income. This may lower the aggregate savings of the economy. These criminal activities may also produce negative effects on social infrastructure and may raise the rate of depreciation of public physical infrastructure. These, in turn, generate negative effects on the investment decision of private firms. We plan to include all these aspects in our future works.

Appendix A

A.1 Stability

The differential equations of adjustments are given by:

$$\dot{u} = \alpha\left[h(\bar{w}, u, z) - \bar{h}\right] \text{ with } \alpha < 0 \tag{A.1}$$

and

$$\dot{\lambda} = \beta\left[\frac{(1-\phi(\lambda)Y)}{z} - pT - w(1-u)\right] \text{ with } \beta > 0.$$

Equation (A.1) implies that firms employ fewer (more) workers when efficiency goes below (above) the specified level, $\bar{h}$. Here $\bar{h}$ is the profit-maximising level of efficiency. The second equation implies that workers join (leave) the criminal sector when the average income from criminal activities exceeds (falls short of) the opportunity cost.

From the second equation in this Appendix A and from Equations (5.1), (5.2) and (5.9) we have

$$\dot{\lambda} = \beta\left[\frac{\lambda Y}{\lambda L} - pT - w(1-u)\right] \text{ with } \beta > 0$$

$$\Rightarrow \dot{\lambda} = \beta\left[\frac{Y}{L} - pT - w(1-u)\right] \text{ with } \beta > 0$$

$$\Rightarrow \dot{\lambda} = \beta\left[\frac{wL(1-\lambda)(1-u) + rK}{L} - pT - w(1-u)\right] \text{ with } \beta > 0 \tag{A.2}$$

$$\Rightarrow \dot{\lambda} = \beta\left[w(1-\lambda)(1-u) + r\frac{K}{L} - pT - w(1-u)\right] \text{ with } \beta > 0$$

$$\Rightarrow \dot{\lambda} = \beta\left[-w\lambda(1-u) + r\frac{K}{L} - pT\right] \text{ with } \beta > 0.$$

Here

$$J = \begin{bmatrix} \frac{\partial \dot{u}}{\partial u} & \frac{\partial \dot{u}}{\partial \lambda} \\ \frac{\partial \dot{\lambda}}{\partial u} & \frac{\partial \dot{\lambda}}{\partial \lambda} \end{bmatrix}$$

is the Jacobian matrix

where

$$\frac{\partial \dot{u}}{\partial u} = \alpha \frac{\partial h}{\partial u} < 0;$$

$$\frac{\partial \dot{u}}{\partial \lambda} = \alpha \frac{\partial h}{\partial z} L > 0;$$

$$\frac{\partial \dot{\lambda}}{\partial u} = \beta w \lambda > 0;$$

and

$$\frac{\partial \dot{\lambda}}{\partial \lambda} = -\beta w (1-u) < 0.$$

The trace of J matrix is given by:

$$\frac{\partial \dot{u}}{\partial u} + \frac{\partial \dot{\lambda}}{\partial \lambda} = \left[\alpha \frac{\partial h}{\partial u} - \beta w (1-u) \right] < 0 \text{ because } \alpha < 0 \text{ and } \beta > 0.$$

The determinant of J matrix is given by:

$$|J| = \left(\frac{\partial \dot{u}}{\partial u}\frac{\partial \dot{\lambda}}{\partial \lambda} - \frac{\partial \dot{u}}{\partial \lambda}\frac{\partial \dot{\lambda}}{\partial u} \right)$$

$$\Rightarrow |J| = \alpha\beta \left\{ -\frac{\partial h}{\partial u} w(1-u) - \frac{\partial h}{\partial z} Lw\lambda \right\}$$

$$\Rightarrow |J| = \alpha\beta \left\{ -\varepsilon_u \frac{h}{u} w(1-u) - \varepsilon_z \frac{h}{z} Lw\lambda \right\}$$

$$\Rightarrow |J| = \alpha\beta h \left\{ -\varepsilon_u \frac{w(1-u)}{u} - \varepsilon_z w \right\}$$

$$\Rightarrow |J| = -\alpha\beta hw \left(\varepsilon_z + \varepsilon_u \frac{(1-u)}{u} \right).$$

Here $\alpha < 0$ and $\beta > 0$. However, $\varepsilon_u > 0$ and $\varepsilon_z < 0$. Hence $|J| > 0$ if $\left(\varepsilon_u \frac{(1-u)}{u} + \varepsilon_z \right) > 0$.

So the equilibrium is stable if $\left(\varepsilon_u \frac{(1-u)}{u} + \varepsilon_z\right) > 0$. In the conventional efficiency wage model, $\varepsilon_z = 0$, and hence $|J|$ is always positive.

Appendix B

From Equations (5.1)–(5.3) and (5.9), we have

$$\begin{aligned}
&\frac{(1-\phi(\lambda))Y}{z} = pT + w(1-u) \\
&\Rightarrow \frac{\lambda Y}{\lambda L} = pT + w(1-u) \\
&\Rightarrow \frac{Y}{L} = pT + w(1-u) \\
&\Rightarrow \frac{wL(1-\lambda)(1-u) + rK}{L} = pT + w(1-u) \\
&\Rightarrow w(1-\lambda)(1-u) + r\frac{K}{L} = pT + w(1-u) \\
&\Rightarrow - w\lambda(1-u) + r\frac{K}{L} = pT.
\end{aligned} \tag{5.B.1}$$

This Equation (5.B.1) is the same as Equation (5.10) in the body of the chapter.

From Equation (5.B.1), we have

$$\frac{-w\lambda(1-u)}{pT}\left(\hat{w} + \hat{\lambda} - \frac{u}{(1-u)}\hat{u}\right) + \frac{r\frac{K}{L}}{pT}\left(\hat{r} + \hat{K} - \hat{L}\right) = \hat{p} + \hat{T}$$

$$\Rightarrow \frac{-w\lambda(1-u)}{pT}\left(\hat{\lambda} - \frac{u}{(1-u)}\hat{u}\right) = -\frac{r\frac{K}{L}}{pT}\left(\hat{K} - \hat{L}\right) + \hat{T} + \hat{p} \tag{5.B.2}$$

$$\Rightarrow \frac{w\lambda u}{pT}\hat{u} - \frac{w\lambda(1-u)}{pT}\hat{\lambda} = -\frac{r\frac{K}{L}}{pT}\left(\hat{K} - \hat{L}\right) + \hat{T} + \hat{p}.$$

This Equation (5.B.2) is the same as Equation (5.17) in the body of the chapter.

Using Equations (5.15) and (5.17), we have

$$\hat{u} = \frac{1}{|D|}\begin{vmatrix} -\frac{r\frac{K}{L}}{pT}\left(\hat{K}-\hat{L}\right)+\hat{T}+\hat{p} & -\frac{w\lambda(1-u)}{pT} \\ -\varepsilon_z\hat{L} & \varepsilon_z \end{vmatrix}$$

$$\Rightarrow \hat{u} = \frac{1}{|D|}\left[\varepsilon_z\left\{-\frac{r\frac{K}{L}}{pT}\left(\hat{K}-\hat{L}\right)+\hat{T}+\hat{p}\right\}-\varepsilon_z\hat{L}\frac{w\lambda(1-u)}{pT}\right] \tag{5.B.3}$$

$$\Rightarrow \hat{u} = \frac{1}{|D|}\left[\varepsilon_z\hat{T}+\varepsilon_z\hat{p}-\frac{r\frac{K}{L}}{pT}\varepsilon_z\hat{K}+\varepsilon_z\left(-\frac{w\lambda(1-u)}{pT}+\frac{r\frac{K}{L}}{pT}\right)\hat{L}\right].$$

This Equation (5.B.3) is the same as Equation (5.18) in the body of the chapter.

We also have

$$\hat{\lambda} = \frac{1}{|D|}\begin{vmatrix} \frac{w\lambda u}{pT} & -\frac{r\frac{K}{L}}{pT}\left(\hat{K}-\hat{L}\right)+\hat{T}+\hat{p} \\ \varepsilon_u & -\varepsilon_z\hat{L} \end{vmatrix}$$

$$\Rightarrow \hat{\lambda} = \frac{1}{|D|}\left[-\frac{w\lambda u}{pT}\varepsilon_z\hat{L}-\left\{-\frac{r\frac{K}{L}}{pT}\left(\hat{K}-\hat{L}\right)+\hat{T}+\hat{p}\right\}\varepsilon_u\right] \tag{5.B.4}$$

$$\Rightarrow \hat{\lambda} = \frac{1}{|D|}\left[-\varepsilon_u\hat{T}-\varepsilon_u\hat{p}+\varepsilon_u\frac{r\frac{K}{L}}{pT}\hat{K}-\frac{1}{pT}\left(w\lambda u\varepsilon_z+\varepsilon_u r\frac{K}{L}\right)\hat{L}\right].$$

This Equation (5.B.4) is the same as Equation (5.20) in the body of the chapter.

From Equations (5.9), (5.19) and (5.20), we have

$$\hat{Y} = \frac{wL(1-\lambda)(1-u)}{Y}\hat{L}-\frac{wL(1-\lambda)(1-u)}{Y}\left(\frac{u}{1-u}\hat{u}+\frac{\lambda}{1-\lambda}\hat{\lambda}\right)+\frac{rK}{Y}\hat{K}$$

$$\Rightarrow \hat{Y} = \frac{wL(1-\lambda)(1-u)}{Y}\hat{L}+\frac{rK}{Y}\hat{K}-\frac{wL(1-\lambda)u}{Y}\frac{1}{|D|}\left(\varepsilon_z\hat{T}+\varepsilon_z\hat{p}-\frac{r\frac{K}{L}}{pT}\varepsilon_z\hat{K}+\varepsilon_z\hat{L}\right)$$

$$-\frac{wL\lambda(1-u)}{Y}\frac{1}{|D|}\left(-\varepsilon_u\hat{T}-\varepsilon_u\hat{p}+\varepsilon_u\frac{r\frac{K}{L}}{pT}\hat{K}-\frac{1}{pT}\left(w\lambda u\varepsilon_z+\varepsilon_u r\frac{K}{L}\right)\hat{L}\right)$$

$$\Rightarrow\hat{Y}=-\frac{wL}{Y|D|}\{\varepsilon_z(1-\lambda)u-\varepsilon_u\lambda(1-u)\}(\hat{T}+\hat{P})$$

$$+\left[\frac{wL(1-\lambda)(1-u)}{Y}-\frac{wL}{Y|D|}\left\{\varepsilon_z(1-\lambda)u-\lambda(1-u)\frac{1}{pT}\left(w\lambda u\varepsilon_z+\varepsilon_u r\frac{K}{L}\right)\right\}\right]\hat{L}$$

$$+\left[\frac{rK}{Y}+\frac{wL}{Y|D|}\frac{r\frac{K}{L}}{pT}\{\varepsilon_z(1-\lambda)u-\varepsilon_u\lambda(1-u)\}\right]\hat{K}$$

$$\Rightarrow\hat{Y}=-\frac{wL}{Y|D|}\{\varepsilon_z(1-\lambda)u-\varepsilon_u\lambda(1-u)\}(\hat{T}+\hat{P})$$

$$+\frac{wL}{Y}\left[(1-\lambda)(1-u)-\frac{1}{|D|}\left\{\varepsilon_z(1-\lambda)u-\lambda(1-u)\frac{1}{pT}\left(w\lambda u\varepsilon_z+\varepsilon_u r\frac{K}{L}\right)\right\}\right]\hat{L}$$

$$+\frac{rK}{Y}\left[1+\frac{w}{pT}\frac{1}{|D|}\{\varepsilon_z(1-\lambda)u-\varepsilon_u\lambda(1-u)\}\right]\hat{K}. \tag{5.B.5}$$

This Equation (5.B.5) is the same as Equation (5.22) in the body of the chapter.

Notes

1 See, for example, Alexopoulos (2003), Brecher et al. (2002), Solow (1979), Summers (1988), Calvo (1979), Shapiro and Stiglitz (1984), Pisauro (1991), Agell and Lundborg (1992, 1995), Salop (1979), Akerlof (1984), Akerlof and Yellen (1990) etc.
2 Obviously there are many other empirical works pointing out the existence of this problem in many other countries. However, we have not surveyed the entire existing empirical literature.
3 The set includes Bassetti et al. (2010), Becker (1968), Burdett et. al. (2003, 2004), Ehrlich (1973), Engelhardt (2010), Engelhardt et al. (2008), Fender (1999), Furlong (1987), Persson and Siven (2001), Allingham and Sandmo (1972) and many others.
4 For the sake of simplicity, it is assumed that a criminal must be punished if he is caught.
5 Derivation of Equation (5.10) is given in the Appendix B.
6 Derivation of Equation (5.17) is given in the Appendix B.
7 Stability of equilibrium is shown in Appendix A.

8 Derivation of Equation (5.20) is shown in Appendix B.
9 Derivation of Equation (5.22) is shown in Appendix B.

References and Notes

Agell, J., & Lundborg, P. (1992). Fair Wages, Involuntary Unemployment and Tax Policy in the Simple General Equilibrium Model. *Journal of Public Economics 47*(3), 299–320.

Agell, J., & Lundborg, P. (1995). Fair Wages in the Open Economy. *Economica 62*(247), 325–351.

Akerlof, G. (1984). Gift Exchange and Efficiency-Wage Theory: Four Views. *The American Economic Review 74*, 79–83.

Akerlof, G. A., & Yellen, J. L. (1990). The Fair Wage-Effort Hypothesis and Unemployment. *The Quarterly Journal of Economics 105*(2), 255–283.

Alexopoulos, M. (2003). Growth and Unemployment in a Shirking Efficiency Wage Model. *The Canadian Journal of Economics/Revue Canadienne d`Economique 36*(3), 728–746.

Allingham, M. G., & Sandmo, A. (1972). Income Tax Evasion: A Theoretical Analysis. *Journal of Public Economics 1*(3–4), 323–338.

Bassetti, T., Corazzini, L., & Cortes, D. (2010). Crime, Immigration and the Labour Market: A General Equilibrium Model. *Marco Fanno Working Paper No. 121*. University of Padova, Italy.

Becker, G. S. (1968). Crime and Punishment: An Economic Approach. *Journal of Political Economy 78*(2), 526–576.

Brecher, R. A., Chen, Z., & Choudhuri, E. H. (2002). Unemployment and Growth in the Long Run: An Efficiency Wage Model with Optimal Savings. *International Economic Review 43*(3), 875–894.

Bukenya, J. O. (2005). Crime Trends and Socio-economic Interactions: A County-Level Analysis. *Criminal Justice Studies 18*(4), 365–378.

Burdett, K., Lagos, R., & Wright, R. (2003). Crime Inequality and Unemployment. *American Economic Review 93*(5), 1764–1777.

Burdett, K., Lagos, R., & Wright, R. (2004). An On-the-Job Search Model of Crime Inequality and Unemployment. *International Economic Review 45*(3), 681–706.

Calvo, G. (1979). Quasi-Walrasian Theories of Unemployment. *The American Economic Review 69*, 102–107.

Carmichael, F., & Ward, R. (2000). Youth Unemployment and Crime in the English Regions and Wales. *Applied Economics 32*(5), 559–571.

Deardorff, A. V. (2002). Policy Implications of the Trade and Wage Debate. *Review of International Economics 8*(3), 478–496.

Ehrlich, I. (1973). Participation in Illegitimate Activities: A Theoretical and Empirical Investigation. *Journal of Political Economy 81*(3), 521–565.

Engelhardt, B. (2010). The Effect of Employment Frictions on Crime. *Journal of Labour Economics 28*(3), 677–718.

Engelhardt, B., Rocheteau, G., & Rupart, P. (2008). Crime and the Labour Market: A Search Model with Optimal Contracts. *Journal of Public Economics 92*(10–11), 1876–1891.

Fender, L. (1999). A General Equilibrium Model of Crime and Punishment. *Journal of Economic Behavior and Organization 39*(4), 437–453.

Furlong, W. (1987). A General Equilibrium Model of Crime Commission and Prevention. *Journal of Public Economics 34*(1), 87–103.

Nilsson, A. (2004). Income Inequality and Crime: The Case of Sweden. *Working Paper Series*. IFAU, Presented at the Department of Economics. Stockholm University, Uppsala.

Papps, K., & Winkelmann, R. (2000). Unemployment and Crime: New Evidence for an Old Question. *New Zealand Economic Papers 34*(1), 53–71.

Persson, M., & Siven, C. (2001). Incentive and Incarceration Effects in a General Equilibrium Model of Crime. *Stockholm University Working Paper*.

Pisauro, G. (1991). The Effects of Taxes on Labour in Efficiency Wage Models. *Journal of Public Economics 46*(3), 329–345.

Rodrik, D. (1997). *Has Globalization Gone Too Far?* Institution for International Economics, Washington, DC.

Sachsida, A., Mendonca, M., Loureiro, P., & Gutierrez, M. (2010). Inequality and Criminality Revisited: Further Evidence from Brazil. *Empirical Economics* (Springer) *39(1)*, 93–109.

Salop, S. C. (1979). A Model of the Natural Rate of Unemployment. *The American Economic Review 69*, 117–125.

Shapiro, C., & Stiglitz, J. (1984). Equilibrium Unemployment as a Worker-Discipline Device. *American Economic Review 74*(3), 433–444.

Solow, R. M. (1979). Another Possible Source of Wage Stickiness. *Journal of Macroeconomics 1*(1), 79–82.

Summers, L. H. (1988). Relative Wages, Efficiency Wages, and Keynesian Unemployment. *The American Economic Review 78*, 383–388.

Witt, R., Clarke, A., & Fielding, N. (1998). Crime, Earnings Inequality and Unemployment in England and Wales. *Applied Economics Letters 5*(4), 265–267.

Wolf, M. (2004). *Why Globalisation Works?* Yale University Press, New Haven, CT.

Wu, D., & Wu, Z. (2012). Crime, Inequality and Unemployment in England and Wales. *Applied Economics 44*(29), 559–571.

6 Crime, Corruption and Capital

A General Equilibrium Analysis in the Presence of Political Cronyism

Sushobhan Mahata, Rohan Kanti Khan, Ranjanendra Narayan Nag, Soumyajit Mandal, Salonkara Chaudhuri

6.1 Introduction

Against the backdrop of globalisation, the nature of organised crime and corruption is changing to adapt to the new circumstances to amass illicit profit and market power. The natural resource-based industry is highly vulnerable to the incidence of crime and corruption when politicians at the local or national level and weak law enforcement allow the existence and functioning of such illegal activities.[1] Given this nexus between crime and corruption, there exists a sceptic view that the positive gains of globalisation may be dominated by its negative effects in terms of accentuating crime (Gupta, 2020). There exist substantial theoretical works on the economics of crime and corruption that analysed several aspects which include the agency theory of corruption (Tirole, 1986; Laffont and Tirole, 1991; Strausz, 1995; Celik, 2009; Khalil, Lawarree and Yun, 2010 etc.), bureaucratic corruption (Shleifer and Vishy, 1993, 1994; Besley and McLaren, 1993; Mookherjee and Png, 1995; Acemoglu and Verdier, 2000 etc.), industrial organisation theory of corruption (Rose-Ackerman, 1975; Bliss and Di Tella, 1997; Amir and Burr, 2015 etc.) and bribe competition (Burguet and Perry, 2007; Koc and Neilson, 2008 etc.) among others.[2] The effect of crime and corruption on foreign investment inflow has also been extensively analysed empirically. Egger and Winner (2005) found a positive association between corruption and inward foreign direct investment (FDI) for a sample of 73 developed and less-developed economies for the period 1995–1999. The main highlight of the Paper is that corruption acts as a stimulus to FDI. A similar positive correlation was found in Moustafa (2021) for the Egyptian economy for the period of study 1970–2019. The opposite result in terms of a negative association between corruption and foreign capital inflow has been found in Habib and Zurawicki (2002) with Germany, Italy, Japan, Korea, Spain, the UK and the USA as host countries. A similar negative association between corruption and FDI was obtained by Alemu (2012) for 16 Asian economies for the period 1995–2009. A few other works that obtained similar results include Sadig (2009), Luu et al. (2019), Canare (2017) and Zander (2021)

DOI: 10.4324/9781003375050-6

which found that corruption hinders FDI inflow in the origin country and is positively correlated with the target country.[3]

Besides corruption, the level of criminal activity in host countries acts as a determinant of foreign capital inflows. Daniele and Marini (2011) using a panel data estimation found that crime represents a deterrent for foreign investors. Blanco, Ruiz and Wooster (2019) found that crime negatively affects foreign investment inflow in the secondary and tertiary sectors in Latin American countries. Brown and Hibbert (2017) empirically obtained a negative association between crime and FDI for a global sample of 62 countries during 1997–2012. Torres, Mollick and Saucedo (2018) found a similar result for 32 Mexican states for the period 2005–2015. On the other hand, Khan et al. (2022) theoretically analysed the reverse causality effect of FDI on crime-corruption nexus using a general equilibrium model. Their paper obtained that when corruption becomes necessary to sustain the criminal sector, capital expansion and deterrence policy augment crime and corruption.

Corruption is also a symptom of wider political dynamics and electoral malpractice and is likely to thrive in conditions where law enforcement and legal institutions are weak or politically paralysed. In this regard, Acemoglu and Robinson (2011) and Rocha Menocal (2013) found a positive and long-term correlation between democracy and higher quality of governance which together lead to a lower incidence of corruption. Dastidar and Mukherjee (2014) analytically demonstrated how corruption always leads to lower quality and lower prices in public procurement auctions by taking into account explicitly the behaviour of the politician. Few other works in this regard include Boerner and Hainz (2009), Harstad and Svensson (2011), Le and Yalcin (2018), Dastidar and Yano (2021), Yu et al. (2021), Chaudhuri, Dastidar and Mahata (2022) etc. among others.

In the domain of Jonesian general equilibrium, there exists a relative dearth of studies on corruption and crime. Few existing works in this domain have focused on the following aspects, namely, the effect of globalisation on criminal activities (Gupta, 2020), the effect of corruption on the pattern of trade (Marjit and Mandal, 2008), the effect of corruption on wage inequality (Mandal and Marjit, 2010) and the effect of foreign capital on crime and corruption (Khan, Mahata and Nag, 2022).

However, the majority of these works are either partial equilibrium analyses or general equilibrium analyses dealing with only one aspect of either crime or corruption in isolation from one another. In this chapter, we attempt to build an analytical structure pertaining to the nature of crime and corruption in an otherwise general equilibrium framework, in which the existence of the organised crime sector becomes necessary to sustain corruption that leads to the formation of the nexus between these two illegal activities in the backdrop of foreign capital inflow. The analytical structure examines how a corporate firm in a completely privatised economy can employ corruption and political cronyism as a means to strategically deter the entry of other firms in the industry that leads to the generation of monopoly rent owing to an increase in the market power of the incumbent firm by exploiting the natural resources. In so doing, a four-stage game-theoretic model is employed to endogenise "corruption", "cronyism" and "the choice of effective enforcement of law and order" in terms of "criminal detention rate" by the legal institutions which are highly influenced by the ruling political party with its direct or indirect interventions. In this setup, criminals are employed by the ruling political party to deter new entrants into the industry which benefits the incumbent firm.[4] The incumbent firm in exchange for this favour donates (or, bribes) the ruling party to support it financially to win the re-election bid in the upcoming general election. However, the politician is always vulnerable to facing some backlash, provided they fail to win and remain out of power. In the general equilibrium structure, the economy is divided into two broad sectors i.e., legal and illegal, where one exists parallelly alongside the other. Given this political and legal distortion, the effect of foreign direct investment is analysed to investigate whether it acts as a panacea to curb corruption and crime endogenously or rather help augment this nexus. We also analytically demonstrate how an inflow of foreign capital influences the internal law and order endogenously from the optimal decision-making of the politician, given its nexus with both the criminal and the corporate sectors.

The itinerary of the chapter is organised as follows. Section 6.2 describes the economic structure and the socio-political environment of the representative developing economy. The equational structure of the model is represented in Section 6.3. The effect of foreign capital inflow and its implications for the economy has been analysed in Section 6.4. Finally, Section 6.5 concludes the chapter.

6.2. Description of the Economy and the Socio-political Environment

This is a small open developing economy with three sectors and three factors of production. The factors of production are land (N), labour (L) and capital (K). The production side of the economy is elucidated as follows. Sector 1 is the agriculture sector that produces output, X_1, using land, labour and capital. Sector 2 is an import-competing secondary sector that produces a final manufacturing commodity, X_2, using labour and capital. Industry M is a vertically integrated sector that produces a non-traded final commodity using labour and capital in an imperfect market. Thus, the manufacturing sector is non-monocentric.

In industry M, two firms compete for the market share – one incumbent firm ($m1$) and one potential entrant ($m2$). The incumbent firm $m1$ bribes the ruling political party to deter the entry of the potential entrant. The rate of bribe is δ per unit of output which is endogenously determined. Against this bribe, on the one hand, the ruling political party influences the legal institutions and exhorts the criminal sector to favour the incumbent firm by imposing an additional damage cost due to criminals on the entrant firm, while, on the other hand, the ruling party chooses the effective enforcement of law and order to maximise its aggregate payoff which is the weighted average of expected political gain and national income.[5] Although industry M produces a legal commodity that makes it a *legal* sector, however, the incumbent firm in this industry uses unfair means of crime and corruption that can be thought of as an indirect *illegal* input into its production process.

The operation of the *illegal criminal* sector of the economy exists parallelly alongside the *legal* sectors and all transactions carried out within this sector are legally prohibited and officially remain unaccounted. This *criminal* sector is funded by the incumbent political party to cover the cost of employing criminals of size Z and capital (K_Z) that is borrowed from illegal sources at some legally prohibited high informal interest rate, g. Let "Υ" be the fraction of criminals who are vulnerable to getting caught and facing legal action that prevents them to participate in the labour market, while "$1-\Upsilon$" fraction of criminals skip vigilance, where $\Upsilon \in [0,1]$. Each criminal is compensated with W_Z for the services provided to criminal sector (sector I). Thus, each worker in the economy has the option either to engage in the legal labour market in sector 1, 2 and M or participate in the criminal sector. The *corruption* in the economy includes the amount of bribe paid to the political party in power (i.e., δX_M), denoted by C. Notice that the total amount of bribes is channelised towards payment to criminals and illegal capital owners, and thus, the measure of corruption automatically includes these two illegal payments.[6]

Against this backdrop, it is indispensable to distinguish between the *shadow* (informal) economy and the illegal sector (activities). The former includes "illegal" activities besides the unreported income from the production of "*legal* goods and services", either from monetary or barter transactions. Shadow economies are all economic activities that would be taxable if reported to tax authorities (Schneider and Enste, 2002). On the other hand, the latter "illegal sector" include those whose sale or purchase are either forbidden by the law, or are unlicensed (see section 6.3, System of National Accounts, 2008). In the present analytical structure, the shadow economy consists of informal labour income in sector 1 that is different from the institutionally determined wage rate in the other two formal sectors (sector 2 and sector M) besides the income distribution in the illegal sector. Thus, all illegal activities are a *subset* of the shadow economy.

6.3 The Model

In this section, the bribe rate (δ) and degree of law enforcement (Υ) are endogenously determined from the strategic interaction among the ruling political party, an incumbent firm and a potential entrant firm. Thereafter, the general equilibrium analogue is built for a representative developing economy in the presence of factor market distortion and capital inflow.

6.3.1 Determination of Demand for the Non-traded Final Commodity

The non-traded final commodity, M, is consumed by both law-abiding labour and criminals beside the other two traded commodities (commodity 1 and 2), where each representative individual within the group is represented by l and z, respectively. Each individual maximises their respective utility in a two-step process. In the first step, the representative ςth individual, where $\varsigma = \{l, z\}$, chooses the consumption level of commodity M, $x_{M\varsigma}$ to maximise the utility V_ς net of expenditure on $x_{M\varsigma}$ for the given level of expected income μ_ς. In the second step, the individual chooses $x_{1\varsigma}$ and $x_{2\varsigma}$ to maximise the sub-utility for a given level of residual income (Q_ς) that is obtained from the first step.

The representative individual solves the following in the first-step optimisation:[7]

$$\underset{\{x_{M\varsigma}\}}{Max} \quad V_\varsigma = a x_{M\varsigma} - \frac{1}{2} x_{M\varsigma}^2 + \mu_\varsigma - P_M x_{M\varsigma} \tag{6.1}$$

$$\text{where } \mu_\varsigma = \begin{cases} W\left(\dfrac{a_{L1} X_1}{\bar{L} - Z}\right) + \bar{W}\left(\dfrac{a_{L2} X_2 + a_{LM} X_M}{\bar{L} - Z}\right) & \text{for } \varsigma = l \\ W_Z[1 - \Upsilon], \text{ otherwise} \end{cases}$$

The first-step optimisation yields the demand function and residual income, respectively, as follows:

$$x_{M\varsigma}(P_M) = a - P_M \tag{6.2}$$

$$Q_\varsigma(\mu_\varsigma, P_M) = \mu_\varsigma - P_M(a - P_M) \tag{6.3}$$

In the second step, the individual solves the optimisation problem for the following sub-utility function:[8]

$$\underset{\{x_{1\varsigma}, x_{2\varsigma}\}}{Max} \quad x_{1\varsigma} x_{2\varsigma}$$

subject to $Q_\varsigma(\mu_\varsigma, P_M) = \mu_\varsigma - P_M(a - P_M)$

The second-step optimisation yields the following demand function for commodities 1 and 2, respectively:

$$x_{1\varsigma}^* = \frac{\mu_\varsigma - P_M(a - bP_M)}{2} \tag{6.4}$$

$$x^*_{2\varsigma} = \frac{\mu_\varsigma - P_M(a - bP_M)}{2P_2} \tag{6.5}$$

Comparing the indirect utilities for the marginal worker, $\varsigma = \{l, z\}$, the following labour relocation equilibrium is obtained:[9]

$$W_Z[1 - \Upsilon] = W(\frac{a_{L1} X_1}{\bar{L} - Z}) + \bar{W}(\frac{a_{L2} X_2 + a_{LM} X_M}{\bar{L} - Z}) \tag{6.6}$$

Given the population size, $\bar{L}$, the aggregate demand for the non-traded commodity M is given by the following:

$$X_M^D(P_M, \bar{L}) = \bar{L}(a - P_M) \tag{6.7}$$

6.3.1.1 *Endogenous Determination of Bribe Rate and Degree of Law Enforcement*

The following four-stage model is considered to endogenously determine the bribe rate and the degree of law enforcement from the strategic interaction between the firms and the ruling political party.

Stage 1: The ruling politician chooses the degree of law enforcement, Υ.
Stage 2: The incumbent firm $m1$ chooses the level of the bribe (cut money) "δ" per unit of output that is to be paid to the political entity.
Stage 3: The potential entrant firm, $m2$, decides whether to enter the market. If it does, it pays an entry cost which consists of a fixed entry cost "ϑ" and cut money "δ". Thus, the aggregate entry cost is $F(\vartheta, \delta)$. Additionally, firm $m2$ also faces a damage cost due to criminals which increases its cost of production by the amount "εZ", that hinders its possible entry, where $\varepsilon > 0$ is the intensity of damage that each criminal can cause.
Stage 4: If firm $m2$ enters, then the incumbent firm $m1$ becomes the Stackelberg leader and the entrant firm becomes the follower. Both play a sequential duopoly game. If firm $m2$ does not enter, then firm $m1$ acts as a monopolist within industry M.[10]

The following assumption is made to determine stage 4 equilibrium value:

Assumption 6.1: $2P_M > a > P_M > (\bar{W}a_{LM} + ra_{KM})$
The intuition behind Assumption 6.1 can be provided as follows. The market price (P_M) must exceed the marginal cost ($\bar{W}a_{LM} + ra_{KM}$) that makes the production of positive output sustainable. The assumption $2P_M > a > P_M$ is required for market power to exist on the elastic part of the average revenue curve.

In stage 4 equilibrium, given Assumption 6.1, if firm $m2$ enters, then the profit of firm $m1$ is obtained as follows:

$$\pi_{m1}^{A} = \frac{\left\{a-(\bar{W}a_{LM}+ra_{KM})\right\}^{2}\bar{L}}{8} \tag{6.8}$$

If firm $m1$ deters the entry of firm $m2$, then the profit of the monopoly firm $m1$ becomes

$$\pi_{m1}^{D} = (a-x_{m1})\bar{L}x_{m1} - (\bar{W}a_{LM}+ra_{KM})x_{m1} - [\kappa\bar{F}+\delta]x_{m1} \tag{6.9}$$

The following assumption is made to determine a (positive) interior solution for stage 3 equilibrium value:

Assumption 6.2: $\left\{a-(\bar{W}a_{LM}+ra_{KM})\right\}\bar{L} > 2\sqrt{\left\{\varepsilon Z+F(\delta,\vartheta)\right\}\bar{L}} > 2\left\{\kappa\bar{F}+\delta\right\}\bar{L}$

In stage 3 equilibrium, the following condition on firm $m2$'s profit $\pi_{m2} = P(X_M)x_{m2} - C(W,r_2,x_{m2}) - \varepsilon\left\{1-\Upsilon\right\}Z - F(\delta,\vartheta) = 0$ solves the value of x_{m1}^{D} that is obtained as follows:

$$x_{m2}^{D} = \left\{a-(\bar{W}a_{LM}+ra_{KM})\right\}\bar{L} - 2\sqrt{\left\{\varepsilon(1-\Upsilon)Z+F(\delta,\vartheta)\right\}\bar{L}} \tag{6.10}$$

Thus, substituting Equation (6.10) in Equation (6.9), it boils down to

$$\pi_{m1}^{D} = \frac{\left[\left\{a-(\bar{W}a_{LM}+ra_{KM})\right\}\bar{L} - 2\sqrt{\left\{\varepsilon(1-\Upsilon)Z+F(\delta,\vartheta)\right\}\bar{L}}\right]\left[\sqrt{\left\{\varepsilon(1-\Upsilon)Z+F(\delta,\vartheta)\right\}\bar{L}} - \left\{\kappa\bar{F}+\delta\right\}\bar{L}\right]}{\bar{L}} \tag{6.11}$$

The following assumptions are made to determine the stage 2 equilibrium value of δ and its properties.

Assumption 6.3: $\dfrac{(\partial F/\partial\delta)}{2\sqrt{\left\{\varepsilon(1-\Upsilon)Z+F(\delta,\vartheta)\right\}\bar{L}}} < 1$

Assumption 6.4: $2\sqrt{\left\{\varepsilon(1-\Upsilon)Z+F(\delta,\vartheta)\right\}\bar{L}} - (\kappa\bar{F}+\delta)\bar{L} > (a-\bar{W}a_{LM}-ra_{KM})\bar{L} - 2\sqrt{\left\{\varepsilon(1-\Upsilon)Z+F(\delta,\vartheta)\right\}}$

Assumption 6.5: $\dfrac{\bar{L}}{\left\{a-(\bar{W}a_{LM}+ra_{KM})\right\}\bar{L} - 2\sqrt{\left\{\varepsilon(1-\Upsilon)Z+F(\delta,\vartheta)\right\}\bar{L}}} > \dfrac{2}{\left\{a-(\bar{W}a_{LM}+ra_{KM})\right\}}$

In stage 2 equilibrium, firm $m1$ juxtapose π_{m1}^{D} and π_{m1}^{A} determine the bribe rate that could deter the entry of firm $m2$, which leads to the following condition:

$$\delta = \delta(r, Z, \Upsilon) \tag{6.12}$$

where $\frac{\partial \delta}{\partial r} < 0$, $\frac{\partial \delta}{\partial \Upsilon} > 0$ and $\frac{\partial \delta}{\partial Z} < 0$.

Lemma 6.1: The rate of the bribe falls with an increase in the cost of capital, increases with the detention rate and falls with an increase in the number of criminals.

Proof. See Appendices A.1–A.3.

Finally, in stage 1 the incumbent political party chooses the effective enforcement of law and order, denoted by "Υ" that maximises the political party's aggregate payoff, Π, which can be expressed as the weighted average of the ruling party's expected payoff from winning the re-election bid and national welfare.

The probability that the political party will win the next general election, denoted by ρ, is a positive function of the aggregate contribution received from the incumbent firm $m1$, denoted by C, which amounts to $\delta(r, Z, \Upsilon)X_M$.

The objective function of the political party is given by the following:

$$\Pi = \alpha\,[\rho(C)\,\Omega - \{1-\rho(C)\}b] + (1-\alpha)Y \qquad (6.13)$$

Here, $\Omega > 0$ is the payoff (political dividend) to the party if it retains power which is positive implying that no political party would like to lose power.[11] If it loses the re-election bid, then the incumbent party faces some backlash (denoted by "b") that it cannot suppress once the party is out of office. The magnitude of backlash (b) increases with an increase in the amount of illegitimate donations (C) from firm $m1$ and the number of non-detained criminals $((1-\Upsilon)Z)$. Thus, the backlash is defined as $b = b(C,(1-\Upsilon)Z)$; $\frac{\partial b}{\partial C} > 0$, $\frac{\partial b}{\partial (1-\Upsilon)Z} > 0$. Here, Y denotes the real national income. The parameter α with $1 > \alpha > 0$ denotes the political party's preference towards political power and national interest. Hence, the first term of the right-hand side of Equation (6.13) is the expected payoff from re-winning the election bid, while the second term is a proxy for its concern towards the economic prosperity of the country. Thus, the aggregate payoff of the incumbent political party is a convex combination of the expected payoff from retaining power and national interest.

Thus, the problem of the incumbent political party in this stage 1 can be stated as follows which is solved by choosing the effective enforcement of law and order, denoted by "Υ".

$$\underset{\{\Upsilon\}}{Max},\ \Pi = \alpha\,[\rho(C)\,\Omega - \{1-\rho(C)\}b] + (1-\alpha)Y$$

The following assumptions are imperative to guarantee the first-order and the second-order optimisation conditions, respectively.[12]

Assumption 6.6: $(\Omega+b)\rho' < (1-\rho)\frac{\partial b}{\partial C}$

Assumption 6.7: $\frac{\partial \delta}{\partial \Upsilon}\frac{\partial b}{\partial C}(1+\frac{\partial \delta}{\partial \Upsilon})X_M < \frac{\partial b}{\partial \tilde{Z}} Z$

The *first-order necessary condition* for an interior solution is given by the following expression:

$$\frac{\partial \delta}{\partial \Upsilon} X_M \left\{(\Omega+b)\rho' - (1-\rho)\frac{\partial b}{\partial C}\right\} + Z(1-\rho)\frac{\partial b}{\partial \tilde{Z}} = 0 \tag{6.14}$$

where $\rho' = \frac{\partial \rho}{\partial C}$ and $\tilde{Z} = (1-\Upsilon)Z$

Rearranging Equation (6.14) leads to the following expression:

$$\underbrace{\frac{\partial \delta}{\partial \Upsilon} X_M(\Omega+b)\rho' + Z(1-\rho)\frac{\partial b}{\partial \tilde{Z}}}_{\text{marginal political gain}} - \underbrace{(1-\rho)\frac{\partial b}{\partial C}}_{\text{marginal political loss}} = 0 \tag{6.14.1}$$

An improvement in the degree of law enforcement implied by an increase in Υ leads to an increase in bribe rate (δ) by the incumbent firm $1m$ (6.12) which augments the political donation, C. This improves the probability of getting re-elected which is captured by the term, $\frac{\partial \delta}{\partial \Upsilon} X_M(\Omega+b)\rho'$. On the other hand, an increase in Υ implies a higher rate of detention of criminals in society, ceteris paribus, this lowers the backlash that the political party might face if it is out of power by an amount $Z(1-\rho)\frac{\partial b}{\partial \tilde{Z}}$. Thus, these two above effects yield marginal political gain to the party. On the other hand, a higher detention rate, Υ, increases the amount of corruption C which increases the possible magnitude of backlash represented by the term, $(1-\rho)\frac{\partial b}{\partial C}$. This is a marginal political loss. At the optimum, the marginal political gain must be equalised with marginal political loss to obtain an interior solution for the detention rate, Υ. Equation (6.14.1) constitutes a first-order necessary condition, while Assumption 6.6 leads to a first-order sufficient condition that implies that an improvement in law enforcement leads to a net fall in the probability of getting re-elected.

Solving Equation (6.14), we obtain the following optimal value:

$$\Upsilon = \Upsilon(X_M, Z) \tag{6.15}$$

Assumption 6.8: $2\left(\frac{\partial b}{\partial C}\right)\left(\frac{\partial \delta}{\partial \Upsilon}\right)X_M < \frac{\partial b}{\partial \tilde{Z}} Z$

Assumption 6.9: $(1-\rho) > Z\rho' X_M \frac{\partial \delta}{\partial Z}$

Lemma 6.2: The enforcement of law and order (in terms of criminal detention rate) is positively associated with an increase in the number of criminals and deteriorates with an expansion of the corruption-ridden industry M's output, i.e., $\frac{\partial \Upsilon}{\partial X_M} < 0$, $\frac{\partial \Upsilon}{\partial Z} > 0$.

Proof. Given the first-order optimality condition in Equation (6.14.1), a higher amount of output produced by the corruption-ridden industry M (a high X_M) leads to an increase in the amount of political donation (corruption), C, that accentuates the marginal gain to the ruling party owing to an improvement in the chances of getting re-elected. On the other hand, a rise in C lowers the probability of losing an election ($1-\rho$ falls) which lowers the marginal gain resulting from a lower b due to a higher Υ. Finally, a fall in $(1-\rho)$ lowers the marginal cost to the political party arising due to an increase in b owing to a higher Υ. To restore the optimality condition (or, stage 1 equilibrium) obtained in Equation (6.14.1), each effect on marginal gain and marginal loss must be countered by an adjustment in the politician's instrumental variable, i.e., Υ. First, an increase in marginal gain (the first term in Equation (6.14.1)) requires an increase in Υ that would cause a fall in b. Second, a fall in marginal gain (the second term in Equation (6.14.1)) must be accompanied by a fall in Υ that would lead to a rise in $(1-\rho)$ by lower the amount of C. Third, a fall in marginal cost must be countered by a fall in Υ that would again lead to an increase in $(1-\rho)$ (last term in Equation (6.14.1)). Provided Assumptions 6.6 and 6.8, it is obtained that the latter two effects dominate the former effect such that Υ falls owing to an increase in X_M. Similarly, given Assumption 6.9 and through the adjustment mechanism in the marginal gain and marginal loss terms, it is obtained that an increase in Z causes a rise in Υ. This proves Lemma 6.1.

6.3.3 The General Equilibrium Analogue

The general equilibrium analogue is elucidated as follows.

The profit-maximisation conditions for sector 1, sector M and sector 2 are represented by the following equations, respectively:

$$Wa_{L1} + Ra_{N1} + ra_{K1} = 1 \tag{6.16}$$

$$k\left(\bar{W} a_{LM} + r a_{KM} + \kappa \bar{F} + \delta\right) = P_M \tag{6.17}$$

$$\bar{W} a_{L2} + r a_{K2} = P_2^* \tag{6.18}$$

where k represents the market power of firm $m1$ in industry M.

The criminal (illegal) sector incurs the cost of hiring criminals ($W_Z Z$) and the cost of borrowing capital from illegal sources at a higher informal interest rate ($g k_Z Z$). The cost in the criminal sector is covered by the contribution made by firm $m1$ in the form of a bribe (political donations) to the incumbent political party. Thus, the break-even condition for the illegal sector is given by the following:

$$\delta(r,Z,\Upsilon)X_M = W_Z Z + gk_Z Z \tag{6.19}$$

The interest rate of the illegally sourced capital is determined by the following rule:[13]

$$g = \alpha + \beta(r) \;;\; \alpha \geq 0,\; \beta' > 1 \;\forall\; r > 0,\; \beta'' > 0 \tag{6.20}$$

The factor market equilibrium conditions for capital and land are obtained as follows, respectively:

$$a_{K1} X_1 + a_{KM} X_M + a_{K2} X_2 = \bar{K} - k_Z Z \tag{6.21}$$

$$a_{N1} X_1 = \bar{N} \tag{6.22}$$

The enforcement of law and order leads to the detention of Υ fraction of the total number of criminals who are prevented from participating in the labour market; thus, the labour market-clearing condition is as follows:

$$a_{L1} X_1 + a_{LM} X_M + a_{L2} X_2 = \bar{L} - \Upsilon(.)Z - \{1 - \Upsilon(.)\}Z \tag{6.23}$$

On simplification of Equation (6.23), it boils down to

$$a_{L1} X_1 + a_{LM} X_M + a_{L2} X_2 = \bar{L} - Z \tag{6.23.1}$$

where $\bar{K}, \bar{N}$ and $\bar{L}$ are exogenously given endowment of capital, land and labour, respectively.

The market-clearing condition for commodity X_M is given by the following:

$$X_M = X_M^D(P_M, \bar{L}) \tag{6.24}$$

Given the trade balance condition and using Equations (6.16)–(6.23), the real national income is obtained as follows:

$$Y = \underbrace{W a_{L1} X_1 + \bar{W}\left(a_{L2} X_2 + a_{LM} X_M\right)}_{\text{Labour income from the legal product sectos}} + \underbrace{W_Z Z}_{\text{Income of criminals}} + \underbrace{R\bar{N} + r\bar{K}}_{\text{Aggregate land and capital income}}$$
$$+ \underbrace{(g - r)k_Z Z}_{\text{Black income generated due to existence of shadow capital market}} + \underbrace{(k-1)\left(\bar{W} a_{LM} + r a_{KM} + \kappa\bar{F} + \delta\right) X_M}_{\text{positive profit in industry M}}$$
$$+ \underbrace{\kappa\bar{F}}_{\text{Lump-sum redistribution of penalties collected by the Government}} \tag{6.25}$$

Equation (6.25) reveals that even the black income which is initially a leakage in the system gets reflected in the national income through various channels of expenditure on the final product of the legally produced sector and the profit of firms. For instance, criminals spent their income on the consumption of commodities that are produced in the legal sectors, and firm $m1$ in industry M pays bribe to the ruling political party that adds to its cost of production which is collected in the form of high commodity price, thus enter in the national income as profit.[14]

In this general equilibrium system, there are 14 main endogenous variables, $W, W_Z, R, r, g, \delta, \Upsilon, P_M, X_1, X_2, X_M, Z, X_M^D$ and Y with the same number of independent equations (i.e., (6.6), (6.7), (6.12), (6.15)–(6.22), (6.23.1), (6.24) and (6.25)). Equation (6.18) solves r. Once r is obtained, g can be determined from Equation (6.20). Equation (6.22) solves X_1. Solving simultaneous Equations (6.21) and (6.23.1), X_2 and X_M are solved in terms of Z. Equations (6.12) and (6.15) solve δ and Υ as a function of Z. Equation (6.17) solves Z as a function of P_M. The final equilibrium value of P_M is solved from Equation (6.24). Once P_M is obtained, the final values of X_2, X_M and Z get determined. Equation (6.19) solves W_Z. Equations (6.6) and (6.16) solve W and R, respectively. Finally, Equation (6.25) solves Y. Given that sector 1 uses a specific input land, thus, its output hinges on the endowment of land, while sector 2 and sector M form a *subsystem* with respect to capital and labour. Non-reversibility of factor-intensity ranking and Walrasian stability for the non-traded commodity ensures the stability of the general equilibrium model. This completes the determination of general equilibrium values and description of the working of the model.

6.4 Foreign Capital Inflow, Crime–Corruption Nexus and Endogenous Enforcement of Law and Order

In this section, we analyse the effect of capital augmentation in terms of an exogenous increase in the inflow of foreign capital on the amount of corruption (C), the bribe rate (δ), the size of the criminal sector measured in terms of the number of criminals (Z) and the effective level of law enforcement measured in terms of detention rate of criminals (Υ).

Taking the total derivative of Equations (6.6), (6.7), (6.12), (6.15), (6.16)–(6.22), (6.23.1) and (6.24)–(6.25) with $\hat{\bar{K}} > 0$, the following propositions are immediate.

Proposition 6.1: An increase in foreign capital inflow which augments the domestic capital endowment of the economy leads to (i) an increase in the bribe rate, (ii) a rise in the rate of returns to the criminals, (iii) a fall in the level of production of the political crony industry M, (iv) a decrease in the number of criminals and (v) a possible fall in the rate of detention.

Proposition 6.2: The number of criminals falls at a cost to an escalation in the incidence of corruption and a deterioration in the effective enforcement of law and order owing to an inflow of foreign capital under certain sufficient conditions.

Proof. See Appendixes C and D.

An intuitive proof of Propositions 6.1 and 6.2 can be offered as follows. An inflow of foreign capital augments the domestic capital endowment of the economy. This causes an expansion of sector 2 and a contraction of sector M owing to the Rybczynski effect, provided sector 2 is relatively more capital-intensive compared to labour than sector M; i.e., $|\lambda|_{KL}^{2M} = (\lambda_{LM}\lambda_{K2} - \lambda_{L2}\lambda_{KM}) > 0$, where λ_{ji} is the physical share of jth factor in the ith sector. This is the primary effect. It follows from *Lemma 6.2* that a fall in the production level of output in sector M causes the politician to choose a higher level of detention rate, Υ (Equation (6.15)). A higher Υ leads to a higher level of bribe rate, δ, offered by firm $m1$ operating in industry M to the incumbent politician (see Lemma 6.1). From Equation (6.24), it follows that a fall in output level, X_M, leads to a rise in P_M such that market equilibrium in industry M gets restored. An increase in P_M causes marginal revenue to rise; thus, to maintain the profit-maximising condition represented in Equation (6.17), δ must increase further such that the marginal cost and marginal revenue parity condition remain stable. This further rise in δ requires adjustment in the number of criminals, Z, which has two opposite effects on δ. First, a fall in Z directly increases δ by proportion $|\varepsilon_Z^\delta|$, where $|\varepsilon_Z^\delta|$ is the elasticity of δ with respect to Z. This is the *direct effect* of change in the size of criminals on the bribe rate. Second, a rise in Z leads to a high detention rate Υ by proportion ε_Z^Υ, where ε_Z^Υ represents the elasticity of Υ with respect to Z. This causes an increase in δ by proportion $\varepsilon_\Upsilon^\delta$ where $\varepsilon_\Upsilon^\delta$ is the elasticity of δ with respect to Υ. This is an *indirect effect* of change in the size of criminals on the bribe rate through a change in detention rate that leads to an increase in δ by $\varepsilon_\Upsilon^\delta\varepsilon_Z^\Upsilon$. Thus, if the direct effect dominates the indirect effect, then Z falls which leads to an increase in δ.

The contracting criminal sector releases capital and labour that need to get absorbed in the legal good producing sector 2 and M. It is reasonable to assume that the criminal sector is labour-intensive, and thus, it releases more labour relative to capital that causes a Rybczynski-type effect which leads to an expansion of sector M and a contraction of sector 2. This is a secondary effect. The primary effect of a fall in X_M dominates the secondary effect of rise in X_M, provided $\lambda_{L2} > |\lambda|_{LK}^{Z2}|A_1|$ (see Appendix C). The amount of corruption, C, defined by δX_M increases due to a rise in δ and decreases due to a fall in X_M. Under the sufficient condition (D.5), the increase in δ is proportionately greater than the decrease in X_M, and thus, C rises. An increase in C causes the left-hand side to increase, while a fall in Z causes the right-hand side to fall in Equation (6.19), and thus, the returns to criminal, W_Z, must rise to restore the equilibrium (break-even condition) in the criminal sector. The final effect on the choice of detention rate by the incumbent politician, Υ, falls provided the sufficient condition (D.6) which implies that proportionate fall in Z dominates the fall in X_M. In the labour relocation equilibrium (Equation (6.6)), on the one hand, the expected wage in the criminal sector escalates due to the rise in W_Z and fall in Υ, and on the other hand, the expected returns from participating in the legal labour market remain ambiguous owing to multiple secondary effects; thus, W remain ambiguous.

6.5 Concluding Remarks

This chapter attempted to offer a theoretical understanding of the role of foreign capital inflow in influencing the incidence of corruption, crime and politicised manipulation of law and order using a four-stage game-theoretic general equilibrium model in the presence of political cronyism. Corruption in this analysis is defined as the aggregate amount of bribe payment/political donations to the ruling party. In exchange for this payment, the ruling party with the help of the criminal sector causes damages to the potential entrant firm to deter its entry into the industry which leads to the generation of monopoly rent to the incumbent firm. The politician does this by choosing optimally the effective enforcement of law and order in terms of criminal detention rate which maximises its expected payoff from winning the re-election bid.

The strategic interaction between the ruling political party, the incumbent party and the potential entrant leads to the following interesting optimal outcomes. The criminal detention rate falls with an increase in the scale of operation of the incumbent firm (crony capitalist) and rises with an increase in the number of criminals. On the other hand, a high rate of bribe payment could be observed with an increase in the rate of criminal detention, while the bribe rate falls if the number of criminals goes up. Given these optimal choices, an inflow of foreign capital leads to decriminalisation in terms of a fall in the number of criminals, however, at the cost of an increase in the amount of corruption and deterioration in the enforcement of law and order. Thus, foreign capital in a democracy with legal distortion alongside economic distortions may be detrimental to the law-and-order situation besides worsening the magnitude and the rate of corruption.

Acknowledgement

The authors are grateful for the constructive comments received from Dr Jayanta Kumar Dwibedi at the Second Annual Economics Conference, St. Xavier's University, Kolkata, Dr Amarjyoti Mahanta at Graduate Research Meet 2021, Indian Institute of Technology, Guwahati, Prof Oguzhan Dincer, Dr Robert Gillanders and Mr Nicolás Jaramillo at the Third Workshop on Corruption, Institute of Corruption Studies, Illinois State University, USA, Dr Biswajit Nag at the Seventh Empirical Issues in International Trade and

Finance Conference, Indian Institute of Foreign Trade, Kolkata, and Dr Shivangi Chandel at Annual Conference on Economics and Public Policy 2021, O.P. Jindal Global University, Haryana, who helped improve and clarify this chapter. The authors remember (Late) Prof Sarbajit Chaudhuri with great fondness and respect for encouraging diverse issue-based research in applied general equilibrium models besides acting as a doctoral supervisor to S. Mahata, R. K. Khan and S. Mandal until his unfortunate demise and an academic guide to S. Chaudhuri and R. N. Nag. However, the usual disclaimer applies.

Appendixes

Appendix A: Determination of the Bribe Rate in the Industry M

A.1 Fourth-Stage Equilibrium with Accommodation

From Equation (6.7), the inverse demand function of sector M is written as

$$P_M = a - \frac{X_M}{\bar{L}} \tag{A.1.1}$$

The profit of firm 2 in industry M is given by:

$$\pi_{m2}^{A} = \left[a - \left(\frac{x_{m1} + x_{m2}}{\bar{L}} \right) \right] x_{m2} - \left(\bar{W} a_{LM} + r a_{KM} \right) x_{m2} \tag{A.1.2}$$

The first-order condition of profit maximisation of firm 2 yields

$$\frac{\partial \pi_{m2}^{A}}{\partial x_{m2}} = a - \left(\frac{x_{m1}}{\bar{L}} \right) - \frac{2x_{m2}}{\bar{L}} - \left(\bar{W} a_{LM} + r a_{KM} \right) = 0$$

$$or, \;\; x_{m2} = \left(\frac{a - \bar{W} a_{LM} - r a_{KM}}{2} \right) \bar{L} - \frac{x_{m1}}{2} \tag{A.1.3}$$

Using Equation (A.1.3), the profit of firm 1 in industry M is obtained as

$$\pi_{m1}^{A} = \left[a - \left(\frac{x_{m1}}{2\bar{L}} \right) - \left(\frac{a - \bar{W} a_{LM} - r a_{KM}}{2} \right) \right] x_{m1} - \left(\bar{W} a_{LM} + r a_{KM} \right) x_{m1} \tag{A.1.4}$$

The first-order condition of profit maximisation of firm 1 yields

$$\frac{\partial \pi_{m1}^{A}}{\partial x_{m1}} = a - \left(\frac{x_{m1}}{\bar{L}} \right) - \left(\frac{a - \bar{W} a_{LM} - r a_{KM}}{2} \right) - \left(\bar{W} a_{LM} + r a_{KM} \right) = 0$$

$$x_{m1}^{A} = \left(\frac{a - \bar{W} a_{LM} - r a_{KM}}{4} \right) \bar{L} \tag{A.1.5}$$

A.2 Third-Stage Equilibrium and Deterrence

To deter the entry of firm 2 in industry M the following condition is required:

$$\pi_{m2}^{D}=\left[a-\left(\frac{x_{m1}}{\bar{L}}\right)-\left(\frac{a-\bar{W}a_{LM}-ra_{KM}}{2}\right)+\left(\frac{x_{m1}}{2\bar{L}}\right)\right]\left[\left(\frac{a-\bar{W}a_{LM}-ra_{KM}}{2}\right)\bar{L}-\frac{x_{m1}}{2}\right]$$
$$-\left(\bar{W}a_{LM}+ra_{KM}\right)\left[\left(\frac{a-\bar{W}a_{LM}-ra_{KM}}{2}\right)\bar{L}-\frac{x_{m1}}{2}\right]-\varepsilon(1-\Upsilon)Z-F(\delta,u)=0$$

(A.2.1)

Equation (A.2.1) solved for x_{m1}^{D} that is given in Equation (6.10).

A.3 Second-Stage Equilibrium and the Determination of the Bribe Rate, δ

Juxtaposing Equations (A.1.3) and (A.1.5) and taking the total derivative we arrive at the following expression that leads to the determination of δ as a function of *r*, *Z* and ϒ

$$dr\left[\frac{a_{KM}\bar{L}}{\left\{a-(\bar{W}a_{LM}+ra_{KM})\right\}\bar{L}-2\sqrt{\left\{\varepsilon(1-\Upsilon)Z+F(\delta,\vartheta)\right\}\bar{L}}}-\frac{2a_{KM}}{\left\{a-(\bar{W}a_{LM}+ra_{KM})\right\}}\right]=$$

$$+d\delta\left[\frac{-\dfrac{\partial F}{\partial\delta}\dfrac{\bar{L}}{\sqrt{\left\{\varepsilon(1-\Upsilon)Z+F(\delta,\vartheta)\right\}\bar{L}}}}{\left\{a-(\bar{W}a_{LM}+ra_{KM})\right\}\bar{L}-2\sqrt{\left\{\varepsilon(1-\Upsilon)Z+F(\delta,\vartheta)\right\}\bar{L}}}+\frac{\dfrac{\bar{L}\dfrac{\partial F}{\partial\delta}}{2\sqrt{\left\{\varepsilon(1-\Upsilon)Z+F(\delta,\vartheta)\right\}\bar{L}}}}{\sqrt{\left\{\varepsilon(1-\Upsilon)Z+F(\delta,\vartheta)\right\}\bar{L}}-\left(\kappa\bar{F}+\delta\right)\bar{L}}\right]$$

$$+\frac{\left[(1-\Upsilon)dZ-Zd\Upsilon\right]}{\sqrt{\left\{\varepsilon(1-\Upsilon)Z+F(\delta,\vartheta)\right\}\bar{L}}}\left[\frac{-\varepsilon\bar{L}}{\left\{a-(\bar{W}a_{LM}+ra_{KM})\right\}\bar{L}-2\sqrt{\left\{\varepsilon(1-\Upsilon)Z+F(\delta,\vartheta)\right\}\bar{L}}}+\frac{\left\{\dfrac{\varepsilon\bar{L}}{2\sqrt{\left\{\varepsilon(1-\Upsilon)Z+F(\delta,\vartheta)\right\}\bar{L}}}\right\}}{\sqrt{\left\{\varepsilon(1-\Upsilon)Z+F(\delta,\vartheta)\right\}\bar{L}}-\left(\kappa\bar{F}+\delta\right)\bar{L}}\right]$$

(A.3.1)

Appendix B: First-Stage Equilibrium

The first-order condition for the optimisation exercise of the political party yields

$$\frac{\partial\Pi}{\partial\Upsilon}=\Omega\rho' X_M\frac{\partial\delta}{\partial\Upsilon}-\{1-\rho(C)\}\left[(-Z)\frac{\partial b}{\partial\tilde{Z}}+X_M\frac{\partial b}{\partial C}\frac{\partial\delta}{\partial\Upsilon}\right]+b\rho' X_M X_M\frac{\partial\delta}{\partial\Upsilon}=0$$

$$or,\ X_M\frac{\partial\delta}{\partial\Upsilon}\left[(\Omega+b)\rho'-\{1-\rho(C)\}\frac{\partial b}{\partial C}\right]+Z\{1-\rho(C)\}\frac{\partial b}{\partial\tilde{Z}}=0 \qquad \text{(B.1)}$$

The second-order condition for optimisation requires

$$\frac{\partial^2\Pi}{\partial\Upsilon^2}=\alpha X_M\left[\frac{\partial\delta}{\partial\Upsilon}\left\{\left(\frac{\partial\delta}{\partial\Upsilon}\rho' X_M+\rho' X_M\right)\frac{\partial b}{\partial C}-\rho' Z\frac{\partial b}{\partial\tilde{Z}}\right\}-X_M Z\frac{\partial\delta}{\partial\Upsilon}\frac{\partial b}{\partial\tilde{Z}}\right]<0$$

Taking the total differential of the first-order condition we get

$$dX_M\left[\frac{\partial\delta}{\partial\Upsilon}\left\{(\Omega+b)\rho'-(1-\rho)\frac{\partial b}{\partial C}\right\}+2\rho'\delta X_M\frac{\partial b}{\partial C}\frac{\partial\delta}{\partial\Upsilon}-\rho'\delta Z\frac{\partial b}{\partial\tilde{Z}}\right]$$

$$+d\Upsilon\left[2X_M^2\rho'\left(\frac{\partial\delta}{\partial\Upsilon}\right)^2\frac{\partial b}{\partial C}-2Z\rho' X_M\frac{\partial\delta}{\partial\Upsilon}\frac{\partial b}{\partial\tilde{Z}}\right]$$

$$+dZ\left[2X_M^2\rho'\frac{\partial\delta}{\partial\Upsilon}\frac{\partial b}{\partial C}\frac{\partial\delta}{\partial Z}+\rho' X_M(1-\Upsilon)\frac{\partial\delta}{\partial\Upsilon}\frac{\partial b}{\partial\tilde{Z}}+\frac{\partial b}{\partial\tilde{Z}}\left\{(1-\rho)-Z\rho' X_M\frac{\partial b}{\partial Z}\right\}\right]=0$$

(B.2)

Appendix C: The General Equilibrium and Equations of Change

From Equations (6.18), (6.20) and (6.22), it is evident that $\hat{r}=0$ and $\hat{g}=0$ and that

$$\hat{X}_1=0 \qquad \text{(C.1)}$$

Equations (6.21) and (6.23.1) give

$$\hat{X}_M=-\left(\frac{\lambda_{L2}}{|\lambda|_{KL}^{2M}}\right)\hat{\bar{K}}-\left(\frac{|\lambda|_{LK}^{Z2}}{|\lambda|_{KL}^{2M}}\right)\hat{Z} \qquad \text{(C.2)}$$

$$\hat{X}_2=\left(\frac{\lambda_{LM}}{|\lambda|_{KL}^{2M}}\right)\hat{\bar{K}}+\left(\frac{|\lambda|_{LK}^{ZM}}{|\lambda|_{KL}^{2M}}\right)\hat{Z} \qquad \text{(C.3)}$$

where $|\lambda|_{KL}^{2M} = (\lambda_{LM}\lambda_{K2} - \lambda_{L2}\lambda_{KM})$, $|\lambda|_{LK}^{Z2} = (\eta_Z\lambda_{K2} - \lambda_{L2}\lambda_{KZ})$, $|\lambda|_{LK}^{ZM} = (\eta_Z\lambda_{KM} - \lambda_{LM}\lambda_{KZ})$ and $\eta_Z = Z/L$.

From (6.12) and (6.15), the following results are determined:

$$\hat{\delta} = -\left(\frac{\varepsilon_{\Upsilon}^{\delta}\varepsilon_{X_M}^{\Upsilon}\lambda_{L2}}{|\lambda|_{KL}^{2M}}\right)\hat{\bar{K}} + \left(\varepsilon_Z^{\delta} + \varepsilon_{\Upsilon}^{\delta}\varepsilon_Z^{\Upsilon} - \frac{\varepsilon_{\Upsilon}^{\delta}\varepsilon_{X_M}^{\Upsilon}|\lambda|_{LK}^{Z2}}{|\lambda|_{KL}^{2M}}\right)\hat{Z} \tag{C.4}$$

$$\hat{\Upsilon} = -\left(\frac{\varepsilon_{X_M}^{\Upsilon}\lambda_{L2}}{|\lambda|_{KL}^{2M}}\right)\hat{\bar{K}} + \left(\varepsilon_Z^{\Upsilon} - \frac{\varepsilon_{\Upsilon}^{\delta}\varepsilon_{X_M}^{\Upsilon}|\lambda|_{LK}^{Z2}}{|\lambda|_{KL}^{2M}}\right)\hat{Z} \tag{C.5}$$

Equation (6.17) gives the following, where $\theta_{\delta}^{M} = \dfrac{k\delta}{P_M}$:

$$\hat{k} = \hat{P}_M(P_M - a) = \hat{P}_M - \theta_{\delta}^{M}\left[\left(\varepsilon_Z^{\delta} + \varepsilon_{\Upsilon}^{\delta}\varepsilon_Z^{\Upsilon} - \frac{\varepsilon_{\Upsilon}^{\delta}\varepsilon_{X_M}^{\Upsilon}|\lambda|_{LK}^{Z2}}{|\lambda|_{KL}^{2M}}\right)\hat{Z} - \left(\frac{\varepsilon_{\Upsilon}^{\delta}\varepsilon_{X_M}^{\Upsilon}\lambda_{L2}}{|\lambda|_{KL}^{2M}}\right)\hat{\bar{K}}\right] \tag{C.6}$$

Equations (6.24) and (6.34) give

$$\hat{P}_M = -\left(\frac{\lambda_{L2}}{\varepsilon_{P_M}^{MD}|\lambda|_{KL}^{2M}}\right)\hat{\bar{K}} - \left(\frac{|\lambda|_{LK}^{Z2}}{\varepsilon_{P_M}^{MD}|\lambda|_{KL}^{2M}}\right)\hat{Z} \tag{C.7}$$

Therefore Equations (C.4) and (C.5) give

$$\hat{Z} = A_1\hat{\bar{K}} \tag{C.8}$$

where $A_1 = \dfrac{\lambda_{L2}}{\dfrac{\left(\varepsilon_Z^{\delta} + \varepsilon_{\Upsilon}^{\delta}\varepsilon_Z^{\Upsilon}\right)\theta_{\delta}^{M}}{\left[\dfrac{(P_M - a - 1)}{\varepsilon_{P_M}^{MD}|\lambda|_{KL}^{2M}} + \left(\dfrac{\varepsilon_{\Upsilon}^{\delta}\varepsilon_{X_M}^{\Upsilon}}{|\lambda|_{KL}^{2M}}\right)\theta_{\delta}^{M}\right]} - |\lambda|_{LK}^{Z2}}$

Using Equations (A.1.1)–(A.3.1) and (B.1), from Equation (6.19) the following result is derived:

$$\hat{W}_Z = A_2 \hat{\bar{K}} \tag{C.9}$$

where $A_2 = \dfrac{1}{\theta_Z}\left[-\left(\dfrac{\overset{\delta}{\varepsilon}_{\Upsilon}\overset{\Upsilon}{\varepsilon}_{X_M}+1}{|\lambda|^{2M}_{KL}}\right)\left(|\lambda|^{Z2}_{LK}A_1+\lambda_{L2}\right)+\left\{\overset{\delta}{\varepsilon}_Z+\overset{\delta}{\varepsilon}_{\Upsilon}\overset{\Upsilon}{\varepsilon}_Z-1\right\}A_1\right]$

Using Equations (6.6) and (6.16), the following results are determined:

$$\hat{W} = \frac{A_3}{\eta_L^1}\hat{\bar{K}} \tag{C.10}$$

$$\hat{R} = -\frac{\theta_{L1}A_3}{\theta_{N1}\eta_L^1}\hat{\bar{K}} \tag{C.11}$$

where $A_3 = \left[\begin{array}{l} A_2 - \dfrac{\eta_Z}{1-\eta_Z}A_1 - \left(\dfrac{\Upsilon}{1-\Upsilon}\right)\left\{\left(\overset{\Upsilon}{\varepsilon}_Z - \dfrac{\overset{\delta}{\varepsilon}_{\Upsilon}\overset{\Upsilon}{\varepsilon}_{X_M}|\lambda|^{Z2}_{LK}}{|\lambda|^{2M}_{KL}}\right)A_1 - \left(\dfrac{\overset{\Upsilon}{\varepsilon}_{X_M}\lambda_{L2}}{|\lambda|^{2M}_{KL}}\right)\right\} \\ -\eta_L^2\left(\dfrac{\lambda_{LM}+|\lambda|^{ZM}_{LK}A_1}{|\lambda|^{2M}_{KL}}\right)+\eta_L^M\left(\dfrac{\lambda_{L2}+|\lambda|^{Z2}_{LK}A_1}{|\lambda|^{2M}_{KL}}\right)\end{array}\right]$,

$\eta_L^1 = \dfrac{Wa_{L1}X_1}{L_I}$, $\eta_L^2 = \dfrac{\bar{W}a_{L2}X_2}{L_I}$, $\eta_L^M = \dfrac{\bar{W}a_{LM}X_M}{L_I}$ and $L_I = \left(Wa_{L1}X_1 + \bar{W}a_{L2}X_2 + \bar{W}a_{LM}X_M\right)$.

The excess demand function in the market for commodity M is given by:

$$ED(P_M) = X_M^D - X_M \tag{C.12}$$

Taking the total derivative of equations (C.11) and (6.7) and using equations (C.1), (C.5) and (C.6) with $\hat{\bar{K}} = 0$, the Walrasian stability condition requires the following sufficient condition:

$$\left|\overset{\delta}{\varepsilon}_Z+\overset{\delta}{\varepsilon}_{\Upsilon}\overset{\Upsilon}{\varepsilon}_Z\right| > \frac{\overset{\delta}{\varepsilon}_{\Upsilon}\left|\overset{\Upsilon}{\varepsilon}_{X_M}\right||\lambda|^{Z2}_{LK}}{|\lambda|^{2M}_{KL}} \tag{C.13}$$

The index of corruption is given by the following expression:

$$C = \delta X_M \tag{C.14}$$

Appendix D: Effect of Capital Inflow: Main Results

Equations (C.1) and (C.2) suggest that $\hat{X}_M < 0$ and $\hat{X}_2 > 0$ under the sufficient condition:

$$\lambda_{L2} > |A_1||\lambda|^{Z2}_{LK} \tag{D.1}$$

Using (C.12), it is evident that $\hat{P}_M > 0$ from Equation (C.6). This implies $\hat{k} > 0$ from Equation (C.5).

From Equation (C.7), it is evident that $\hat{Z} < 0$ under the following sufficient conditions:

$$\left|\varepsilon^{\delta}_{Z}\right| > \varepsilon^{\delta}_{\Upsilon}\varepsilon^{\Upsilon}_{Z} \tag{D.2}$$

$$\frac{|P_M - a - 1|}{\varepsilon^{MD}_{P_M}} > \frac{\varepsilon^{\delta}_{\Upsilon}\left|\varepsilon^{\Upsilon}_{X_M}\right|}{|\lambda|^{2M}_{KL}}\theta^{M}_{\delta} \tag{D.3}$$

From Equation (C.8), using condition (D.1) it is obtained that $\hat{W}_Z > 0$ if the following sufficient condition is satisfied

$$\varepsilon^{\delta}_{\Upsilon}\left|\varepsilon^{\Upsilon}_{X_M}\right| < 1 \tag{D.4}$$

It is evident from Equation (C.11) that $\hat{C} > 0$ if

$$\left(\varepsilon^{\delta}_{Z} + \varepsilon^{\delta}_{\Upsilon}\varepsilon^{\Upsilon}_{Z}\right)A_1 > \left(1 + \varepsilon^{\delta}_{\Upsilon}\varepsilon^{\Upsilon}_{X_M}\right)\frac{\left|-\lambda_{L2} + |\lambda|^{Z2}_{LK}|A_1|\right|}{|\lambda|^{2M}_{KL}} \tag{D.5}$$

Equation (C.4) suggests that $\hat{\Upsilon} < 0$ if

$$\left(\varepsilon^{\Upsilon}_{Z} - \frac{\varepsilon^{\delta}_{\Upsilon}\varepsilon^{\Upsilon}_{X_M}|\lambda|^{Z2}_{LK}}{|\lambda|^{2M}_{KL}}\right)|A_1| > \left(\frac{\left|\varepsilon^{\Upsilon}_{X_M}\right|\lambda_{L2}}{|\lambda|^{2M}_{KL}}\right) \tag{D.6}$$

Equations (C.9) and (C.10) suggest that $\hat{W} > (<)$ and $\hat{R} < (>)$ if $A_3 > (<) 0$.

Notes

1 For example, the existence of crime–corruption–political nexus in natural resource-based industry in different countries can be found in many scholarly works. Dutt and Williams (2005), Dutt (2007; 2014), Long et al. (2012), White and Michelutti (2019), Mahadevan (2019) and Zabyelina and Uhm (2020) are some of the well documented studies that investigate the nexus to a greater extent.

2 For an extensive review of the above-mentioned analytical approaches in the study of corruption, see Burguet, Ganuza and Montalvo (2016).

3 For an extensive review of more evidence-based studies on corruption and its several aspects, see Enste and Heldman (2017).

4 The present chapter makes no distinction between politician, number of party members and a political party which is out of scope of this chapter. Thus, the term "ruling politician" or "ruling political party" has been interchangeably used to denote the "political entity" in power.

5 In developing economy like India, such politicised manipulation of regulative laws and selective enforcement failure is usual practice among ruling politicians. This was evident in 2G spectrum scam in the telecom industry, Colgate scam (Coal blocks allocation scam) etc. See White and Michelutti (2019) (eds), "The Wild East: Criminal political economies in South Asia" for detailed descriptions of such scams and political cronyisms.

6 Besides the (illegal) criminal sector, there exists an informal legal commodity producing sector 1. Labour in sector 1 are compensated with informal wage rate, W, while its counterpart in sector 2 and M earn formal institutionally wage rate, $\bar{W}$. Ideally, by the definition of law, any wage payment other than the legally determined, $\bar{W}$ is illegal and can be considered as part of corruption. In other words, employer in sector 1 by paying a less than legally determined wage earns a surplus of $(\bar{W} - W)$ that constitute part of illegal income. However, in broad sense, the definition of corruption is relative and perception based. We have assumed that the informal wage payment does not constitute part of corruption. This is because had sector 1 provided formal legal wage, $\bar{W}$, there would arise open unemployment in the legal sectors on one hand, or this would motivate unemployed labour to move to the criminal sector, thereby increasing criminalization of labour force. In this sense, a lower W restricts some of the labour from becoming potential criminals besides providing them means of livelihood rather than remaining unemployed.

7 The utility function is a modified version of Dixit (1979) utility function.

8 The sub-utility function for the other two commodities produced in the competitive sector is assumed to take a Cobb–Douglas form; however, the results of the model are invariant to the form of the sub-utility function. This is because these commodities produced in sectors 1 and 2 are internationally traded, and given the small-open economy assumption, prices are internationally determined. Thus, any change in demand for these products would leave the domestic terms of trade unchanged and hence no effects will be generated on the other variables in the model.

9 The right-hand side of Equation (6.6) represent the expected income from participating in the legal labour market; on the other hand, the criminal skips the vigilant authorities with probability, $\{1 - \Upsilon\}$, and thus, the expected income in the criminal sector is represented by the left-hand side expression in Equation (6.6). Here, we assume for simplicity that if the criminal gets caught, then the criminal is barred from participating in the labour market; however, no fine/penalty is imposed. Even if space for penalty is included (say at rate $\bar{\Gamma}$), then it will only lower the LHS by $\Upsilon\bar{\Gamma}$. If the $\bar{\Gamma}$ is positive constant, then inclusion of this will have no qualitative effect except for quantitative changes in the result.

10 Here, it is assumed that the incumbent firm is crony of the ruling political party and it bribes (donates funds) to the political party to deter entry of the potential entrant. Such initial ties between businesses and political party pre-exist due to factors such as belonging to the same ethnic group/caste/religion etc. For example, Lehne, Shapiro and Eynde (2018) found evidence in India of biased road construction contracts to contractors who share a common surname (belonging to the same caste) with the member of parliament/member of legislative assembly.

11 If the party remains out of office, its payoff is $\Pi' = (1-\alpha)Y$ which is less than the payoff had it been an office holder, i.e., $\Pi = \alpha\,[\rho(C)\,\Omega - \{1-\rho(C)\}b] + (1-\alpha)Y$. Given that $\Omega > 0$ which implies $\Pi > \Pi'$, and hence no party would like to lose power and remain out of office.
12 See Appendix B for detailed derivation.
13 See Gupta and Chaudhuri (1997) for partial equilibrium determination of informal interest rate and its association with the formal interest rate in the presence of corrupt officials and informal moneylenders. For similar treatment of informal interest rate, see Gupta (1993), Marjit and Acharyya (2003), Chaudhuri and Gupta (2014), Chaudhuri and Chaudhuri (2019) and Mahata, Khan and Nag (2020) among others.
14 Mendez and Sepulveda (2006) found that for a sample of 130 free countries for the period 1960–2000 corruption augments economic growth at a low incidence of corruption and detrimental to growth at high levels of incidence which implies the existence of a non-monotonic relationship between corruption and economic growth. Equation (6.25) is an analytical representation of this non-monotonic relationship.

References and Notes

Acemoglu, D. and Robinson, J. (2011). *Why Nations Fail: The Origins of Power, Prosperity, and Poverty*. New York: Crown Publishers.

Acemoglu, D. and Verdier, T. (2000). The choice between market failures and corruption. *American Economic Review*. 90(1). 194–211.

Alemu, A. M. (2012). Effects of corruption on FDI inflow in Asian economies. *Seoul Journal of Economics*. 25(4). 387–412.

Amir, R. and Burr, C. (2015). Corruption and socially optimal entry. *Journal of Public Economics*. 123. 30–41.

Besley, T. and McLaren, J. (1993). Taxes and bribery: The role of wage incentives. *Economic Journal*. 103(416). 119–141.

Blanco, L. R., Ruiz, I. and Wooster, R. B. (2019). The effect of violent crime on sector-specific FDI in Latin America. *Oxford Development Studies*. 47(4). 420–434.

Bliss, C. and Tella, R. D. (1997). Does competition kill corruption? *Journal of Political Economy*. 105(5). 1001–1023.

Boerner, K. and Hainz, C. (2009). The political economy of corruption and the role of economic opportunities 1. *Economics of Transition*. 17(2). 213–240.

Brown, L. and Hibbert, K. (2017). The effect of crime on foreign direct investment: A multi-country panel data analysis. *The Journal of Developing Areas*. 51(1). 295–307.

Burguet, R., Ganuza, J. J. and Montalvo, J. G. (2016). The microeconomics of corruption: A review of thirty years of research. *Barcelona GSE Working Paper Series 908,* Barcelona.

Burguet, R. and Perry, M. K. (2007). Bribery and favoritism by auctioneers in sealed-bid auctions. *The B E Journal of Theoretical Economics*. 7(1). pp. 00001022021935170412l9

Canare, T. (2017). The effect of corruption on foreign direct investment inflows: Evidence from a panel of Asia-Pacific countries. In Rama, M. D. and Rowley, C. (editors) *The Changing Face of Corruption in the Asia Pacific: Current Perspective and Future Challenges*. 35–55. https://www.sciencedirect.com/book

/9780081011096/the-changing-face-of-corruption-in-the-asia-pacific#book-description

Celik, G. (2009). Mechanism design with collusive supervision. *Journal of Economic Theory*. 144(1). 69–95.

Chaudhuri, S. and Chaudhuri, S. (2019). Foreign direct investment and credit market reform in a developing economy: Could these be alternative policies? *International Review of Economics and Finance*. 62. 321–331.

Chaudhuri, S., Dastidar, K. G. and Mahata, S. (2022). Cronyism and corruption in India: A game-theoretic analysis. *Managerial and Decision Economics*. https://doi.org/10.1002/mde.3550.

Chaudhuri, S. and Gupta, M. R. (2014). International factor mobility, informal interest rate and capital market imperfection: A general equilibrium analysis. *Economic Modelling*. 37. 184–192.

Daniele, V. and Marani, U. (2011). Organized crime, the quality of local institutions and FDI in Italy: A panel data analysis. *European Journal of Political Economy*. 27(1). 132–142.

Dastidar, K. G. and Mukherjee, D. (2014). Corruption in delegated public procurement auctions. *European Journal of Political Economy*. 35. 122–127.

Dastidar, K. G. and Yano, M. (2021). Corruption, market quality, and entry-deterrence in emerging economies. *International Journal of Economic Theory*. 17(1). 101–117.

Dixit, S. (1979). A model of duopoly suggesting a theory of entry barriers. *The Bell Journal of Economics*. 10(1). 20–32.

Dutt, K. L. (2007). Illegal coal mining in Eastern India: Rethinking legitimacy and limits of justice. *Economic and Political Weekly*. 42(49). 57–66.

Dutt, K. L. (ed.). (2014). *The Coal Nation Histories, Ecologies and Politics of Coal in India*. Ashgate Publishing Limited, India. https://www.routledge.com/The-Coal-Nation-Histories-Ecologies-and-Politics-of-Coal-in-India/Lahiri-Dutt/p/book/9781138272033

Dutt, K. L. and Williams, D. J. (2005). The coal cycle: Small scale illegal coal supply in eastern India. *Journal of Resources, Environmental and Development*. 2(2). 93–105.

Egger, P. and Winner, H. (2005). Evidence on corruption as an incentive for foreign direct investment. *European Journal of Political Economy*. 21(4). 932–952.

Enste, D. and Heldman, C. (2017). Causes and consequences of corruption: An overview of empirical results. *IW-Report No. 2/2017*. Cologne: German Economic Institute (IW).

Gupta, M. R. (1993). Rural-urban migration, informal sector and development policies: A theoretical analysis. *Journal of Development Economics*. 41(1). 137–151.

Gupta, M. R. (2020). Globalisation, crime and wage inequality: A theoretical analysis. *Indian Growth and Development Review*. 14(1). 97–121.

Gupta, M. R. and Chaudhuri, S. (1997). Evidence on corruption as an incentive for foreign direct investment. *Economica*. 64(254). 331–343.

Habib, M. and Zurawicki, L. (2002). Corruption and foreign direct investment. *Journal of International Business Studies*. 33(2). 291–307.

Harstad, B. and Svensson, J. (2011). Bribes, lobbying and development. *American Political Science Review*. 105(1). 46–63.

Khalil, F., Lawarree, J. and Yun, S. (2010). Bribery versus extortion: Allowing the lesser of two evils. *The RAND Journal of Economics*. 41(1). 179–198. http://www.jstor.org/stable/40649276.

Khan, R. K., Mahata, S. and Nag, R. N. (2022). Capital and crime-corruption nexus in the shadow of the law: A theoretical analysis of public policy. *Public Finance Review*. [OnlineFirst] https://doi.org/10.1177/10911421221127098

Koc, S. A. and Neilson, W. S. (2008). Interim bribery in auctions. *Economics Letters*. 99(2). 238–241.

Laffont, J. J. and Tirole, J. (1991). The politics of government decision-making: A theory of regulatory capture. *Quarterly Journal of Economics*. 196(4). 1089–1127.

Le, T. and Yalcin, E. (2018). Lobbying, campaign contributions, and electoral competition. *European Journal of Political Economy*. 55. 559–572.

Lehne, J., Shapiro, J. N. and Eynde, O. V. (2018). Building connections: Political corruption and road construction in India. *Journal of Development Economics*. 131. 62–78.

Long, M. A., Stretesky, P. B., Lynch, M. J. and Fenwick, E. (2012). Crime in the coal industry: Implications for green criminology and treadmill of production. *Organization and Environment*. 25(3). 328–346.

Luu, H. N., Nguyen, N. M., Ho, H. H. and Nam, V. H. (2019). The effect of corruption on FDI and its modes of entry. *Journal of Financial Economic Policy*. 11(2). 232–250.

Mahadevan, P. (2019). *Sand Mafias in India: Disorganized Crime in a Growing Economy*. Switzerland: The Global Initiative Against Transnational Organized Crime.

Mahata, S., Khan, R. K. and Nag, R. N. (2020). Economic recession, informal sector and skilled–unskilled wage disparity in a developing economy: A trade-theoretical analysis. *Foreign Trade Review*. 55(2). 168–188.

Mandal, B. and Marjit, S. (2010). Corruption and wage inequality? *International Review of Economics and Finance*. 19(1). 166–172.

Marjit, S. and Acharyya, R. (2003). Chapter 8. In *International Trade, Wage Inequality and the Developing Economy: A General Equilibrium Approach*. Heidelberg: Springer-Verlag Berlin Heidelberg.

Marjit, S. and Mandal, B. (2008). Corruption and trade in general equilibrium. *Research Paper Series* no. 15. The University of Nottingham, Nottingham.

Mendez, F. and Sepulveda, F. (2006). Corruption, growth and political regimes: Cross country evidence. *European Journal of Political Economy*. 22(1). 82–98.

Mookherjee, D. and Png, I. P. L. (1995). Corruptible law enforcers: How should they be compensated? *Economic Journal*. 105(428). 145–159.

Moustafa, E. (2021). The relationship between perceived corruption and FDI: A longitudinal study in the context of Egypt. *Transnational Corporations*. 28(2). 97–129.

Rocha Menocal, A. (2013). *Governance and Growth: Institutions Yes, but Which Ones?* Report prepared for the World Bank. London: ODI.

Rose-Ackerman, S. (1975). The economics of corruption. *Journal of Public Economics*. 4(2). 187–203.

Sadig, A. (2009). The effects of corruption on FDI inflows. *Cato Journal*. 29(2). 267–294.

Shleifer, A. and Vishny, R. W. (1993). Corruption. *The Quarterly Journal of Economics*. 108(3). 599–617.

Shleifer, A. and Vishny, R. W. (1994). Politicians and firms. *Quarterly Journal of Economics*. 109(4). 995–1025.

Strausz, R. (1995). *Collusion and Renegotiation in a Principal-Supervisor-Agent Relationship*. Center for Economic Research discussion paper, No. 9548. The Netherlands: Tilburg University.

System of National Accounts (2008). European Commission-United Nations-International Monetary Fund-Organization for Economic Co-operation and Development-World Bank, New York, 2008. https://unstats.un.org/unsd/nationalaccount/docs/sna2008.pdf ISBN 978-92-1-161522-7

Tirole, J. (1986). Hierarchies and bureaucracies: On the role of collusion in organizations. *Journal of Law, Economics and Organization*. 2(2). 181–214.

Torres, R. C., Mollick, A. V. and Saucedo, E. (2018). *The Impact of Crime and Other Economic Forces on Mexico's Foreign Direct Investment Inflows*. Working Papers, No. 2018-24. Mexico City: Bank of Mexico. https://www.econstor.eu/bitstream/10419/240665/1/wp2018-24.pdf.

White, B. H. and Michelutti, L. (eds.). (2019). *The Wild East: Criminal Political Economies in South Asia*. London: UCL Press, University College London.

Yu, J., De Klerk, S. and Hess, M. (2021). The influence of cronyism on entrepreneurial resource acquisition. *Asia Pacific Journal of Management*. https://doi.org/10.1007/s10490-021-09769-7.

Zabyelina, Y. and Uhm, D. V. (eds.). (2020). *Legal Mining Organized Crime, Corruption, and Ecocide in a Resource-Scarce World*. Palgrave Macmillan, Cham, Switzerland

Zander, T. (2021). Does corruption matter for FDI flows in the OECD? A gravity analysis. *International Economics and Economic Policy*. 18(2). 347–377.

7 Asymmetric Adjustment Costs and the Gender Wage Gap

With Fragmentation in a Simple General Equilibrium Model

Hamid Beladi, Avik Chakrabarti and Daniel Hollas

7.1 Introduction

Rising socio-economic concerns surrounding persistent wedges between the wages earned by male and female workers have multiple facets, though the differential impact of international trade on labour market rewards is typically explained by economists in terms of differences in workers' skills. One of the earliest explanations of gender wage gaps can be traced back to the works of Becker (1971) who offered an explanation for the existence of such economic gaps in terms of employers having a socially biased preference for discrimination even in apparently advanced economies whose legal institutions promise to protect the rights to equal opportunities. However, in the rapidly integrating global economy, international trade has fostered an all-round competition, making it increasingly costly for employers to sustain such discrimination: Gender wage gaps, unexplained by differences in educational attainment, cannot persist in the long run.[1]

The global male–female wage gap has been declining since the 1990s, a period during which the world has become increasingly integrated through international trade, albeit with wide variations across countries (Figure 7.1). While a vast literature has looked into the links between wage inequality[2] and trade, it is not surprising that one of the visible strands of the ongoing economic debate surrounding the issue of male–female wage inequality poses a demanding question: Why does a gender bias in wages persist even in advanced open economies? The objective of this chapter is to seek a reasonable answer to this question, contributing to the relevant literature on gender-based inequality of income, within the boundaries of a tractable general equilibrium model of production and trade. We take the structure of simple general equilibrium models, befitting a formal exposition of the Heckscher–Ohlin–Samuelson (H-O-S) theory, as our analytical point of reference. Within the confines of the classic H-O-S theory, gender wage inequalities would not exist in competitive markets. Our analysis departs from any conventional modelling of the H-O-S structure to the extent that we

DOI: 10.4324/9781003375050-7

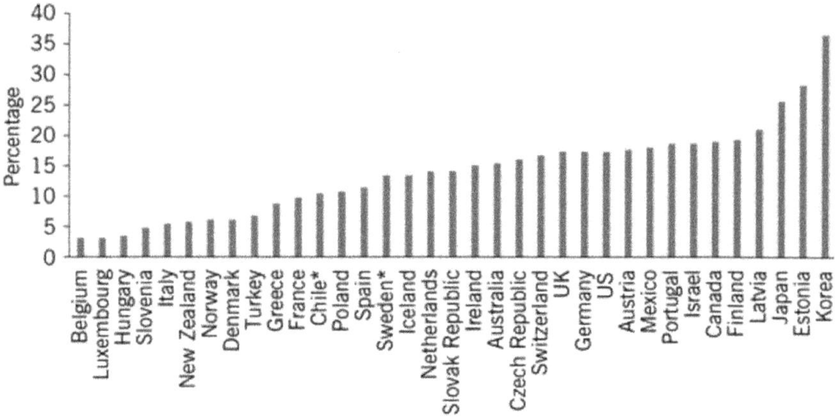

Figure 7.1 Male–female wage gap: Organization for Economic Cooperation and Development (OECD) countries Source: Pieters (2018)

look at the links between fragmentation and gender inequality, allowing imperfect inter-sectoral mobility of physical capital. In the next section we present our model and discuss some propositions that follow. The final section summarises our conclusion.

7.2 Model and Propositions

Consider, following Chakrabarti (2004), land and physical capital to be quasi-fixed inputs in the sense that adding new land or physical capital, removing existing land or physical capital and/or moving land or physical capital from one sector to another entails an adjustment cost.[3] Moving land or physical capital from one sector to another involves the addition of the released land and/or capital requiring an adjustment the cost of which is borne exclusively by the recipient sector; as well as the removal of land and/ or physical capital from one sector entailing an adjustment cost that is borne exclusively by the releasing sector.[4]

Suppose an industry (A) offers a non-tradable service that transforms physical capital (new or released) and land to fit their use in production: K_j^A represents the amount of physical capital used by A exclusively for adjustment in the output of sector j; T_j^A represents the amount of land used by A exclusively for adjustment in the output of sector j; and P_{Aj} is the unit cost of adjustment for sector j, i.e. the price paid by sector j to A in transforming capital to support a unit change in the output of sector j. We abstract from any difference in adjustment cost between (a) the addition of new land and/or physical capital to a sector and the addition of land and/or capital to the same sector released by the other, and (b) the addition of land and/or physical capital to a sector and removal of land and/or capital from the same sector. We also assume that physical capital is the only factor employed in *A*. The adjustment technology is specified as:

$$\mathbf{K} = \alpha.\Delta$$

where $\mathbf{K} = \{K_J^A\}, \alpha = \{\alpha_j\}, \Delta = \{dj\}, \alpha_j = \begin{cases} +\alpha^j \, for \, dj \geq 0 \\ -\alpha^j \, for \, dj \leq 0 \end{cases}$, and $\alpha^j \geq 0$ are constants.[5]

Following Marjit, Beladi, and Chakrabarti (2004), let the home country consist of four sectors, each producing a single good. The goods are *X* that is male-labour-intensive and is exported; *Y* which is import-competing good; *Z* that is female-labour-intensive and is exported; and *I* which is a non-traded intermediate input used in the male-labour-intensive export good sector. There are four factors of production: Male labour (*M*), female labour (*F*), land (*T*) and physical capital (*K*). The home country, in effect, can export both male-labour-intensive and female-labour-intensive goods. Sector *I* uses male labour and physical capital, *X* uses male labour and the intermediate input, *Y* uses female labour and physical capital and *Z* uses female labour and land.

Our model permits the reallocation of resources between industries without affecting factor prices as long as the factor use envelope contains the factor endowment envelope with the factor use matrix having full rank, in the absence of any asymmetry in adjustment costs.[6] The production functions are subject to diminishing returns to each factor of production and constant returns to scale. All markets are perfectly competitive. Other notations, used in this chapter, include

w_M = male wage

w_F = female wage

r_K = return to capital

r_T = rent on land

P_j = price of the *j*-th product, *j* = *X*, *I*, *Y*, *Z*

a_{ij}'s are unit factor requirements. Any variable with , á la Jones (1965), denotes the percentage change in that variable.

Equations (7.1) through (7.4) represent competitive markets and equilibrium conditions:

$$w_M M_I + r_K K_I + P_{AI} dI = P_I I \tag{7.1}$$

$$w_M a_{MX} + P_I a_{IX} = P_X \tag{7.2}$$

$$w_F F_Y + r_K K_Y + P_{AY} dY = P_Y Y \tag{7.3}$$

$$w_F F_Z + r_T T_Z + P_{AZ} dZ = P_z Z \tag{7.4}$$

Equations (7.5) through (7.8) ensure full employment

$$a_{MX}X + a_{MI}I = M \tag{7.5}$$

$$a_{KI}I + a_{KY}Y + K_M^A + K_Y^A + K_Z^A = K \tag{7.6}$$

$$a_{FY}Y + a_{FZ}Z = F \tag{7.7}$$

$$a_{TZ}Z = T \tag{7.8}$$

Equation (7.9) defines the market clearing condition for the local intermediate

$$a_{mx}X = M \tag{7.9}$$

θ_{ij} measures the distributive share of factor *i* in industry *j*; $\theta_{Aj} = \left(\alpha_j r \middle/ P_j \right)$; λ_{ij} is the fraction of input *i* employed in industry *j*; σ_j is the elasticity of factor substitution in industry *j*; $\lambda_{Kj}^A = \dfrac{K_j^A}{K}$; and $\tilde{\lambda}_{Kj} = (\lambda_{Kj} + \lambda_{Kj}^A)$. Let $P_{AZ} = 0$ and $K_Z^A = 0$.

A rise (fall) in the marginal cost of male-labour-intensive exports, given prices, results in a fall (rise) in its output which lowers (raises) the demand for male workers. Lemma 7.1 follows.

Lemma 7.1: Male wage and the price of the intermediate input are inversely related.

Proof: From (7.2), $\theta_{MX}\hat{w}_M + \theta_{IX}\hat{P}_I = 0 \Rightarrow \hat{w}_M = -\dfrac{\theta_{IX}}{\theta_{MX}}\hat{P}_I > 0.$

If the price of the intermediate input falls, so would the price of physical capital. This would lead to an expansion of the import-competing sector, given the price of the import-competing commodity, which absorbs physical capital. The demand for women workers would be higher, and consequently their wages would rise, in the absence of any cost of adjustment. However, the increase in female wages will be dampened if the costs associated with adjustment are high. For a sufficiently high adjustment cost, the absorption of capital in the import-competing sector must be compensated by a reduction in the wages of female labour. Lemma 7.2 follows.

Lemma 7.2: Female wage and the price of the intermediate input are positively related if $\dfrac{\theta_{AY}}{\tilde{\lambda}_{KY}} > \dfrac{\theta_{KY}}{\lambda_{KY}\theta_{FY}\sigma_Y + \lambda_{KI}\theta_{MI}\sigma_I}$

Proof:From(7.1)–(7.3),and(7.6), $\hat{w}_F = \dfrac{1}{1+\Delta}\left[\left(\dfrac{(\theta_{FY}\Delta - \theta_{KY})\Phi}{\theta_{FY}}\right) + \Delta\dfrac{\theta_{IX}}{\theta_{MX}}\right]\hat{P}_I$

where $\Delta = \dfrac{\theta_{AY}\left(\lambda_{KY}\theta_{FY}\sigma_Y + \lambda_{KM}\theta_{MI}\sigma_I\right)}{\theta_{FY}\tilde{\lambda}_{KY}}$ and $\Phi = \left[\dfrac{1}{\theta_{KI}} + \dfrac{\theta_{MI}\theta_{IX}}{\theta_{MX}}\right].$

Therefore,

$$\frac{\theta_{AY}}{\tilde{\lambda}_{KY}} > \frac{\theta_{KY}}{\lambda_{KY}\theta_{FY}\sigma_Y + \lambda_{KI}\theta_{MI}\sigma_I} \Rightarrow \theta_{LY}\Delta - \theta_{KY} > 0 \Rightarrow \hat{w}_F < 0.$$

Suppose $P_I > P_I^*$, i.e. the price of the intermediate good in the home country, exceeds the price of the same intermediate good in a foreign country. The intermediate input is produced at home as long as the incentive for accessing the lower-priced intermediate from abroad is impeded by a sufficiently high cost associated with friction, e.g. transportation and communication. Offshore outsourcing takes place, in our model, through "fragmentation" (i.e. slicing the value chain in a way that allows different countries to specialise in different fragments of the production of a commodity) when a decline in the costs associated with friction is sufficient to induce imports of *i* which, in effect, lowers the price of the intermediate good to P_I^*.

Returns to physical capital decline, in the absence of perfect mobility of capital across borders, when physical capital is released due to offshore outsourcing of the intermediate input. Physical capital would leave the home country if perfect international mobility of physical capital were allowed. This would offset the decline in the return to capital which, in effect, would leave the wages of the female workers unchanged. Proposition 7.1 follows.

Proposition 7.1. An increase in capital outflow, induced by fragmentation, raises gender inequality in wages.

Proof: Follows directly from Lemma 7.1.

Now, suppose offshore outsourcing of the production of the intermediate good causes the foreign price of the intermediate input to rise. The incentives for the expansion of the male-labour-intensive export sector, in the face of fragmentation, will then be reduced which will dampen the fragmentation-induced rise in the wages of male workers. The rise in the international price of the intermediate input does not affect female wages since the import-competing sector must absorb the released physical capital. Proposition 7.2 follows.

Proposition 7.2: *A fall in the domestic price of the intermediate input dampens any fragmentation-induced gender gap in wages.*

Proof: Follows directly from Lemmas 7.1 and 7.2 since $P_I = P_I^*$.

If the production of the intermediate input is outsourced, physical capital released from the intermediate goods sector must be absorbed by the import-competing sector when physical capital is not perfectly mobile across borders. This would raise the wages of the women workers if adjustment costs were nil. However, a sufficiently high adjustment cost will dampen the rise in female wages causing the male–female wage gap to widen. Proposition 7.3 follows.

Proposition 7.3. Fragmentation will induce a widening of the gender gap in wages for sufficiently high costs of adjustment in the import-competing sector.

Proof: Follows directly from Lemmas 7.1 and 7.2.

The absorption of physical capital by the import-competing sector must be accompanied by an offsetting rise in the wages of the female workers if the cost of adjustment falls. This would not affect the wages of the male workers and, in consequence, reduce the male–female wage gap. Hence, our final proposition.

Proposition 7.4. A lower cost of adjustment in the import-competing sector reduces any fragmentation-induced gender gap in wages.

Proof: Follows from Proposition 7.1 since $\frac{\partial}{\partial \alpha^{Y}}\left(\frac{\theta_{AY}}{\tilde{\lambda}_{KY}}\right) > 0$.

7.3 Conclusion

This chapter constructs a simple general equilibrium model to capture the effects of fragmentation on male–female wage inequality when costs of adjustment are asymmetric in an otherwise H-O-S structure. We show that a rise in the price of an outsourced intermediate input can reduce any gender wage inequality. Fragmentation can widen the gap between the wages of male and female workers when the costs of adjustment are high in the import-competing sector. A lower cost of adjustment in the import-competing sector reduces any fragmentation-induced wedge between the wages of the men and women workers. A couple of interesting extensions of our work may include (a) imperfect mobility of labour[7] and/or (b) divisionalisation.[8]

Notes

1 The evidence is mixed. For instance, Black and Brainerd (2004) provided evidence supporting the contention that increased competition from trade benefits females by reducing employers' power to discriminate. In comparison, Berik Rodgers and Zveglich (2004) observed that trade in competitive industries is positively associated with wage discrimination against females in South Korea and China, two large open economies.

2 See Yabuuchi and Chaudhuri (2007, 2009) and Noria (2015).

3 Similar production structures have been adapted by Chakrabarti and Mitra (2010), Beladi and Chakrabarti (2010), Marjit and Mandal (2012) and Mandal (2015).

4 Chakrabarti (2004) proved that the introduction of asymmetric adjustment costs (AAC) in a simple general equilibrium framework breaks the analytically convenient dichotomy of the Heckscher-Ohlin-Samuelson (H-O-S) theory and establishes a meaningful link between the determination of input prices and outputs. Chakrabarti (2009) presented empirical evidence upholding the hypothesis of AAC.

5 See Kierzkowski (2005) for theoretical foundations of fragmentation without adjustment costs.

6 See Chakrabarti (2006) for the earliest generalization of the factor price equalization (FPE) theorem which identifies a condition, stated in terms of the allocation of factor endowments across countries relative to the demand for and the factor intensities of goods, that is both *necessary* and *sufficient* for FPE in a world with arbitrary number of countries, goods and factors.
7 See Gilbert and Oladi (2009).
8 See Beladi and Chakrabarti (2019).

References

Becker, G. (1971), *The Economics of Discrimination*. Chicago: University of Chicago Press.

Beladi, H. and A. Chakrabarti (2019), Multidivisional Firms, Internal Competition, and Comparative Advantage. *Journal of International Economics*, 116, 50–57.

Beladi, H., A. Chakrabarti and S. Marjit (2010), Skilled-Unskilled Wage Inequality and Urban Unemployment. *Economic Inquiry*, 48(4), 997–1007.

Berik, G., Y. M. Rodgers and J. Zveglich (2004), International Trade and Gender Wage Discrimination: Evidence from East Asia. *Review of Development Economics*, 8(2), 237–254.

Black, S. and E. Brainerd (2004), Importing Equality? The Impact of Globalization on Gender Discrimination. *Industrial and Labor Relations Review*, 57(4), 540–559.

Chakrabarti, A. (2004), Asymmetric Adjustment Costs in Simple General Equilibrium Models. *European Economic Review*, 48(1), 63–73.

Chakrabarti, A. (2006), Factor Price Equalization Beyond a "Cubic" World. *Economic Theory*, 27(2), 483–491.

Chakrabarti, A. (2009), Internal Adjustment Costs in Capital-Intensive and Labor-Intensive Industries. *Economics Letters*, 102(2), 76–77.

Chakrabarti, A. and R. Mitra (2010), Skilled–Unskilled Wage Inequality and Offshore Outsourcing with Asymmetric Adjustment Costs. *International Review of Economics and Finance*, 19(2), 340–345.

Gilbert, J. and R. Oladi (2009), Capital Specificity, Imperfect Labor Mobility and Growth in Developing Economies. *International Review of Economics and Finance*, 18(1), 113–122.

Jones, R. W. (1965), The Structure of Simple General Equilibrium Models. *Journal of Political Economy*, 73(6), 557–572.

Kierzkowski, H. (2005), Outsourcing and Fragmentation: Blessing or Threat? *International Review of Economics and Finance*, 14(3), 233–235.

Mandal, B. (2015), Distance, Production, Virtual Trade and Growth: A Note. *Economics*, 9(1), 1–122.

Marjit, S., H. Beladi, and A. Chakrabarti (2004), Trade and Wage Inequality in Developing Countries. *Economic Inquiry*, 42(2), 295–303.

Marjit, S. and B. Mandal (2012), Domestic Trading Costs and Pure Theory of International Trade. *International Journal of Economic Theory*, 8(2), 165–178.

Noria, G. L. (2015), The Effect of Trade and FDI on Inter-industry Wage Differentials: The Case of Mexico. *North American Journal of Economics and Finance*, 34, 381–397.

Pieters, J. (2018), *Trade Liberalization and Gender Inequality*. IZA World of Labor, Bonn, Germany.

Yabuuchi, S. and S. Chaudhuri (2007), International Migration of Labour and Skilled–Unskilled Wage Inequality in a Developing Economy. *Economic Modelling*, 24(1), 128–137.

Yabuuchi, S. and S. Chaudhuri (2009), Skill Formation, Capital Adjustment Cost and Wage Inequality. *Review of Urban & Regional Development Studies*, 21(1), 2–13.

8 Skilled–Unskilled Wage Inequality, Unemployment and Tourism Development

A Theoretical Analysis

Priya Brata Dutta and Swaraj Das

8.1 Introduction

Tourism industry is one of the world's largest and most complex industries, and the reason for this complexity is its strong bond with social, political and environmental issues. In order to achieve the goal of sustainable tourism, attention should be given to understand both the positive and negative effects of tourism on the environment. There are many countries in this world where tourism is the primary source of employment opportunities for domestic labour and income, a major source of growth and the primary driving force of that particular country so that it can attain its economic aim. It is also an important source of earning foreign exchange. Expenditure made by the tourists in the recipient countries mostly on non-traded goods and services boosts consumption and helps the economy to recover from an economic downturn. The recent recovery of Hong Kong economy can be mentioned in this respect. The Asian Financial Crisis in 1997 and the severe acute respiratory syndrome (SARS) outbreak in 2003 worldwide made their situation worse and unemployment rose. The consequent tourism boom aftermath had made the situation manageable. Besides large countries such as Canada or India, there are small and less developed island counties whose economy is heavily reliant on tourism, such as Macau and Maldives where tourism accounts for 47.2% and 44.6% (2021) of its economy (World travel and tourism council report). Tourism and related service industries contributed a considerable extent to the gross domestic product (GDP) in Peru (5.6% in 2021), Egypt (5.1% in 2021) and Cambodia (4.7% in 2021) (World Travel and Tourism Council Report). In a developed country like Spain, tourism activity represents 8.5% in 2021 of the gross domestic product and 12.7% in 2021 of total employment in 2014.

Many empirical literature studies point out the effect of tourism development policies on both unemployment and inequality. The causes and explanations of growing unemployment worldwide are one of the pivotal research areas in the realm of development economics. The empirical research works from the perspective of developing countries which

DOI: 10.4324/9781003375050-8

investigate the effect of tourism development on labour unemployment did not categorise unemployment into skilled and unskilled labour unemployment; nevertheless, their contribution is significant in forming an overall idea about the situation of unemployment due to tourism development. Some empirical works like Snyman (2012), Xaba, Selepe and Mdiniso (2018), Nestorovic and Anivic (2019), and Qin, Su and Zhang (2020) show that tourism development lowers the unemployment problem. Similar to unemployment, economic inequality is another major potboiler in the literature of development economics. Tourism development is believed to increase employment opportunities and raise income levels, but it can also generate inequality in income since the benefits of tourism may not always percolate into every stratum of the society. Some major research works which presented a positive picture of tourism development in reducing regional inequality include Li, Chen, Li and Goh (2016) and Zhike (2019). There are other papers like Wattanakuljarus and Coxhead (2008) and Guimaraes and Silva (2016) who found out that tourism development raised household income but worsened the distribution of income, hence increased inequality.[1]

The major theoretical literature dealing with the issue of growing unemployment which motivates us in this regard is the work by Gupta and Dutta (2017) which develop a Harris–Todaro type theoretical model to analyse the effect of tourism development on urban unemployment taking intersectoral capital mobility into account. Their analyses show that the effects of tourism development on unemployment and national income not only depend on the capital intensity rankings of different sectors but also depend on the nature of capital mobility among different sectors. Another theoretical literature dealing with the issue of unemployment is given by Copeland (1991), which tried to find the effect of the expansion of tourism on welfare, factor prices and output in the host country using a static general equilibrium model. They conclude that in order for a tourist influx to yield significant benefits, local residents must obtain gains from an improvement in the terms of trade pertaining to tourism (the real exchange rate). It is only in the absence of taxation and distortions such as unemployment, the appreciation of the real exchange rate is possible and is the only mechanism by which tourism can benefit the economy. There exist other theoretical works dealing with the issue of this growing wage inequality. Based on the framework of static competitive general equilibrium models with two different types of labour – skilled and unskilled, it is divided into two groups. One group of models assumes full employment of both types of labour and this group includes works of Gupta and Dutta (2010a, 2010b), Marjit and Acharyya (2003, 2006) and Marjit and Kar (2005). However, Chaudhuri and Yabuuchi (2008) and Marjit and Acharyya (2003) introduced non-traded goods in their models and assumed them to be produced by unskilled labour. The second group of models considers Harris and Todaro (1970) type unemployment of unskilled labour; and this group includes works of Marjit and Acharyya (2003), Beladi et al. (2008)

and Chaudhuri (2008, 2004) and these models assume full employment of skilled labour. Chaudhuri and Banerjee (2010) explain unemployment of skilled labour with the help of efficiency wage hypothesis and unemployment of unskilled labour using Harris and Todaro (1970) migration mechanism but they do not consider non-traded goods.

The present model is a static competitive general equilibrium model of a small open economy with skilled labour, unskilled labour and physical capital being the three primary factors of production. We capture the phenomenon of both rural and urban tourism development, and for that we prepare two variations of our model. In the urban tourism development model or in our basic model, there are three sectors – an urban manufacturing sector employing physical capital and skilled labour, a rural agricultural sector employing unskilled labour and physical capital, and an urban non-traded tourism goods sector employing skilled labour and physical capital. Our second model is the extension of our basic model where we consider the case of rural tourism development and there are three sectors – an urban manufacturing sector employing physical capital and skilled labour, a rural agricultural sector employing unskilled labour and physical capital, and a rural non-traded tourism goods sector employing unskilled labour and physical capital. In both rural and urban tourism models, physical capital is perfectly mobile between all three sectors and the urban manufacturing sector has the highest capital intensity. Skilled labour is mobile between skilled goods-utilising sectors and unskilled labour is mobile between unskilled goods-utilising sectors. Tourism sector is more capital intensive than the rural agricultural sector in both of our models. The improvisation which we made in our model is that along with unemployment we have analysed the effect of tourism on wage inequality. Another variation which we made in our model is while the previous theoretical papers analysed the effect of tourism development on unemployment problem using the Harris–Todaro (1970) framework, we have used static general equilibrium framework using efficiency wage in our model. Efficiency wage hypothesis[2] says that the efficiency of a labour in a labour market varies positively with its wage rate and unemployment. The non-traded good is assumed to be a non-inferior final good whose demand varies positively with the disposable income of consumers, and thus increase in factor prices and/or factor endowments produces positive effects on the demand for the non-traded good and consequently on its equilibrium price. The skilled–unskilled wage ratio and unemployment rates in two labour markets are affected by this change in equilibrium price.

We derive two interesting results from both the urban and rural tourism models on how tourism development affects unemployment and wage inequality conditional on assumptions of factor intensity. From the urban tourism model, there is a positive relationship between foreigner's income and skilled–unskilled labour wage inequality and an inverse relationship between foreigner's income and both skilled and unskilled labour unemployment rates. We have got a contrary result in the case of rural tourism where there is an inverse relationship between foreigner's income and both skilled–unskilled labour wage inequality and a positive relationship between foreigner's income and both skilled and unskilled labour unemployment rates.

In Section 8.2, we introduce the urban tourism model and its comparative statics. Rural tourism and its comparative statics are analysed in Section 8.3. Concluding remarks are made in Section 8.4.

8.2 The Urban Tourism Model

8.2.1 Description

We consider a small open economy (Home country) with three sectors and three factors – skilled labour, unskilled labour and capital. Sectors 1 and 2 use skilled labour and capital in their production as inputs and sector 3 uses unskilled labour and capital as inputs in its production. So capital is mobile among all these three sectors and skilled labour is mobile between Sectors 1 and 2. However, unskilled labour is specific to sector 3 only. Production in each sector satisfies all the standard neo-classical properties including constant returns to scale. Sector 1 produces manufacturing goods and this sector is located in an urban sector, sector 2 produces tourism goods and sector 3 produces agricultural goods and this sector is located in a rural area. All factor endowments are exogenously given. Both skilled and unskilled labourers are measured in efficiency units and both wage rates are perfectly flexible. There exists unemployment in both these two labour markets, and this is explained by efficiency wage hypothesis, which says that the efficiency of both types of labour is a positive function of its wage rate and unemployment rate. A higher wage rate encourages a labourer to work hard, and a high unemployment rate increases the disutility in the presence of a threat of firing and thus makes him more disciplined. Since the rental rate on capital is perfectly flexible, this flexibility ensures full utilisation of capital stock. All markets are competitive. The objectives of the representative firms in all these three sectors are to maximise profit subject to budget constraints. We are using this model as an urban tourism model as here non-traded tourism sector uses skilled labour.

We follow the following notations:

a_{Ki}: Capital output ratio in the ith sector for i = 1, 2, 3

a_{Si}: Skilled labour output ratio in the ith sector for i = 1, 2

a_{N3}: Unskilled labour output ratio in the ith sector for sector 3

P_i: Effective producer's price of the product produced by the ith sector for i = 1, 2, 3

h: Efficiency of the skilled labour

f: Efficiency of the unskilled labour

W_S: Wage rate of skilled labour

W_u: Wage rate of unskilled labour

$\frac{W_S}{h}$: Wage rate per efficiency unit of skilled labour

$\frac{W_u}{f}$: Wage rate per efficiency unit of unskilled labour

r: Common rate of return on capital employed in all three sectors

D_2: Demand function for commodity 2

Y: Total factor income/output of the home country

X_i: Amount of output produced by the ith sector for i = 1, 2, 3

$\bar{S}$: Endowment of skilled labourer given exogenously

$\bar{K}$: Endowment of capital given exogenously

$\bar{N}$: Endowment of unskilled labourer given exogenously

V_S: Unemployment rate of skilled labour

V_U: Unemployment rate of unskilled labour

Y_N: Income of the foreigners

θ_{ij}: Distributive share of the jth input in the ith sector for j = S, K, N and i = 1, 2, 3

λ_{ji}: Proportion of the jth input involved in the ith sector for j = S, K, N and i = 1, 2, 3

S_{ji}^{h}: The elasticity of factor output coefficient of the jth factor in the hth sector with respect to the price of the ith factor, for i, j = S, K, N and h = 1, 2, 3. For example $S_{SK}^{1} = \left(\frac{r}{a_{S1}}\right)\left(\frac{\partial a_{S1}}{\partial r}\right).S_{jj}^{h}\langle 0, S_{ji}^{h}\rangle 0;\ i \neq j$

The following equations describe the model.

Competitive market equilibrium conditions:

$$P_1 = a_{S1}\left(\frac{W_S}{h}\right) + a_{K1}r, \tag{8.1}$$

$$P_2 = a_{S2}\left(\frac{W_S}{h}\right) + a_{K2}r, \tag{8.2}$$

$$P_3 = a_{N3}\left(\frac{W_u}{f}\right) + a_{K3}r. \tag{8.3}$$

Efficiency functions:

$$h = h(W_S, v_S), \tag{8.4}$$

$$\text{, with } \frac{\partial h}{\partial W_S} = h_1 > 0, \frac{\partial^2 h}{\partial {W_S}^2} = h_{11}\left\langle 0, \frac{\partial h}{\partial v_S} = h_2\right\rangle 0, \frac{\partial^2 h}{\partial {v_S}^2} = h_{22} < 0.$$

$$f = f(W_U, v_U,) \tag{8.5}$$

$$\text{, with } \frac{\partial f}{\partial W_u} = f_1 > 0, \frac{\partial^2 f}{\partial {W_u}^2} = f_{11}\left\langle 0, \frac{\partial f}{\partial v_u} = f_2\right\rangle 0, \frac{\partial^2 f}{\partial {v_u}^2} = f_{22} < 0 \quad .$$

$$\frac{\partial h}{\partial W_S}\cdot\frac{W_S}{h}=1, \tag{8.6}$$

$$\frac{\partial f}{\partial W_U}\cdot\frac{W_U}{f}=1. \tag{8.7}$$

Factor market clearing conditions:

$$a_{K1}X_1+a_{K2}X_2+a_{K3}X_3=\bar{K}, \tag{8.8}$$

$$a_{S1}X_1+a_{S2}X_2=\bar{S}(1-v_S)h, \tag{8.9}$$

$$a_{N3}X_3=\bar{N}(1-v_u)f. \tag{8.10}$$

Total factor income:

$$Y=W_S\bar{S}(1-v_S)+r\bar{K}+W_u\bar{N}(1-v_U). \tag{8.11}$$

Demand–supply equation:

$$D_2(P_2,Y,Y_N)=X_2, \tag{8.12}$$

$$\text{, with }\frac{\partial D_2}{\partial P_2}\cdot\frac{P_2}{D_2}=e_{P_2}\left\langle 0,\frac{\partial D_2}{\partial Y}\cdot\frac{Y}{D_2}=e_Y\right\rangle 0,\frac{\partial D_2}{\partial Y_N}\cdot\frac{Y_N}{D_2}=e_{Y_N}>0 \quad .$$

Here Equations (8.1)–(8.3) represent the profit-maximising conditions of competitive firms in sectors 1–3. Equations (8.4) and (8.5) represent the efficiency functions of skilled labour and unskilled labour, respectively. Each of these two efficiency functions is a positive and concave function in terms of every variable. These two efficiency functions are assumed to be similar. Effective unit costs of employing skilled labour and unskilled labour are $\frac{W_S}{h}$ and $\frac{W_u}{f}$, respectively. Equations (8.6) and (8.7) are basic two Solow (1979) conditions implying that wage elasticities of efficiency are equal to unity in these two labour markets. We get Equations (8.6) and (8.7) by minimising $\frac{W_S}{h}$ and $\frac{W_u}{f}$ with respect to W_S and W_u, respectively. Equation (8.8) implies equilibrium condition in the capital market. Equations (8.9) and (8.10) are efficiency-adjusted equilibrium conditions in the skilled and unskilled labour market, respectively. Equation (8.11) represents total factor income (national income at factor cost in the absence of taxes and subsidies), and Equation (8.12) implies the supply–demand equality in market for tourism goods.

In our model, P_1 and P_3 are internationally given and P_2 is endogenously determined by the demand–supply mechanism. There are 12 unknowns in the model: W_S, W_U, r, h, f, V_S, V_U, X_1, X_2, X_3, Y and P_2. The parameters of this system are P_1, P_3, $\bar{N}$, $\bar{S}$, $\bar{K}$ and Y_N. There are 12 independent equations with 12 unknowns and so the system is determinate. The production structure does not possess the decomposition property and so factor prices cannot be solved independently of factor endowments.

The working of the general equilibrium model is described as follows. Given P_1 and P_2, W_S, W_u, V_S, V_u, h and f are determined simultaneously from Equations (8.1)–(8.7) as functions of P_2. Now from Equation (8.10), we obtain X_3 and Equations (8.8) and (8.9) simultaneously solve X_1 and X_2 as functions of P_2, given N, S and K. Then from Equation (8.11), we find Y as a function of P_2. Since Y and X_2 are determined as a function of P_2, we solve for P_2 from Equation (8.12).

Using Equations (8.1)–(8.3) and (8.8)–(8.11), it can be easily shown that $P_1X_1 + P_2X_2 + P_3X_3 = Y$, which is the aggregate sales revenue that is equal to the national income at product prices in the absence of commodity taxes and subsidies.

8.2.2 *Comparative Static Exercise*

In this section, we examine the consequences of an exogenous increase in foreigner's income (Y_N) on both skilled and unskilled unemployment rate and skilled–unskilled wage inequality.

Using Equations (8.1)–(8.7), (8.11) and (8.12), we get both skilled and unskilled unemployment rates, respectively, as

$$\hat{V}_S = \frac{1}{\varepsilon_{VS}}\left\{\frac{\theta_{K1}}{|\theta|}\left(\beta\hat{Y}_N\right)\right\} < 0 \tag{8.13}$$

and

$$\hat{V}_u = \frac{1}{\varepsilon_{vu}}\left\{\frac{\theta_{K3}\theta_{S1}}{\theta_{N3}|\theta|}\left(\beta\hat{Y}_N\right)\right\} < 0 \tag{8.14}$$

Here $|\theta| = (\theta_{S1}\theta_{K2} - \theta_{K1}\theta_{S2})$ is the factor intensity ranking between sector 1 and sector 2 and it is negative since sector 1 is relatively capital intensive than sector 2. Equations (8.13) and (8.14) indicate the inverse relationship between Y_N, V_s and Y_N, V_U.

Equations (8.1)–(8.7), (8.11) and (8.12) also give the skilled–unskilled wage inequality

$$\hat{W}_S - \hat{W}_u = \frac{\beta}{\theta_{N3}|\theta|}\left\{\frac{h\theta_{K1}\theta_{N3}}{W_S^2 h_{11}} - \frac{f\theta_{K3}\theta_{S1}}{W_U^2 f_{11}}\right\}\hat{Y}_N. \tag{8.15}$$

Here, $\left\{\frac{h\theta_{K1}\theta_{N3}}{W_S^2 h_{11}} - \frac{f\theta_{K3}\theta_{S1}}{W_u^2 f_{11}}\right\}$ represents the efficiency-adjusted capital intensity ranking between sector 1 and sector 3.[3] However, $h_{11} < 0$ and $f_{11} < 0$, if we assume sector 1 is more capital intensive than sector 3, then $\left\{\frac{h\theta_{K1}\theta_{N3}}{W_S^2 h_{11}} - \frac{f\theta_{K3}\theta_{S1}}{W_u^2 f_{11}}\right\} < 0$. So rise in Y_N raises $\hat{W}_S - \hat{W}_u$.

We can clearly see from Equations (8.13) and (8.14) that the change in both skilled and unskilled unemployment rates is negatively related to the change in foreigner's income, which is exogenous in nature and not under the control of a foreign country. Equation (8.15) shows how a change in foreigner's income affects the skilled–unskilled wage inequality. The sign of $\hat{W}_S - \hat{W}_u$ depends on two features (i) capital intensity ranking between sector 1 and sector 2 and (ii) efficiency-adjusted capital intensity ranking between sector 1 and sector 3 which use two different kinds of labour with two different efficiency functions and the term inside the parenthesis of Equation (8.15),), $\left\{\frac{h\theta_{K1}\theta_{N3}}{W_S^2 h_{11}} - \frac{f\theta_{K3}\theta_{S1}}{W_u^2 f_{11}}\right\}$, represents the efficiency-adjusted capital intensity ranking between sector 1 and sector 3. $|\theta|<0$, since sector 1 is capital intensive than sector 2 by our assumption. So the effect of the change in foreigner's income on wage inequality is positive in nature and this positive relationship between $\hat{Y}_N$ and $\hat{W}_S - \hat{W}_U$ occurs due to the term inside the parenthesis of Equation (8.15), which is less than zero if sector 1 is more capital intensive than sector 3.

Proposition 8.1: An exogenous increase in foreigner's income lowers the skilled and unskilled unemployment rates but raises the skilled–unskilled wage inequality.

We now provide intuitive explanations behind the proposition. When foreigner's income (Y_N) increase (decrease), there is a demand for tourism services in the home country. This leads to a rise (fall) in the price of tourism services. Now since sector 2 in the home country is a skilled labour-intensive sector, there is a Stolper–Samuelson trade effect and as a result the return to skilled labour, i.e. $\frac{W_S}{h}$ increases (decreases) and rental rate (r) decreases (increases). As $\frac{W_s}{h}$ rises (falls), rise (fall) in W_s must be more than rise (fall) in h. So there is a relative fall (rise) in h. From the efficiency function, we see that if the skilled unemployment rate (V_s) falls then the efficiency of the skilled labourer (h) falls. So as V_s is falling, there is an inverse relationship between Y_N and V_s. Now as V_s is falling if the employer wants to minimise $\frac{W_s}{h}$ with respect to W_s, then W_s must rise to raise h. So there is a positive relationship between Y_N and W_s. Using similar logic, we get an inverse relationship between Y_N and V_u and a direct relationship between Y_N and W_u.

From the profit-maximising condition, Equation (8.3), mathematically we can see, since P_3 fixed $\left(\hat{P}_3 = 0\right)$ and rental rate (r) falls, $\left(\frac{W_u}{f}\right)$ bound to rise also. As sector 1 is more capital intensive than sector 3, so fall in rental rate (r) is more in sector 1. So rise in W_s is more than rise in W_U. And, skilled–unskilled wage inequality rises.

8.3 The Rural Tourism Model

8.3.1 Description

The difference between this extension model and the basic model is that for non-traded tourism goods sector 2 uses skilled labour in the urban tourism model whereas sector 2 in this extension model uses unskilled labour. So here skilled labour is specific to the manufacturing sector and unskilled labour is mobile between tourism sector and agricultural sector. All other assumptions are the same as the basic model.

The following two notations are different compared to the first model in Section 2:

a_{S1}: Skilled labour output ratio in the ith sector for sector 1

a_{Ni}: Unskilled labour output ratio in the ith sector for sector i = 2, 3

The following equations describe the model.

Competitive market clearing conditions:

$$P_1 = a_{S1}\left(\frac{W_S}{h}\right) + a_{K1}r, \tag{8.16}$$

$$P_2 = a_{N2}\left(\frac{W_u}{f}\right) + a_{K2}r \tag{8.17}$$

and

$$P_3 = a_{N3}\left(\frac{W_u}{f}\right) + a_{K3}r. \tag{8.18}$$

Efficiency functions:

$$h = h\left(W_S, v_S\right), \tag{8.19}$$

$$\text{with} \frac{\partial h}{\partial W_S} = h_1 > 0, \frac{\partial^2 h}{\partial {W_S}^2} = h_{11}\left\langle 0, \frac{\partial h}{\partial v_S} = h_2 \right\rangle 0, \frac{\partial^2 h}{\partial {v_S}^2} = h_{22}.$$

$$f = f\left(W_U, v_U,\right) \tag{8.20}$$

$$, \text{with} \frac{\partial f}{\partial W_u} = f_1 > 0, \frac{\partial^2 f}{\partial W_u^{\,2}} = f_{11} \left\langle 0, \frac{\partial f}{\partial v_u} = f_2 \right\rangle 0, \frac{\partial^2 f}{\partial v_u^{\,2}} = f_{22}.$$

$$\frac{\partial h}{\partial W_S} \cdot \frac{W_S}{h} = 1 \tag{8.21}$$

and

$$\frac{\partial f}{\partial W_u} \cdot \frac{W_U}{f} = 1. \tag{8.22}$$

Factor market clearing conditions:

$$a_{K1}X_1 + a_{K2}X_2 + a_{K3}X_3 = \bar{K}, \tag{8.23}$$

$$a_{S1}X_1 = \bar{S}\left(1 - v_S\right)h \tag{8.24}$$

and

$$a_{N2}X_2 + a_{N3}X_3 = \bar{N}(1 - v_U)f \tag{8.25}$$

Total factor income:

$$Y = W_S\bar{S}\left(1 - v_S\right) + r\bar{K} + W_U\bar{N}\left(1 - v_U\right). \tag{8.26}$$

Demand–supply equation:

$$D_2\left(P_2, Y, Y_N\right) = X_2 \tag{8.27}$$

$$, \text{ with} \frac{\partial D_2}{\partial P_2} \cdot \frac{P_2}{D_2} = e_{P_2} \left\langle 0, \frac{\partial D_2}{\partial Y} \cdot \frac{Y}{D_2} = e_Y \right\rangle 0, \frac{\partial D_2}{\partial Y_N} \cdot \frac{Y_N}{D_2} = e_{Y_N} > 0.$$

There are 12 unknowns in the model: W_S, W_U, r, $\underline{h}$, $\underline{f}$, $v_{\underline{S}}$, v_U, X_1, X_2, X_3, Y and P_2. The parameters of this system are P_1, P_3, $\bar{N}$, $\bar{S}$, $\bar{K}$ and Y_N. There are 12 independent equations with 12 unknowns and so the system is determinate. The production structure does not possess the decomposition property and so factor prices cannot be solved independently of factor endowments.

The working of the general equilibrium model is described as follows. Given P_1 and P_2, W_S, W_u, V_S, V_u, h and f are determined simultaneously from Equations (8.16) to (8.22) as functions of P_2. Now from Equation (8.25), we obtain X_3 and Equations (8.23) and (8.24) simultaneously solve X_1 and X_2 as functions of P_2 given N, S and K. Then from Equation (8.26), we find Y as a function of P_2. Since Y and X_2 are determined as a function of P_2, we solve for P_2 from Equation (8.27).

8.3.2 Comparative Static Exercise

In this section, we examine the consequences of an exogenous increase in foreigner's income (Y_N) on both skilled and unskilled unemployment rate and skilled–unskilled wage inequality.

Using Equations (8.16)–(8.22), (8.26) and (8.27), we get both skilled and unskilled unemployment rates, respectively, as

$$\hat{V}_S = -\frac{1}{\varepsilon_{VS}}\left\{\frac{\theta_{K1}\theta_{N3}}{\theta_{S1}|\theta|}\left(\beta\hat{Y}_N\right)\right\} > 0 \tag{8.28}$$

and

$$\hat{V}_U = -\frac{1}{\varepsilon_{Vu}}\left\{\frac{\theta_{K3}}{|\theta|}\left(\beta\hat{Y}_N\right)\right\} > 0. \qquad (8.29),$$

Here $|\theta| = (\theta_{N2}\theta_{K3} - \theta_{K2}\theta_{N3})$ represents the capital intensity ranking between sector 2 and sector 3. Equations (8.28) and (8.29) indicate the direct relationship between Y_N, V_s and Y_N, V_u

Using Equations (8.16)–(8.22), (8.26) and (8.27) gives the skilled–unskilled wage inequality:

$$\hat{W}_S - \hat{W}_U = \frac{\widehat{\beta Y_N}}{\theta_{S1}|\theta|}\left\{\frac{f\theta_{K3}\theta_{S1}}{W_u^2 f_{11}} - \frac{h\theta_{K1}\theta_{N3}}{W_S^2 h_{11}}\right\} \tag{8.30}$$

Here, $\left\{\frac{f\theta_{K3}\theta_{S1}}{W_u^2 f_{11}} - \frac{h\theta_{K1}\theta_{N3}}{W_S^2 h_{11}}\right\}$ represents efficiency-adjusted capital intensity ranking between sector 1 and sector 3. However, $h_{11} < 0$ and $f_{11} < 0$, if we assume sector 1 is more capital intensive than sector 3, then $\left\{\frac{f\theta_{K3}\theta_{S1}}{W_u^2 f_{11}} - \frac{h\theta_{K1}\theta_{N3}}{W_S^2 h_{11}}\right\} > 0$. So rise in Y_N lowers $\widehat{W}_S - \hat{W}_u$.

When $f_{11}, h_{11} < 0$ as clear from second-order conditions of Equations (8.4) and (8.5), $|\theta| < 0, \beta > 0$.

And $|\theta| = (\theta_{S1}\theta_{K2} - \theta_{K1}\theta_{S2})$ is the factor intensity ranking between sector 1 and sector 2 and it is negative since sector 1 is relatively capital intensive than sector 2.

And $\beta = -\frac{e_{Y_N}}{(e_{P_2} + e_Y A_5 - A_4)}$, where $e_{Y_N} > 0$ and $(e_{P_2} + e_Y A_5 - A_4) < 0$ for the stability in the market for non-traded goods.

We can clearly see from Equations (8.28) and (8.29) that the change in both skilled and unskilled unemployment rates is positively related to the change in foreigner's income, which is exogenous in nature and not under the control of foreign country. Equation (8.30) shows how change in foreigner's income affects the skilled–unskilled wage inequality. The sign of $\hat{W}_S - \hat{W}_U$ depends on two features: (i) capital intensity ranking between sector 1 and sector 2 and (ii) efficiency-adjusted capital intensity ranking between sector 1 and sector 3 who uses two different kinds of labour with two different efficiency functions and the term inside the parenthesis of Equation (8.30). $\left\{\frac{f\theta_{K3}\theta_{S1}}{W_u^2 f_{11}} - \frac{h\theta_{K1}\theta_{N3}}{W_S^2 h_{11}}\right\}$ represents the efficiency-adjusted capital intensity ranking between sector 1 and sector 3. $|\theta|<0$, since sector 2 is more capital intensive than sector 3 by our assumption. So the effect of the change in foreigner's income on wage inequality is negative in nature and this negative relationship between $\widehat{Y}_N$ and $\widehat{W}_S - \widehat{W}_U$ occurs due to the term inside the parenthesis of Equation (8.30), which is greater than zero from our assumption of the basic model that sector 1 is more capital intensive compare to sector 3.

Proposition 8.2: An exogenous increase in foreigner's income raises the skilled and unskilled unemployment rate but lowers the skilled–unskilled wage inequality.

We now provide intuitive explanations behind the proposition. When foreigner's income (Y_N) increases (decreases), the demand for tourism goods (non-traded goods) in the foreign country increases (decreases), as a result there is excess (lack of) demand for tourism goods in the foreign country which result in the increase (decrease) in the price (P_2) of tourism-related (non-traded) goods in the home country. Now since sector 2 in the home country is a capital-intensive sector, there is Stolper–Samuelson trade effect, and as a result the return to unskilled labour; i.e. $\frac{W_u}{f}$ decreases (increases) and rental rate (r) increases (decreases). As r increases (decreases), from Equation (8.1) we see that $\frac{W_s}{h}$ falls (rises). Since $\frac{W_s}{h}$ falls (rise), a fall (rise) in W_s must be more than fall (rise) in h. So there is a relative rise (fall) in h. From the efficiency function, we see that if skilled unemployment rate (V_s) rises (falls), the efficiency of the unskilled labourer (h) also rises (falls). So as V_s is rising (falling), there is a direct relationship between V_s and Y_N. Now if the employer wants to minimise $\frac{W_s}{h}$ with respect to W_s, W_s must rise to raise h. So as rise in h lowers $\frac{W_s}{h}$, there is an inverse relationship between Y_N and W_s. Using similar logic, we get an inverse relationship between W_u and Y_N and a direct relationship between V_u and Y_N.

From the profit-maximising condition Equation (8.3), mathematically we see, sinceP_3 is fixed $\left(\widehat{P_3} = 0\right)$ and rental rate(r) rises, $\frac{W_u}{f}$ bound to fall also. As sector 1 is more capital intensive than sector 3, so rise in rental rate(r) is more in sector 1. So rise in W_s is less than the rise in W_U and skilled–unskilled wage inequality falls.

So from the abovementioned two models, we conclude that the improvement of tourism has completely different impacts on skilled–unskilled unemployment rate and skilled–unskilled wage inequality depending on the nature of tourism improvement. Due to upgradation of urban tourism, i.e. when tourism sector uses skilled labour, the unemployment rate of skilled labour and unskilled labour decreases and skilled–unskilled wage inequality increases, but due to upgradation of rural tourism, i.e. when the tourism sector uses unskilled labour, the unemployment rate of skilled labour and unskilled labour increases and skilled–unskilled wage inequality decreases.

8.4 Conclusion

This chapter develops a static three-sector and three-factor competitive general equilibrium urban tourism model of a small open economy in which skilled labour is specific to traded goods sector (urban manufacturing) and non-traded goods sector (tourism), whereas unskilled labour is specific to another non-traded goods sector (rural agriculture). Capital is mobile and common factor of production among all three sectors. We have also made a variation of our model and named it as rural tourism model where skilled labour is specific to traded good sectors (urban manufacturing) and unskilled labour is specific to another non-traded goods sector (rural agriculture) and non-traded goods sector (tourism) and again capital is mobile and common factor of production among all three sectors.

Gupta and Dutta (2017) and Copeland (1991) are the two major theoretical works which are closest to ours among all other existing contributions. Our work differs from Gupta and Dutta (2017) with respect to the theoretical model framework, where we develop a static general equilibrium model to show how there are effects of tourism development on both rural and urban unemployment and wage inequality and they have developed a Harris–Todaro type theoretical model to analyse the effect of tourism development on urban unemployment taking intersectoral capital mobility into account. Their analyses show that the effects of tourism development on unemployment and national income not only depend on the capital intensity rankings of different sectors but also on the nature of capital mobility among different sectors. Another theoretical literature dealing with the issue of unemployment is Copeland (1991) which investigates the effect of the expansion of tourism on welfare, factor prices and output in the host country using a static general equilibrium model. Just like Copeland (1991), we also use the framework of the general equilibrium model but instead of factor price our major focus was to analyse the effect of tourism development on both rural and urban unemployment and wage inequality. Both Gupta and Dutta (2017) and Copeland (1991) do not consider efficiency wage in their model, but in our model we take efficiency wage instead of nominal wage, as the efficiency of a labour has a significant effect on his/her quality of work. So we have tried to capture the qualitative aspect of labour in our model and shown the effect of tourism development on the efficiency factor of labour also.

In our urban tourism model, we derive an interesting result. An exogenous increase in foreigner's income lowers the skilled and unskilled unemployment rate but raises the skilled–unskilled wage inequality. On the other hand, in our rural tourism model where we use unskilled labour in the production of non-traded goods, we have got a contrary result to our rural tourism model. An exogenous increase in foreigner's income raises the skilled and unskilled unemployment rate but lowers the skilled–unskilled wage inequality.

However, our model does not introduce many important aspects of reality. The problem of imperfection of markets is not considered here. Also, we consider a static model where skilled labour and capital do not accumulate over time. In this model, skilled labour and unskilled labour are assumed to be two different non-substitute factors of production. We plan to do further research in the future attempting to remove the above major problems.

Appendix A

A.1 Intensity Ranking

Here sector 1 (manufacturing sector) and sector 2 (tourism sector) both use skilled labour and capital as inputs. We assume sector 1 is capital intensive compared to sector 1.

Mathematically,

$$\frac{\theta_{K1}}{\theta_{S1}} > \frac{\theta_{K2}}{\theta_{S2}},$$

$$\Rightarrow \theta_{K1}\theta_{S2} > \theta_{S1}\theta_{K2},$$

$$\Rightarrow \theta_{S1}\theta_{K2} < \theta_{K1}\theta_{S2},$$

$$\Rightarrow \left(\theta_{S1}\theta_{K2} - \theta_{K1}\theta_{S2}\right) < 0,$$

$$\Rightarrow |\theta| < 0,$$

where $|\theta| = \theta_{S1}\theta_{K2} - \theta_{K1}\theta_{S2}$ and θ_{ji} are the distributive shares, for example $\theta_{S1} = \frac{a_{S1}}{P_1}\frac{W_S}{h}$.

Similarly,

$$\frac{\lambda_{K1}}{\lambda_{S1}} > \frac{\lambda_{K2}}{\lambda_{S2}},$$

$$\Rightarrow \left(\lambda_{K1}\lambda_{S2} - \lambda_{S1}\lambda_{K2}\right) > 0,$$

$\Rightarrow |\lambda|>0$, where $|\lambda| = (\lambda_{K1}\lambda_{S2} - \lambda_{S1}\lambda_{K2})$ and λ_{ji} is the proportion of the jth input in the ith sector.

For example, $\dfrac{a_{S1}X_1}{S(1-V_S)h} = \lambda_{S1}$.

Differentiating Equations (1)–(3) and using profit-maximising conditions, we obtain the following equations:

$$\theta_{S1}\left(\widehat{W}_S - \hat{h}\right) + \theta_{K1}\hat{r} = \widehat{P}_1, \qquad (A.8.1)$$

$$\theta_{S2}\left(\widehat{W}_S - \hat{h}\right) + \theta_{K2}\hat{r} = \widehat{P}_2 \qquad (A.8.2)$$

and

$$\theta_{N3}\left(\widehat{W}_u - \hat{f}\right) + \theta_{K3}\hat{r} = \hat{P}_3. \qquad (A.8.3)$$

Using Equations (A.8.1) and (A.8.2), we get

$$\widehat{W}_S - \hat{h} = \frac{\begin{vmatrix} 0 & \theta_{K1} \\ \hat{P}_2 & \theta_{K2} \end{vmatrix}}{\begin{vmatrix} \theta_{S1} & \theta_{K1} \\ \theta_{S2} & \theta_{K2} \end{vmatrix}}$$

$$\Rightarrow \widehat{W}_S - \hat{h} = \frac{-\theta_{K1}\hat{P}_2}{(\theta_{S1}\theta_{K2} - \theta_{S2}\theta_{K1})} = \frac{-\theta_{K1}\hat{P}_2}{|\theta|}. \qquad (A.8.4)$$

$$\text{Similarly, } \hat{r} = \frac{\begin{vmatrix} \theta_{s1} & 0 \\ \theta_{s2} & \hat{P}_2 \end{vmatrix}}{\begin{vmatrix} \theta_{S1} & \theta_{K1} \\ \theta_{S2} & \theta_{K2} \end{vmatrix}} = \frac{\theta_{S1}\hat{P}_2}{(\theta_{S1}\theta_{K2} - \theta_{S2}\theta_{K1})} = \frac{\theta_{S1}\hat{P}_2}{|\theta|}. \qquad (A.8.5)$$

Using Equations (A.8.3), (A.8.5), we get

$$\left(\widehat{W}_u - \hat{f}\right) = \frac{-\theta_{K3}\theta_{S1}\hat{P}_2}{\theta_{N3}|\theta|}. \qquad (A.8.6)$$

Now differentiating Equation (8.4) and using Equation (8.6), we have

$$-\varepsilon_{VS}\widehat{V}_S = \hat{W}_S - \hat{h}. \qquad (A.8.7)$$

Similarly differentiating Equation (8.5) and using Equation (8.7), we have

$$-\varepsilon_{VU}\widehat{V}_U = \hat{W}_U - \hat{f}. \tag{A.8.8}$$

Using Equations (A.8.7) and (A.8.8) with (A.8.4) and (A.8.6), respectively, we get

$$\widehat{V}_S = \frac{\theta_{K1}\widehat{P}_2}{\varepsilon_{VS}|\theta|} \tag{A.8.9}$$

and

$$\widehat{V}_U = \frac{\theta_{K3}\theta_{S1}}{\varepsilon_{VU}\theta_{N3}|\theta|}\widehat{P}_2 . \tag{A.8.10}$$

Totally differentiating Equation (8.6), we get

$$\frac{\partial^2}{\partial W_S^2}\frac{dW_S}{W_S}\frac{W_S^2}{h} + \frac{\partial h}{\partial W_S}\frac{dW_S}{W_S}\frac{W_S}{h} - \frac{\partial h}{\partial W_S}\frac{W_S}{h^2}\left\{\frac{\partial h}{\partial W_S}\frac{dW_S}{W_S}W_S + \frac{\partial h}{\partial V_S}\frac{dV_S}{V_S}V_S\right\} = 0 \ .$$

$$\Rightarrow \frac{W_S^2 h_{11}\widehat{W_S} - h\varepsilon_{vs}\widehat{V_S}}{h} = 0$$

$$\Rightarrow \widehat{W}_s = \frac{h\left(\varepsilon_{vs}\widehat{V_S}\right)}{W_S^2 h_{11}}. \tag{A.8.11}$$

Similarly differentiating Equation (8.7), we have

$$\widehat{W}_U = \frac{h\left(\varepsilon_{vU}\widehat{V}_U\right)}{W_U^2 f_{11}}. \tag{A.8.12}$$

Using Equations (A.8.8), (A.8.9), and (A.8.10), we get

$$\widehat{W}_S = \frac{\widehat{P}_2 h\theta_{K1}}{|\theta| W_S^2 h_{11}} \tag{A.8.13}$$

and

$$\widehat{W}_U = \frac{\widehat{P}_2 f\theta_{K3}\theta_{S1}}{\theta_{N3}|\theta| W_U^2 f_{11}}. \tag{A.8.14}$$

Using Equations (A.8.13), (A.8.14), (A.8.4) and (A.8.6), we get

$$\hat{h} = \frac{\widehat{P}_2}{|\theta|}\theta_{K1}\left(1 + \frac{h}{W_S^2}\frac{1}{h_{11}}\right) \tag{A.8.15}$$

and

$$\hat{f} = \frac{\hat{P}_2}{|\theta|\theta_{N3}}\theta_{K3}\theta_{S1}\left(1+\frac{f}{W_U^2}\frac{1}{f_{11}}\right). \tag{A.8.16}$$

Now the elasticity of $\frac{\partial f}{\partial W_U}$ with respect to W_U is given as

$$\frac{\partial^2 f}{\partial W_U^2}\frac{W_U}{\frac{\partial f}{\partial W_U}} = f_{11}\frac{W_U}{\frac{\partial f}{\partial W_U}\frac{W_U}{f}\frac{f}{W_U}} = f_{11}\frac{W_U^2}{f}\text{since}\frac{\partial f}{\partial W_U}\frac{W_U}{f} = 1\ .$$

The inverse of the term is $\frac{f}{f_{11W_U^2}}$ and we assume $\left|\frac{f}{f_{11W_U^2}}\right| > 1$.

Now $f_{11} < 0$ implies $\left(1+\frac{f}{W_U^2 f_{11}}\right) < 0$, similarly we show that

$$\frac{\partial^2 h}{\partial W_S^2}\frac{W_S}{\frac{\partial h}{\partial W_S}} = h_{11}\frac{W_S}{\frac{\partial h}{\partial W_S}\frac{W_S}{h}\frac{h}{W_S}} = h_{11}\frac{W_U^2}{f}\text{since}\frac{\partial h}{\partial W_S}\frac{W_S}{h} = 1\ .$$ Now $h_{11} < 0$ implies $\left(1+\frac{h}{W_s^2 h_{11}}\right) < 0$

Differentiating Equation (8.10), we get

$$\lambda_{N3}\widehat{X}_3 = \left\{\hat{f}+\hat{N}-\lambda_{K3}\hat{a}_{N3}-\frac{V_U}{1-V_U}\widehat{V}_U\right\}. \tag{A.8.17}$$

Now, $a_{N3} = a_{N3}\left\{\left(\frac{W_U}{f}\right), r\right\}$.

Differentiating a_{N3} and dividing it by a_{N3}, we get

$\hat{a}_{N3} = S_{NN}^3\left(\widehat{W}_S - \hat{f}\right) + S_{NK}^3\hat{r}$ where $S_{NN}^3 < 0$, $S_{NK}^3 > 0$.

Using Equations (A.8.4) and (A.8.5) in $\lambda_{N3}\widehat{a_{N3}}$, we get

$$\hat{a}_{N3}\lambda_{N3} = \lambda_{N3}\frac{\hat{P}_2}{|\theta|}\left(S_{NK}^3\theta_{S1} - S_{NN}^3\theta_{K1}\right).$$

$\widehat{\hat{N}} = 0$, since we are considering no change in N.

Therefore, putting (A.8.10), we get $\frac{V_U}{1-V_U}\widehat{V}_U = \frac{V_U}{(1-V_U)\varepsilon_{VU}}\left(\frac{\theta_{K3}\theta_{S1}}{\theta_{N3}|\theta|}\hat{P}_2\right)$

So, putting the values of $\hat{a}_{N3}$, $\hat{f}$ and $\frac{V_U}{1-V_U}\widehat{V}_U$ in Equation (A.8.17), we get

$$\lambda_{N3}\widehat{X}_3 = \frac{\hat{P}_2}{|\theta|\theta_{N3}}\theta_{K3}\theta_{S1}\left(1+\frac{f}{W_U^2}\frac{1}{f_{11}}\right) - \lambda_{N3}\frac{\hat{P}_2}{|\theta|}\left(S_{NK}^3\theta_{S1} - S_{NN}^3\theta_{K1}\right)$$

$$-\frac{V_U}{(1-V_U)\varepsilon_{VU}}\left(\frac{\theta_{K3}\theta_{S1}}{\theta_{N3}|\theta|}\hat{P}_2\right)$$

$$\Rightarrow \begin{array}{l}\widehat{X}_3 = \dfrac{\hat{P}_2}{\lambda_{N3}|\theta|\theta_{N3}}\theta_{K3}\theta_{S1}\left(1+\dfrac{f}{W_u^2}\dfrac{1}{f_{11}}\right) - \dfrac{\hat{P}_2}{|\theta|}\left(S_{NK}^3\theta_{S1} - S_{NN}^3\theta_{K1}\right) \\ -\dfrac{V_U}{\lambda_{N3}(1-V_U)\varepsilon_{Vu}}\left(\dfrac{\theta_{K3}\theta_{S1}}{\theta_{N3}|\theta|}\hat{P}_2\right)\end{array},$$

$$\Rightarrow \overline{\widehat{X}}_3 = A_1\hat{P}_2, \tag{A.8.18}$$

where

$$A_1 = \left\{\frac{\theta_{K3}\theta_{S1}}{\lambda_{N3}|\theta|\theta_{N3}}\left(1+\frac{f}{W_U^2}\frac{1}{f_{11}}\right) - \frac{\left(S_{NK}^3\theta_{S1} - S_{NN}^3\theta_{K1}\right)}{\lambda_{N3}|\theta|} - \frac{V_U}{\lambda_{N3}(1-V_U)\varepsilon_{VU}}\left(\frac{\theta_{K3}\theta_{S1}}{\theta_{N3}|\theta|}\right)\right\} > 0.$$

Now the elasticity of $\frac{\partial f}{\partial W_U}$ with respect to W_u is given as

$$\frac{\partial^2 f}{\partial W_U^2}\frac{W_u}{\frac{\partial f}{\partial W_U}} = f_{11}\frac{W_u}{\frac{\partial f}{\partial W_U}\frac{W_u}{f}\frac{f}{W_u}} = f_{11}\frac{W_u^2}{f}\text{ since }\frac{\partial f}{\partial W_u}\frac{W_u}{f} = 1.$$

The inverse of the term is $\frac{f}{f_{11W_u^2}}$ and we assume $\left|\frac{f}{f_{11W_u^2}}\right| > 1$.

Now $f_{11} < 0$ implies $\left(1+\frac{f}{W_u^2 f_{11}}\right) < 0$.

Now as $|\theta| < 0$, we can say that $A_1 > 0$ and $B_1 > 0$ since $\varepsilon_{Vu} > 0, S_{NK}^3 > 0, S_{NN}^3 < 0$.

Differentiating Equation (8.8), we get

$$\lambda_{K1}\widehat{X}_1 + \lambda_{K2}\widehat{X}_2 = \widehat{\overline{K}} - \lambda_{K1}\left\{S_{KK}^1\hat{r} - S_{KS}^1\left(\varepsilon_{VS}\widehat{V}_S\right)\right\} - \lambda_{K2}\left\{S_{KK}^2\hat{r} - S_{KS}^2\left(\varepsilon_{VS}\widehat{V}_S\right)\right\}$$

$$-\lambda_{K3}\left\{S_{KK}^3\hat{r} - S_{KS}^3\left(\varepsilon_{VS}\widehat{V}_S\right)\right\} - \lambda_{K3}\widehat{X}_3,$$

$$\Rightarrow \lambda_{K1}\widehat{X}_1 + \lambda_{K2}\widehat{X}_2 = -\left(\lambda_{K1}S_{KK}^1 + \lambda_{K2}S_{KK}^2 + \lambda_{K3}S_{KK}^3\right)\hat{r} + \varepsilon_{VS}\left(\lambda_{K1}S_{KS}^1 + \lambda_{K2}S_{KS}^2\right)\widehat{V}_S$$

$$+\lambda_{K3}S_{KN}^3\varepsilon_{VU}\widehat{V}_U - \lambda_{K3}\widehat{X}_3 \tag{A.8.19}$$

Using Equations (A.8.5), (A.8.9), (A.8.10), (A.8.14) and (A.8.18), we get

$$\lambda_{K1}\widehat{X}_1 + \lambda_{K2}\widehat{X}_2 = -\left(\lambda_{K1}S^1_{KK} + \lambda_{K2}S^2_{KK} + \lambda_{K3}S^3_{KK}\right)\frac{\hat{P}_2\theta_{S1}}{|\theta|} + \left(\lambda_{K1}S^1_{KS} + \lambda_{K2}S^2_{KS}\right)\frac{\hat{P}_{2,\,K1}}{|\theta|}$$

$$+\lambda_{K3}S^3_{KN}\frac{\hat{P}_2\theta_{K3}\theta_{S1}}{|\theta|\,\theta_{N3}} - \lambda_{K3}A_1\hat{P}_2,$$

$$\Rightarrow \lambda_{K1}\widehat{X}_1 + \lambda_{K2}\widehat{X}_2 = A_2\hat{P}_2 \qquad \text{(A.8.20)}$$

and

$$A_2 = \left\{\frac{(\lambda_{K1}S^1_{KS} + \lambda_{K2}S^2_{KS})\theta_{K1}}{\lambda_{N3}|\theta|} + \frac{\lambda_{K3}S^3_{KN}\theta_{K3}\theta_{S1}}{\lambda_{N3}|\theta|\theta_{N3}} - \lambda_{K3}A_1 - \frac{\left(\lambda_{K1}S^1_{KK} + \lambda_{K2}S^2_{KK} + \lambda_{K3}S^3_{KK}\right)\theta_{S1}}{\lambda_{N3}|\theta|}\right\} < 0$$

since $A_1 > 0$.

From Equation (8.9), we get

$$\lambda_{S1}\widehat{X}_1 + \lambda_{S2}\widehat{X}_2 = S(1-V_S)\hat{h} - Sh\widehat{V}_S - \lambda_{S1}\hat{a}_{S1} - \lambda_{S2}\hat{a}_{S2} \qquad \text{(A.8.21)}$$

where $\lambda_{S1} = \dfrac{a_{S1}}{S(1-V_S)h}X_1$ and $\lambda_{S2} = \dfrac{a_{S2}}{S(1-V_S)h}X_2$.

Using $\hat{h} = \dfrac{\widehat{P_2}}{|\theta|}\theta_{K1}\left(1 + \dfrac{h}{W_S^2}\dfrac{1}{h_{11}}\right)$,

$$S(1-V_S)\hat{h} = S(1-V_S)\frac{\widehat{P_2}}{|\theta|}\theta_{K1}\left(1 + \frac{h}{W_S^2}\frac{1}{h_{11}}\right)$$

and $Sh\widehat{V_S} = Sh\widehat{V_S} = \dfrac{Sh}{\varepsilon_{VS}}\left(\dfrac{\theta_{k1}}{|\theta|}\widehat{P_2}\right)$

since $a_{S1} = a_{S1}\left(\dfrac{W_S}{h}, r\right)$ implies $\widehat{a_{S1}} = S^1_{SS}\left(\widehat{W_S} - \hat{h}\right) + S^1_{SK}\hat{r}$.

Using Equations (A.8.4) and (A.8.5) in $\widehat{a_{S1}} = S^1_{SS}\left(\widehat{W_S} - \hat{h}\right) + S^1_{SK}\hat{r}$, we get

$$\widehat{a_{S1}}\lambda_{S1} = \lambda_{S1}\frac{\widehat{P_2}}{|\theta|}\left(S^1_{SK}\theta_{S1} - S^1_{SS}\theta_{K1}\right). \qquad \text{(A.8.22)}$$

Similarly, we derive

$$\widehat{a_{S2}}\lambda_{S2} = \lambda_{S2}\frac{\widehat{P_2}}{|\theta|}\left(S^2_{SK}\theta_{S1} - S^2_{SS}\theta_{K1}\right) \qquad \text{(A.8.23)}$$

Using Equations (A.8.9), (A.8.15), (A.8.19)–(A.8.21), we get

$$\lambda_{S1}\widehat{X_1}+\lambda_{S2}\widehat{X_2}=S(1-V_S)\frac{\theta_{K1}}{|\theta|}\left(1+\frac{h}{W_S^2h_{11}}\right)\widehat{P_2}-\frac{Sh}{\varepsilon_{VS}}\frac{\theta_{K1}}{|\theta|}\widehat{P_2}$$

$$-\lambda_{S1}\frac{\widehat{P_2}}{|\theta|}\left(S_{SK}^1\theta_{S1}-S_{SS}^1\theta_{K1}\right)-\lambda_{S2}\frac{\widehat{P_2}}{|\theta|}\left(S_{SK}^2\theta_{S1}-S_{SS}^2\theta_{K1}\right).$$

We get $\lambda_{S1}\widehat{X_1}+\lambda_{S2}\widehat{X_2}=A_3\widehat{P_2}$, (A.8.24)

where

$$A_3=\left\{-\frac{\lambda_{S2}\left(S_{SK}^2\theta_{S1}-S_{SS}^2\theta_{K1}\right)}{|\theta|}-\frac{\lambda_{S1}\left(S_{SK}^1\theta_{S1}-S_{SS}^1\theta_{K1}\right)}{|\theta|}-\frac{Sh}{\varepsilon_{VS}}\frac{\theta_{K1}}{|\theta|}+S(1-V_S)\frac{\theta_{K1}}{|\theta|}\left(1+\frac{h}{W_S^2h_{11}}\right)\right\}$$

and $A_3>0$.

Therefore, we get

$$\widehat{X_3}=A_1\widehat{P_2}, \quad \text{(A.8.18)}$$

$$\lambda_{K1}\widehat{X_1}+\lambda_{K2}\widehat{X_2}=A_2\widehat{P_2}, \quad \text{(A.8.20)}$$

$$\lambda_{S1}\widehat{X_1}+\lambda_{S2}\widehat{X_2}=A_3\widehat{P_2}. \quad \text{(A.8.24)}$$

We get,

$$\widehat{X_2}=\frac{\begin{vmatrix}\lambda_{K1} & A_2\widehat{P_2}\\ \lambda_{S1} & A_3\widehat{P_2}\end{vmatrix}}{\begin{vmatrix}\lambda_{K1} & \lambda_{K2}\\ \lambda_{S1} & \lambda_{S2}\end{vmatrix}}=\frac{(\lambda_{K1}A_3-\lambda_{S1}A_2)\widehat{P_2}}{|\lambda|}=\widehat{X_2}=A_4\widehat{P_2}, \quad \text{(A.8.25)}$$

where $A_4=\dfrac{A_3\lambda_{K1}-A_2\lambda_{s1}}{|\lambda|}>0$, $|\lambda|>0$ since $A_3>0$ and $A_2<0$.

Similarly, we derive $\widehat{X_1}=\dfrac{\begin{vmatrix}A_2\widehat{P_2} & \lambda_{K2}\\ A_3\widehat{P_2} & \lambda_{S2}\end{vmatrix}}{\begin{vmatrix}\lambda_{K1} & \lambda_{K2}\\ \lambda_{S1} & \lambda_{S2}\end{vmatrix}}=\dfrac{(\lambda_{S2}A_2-\lambda_{K2}A_3)\widehat{P_2}}{|\lambda|}=A_5\widehat{P_2}$

(A.8.26)

$A_5<0$, since $A_3>0$ and $A_2<0$ and $|\lambda|>0$.

Totally differentiating Equation (8.11), we get

$$\hat{Y} = \frac{W_S\bar{S}(1-V_S)}{Y}\left(\hat{\bar{S}} + \widehat{W_S}\right) + \frac{r\bar{K}}{Y}\left(\hat{\bar{K}} + \hat{r}\right) + \frac{W_U\bar{N}(1-V_U)}{Y}\left(\hat{\bar{N}} + \widehat{W_U}\right)$$

$$-\frac{W_S\bar{S}V_S}{Y}\widehat{V_S} - \frac{W_U\bar{N}V_U}{Y}\widehat{V_U}.$$

Now $\hat{S} = \hat{N} = \hat{K} = 0$

$$\text{Therefore, } \hat{Y} = \frac{W_S\bar{S}(1-V_S)}{Y}\left(\widehat{W_S}\right) + \frac{r\bar{K}}{Y}(\hat{r}) + \frac{W_U\bar{N}(1-V_U)}{Y}\left(\widehat{W_U}\right) - \frac{W_S\bar{S}V_S}{Y}\widehat{V_S}$$

$$-\frac{W_U\bar{N}V_U}{Y}\widehat{V_U}. \tag{A.8.27}$$

Using Equations (A.8.5), (A.8.9), (A.8.10), (A.8.13), (A.8.14) and (A.8.27), we get

$$\hat{Y} = A_6\widehat{P_2} \tag{A.8.28}$$

where

$$A_5 = \left\{\frac{W_S\bar{S}(1-V_S)}{Y|\theta|}\frac{h\theta_{K1}}{W_S^2 h_{11}} + \frac{rK}{Y}\frac{\theta_{S1}}{|\theta|} + \frac{W_U\bar{N}(1-V_U)}{Y|\theta|}\frac{f\theta_{S1}\theta_{K3}}{W_U^2 f_{11}} - \frac{W_S\bar{S}V_S}{Y|\theta|\varepsilon_{VS}}\theta_{K1} - \frac{W_U\bar{N}V_U}{Y|\theta|\varepsilon_{VU}}\theta_{S1}\theta_{K3}\right\}$$

is ambiguous.

Differentiating Equation (8.12), we obtain

$$\widehat{X_2} = e_{P_2}\widehat{P_2} + e_Y\hat{Y} + e_{Y_N}\widehat{Y_N}. \tag{A.8.29}$$

Here $e_{P_2} < 0$ and $e_{Y_N} > 0$, and these two represent the price elasticity of demand and foreign income elasticity of demand for the non-traded good, respectively.

$$\frac{\partial D_2}{\partial P_2}.\frac{P_2}{D_2} = e_{P_2}\left\langle 0, \frac{\partial D_2}{\partial Y}.\frac{Y}{D_2} = e_Y\right\rangle 0, \frac{\partial D_2}{\partial Y_N}.\frac{Y_N}{D_2} = e_{Y_N} > 0.$$

Finally, using Equations (A.8.25) and A.8.28) in Equation (A.8.29), we get

$$e_{P_2}\widehat{P_2} + e_Y\hat{Y} + e_{Y_N}\widehat{Y_N} = \widehat{X_2},$$

$$\Rightarrow (e_{P_2} + e_Y A_5 - A_4)\widehat{P_2} = -e_{Y_N}\widehat{Y_N}$$

$$\Rightarrow \widehat{P_2} = -\frac{e_{Y_N}}{\left(e_{P_2} + e_Y A_5 - A_4\right)}\hat{Y}_N$$

$$\Rightarrow \widehat{P_2} = \beta\hat{Y}_N,, \tag{A.8.30}$$

where $\beta = -\dfrac{e_{Y_N}}{\left(e_{P_2} + e_Y A_5 - A_4\right)} > 0.$

Now $\dfrac{e_{Y_N}}{\left(e_{P_2} + e_Y A_5 - A_4\right)} < 0$ and due to stability condition $\left(e_{P_2} + e_Y A_5 - A_4\right) < 0$ and $e_{Y_N} > 0$.

Therefore, $\hat{Y}_N$ has a positive relationship with $\widehat{P_2}$.

So using Equations (A.8.5), (A.8.9), (A.8.10), (A.8.13)–(A.8.16), (A.8.18), (A.8.25), (A.8.26), (A.8.28) and (A.8.30), we get the following equations:

$$\hat{r} = \frac{\theta_{s1}}{|\theta|}\beta\hat{Y}_N < 0 \text{ Since } |\theta| < 0. \tag{A.8.31}$$

$$\hat{W}_S = \frac{\beta\hat{Y}_N h\theta_{K1}}{|\theta| W_S^2 h_{11}} > 0 \text{ since } |\theta| < 0. \tag{A.8.32}$$

$$\hat{V}_S = \frac{1}{\varepsilon_{VS}}\left\{\frac{\theta_{K1}}{|\theta|}\left(\beta\hat{Y}_N\right)\right\} < 0 \text{ since } |\theta| < 0. \tag{A.8.33}$$

Equation (A.8.33) is the same as Equation (8.13) in the body of this chapter.

$$\hat{W}_U = \frac{\beta\hat{Y}_N f\theta_{K3}\theta_{S1}}{\theta_{N3}|\theta| W_U^2 f_{11}} > 0 \text{ since } |\theta| < 0. \tag{A.8.34}$$

$$\hat{V}_U = \frac{1}{\varepsilon_{VU}}\left\{\frac{\theta_{K3}\theta_{S1}}{\theta_{N3}|\theta|}\left(\beta\hat{Y}_N\right)\right\} < 0 \text{ since } |\theta| < 0. \tag{A.8.35}$$

Equation (A.8.35) is the same as Equation (8.14) in the body of this chapter.

$$\hat{h} = \frac{\beta\widehat{Y_N}}{|\theta|}\theta_{K1}\left(1 + \frac{h}{h_{11}W_S^2}\right) > 0 \text{ since } |\theta| < 0, \tag{A.8.36}$$

$$\hat{f} = \frac{\beta\widehat{Y_N}}{|\theta|\theta_{N3}}\theta_{K3}\theta_{S1}\left(1 + \frac{f}{f_{11}W_u^2}\right) > 0 \text{ since } |\theta| < 0, \tag{A.8.37}$$

$$\hat{Y} = A_6\beta\hat{Y}_N; \text{ ambiguous since } A_6 \text{ is ambiguous.} \tag{A.8.38}$$

$$\hat{X}_2 = A_4\left(\beta\hat{Y}_N\right) > 0 \text{ since } A_4 > 0. \tag{A.8.39}$$

$$\hat{X}_1 = A_5\beta\hat{Y}_N < 0 \text{ since } A_5 < 0. \tag{A.8.40}$$

$$\widehat{X_3} = A_1\beta\hat{Y}_N > 0 \text{ since } A_1 > 0. \tag{A.8.41}$$

Using Equations (A.8.32) from (A.8.34), we get

$$\hat{W}_S - \hat{W}_U = \frac{\beta h \theta_{K1}}{|\theta| W_S^2 h_{11}} \hat{Y}_N - \frac{\beta f \theta_{K3} \theta_{S1}}{\theta_{N3} |\theta| W_U^2 f_{11}} \hat{Y}_N = \frac{\beta}{|\theta| \theta_{N3}} \left\{ \frac{h\theta_{K1}\theta_{N3}}{W_S^2 h_{11}} - \frac{f\theta_{K3}\theta_{S1}}{W_U^2 f_{11}} \right\} \hat{Y}_N < 0 \quad \text{(A.8.42)}$$

since $|\theta| < 0$, $f_{11}, h_{11} < 0$ and $\left\{ \frac{h\theta_{K1}\theta_{N3}}{W_S^2 h_{11}} - \frac{f\theta_{K3}\theta_{S1}}{W_U^2 f_{11}} \right\} < 0$,

where $\left\{ \frac{h\theta_{K1}\theta_{N3}}{W_S^2 h_{11}} - \frac{f\theta_{K3}\theta_{S1}}{W_u^2 f_{11}} \right\}$ represents the efficiency-adjusted capital intensity ranking between sector 1 and sector 3 and we assume sector 1 is more capital intensive than sector 3, so it is negative.

Equation (A.8.42) is the same as Equation (8.15) in the body of this chapter.

Appendix B

B.1 Intensity Ranking

In this model, both sector 3 (agricultural sector) and sector 2 use unskilled labour and capital as inputs. We assume that sector 2 is more capital intensive compared to sector 3.

Mathematically,

$$\frac{\theta_{K2}}{\theta_{N2}} > \frac{\theta_{K3}}{\theta_{N3}},$$

$$\Rightarrow \theta_{K2}\theta_{N3} > \theta_{N2}\theta_{K3},$$

$$\Rightarrow \theta_{N2}\theta_{K3} < \theta_{K2}\theta_{N3},$$

$$\Rightarrow (\theta_{N2}\theta_{K3} - \theta_{K2}\theta_{N3}) < 0,$$

$$\Rightarrow |\theta| < 0,$$

where $|\theta| = \theta_{N2}\theta_{K3} - \theta_{K2}\theta_{N3}$.

Similarly,

$$\frac{\lambda_{K2}}{\lambda_{N2}} > \frac{\lambda_{K3}}{\lambda_{N3}}$$

$$\Rightarrow (\lambda_{K2}\lambda_{N3} - \lambda_{N2}\lambda_{K3}) > 0$$

$$\Rightarrow |\lambda| > 0,$$

where $|\lambda| = (\lambda_{K2}\lambda_{N3} - \lambda_{N2}\lambda_{K3})$.

Differentiating Equations (8.16)–(8.18) and using profit-maximising conditions, we obtain the following equations:

$$\theta_{S1}\left(\widehat{W_S} - \hat{h}\right) + \theta_{K1}\hat{r} = \widehat{P_1}, \quad \text{(B.8.1)}$$

$$\theta_{N2}\left(\widehat{W_u}-\hat{f}\right)+\theta_{K2}\hat{r}=\widehat{P_2} \tag{B.8.2}$$

and

$$\theta_{N3}\left(\widehat{W_u}-\hat{f}\right)+\theta_{K3}\hat{r}=\widehat{P_3}. \tag{B.8.3}$$

Using Equations (8.16)–(8.18) and (8.23)–(8.26), it can be easily shown that $P_1X_1+P_2X_2+P_3X_3=Y$, which is the aggregate sales revenue (national income at product prices in the absence of commodity taxes and subsidies.

Using Equations (B.8.1)–(B.8.3), we have

$$\widehat{W_u}-\hat{f}=\frac{\begin{vmatrix}\widehat{P_2} & \theta_{K2}\\ 0 & \theta_{K3}\end{vmatrix}}{\begin{vmatrix}\theta_{N2} & \theta_{K2}\\ \theta_{N3} & \theta_{K3}\end{vmatrix}}=\frac{\theta_{K3}\widehat{P_2}}{\theta_{N2}\theta_{K3}-\theta_{N3}\theta_{K2}}=\frac{\theta_{K3}\widehat{P_2}}{|\theta|}, \tag{B.8.4}$$

$$\hat{r}=\frac{\begin{vmatrix}\theta_{N2} & \widehat{P_2}\\ \theta_{N3} & 0\end{vmatrix}}{\begin{vmatrix}\theta_{N2} & \theta_{K2}\\ \theta_{N3} & \theta_{K3}\end{vmatrix}}=-\frac{\theta_{N3}\widehat{P_2}}{\theta_{N2}\theta_{K3}-\theta_{N3}\theta_{K2}}=-\frac{\theta_{N3}\widehat{P_2}}{|\theta|} \tag{B.8.5}$$

and

$$\widehat{W_S}-\hat{h}=\frac{\theta_{K1}\theta_{N3}\widehat{P_2}}{\theta_{S1}\left(\theta_{N2}\theta_{K3}-\theta_{K2}\theta_{N3}\right)}=\frac{\theta_{N3}\theta_{K1}\widehat{P_2}}{\theta_{S1}|\theta|}. \tag{B.8.6}$$

Now differentiating Equations (8.19) and (8.21), we have

$$-\varepsilon_{VS}\widehat{V_S}=\hat{W}_S-\hat{h}. \tag{B.8.7}$$

Similarly differentiating Equation (8.20) and using Equation (8.22), we have

$$-\varepsilon_{VU}\widehat{V_U}=\hat{W}_U-\hat{f}.. \tag{B.8.8}$$

Using Equations (B.8.4) and (B.8.6) with (B.8.8) and (B.8.7), we get

$$\widehat{V_S}=-\frac{1}{\varepsilon_{VS}}\frac{\theta_{K1}\theta_{N3}\widehat{P_2}}{\theta_{S1}|\theta|} \tag{B.8.9}$$

and

$$\widehat{V_u}=-\frac{1}{\varepsilon_{VU}}\frac{\theta_{K3}\widehat{P_2}}{|\theta|}. \tag{B.8.10}$$

Totally differentiating Equation (8.21), assuming cross terms = 0, we get

$$\frac{\partial^2}{\partial W_S^2}\frac{dW_S}{W_S}\frac{W_S^2}{h}+\frac{\partial h}{\partial W_S}\frac{dW_S}{W_S}\frac{W_S}{h}-\frac{\partial h}{\partial W_S}\frac{W_S}{h^2}\left\{\frac{\partial h}{\partial W_S}\frac{dW_S}{W_S}W_S+\frac{\partial h}{\partial V_S}\frac{dV_S}{V_S}V_S\right\}=0,$$

$$\Rightarrow \frac{W_S^2 h_{11}\widehat{W_S}-h\varepsilon_{vs}\widehat{V_S}}{h}=0,$$

$$\widehat{W_S}=\frac{h\left(\varepsilon_{vs}\widehat{V_S}\right)}{W_S^2 h_{11}}. \tag{B.8.11}$$

Similarly by totally differentiating Equation (8.22),

we can derive $\widehat{W_U}=\dfrac{h\left(\varepsilon_{vU}\widehat{V_U}\right)}{W_U^2 f_{11}}$. (B.8.12)

Using Equations (B.8.9)–(B.8.12), we get

$$\widehat{W_S}=-\frac{\widehat{P_2}h\theta_{K1}\theta_{N3}}{\theta_{S1}\left|\theta\right|W_S^2 h_{11}} \tag{B.8.13}$$

and

$$\widehat{W_u}=-\frac{\widehat{P_2}f\theta_{K3}}{\left|\theta\right|W_U^2 f_{11}}. \tag{B.8.14}$$

Using Equations (B.8.13), (B.8.14), (B.8.6) and (B.8.4), we have

$$\hat{h}=-\frac{\widehat{P_2}}{\left|\theta\right|\theta_{S1}}\theta_{K1}\theta_{N3}\left(1+\frac{h}{W_S^2}\frac{1}{h_{11}}\right) \tag{B.8.15}$$

and

$$\hat{f}=-\frac{\widehat{P_2}}{\left|\theta\right|}\theta_{K3}\left(1+\frac{f}{W_u^2}\frac{1}{f_{11}}\right). \tag{B.8.16}$$

Now elasticity of $\dfrac{\partial f}{\partial W_U}$ with respect to W_U is given as

$$\frac{\partial^2 f}{\partial W_U^2}\frac{W_U}{\frac{\partial f}{\partial W_U}}=f_{11}\frac{W_U}{\frac{\partial f}{\partial W_U}\frac{W_U}{f}\frac{f}{W_U}}=f_{11}\frac{W_U^2}{f}\text{since}\frac{\partial f}{\partial W_U}\frac{W_U}{f}=1.$$

The inverse of the term is $\dfrac{f}{f_{11W_U^2}}$ and we assume $\left|\dfrac{f}{f_{11W_U^2}}\right|>1.$

Now $f_{11}<0$ implies $\left(1+\dfrac{f}{W_u^2 f_{11}}\right)<0.$

Similarly, we show that

$$\frac{\partial^2 h}{\partial W_S^2}\frac{W_S}{\frac{\partial h}{\partial W_S}} = h_{11}\frac{W_S}{\frac{\partial h}{\partial W_S}\frac{W_S}{h}\frac{h}{W_S}} = h_{11}\frac{W_U^2}{f} \text{ since } \frac{\partial h}{\partial W_S}\frac{W_S}{h} = 1; \quad \text{now} \quad h_{11} < 0$$

implies $\left(1 + \frac{h}{W_s^2 h_{11}}\right) < 0.$

From Equation (B.8.9), we get

$$\lambda_{S1}\widehat{X_1} = S(1 - V_S)\hat{h} - Sh\widehat{V_S} - \lambda_{S1}\widehat{a_{S1}},$$

here $a_{S1} = a_{S1}\left(\frac{W_S}{h}, r\right)$.

Differentiating a_{S1} and putting (B.8.5) and (B.8.6), we get $\widehat{a_{S1}} = \frac{\widehat{P_2}\theta_{N3}}{|\theta|}\left\{S_{SS}^1\frac{\theta_{K1}}{\theta_{S1}} - S_{SK}^1\right\}.$

Therefore,

$$\lambda_{S1}\widehat{X_1} = S(1 - V_S)\left\{-\frac{\theta_{K1}\theta_{N3}}{|\theta|\theta_{S1}}\widehat{P_2}\left(1 + \frac{h}{W_S^2 h_{11}}\right)\right\} - Sh\left\{-\frac{\theta_{K1}\theta_{N3}}{\varepsilon_{vs}|\theta|\theta_{S1}}\right\}\widehat{P_2}$$

$$-\lambda_{S1}\frac{\widehat{P_2}}{|\theta|}\theta_{N3}\left\{S_{SS}^1\frac{\theta_{K1}}{\theta_{S1}} - S_{SK}^1\right\}$$

$$\Rightarrow \widehat{X_1} = A_1\widehat{P_2}, \tag{B.8.17}$$

where

$$A_1 = S(1 - V_S)\left\{-\frac{\theta_{K1}\theta_{N3}}{\lambda_{S1}|\theta|\theta_{S1}}\left(1 + \frac{h}{W_S^2 h_{11}}\right)\right\} - Sh\left\{-\frac{\theta_{K1}\theta_{N3}}{\lambda_{S1}\varepsilon_{vs}|\theta|\theta_{S1}}\right\} - \frac{\theta_{N3}}{|\theta|}\left\{S_{SS}^1\frac{\theta_{K1}}{\theta_{S1}} - S_{SK}^1\right\} < 0.$$

Differentiating Equation (B.8.8), we get (putting $\hat{\hat{K}} = 0$)

$$\lambda_{K2}\widehat{X_2} + \lambda_{K3}\widehat{X_3} = -\lambda_{K1}\left\{S_{KS}^1\left(\widehat{W_S} - \hat{h}\right) - S_{KK}^1\hat{r}\right\} - \lambda_{K2}\left\{S_{KN}^2\left(\widehat{W_U} - \hat{f}\right) + S_{KK}^2\hat{r}\right\}$$

$$-\lambda_{K3}\left\{S_{KN}^3\left(\widehat{W_U} - \hat{f}\right) + S_{KK}^3\hat{r}\right\} - \lambda_{K1}\widehat{X_1}. \tag{B.8.18}$$

Using Equations (B.8.4)–(B.8.6), (B.8.17) and (B.8.18), we get

$$\lambda_{K2}\widehat{X_2}+\lambda_{K3}\widehat{X_3}=-\lambda_{K1}\left\{S^1_{KS}\frac{\theta_{K1}\theta_{N3}}{\theta_{S1}|\theta|}-S^1_{KK}\frac{\theta_{N3}}{|\theta|}\right\}\widehat{P_2}-\lambda_{K2}\left\{S^2_{KN}\frac{\theta_{K3}}{|\theta|}-S^2_{KK}\frac{\theta_{N3}}{|\theta|}\right\}\widehat{P_2}$$

$$-\lambda_{K3}\left\{S^3_{KN}\frac{\theta_{K3}}{|\theta|}-S^3_{KK}\frac{\theta_{N3}}{|\theta|}\right\}\widehat{P_2}-\lambda_{K1}A_1\widehat{P_2}$$

$$\Rightarrow \lambda_{K2}\widehat{X_2}+\lambda_{K3}\widehat{X_3}=A_2\widehat{P_2}, \tag{B.8.19}$$

where
$$A_2=\begin{bmatrix}-\lambda_{K1}\left\{S^1_{KS}\frac{\theta_{K1}\theta_{N3}}{\theta_{S1}|\theta|}-S^1_{KK}\frac{\theta_{N3}}{|\theta|}\right\}-\lambda_{K2}\left\{S^2_{KN}\frac{\theta_{K3}}{|\theta|}-S^2_{KK}\frac{\theta_{N3}}{|\theta|}\right\}\\ -\lambda_{K3}\left\{S^3_{KN}\frac{\theta_{K3}}{|\theta|}-S^3_{KK}\frac{\theta_{N3}}{|\theta|}\right\}-A_1\lambda_{K1}\end{bmatrix}>0$$

From Equation (B.8.10), we get

$$\lambda_{N2}\widehat{X_2}+\lambda_{N3}\widehat{X_3}=N(1-V_U)\hat{f}-Nf\widehat{V_u}-\lambda_{N2}\widehat{a_{N2}}-\lambda_{N3}\widehat{a_{N3}}, \tag{B.8.20}$$

where $\lambda_{N2}=\frac{a_{N2}}{N(1-V_u)f}X_2$ and $\lambda_{N3}=\frac{a_{N3}}{N(1-V_u)f}X_3$.

Since $a_{N2}=a_{N2}\left(\frac{W_u}{f},r\right)$ implies $\widehat{a_{N2}}=S^2_{NN}\left(\widehat{W_u}-\hat{f}\right)+S^2_{NK}\hat{r}$

therefore,

$$\lambda_{N2}\widehat{a_{N2}}=\lambda_{N2}\left\{S^2_{NN}\left(\widehat{W_u}-\hat{f}\right)+S^2_{NK}\hat{r}\right\}. \tag{B.8.21}$$

Similarly,

$$a_{N3}=a_{N3}\left(\frac{W_u}{f},r\right)\text{ implies }\hat{a}_{N3}=S^3_{NN}\left(\widehat{W_u}-\hat{f}\right)+S^3_{NK}\hat{r}$$

$$\text{and }\lambda_{N3}\widehat{a_{N3}}=\lambda_{N3}\left\{S^2_{NN}\left(\widehat{W_u}-\hat{f}\right)+S^2_{NK}\hat{r}\right\}. \tag{B.8.22}$$

Therefore,

$$\lambda_{N2}\widehat{X_2}+\lambda_{N3}\widehat{X_3}=N(1-V_u)\hat{f}-Nf\widehat{V_u}-\lambda_{N2}\left\{S^2_{NN}\left(\widehat{W_u}-\hat{f}\right)+S^2_{NK}\hat{r}\right\}$$

$$-\lambda_{N3}\left\{S^3_{NN}\left(\widehat{W_u}-\hat{f}\right)+S^3_{NK}\hat{r}\right\}. \tag{B.8.23}$$

Using Equations (B.8.4), (B.8.5), (B.8.10) and (B.8.16) in (B.8.23), we get

$$\lambda_{N2}\widehat{X_2}+\lambda_{N3}\widehat{X_3}=-N(1-V_U)\left\{\frac{\widehat{P_2}}{|\theta|}\theta_{K3}\left(1+\frac{f}{W_U^2}\frac{1}{f_{11}}\right)\right\}+Nf\left\{\frac{\theta_{N3}}{|\theta|\varepsilon_{VU}}\right\}\widehat{P_2}$$

$$-\lambda_{N2}\left\{S_{NN}^2\frac{\theta_{K3}}{|\theta|}-S_{NK}^2\frac{\theta_{N3}}{|\theta|}\right\}\widehat{P_2}-\lambda_{N3}\left\{S_{NN}^3\frac{\theta_{K3}}{|\theta|}-S_{NK}^3\frac{\theta_{N3}}{|\theta|}\right\}\widehat{P_2},$$

$$\Rightarrow \lambda_{N2}\widehat{X_2}+\lambda_{N3}\widehat{X_3}=A_3\widehat{P_2}, \tag{B.8.24}$$

where

$$A_3=-N(1-V_u)\left\{\frac{1}{|\theta|}\theta_{K3}\left(1+\frac{f}{W_U^2}\frac{1}{f_{11}}\right)\right\}+Nf\left\{\frac{\theta_{N3}}{|\theta|\varepsilon_{VU}}\right\}-\lambda_{N2}\left\{S_{NN}^2\frac{\theta_{K3}}{|\theta|}-S_{NK}^2\frac{\theta_{N3}}{|\theta|}\right\}$$

$$-\lambda_{N3}\left\{S_{NN}^3\frac{\theta_{K3}}{|\theta|}-S_{NK}^3\frac{\theta_{N3}}{|\theta|}\right\}<0$$

Now from the equations

$$\widehat{X_1}=A_1\widehat{P_2}, \tag{B.8.17}$$

$$\lambda_{K2}\widehat{X_2}+\lambda_{K3}\widehat{X_3}=A_2\widehat{P_2} \tag{B.8.19}$$

and

$$\lambda_{N2}\widehat{X_2}+\lambda_{N3}\widehat{X_3}=A_3\widehat{P_2}. \tag{B.8.24}$$

Solving $\widehat{X_2}$ and $\widehat{X_3}$ from (B.8.14) and (B.8.17), we get

$$\widehat{X_2}=\frac{\begin{vmatrix}A_2\widehat{P_2} & \lambda_{K3}\\ A_3\widehat{P_2} & \lambda_{N3}\end{vmatrix}}{\begin{vmatrix}\lambda_{K2} & \lambda_{K3}\\ \lambda_{N2} & \lambda_{N3}\end{vmatrix}}$$

$$\Rightarrow \widehat{X_2}=\frac{\lambda_{N3}A_2-\lambda_{K3}A_3}{\lambda_{K2}\lambda_{N3}-\lambda_{K3}\lambda_{N2}}\widehat{P_2}=\frac{\lambda_{N3}A_2-\lambda_{K3}A_3}{|\lambda|}\widehat{P_2}=A_4\widehat{P_2}, \tag{B.8.25}$$

where

$$A_4=\frac{\lambda_{N3}A_2-\lambda_{K3}A_3}{|\lambda|}>0 \text{ since } |\lambda|>0 \text{ and } A_2>0 \text{ and } A_3<0;$$

and

$$\widehat{X_3} = \frac{\begin{vmatrix} \lambda_{K2} & A_2\hat{P}_2 \\ \lambda_{N2} & A_3\widehat{P_2} \end{vmatrix}}{\begin{vmatrix} \lambda_{K2} & \lambda_{K3} \\ \lambda_{N2} & \lambda_{N3} \end{vmatrix}},$$

$$\widehat{X_3} = \frac{\lambda_{K2}A_3 - \lambda_{N2}A_2}{\lambda_{K2}\lambda_{N3} - \lambda_{K3}\lambda_{N2}}\widehat{P_2} = \frac{\lambda_{K2}A_3 - \lambda_{N2}A_2}{|\lambda|}\widehat{P_2} = A_5\widehat{P_2}, \tag{B.8.26}$$

where $A_5 = \frac{\lambda_{K3}A_3 - \lambda_{N2}A_2}{|\lambda|} < 0$ since $|\lambda| > 0$,

Totally differentiating equation (B.8.11), we get

$$\hat{Y} = \frac{W_S\bar{S}(1-V_S)}{Y}\left(\hat{\bar{S}} + \widehat{W_S}\right) + \frac{r\bar{K}}{Y}\left(\hat{\bar{K}} + \hat{r}\right) + \frac{W_U\bar{N}(1-V_U)}{Y}\left(\hat{\bar{N}} + \widehat{W_U}\right)$$

$$-\frac{W_S\bar{S}V_S}{Y}\widehat{V_S} - \frac{W_U\bar{N}V_U}{Y}\widehat{V_U} \qquad .$$

Now $\hat{\bar{S}} = \hat{\bar{N}} = \hat{\bar{K}} = 0$

Therefore,

$$\hat{Y} = \frac{W_S\bar{S}(1-V_S)}{Y}\left(\widehat{W_S}\right) + \frac{r\bar{K}}{Y}(\hat{r}) + \frac{W_U\bar{N}(1-V_U)}{Y}\left(\widehat{W_U}\right) - \frac{W_S\bar{S}V_S}{Y}\widehat{V_S} - \frac{W_U\bar{N}V_U}{Y}\widehat{V_U}. \tag{B.8.27}$$

Using Equations (B.8.5), (B.8.9), (B.8.10), (B.8.13), (B.8.14) and (B.8.27), we get

$$\hat{Y} = -\frac{W_S\bar{S}(1-V_S)}{Y}\frac{\theta_{K1}\theta_{N3}}{|\theta|\theta_{S1}}\frac{h}{W_S^2h_{11}}\hat{P}_2 - \frac{r\bar{K}}{Y}\frac{\theta_{N3}}{|\theta|}\widehat{P_2} - \frac{W_U\bar{N}(1-V_U)}{Y|\theta|}\frac{f\theta_{K3}}{W_U^2f_{11}}\hat{P}_2$$

$$+\frac{W_S\bar{S}V_S}{Y}\frac{\theta_{K1}\theta_{N3}}{|\theta|\theta_{S1}\varepsilon_{VS}}\widehat{P_2} + \frac{W_U\bar{N}V_U}{Y}\frac{\theta_{K3}}{|\theta|\varepsilon_{VU}}\widehat{P_2} \qquad ,$$

$\hat{Y} = A_6\widehat{P_2}$ (B.8.28)

where

$$A_6 = \left\{\begin{aligned} &-\frac{W_S\bar{S}(1-V_S)}{Y}\frac{\theta_{K1}\theta_{N3}}{|\theta|\theta_{S1}}\frac{h}{W_S^2h_{11}} - \frac{r\bar{K}}{Y}\frac{\theta_{N3}}{|\theta|} - \frac{W_U\bar{N}(1-V_U)}{Y|\theta|}\frac{f\theta_{K3}}{W_U^2f_{11}} \\ &+\frac{W_S\bar{S}V_S}{Y}\frac{\theta_{K1}\theta_{N3}}{|\theta|\theta_{S1}\varepsilon_{VS}} + \frac{W_U\bar{N}V_U}{Y}\frac{\theta_{K3}}{|\theta|\varepsilon_{VU}} \end{aligned}\right\} \text{ is}$$

ambiguous.

$A_1 < 0, A_2 > 0,\ A_3 < 0, A_4 > 0, A_5 < 0, A_6$ is ambiguous.

Differentiating Equation (8.27), we have

$e_{P_2}\widehat{P_2} + e_Y\hat{Y} + e_{Y_N}\widehat{Y_N} = \widehat{X_2}$. (B.8.29)

Using Equations (B.8.25) and (B.8.28) in Equation (B.8.29), we get

$$e_{P_2}\widehat{P_2} + e_Y\hat{Y} + e_{Y_N}\widehat{Y_N} = \widehat{X_2},$$

$$\Rightarrow e_{P_2}\widehat{P_2} + e_Y\hat{Y} + e_{Y_N}\widehat{Y_N} = A_4\widehat{P_2},$$

$$\Rightarrow (e_{P_2} + e_Y A_6 - A_4)\widehat{P_2} = -e_{Y_N}\widehat{Y_N},$$

$$\Rightarrow \widehat{P_2} = -\frac{e_{Y_N}}{\left(e_{P_2} + e_Y A_6 - A_4\right)}\hat{Y}_N,$$

$$\Rightarrow \widehat{P_2} = \beta\hat{Y}_N, \text{ (B.8.30)}$$

where $\beta = -\dfrac{e_{Y_N}}{\left(e_{P_2} + e_Y A_5 - A_4\right)} > 0$ since $e_{P_2} + e_Y A_5 - A_4 < 0$ for stability and $e_{Y_N} > 0$.

Therefore, $\hat{Y}_N$ has a positive relationship with $\widehat{P_2}$.

So using Equations (B.8.5), (B.8.9), (B.8.10), (B.8.13), (B.8.14), (B.8.15), (B.8.16), (B.8.17), (B.8.25), (B.8.26), (B.8.27) and (B.8.30), we get

$$\hat{r} = -\frac{\theta_{N3}}{|\theta|}\beta\hat{Y}_N > 0 \text{ since } |\theta| < 0. \text{ (B.8.31)}$$

$$\hat{W}_S = -\frac{\beta\hat{Y}_N h\theta_{K1}\theta_{N3}}{\theta_{S1}|\theta| W_S^2 h_{11}} < 0 \text{ since } |\theta| < 0, h_{11} < 0. \text{ (B.8.32)}$$

$$\hat{V}_S = -\frac{1}{\varepsilon_{VS}}\left\{\frac{\theta_{K1}\theta_{N3}}{\theta_{S1}|\theta|}\left(\beta\hat{Y}_N\right)\right\} > 0 \text{ since } |\theta| < 0. \text{ (B.8.33)}$$

Equation (B.8.33) is the same as Equation (8.28) in the body of this chapter:

$$\hat{W}_U = -\frac{\beta\hat{Y}_N f\theta_{K3}}{|\theta| W_U^2 f_{11}} < 0, \text{ since } |\theta| < 0. \text{ (B.8.34)}$$

$$\hat{V}_U = -\frac{1}{\varepsilon_{VU}}\left\{\frac{\theta_{K3}}{|\theta|}\left(\beta\hat{Y}_N\right)\right\} > 0 \text{ since } |\theta| < 0. \text{ (B.8.35)}$$

Equation (B.8.35) is the same as Equation (8.29) in the body of this chapter:

$$\hat{Y} = A_6\beta\hat{Y}_N \text{ is ambiguous, since } A_6 \text{ is ambiguous. (B.8.36)}$$

$$\hat{h} = -\frac{\beta\hat{Y}_N}{|\theta|\theta_{S1}}\theta_{K1}\theta_{N3}\left(1 + \frac{h}{W_S^2}\frac{1}{h_{11}}\right) < 0. \qquad \text{(B.8.37)}$$

$$\hat{f} = -\frac{\beta\hat{Y}_N}{|\theta|}\theta_{K3}\left(1+\frac{f}{W_U^2}\frac{1}{f_{11}}\right) < 0. \qquad \text{(B.8.38)}$$

$$\hat{X}_1 = A_1\beta\hat{Y}_N < 0 \text{ since } A_1 < 0. \qquad \text{(B.8.39)}$$

$\hat{X}_2 = A_4\beta\hat{Y}_N >$ since $A_4 > 0$. (B.8.40)

$\hat{X}_3 = A_5\widehat{P_2} < 0$ since $A_5 < 0$. (B.8.41)

Subtracting (B.8.32) from (B.8.34), we get

$$\hat{W}_S - \hat{W}_U = \frac{\beta\widehat{Y_N}}{\theta_{S1}|\theta|}\left\{\frac{f\theta_{K3}\theta_{S1}}{W_u^2 f_{11}} - \frac{h\theta_{K1}\theta_{N3}}{W_S^2 h_{11}}\right\} > 0 \qquad \text{(B.8.42)}$$

Since $|\theta| < 0$ and $h_{11}f_{11} < 0$ and $\left\{\frac{f\theta_{K3}\theta_{S1}}{W_U^2 f_{11}} - \frac{h\theta_{K1}\theta_{N3}}{W_S^2 h_{11}}\right\} > 0$

where $\left\{\frac{f\theta_{K3}\theta_{S1}}{W_u^2 f_{11}} - \frac{h\theta_{K1}\theta_{N3}}{W_S^2 h_{11}}\right\}$ represents efficiency-adjusted capital intensity ranking between sector 1 and sector 3 and we assume sector 1 is more capital intensive than sector 3, so it is positive.

Equation (B.8.42) is the same as Equation (8.30) in the main body of this chapter.

Notes

1 See works of Alam and Paramati (2016), Mahadevan, Amir and Nugroho (2016), Kiyonondo and Pelizzo (2015), etc., which did not explicitly declare tourism development policies as the driving force for increasing inequality, but advocated more equitable government intervention in order to distribute the profits from tourism among the masses through social welfare programmes.
2 See works of Shapiro and Stiglitz (1984), Pisauro (1991), Agell and Lundborg (1992, 1995), Gupta (2000), Gupta and Gupta (2001), Chaudhuri and Banerjee (2010), etc.
3 See Gupta and Dutta (2011) in this context.

References

Agell, J., Lundborg, P., 1992. Fair wages, involuntary unemployment and tax policy in the simple general equilibrium model. *Journal of Public Economics* 47(3), 299–320.

Agell, J., Lundborg, P., 1995. Fair wages in the open economy. *Economica* 62(247), 325–351.

Alam, M.S., Paramati, S.R., 2016. The impact of tourism on income inequality in developing economies: Does Kuznets curve hypothesis exist? *Annals of Tourism Research* 61, 111–126.

Beladi, H., Chaudhuri, S., Yabuuchi, S., 2008. Can international factor mobility reduce wage inequality in a dual economy? *Review of International Economics* 16(5), 893–903.

Chaudhuri, S., 2004. International migration of skilled and unskilled labour, welfare and skilled–unskilled wage inequality: A simple model. *Journal of Economic Integration* 19(4), 726–741.

Chaudhuri, S., 2008. Wage inequality in a dual economy and international mobility of factors: Do factor intensities always matter? *Economic Modelling* 25(6), 1155–1164.

Chaudhuri, S., Banerjee, D., 2010. Foreign capital inflow, skilled–unskilled wage inequality and unemployment of unskilled labour in a fair wage model. *Economic Modelling* 27(1), 477–486.

Chaudhuri, S., Yabuuchi, S., 2008. Foreign capital and skilled–unskilled wage inequality in a developing economy with non-traded goods. In Marjit, S., Yu, E. (Eds.), *Contemporary and Emerging Issues in Trade Theory and Policy*. Emerald Group Publishing Limited, Bingley,West Yorkshire UK.

Copeland, B.R., 1991. Tourism, welfare and de-industrialization in a small open economy. *Economica* 58(232), 515–529.

Guimaraes, C.R.F.F., Silva, J.R., 2016. Pay gap by gender in the tourism industry of Brazil. *Tourism Management* 52, 440–450.

Gupta, M.R., 2000. Duty free zone and unemployment in fair wage model. *Keio Economic Studies* 37, 33–44.

Gupta, M.R., Gupta, K., 2001. Tax policies and unemployment in a dynamic efficiency wage model. *Hitotsubashi Journal of Economics* 42, 65–79.

Gupta, M.R., Dutta, P.B., 2011. Skilled unskilled wage inequality and unemployment: A general equilibrium analysis. *Economic Modelling* 28(4), 1977–1983.

Gupta, M.R., Dutta, P.B., 2017. Capital mobility, urban unemployment & tourism development. *Keio Economic Studies* 53, 1–17.

Harris, J.R., Todaro, M.P., 1970. Migration, unemployment and development a two sector analysis. *The American Economic Review* 59, 126–142.

Kinyondo, A., Pelizzo, R., 2015. Tourism, development, and inequality: The case of Tanzania. *Poverty and Public Policy*, 7(1), 1944–2858.

Li, H., Chen, J.L., Li, G., Goh, C., 2016. Tourism and regional income inequality: Evidence from China. *Annals of Tourism Research* 58, 81–99.

Mahadevan, R., Amir, H., Nugroho, A., 2016. Regional impacts of tourism-led growth on poverty and income: Inequality: A dynamic general equilibrium analysis for Indonesia. *Tourism Economics*, 23(3), 1–18.

Marjit, S., Acharyya, R., 2003. *International Trade, Wage Inequality and the Developing Countries: A General Equilibrium Approach*. Physica/Springer Verlag, Heidelberg.

Marjit, S., Acharyya, R., 2006. Trade liberalization, skill-linked intermediate production and the two-sided wage gap. *The Journal of Policy Reform* 9(3), 203–217.

Marjit, S., Kar, S., 2005. Emigration and wage inequality. *Economics Letters* 88(1), 141–145.

Nestorovic, O., Anivic, D., 2019. Development of tourism in the function of reducing unemployment in Serbia. In *Tourism as a Generator of Employment - Thematic Proceedings, Vrnjačka Banja - TISC*, 4(1), 97–112.June.

Pisauro, G., 1991. The effects of taxes on labour in efficiency wage models. *Journal of Public Economics* 46(3), 329–345.

Qin, M., Su, C.W., Zhang, S.P., 2020. Tourism and unemployment in Hong Kong: Is there any interaction? *Asian Economics Letters* 1(1).

Shapiro, C., Stiglitz, J.E., 1984. Equilibrium unemployment as a worker discipline device. *American Economic Review* 74, 433–444.

Snyman, S.L., 2012. The role of tourism employment in poverty reduction and community perceptions of conservation and tourism in southern Africa. *Journal of Sustainable Tourism* 20(3), 395–416.

Wattanakuljarus, A., Coxhead, I., 2008. Is tourism-based development good for the poor? A general equilibrium analysis for Thailand. *Journal of Policy Modeling* 30(6), 929–955.

World travel and tourism council report, Annual report 2022: Key highlights.

Xaba, F., Selepe, M., Mdiniso, J., 2018. Ecotourism as a vehicle to reduce unemployment and poverty: The role of the community and employees. *African Journal of Hospitality, Tourism and Leisure* 7(5).

Zhike, L.V., 2019. Deepening or lessening? The effects of tourism on regional inequality. *Tourism Management* 72, 23–26.

9 Globalisation, Pandemic Crisis, Income Distribution and Unemployment

A General Equilibrium Analysis

Ranjanendra Narayan Nag, Damayanti Sau, Asmita Das, Tavishi Rupani, Shyani Mukherjee

9.1 Introduction

The past three decades have been associated with greater openness in global markets, as globalisation has arguably become one of the most significant trends influencing the world today. This global integration has had an effect on international trade, investment, income, employment and growth, with an impact on the yardsticks of development such as poverty and inequality. Over the twentieth century, several developing countries liberalised their macroeconomic and trade policies in order to promote growth and peaceful inter-country ties. This global trend towards increased globalisation, since the 1990s, appears to have two distinct repercussions. On the one hand, income disparity between nations has declined, while domestic inequality within countries, on the other hand, has worsened.[1] However, the COVID-19 pandemic has disrupted the global value chain and created a situation conducive to increased protectionism.

Given this backdrop, we construct a three-sector general equilibrium model that accounts for some specific features of a small developing economy, like diverse trade patterns, labour market imperfections and the presence of a non-traded sector producing goods for mass consumption. We use this structure to analyse the effects of trade-related policies like reducing tariff protection on the import-competing manufacturing sector, foreign capital inflow and agricultural trade liberalisation on the skilled–unskilled wage gap and the unemployment of skilled labour. We then analyse the effects of technological innovation in the export-led agricultural sector.

The volume of literature on income inequality is copious and there exists a wide heterogeneity among economists regarding whether such a process of globalisation is associated with narrowing or widening income disparities within developing countries. One viewpoint is that globalisation fosters economic progress and social welfare by allowing emerging countries to join the global economy.[2] Jagdish Bhagwati (2004) recognises the prevalent

DOI: 10.4324/9781003375050-9

misconception that trade in labour-intensive goods will result in an infinite accumulation of exports from impoverished nations, resulting in decreasing prices and lower real wages. In reality, because of technical change and capital accumulation in the countries emerging out of poverty (e.g., East Asia in the 1970s and 1980s), the entry of new exports of labour-intensive goods by poor countries is offset by the withdrawal of exports of labour-intensive goods by these rapidly growing countries. Chakrabarti (2000) observed that greater participation in trade significantly reduces income inequality. There is a lack of strong negative association between trade and inequality because countries that have a more egalitarian distribution of income engage in more trade, and the consequent growth further reduces inequality by raising both initial income and subsequent growth. The other viewpoint is that globalisation has an adverse impact on the wage inequality scenario in developing countries owing to the features of labour market imperfections, the nature of capital mobility, structures of production, etc. Marjit, Beladi and Chakrabarti (2004) find that if the vertically integrated skilled export sector is more capital intensive than the import-competing sector, then in the absence of trade fragmentation, improvements in terms of trade or foreign capital inflows might worsen wage inequality. Chaudhuri and Yabuuchi (2007) obtained that foreign capital inflow improves wage inequality, provided the low-skill sector is capital intensive with imperfections in the market for unskilled labour. Also, when the non-traded sector produces a final commodity, inequality worsens in the presence of a capital-intensive, low-skilled sector. Rojas-Vallejos and Turnovsky (2017) obtain a weak positive relationship between tariff liberalisation and inequality. Marjit and Ahuja (2021) found that when the skilled sector is capital intensive relative to the unskilled sector, the wage gap always increases independent of the sequence of reforms (reforms related to trade and capital-account liberalisation), but the extent of such increase may vary according to the chosen sequence.

Our departure from Chaudhuri and Yabuuchi (2007) is in terms of the existence of imperfections in the skilled labour market rather than in the unskilled labour market, which is in accordance with the luxury unemployment hypothesis. The traditional view states that unemployment rates in developing countries are low because they mostly affect skilled workers who can afford extensive periods of job searching to find suitable jobs. Most job seekers, on the other hand, will quickly settle for the first job that comes along in traditional occupations or self-employment.[3]

One of the characteristic features of a developing economy is the non-traded sector. It usually employs old and backward production technologies and is unskilled labour intensive. When a non-traded sector produces a final good, the purchasing power of the consumers determines how the sector will fare. Thus, price changes in the non-traded sector have significant effects on relative wages.

The model has been extended to analyse the consequences of the COVID-19 crisis. The labour market has been one of the worst hit globally due to

COVID-19. There has been an unprecedented global employment loss in the year 2020,[4] which, among other factors, can beattributed to the lockdown.[5] The efficiency of labour has also been hampered due to reasons like stressful work conditions and the long-lasting effects of COVID known as the "Covid Long Haulers."[6] With a significant transformation of the workplace, the "new normal" of "work from home" has emerged as the need of the hour and most employees have been forced to work remotely, often under stressful and poor working conditions. According to Dasgupta and Murali (2020), this unconventional way of working has led to inequality as all jobs cannot be performed remotely. Capital formation has significantly deteriorated as the "global risk-appetite waned." Even though the government has undertaken fiscal stimulus measures,[7] increased government spending[8] has also not been able to stimulate enough demand or investment. Chaudhuri et al. (2021) have also found that unplanned attempts to the creation of additional jobs have not only accentuated unemployment but also worsened social welfare.

The rest of the chapter has been organised as follows. The basic model is developed in Section 9.2. In Section 9.3, we carry out several comparative static exercises. In Section 9.4, we extend the model to focus on the impacts of the COVID-19 crisis. Finally, Section 9.5 concludes the chapter.

9.2 The General Equilibrium Model

We consider a small open developing economy with three sectors: two traded sectors X and and a non-traded sector Y. Sector X is an import-competing manufacturing sector which uses skilled labour (S) and capital (K). Sector Y is the non-farm sector producing a non-traded good for mass consumption using unskilled labour (L) and capital. Finally, Sector Z is the export-oriented agricultural sector which uses land (T) and unskilled labour to produce a commodity, sold entirely in foreign markets. Skilled labour and land are specific factors in sectors X and Z, respectively, while unskilled labour is mobile between sectors Y and Z. Skilled workers earn an institutionally given wage rate $\overline{W}_s$, while unskilled labour earns a competitive wage, w. r is the interest earned on capital holdings and R is the rent received by landowners. We have assumed prices of sectors $X(P_x^*)$ and $Z(P_z^*)$ to be internationally given owing to the small economy assumption, while the price of the non-traded commodity (P_y) is endogenously determined. Sector X is protected with the help of an exogenously determined tariff rate, and there exists unemployment among skilled workers (V) who are specific to this sector. Considering the "Luxury Unemployment Hypothesis," we assume full employment of unskilled labour at all times.[9] Production functions exhibit constant returns to scale with diminishing marginal productivity to each factor.

The following symbols will be used for the formal presentation of the model:

a_{Sx}= Skilled labour–output ratio in the sector X
a_{Li}= Unskilled labour–output ratio in the sector i, where i=Y, Z
a_{Ki}= Capital–output ratio in the sector i, where i=X, Y
a_{Tz}= Land–output ratio in the sector Z
$\overline{W}_s$ = Institutionally given wage rate of skilled labour
w = Wage rate of unskilled labour
r = Returns to capital
R= Returns to land
$\overline{L}$= Endowment of unskilled labour
$\overline{S}$ = Endowment of skilled labour
$\overline{K}$= Endowment of capital
$\overline{T}$= Endowment of land
λ= Technology parameter
V= Unemployment of skilled labour
P_x^*= World price of commodity X
P_y= Price of commodity Y determined in the domestic market
P_z^*= World price of commodity Z
t= Tariff rate on imports of X
α =Share of income of unskilled workers spent on good Y
θ_{ji} = Distributive share of the jth input in the ith sector, where $j = S, L, K, T$ and $i = X, Y, Z$
λ_{ji} = Proportion of the jth input employed in the ith sector, where $j = S, L, K, T$ and $i = X, Y, Z$
S_{ji}^k = Degree of substitution between factors j and i in the kth sector; $j, i = L, K$; and $k = Y$. For example, $S_{LK}^y = \left(\partial a_{Ly} / \partial r\right)\left(r / a_{Ly}\right)$, $S_{LL}^y = \left(\partial a_{Ly} / \partial w\right)\left(w / a_{Ly}\right)$, etc. $S_{ji}^k > 0$ for $i \neq j$ and $S_{jj}^k < 0$
"∧" = Proportional change

The general equilibrium structure of the model is as follows:

Given the assumption of perfect competition, we have zero profit, and hence price equals the unit cost of production. Accordingly, the price system is represented by Equations (9.1)–(9.3) as follows:

$$P_x^*\left(1+t\right) = \overline{W_S} a_{Sx} + r a_{Kx} \tag{9.1}$$

$$P_y = w a_{Ly} + r a_{Ky} \tag{9.2}$$

$$P_z^* = w a_{Lz} + R a_{Tz} \tag{9.3}$$

All factor coefficients other than a_{ly} and a_{ky} are constant.

We assume that capital endowment includes both domestic and foreign capitals, and these are perfect substitutes, i.e., $\overline{K} = K_d + K_f$.

The endowment equations for skilled labour, unskilled labour, capital and land are given by Equations (9.4)–(9.7), respectively:

$$\overline{S} = a_{Sx} X + V \tag{9.4}$$

$$\bar{L} = a_{Ly}Y + a_{Lz}Z \tag{9.5}$$

$$\bar{K} = a_{Kx}X + a_{Ky}Y \tag{9.6}$$

$$\lambda\bar{T} = a_{Tz}Z,\ \lambda \geq 1 \tag{9.7}$$

Finally, the demand function for Y is given as follows:

$$Y = \frac{\alpha\left(w\bar{L}\right)}{P_y}, 0 < \alpha \leq 1 \tag{9.8}$$

9.2.1 *Working of the Model*

In the system, we have eight endogenous variables : w, r, R, P_y, V, X, Y and Z. The parameters of the system are $t, \overline{W_s}, P_x^*, P_z^*, \bar{S}, \bar{L}, \bar{K}, \bar{T}, \lambda$ and α which are exogenously given. The production structure possesses a non-decomposable property, as factor prices depend on both commodity prices and endowment equations.

The production levels of goods in the economy are determined using the endowment equations. Since all terms except Z, are constants in Equation (9.7), we obtain the value of Z. Substituting this value of Z in Equation (9.5), we get the total production of non-traded good, Y. The total production of traded industrial good, X, is hence obtained by substituting the value of Y in Equation (9.6). From Equation (9.4), we obtain the level of unemployment, V, in the skilled labour market.

We determine the rental rate r from Equation (9.1). On substituting this value of r in Equation (9.2), we obtain the wage of unskilled workers (w) as a function of P_y. The rent on land, i.e., R is obtained as a function of P_y by substituting $w(P_y)$ in Equation (9.3). Consequently, we get the price of commodity Y from Equation (9.8). Substituting this value of P_y in w (P_y) and $R(P_y)$, we obtain the wage of unskilled labour and rent on land, respectively. As a_{Ly} and a_{Ky} are functions of factor prices, we can obtain them automatically.

9.3 Comparative Static Exercises

In this section, we shall intuitively analyse the effects of different liberalisation policies and a land-augmenting technological progress on the skilled–unskilled wage gap, income distribution and the unemployment of skilled labour. The liberalisation policies involve a reduction in the protection of the import-competing sector, an increase in the world price of the traded agricultural good, and an inflow of foreign capital.

9.3.1 *Tariff Liberalisation*

Here we consider a reduction in the tariff rate in order to promote imports in the domestic economy. A reduction in the import tariff, t, lowers the tariff-inclusive price of commodity X. Since wage of skilled labour, $\overline{W_s}$, is institutionally given, the rental price of capital, r, falls to satisfy the zero-profit condition in this sector. In order to maintain the zero-profit condition in sector Y, the wage of unskilled labour falls, and as a result, there is a decrease in P_y.[10] The fall in the unskilled wage rate, w, in turn leads to a rise in the rent of land, R.

In this particular case, the magnitudes of change in P_y and w are equal, such that the elasticity of the demand curve calculated from Equation (9.8) is found to be zero. As a result, there is no expansion or contraction in the production of commodity Y. This along with no change in the total capital endowment of the economy keeps production in the sector X unchanged. Consequently, the unemployment of skilled workers also remains unaffected.

As r falls, capital owners lose out; the fall in w decreases the wages of unskilled workers, and the rise in "R" leads to a gain in the income of the land owners. Thus, the wage gap between skilled and unskilled workers increases (beginning from $\overline{W_s} > w$) because w falls while $\overline{W_s}$ remains unchanged. This result is in accordance with the standard "trade view" on wage inequality where tariff liberalisation (i.e., increased openness of a small domestic economy to the world economy) causes a rise in the incidence of poverty and wage inequality.

Proposition 9.1: Tariff liberalisation in the import-competing sector of an economy only leads to an increase in the wage gap between skilled and unskilled workers and has no impact on the unemployment of skilled workers. Likewise, capital owners lose out whereas land owners are benefitted.

9.3.2 *Agricultural Trade Liberalisation*

Here we consider a rise in P_z^*, the price of commodity Z, as a means for agricultural trade liberalisation. Since the wage of skilled labour, $\overline{W_s}$, is institutionally fixed, the rate of return for capital remains unchanged as the tariff-inclusive price of the import-competing commodity is fixed. Hence, producers have no incentive to substitute one factor of production for another in sector Y. As a result, the wage of unskilled labour, w, and the price of commodity Y, P_y, remain unchanged. The return to land, R, rises following the Stolper–Samuelson effect, as sector Z is land intensive. This improves land owner's incomes.

On the other hand, since the factor prices of the inputs required in sector Y remain unchanged, there is no change in the production of commodity Y. Production of commodity X also remains unchanged following which the unemployment of skilled labour also remains fixed.[11]

Proposition 9.2: A policy leading to agricultural trade liberalisation has no effect on the wage gap or unemployment of skilled labour. Rather, it has resulted in an increase in the income of the landowners.

9.3.3 Capital Account Liberalisation

Here we consider an inflow of foreign capital in the domestic economy, i.e., an increase in K_f. We assume that skilled labour and capital used in sector X are perfect complements. Since the wage rate of skilled labour $(\overline{W_s})$ is institutionally given, the rental rate of capital, r, changes only if there is a change in the protectionist policy or in the world price of commodity X, so, here the rental rate of capital remains unchanged. As a result, producers have no incentive to substitute between the two factors. Hence, the wage rate of unskilled labour also remains unchanged, following which the domestically determined price of Y does not change. The return to land, R, remains unchanged as well.

An inflow of foreign capital does not affect production in the Z sector. Consequently, the production in sector Y remains unaltered. Since capital is used only in sectors X and Y, sector X expands to match the increase in capital endowment. As a result, the unemployment of skilled labour falls due to an increase in the requirement for skilled workers who are intensively used in the production of this sector[12].

Proposition 9.3: An increase in the foreign inflow of capital does not affect the skilled–unskilled wage gap, rather capital inflow has resulted in an increase in the production of the import-competing commodity and a reduction in unemployment of the skilled workers.

9.3.4 Technological Innovation in the Agricultural Sector

Here we consider a progress in the land-augmenting technology in the traded agricultural sector, i.e., an increase in λ. Since the endowment of land is fixed, an increase in λ leads to an equally proportionate increase in the production of the exported commodity, Z, which in turn leads to an increase in the number of unskilled workers employed in this sector, given by $a_{Lz}Z$. Total endowment of unskilled workers remains constant, and there is a fall in the number of unskilled workers employed in the Y sector, i.e., $a_{Ly}Y$. Whether the Y sector expands or contracts depends crucially on the change in the labour–output ratio of sector Y, i.e., a_{Ly}. Hence, when $\theta_{Ky} < S^{y}_{LK}$, the production in sector Y increases and there is a fall in a_{Ly}, as a result $a_{Ly}Y$ falls and equilibrium is maintained. Under this sufficient condition, the X sector contracts and increases the unemployment of skilled workers. On the other hand, since the wage rate of skilled labour $(\overline{W_s})$ is institutionally given, the rental rate of capital remains unchanged. Now, under the afore-mentioned condition, as the labour–output ratio, a_{Ly} falls, the wage rate of unskilled workers, w, increases. This is turn raises the price of commodity Y, i.e., P_y, and lowers the return on land, R. The results are reversed, when $\theta_{Ky} > S^y_{LK}$.[13]

It can be noted that P_y and Y move in the same direction, under both conditions. The reason is that an increase (decrease) in P_y leads to an increase (decrease) in w, i.e., unskilled workers now earn more (less) income. As a result, their demand for the domestically produced commodity increases (decreases), and Y goes up (down).

Proposition 9.4: Technological innovation in the agricultural sector reduces the skilled–unskilled wage gap but increases unemployment. The rentier class are worse-off. The production of import-competing commodity reduces and the non-traded sector is better off when $\theta_{Ky} < S^y_{LK}$.

9.4 An Analysis of COVID-19

In this section, we extend the model built in Section 9.2 to analyse the adverse impacts of the COVID-19 pandemic. First, we introduce an efficiency parameter e, which indicates the efficiency of unskilled labour. Second, in an attempt to explain whether fiscal stimulus aimed at recovery of the economy from recession has been effective or not, we introduce government expenditure on non-traded good, G. Besides, we consider the technology parameter, λ, to be unity in this case.

In addition to the symbols that we have used in Section 9.2, we use the following symbols:

G = Real government expenditure

e = Efficiency parameter of unskilled labour

The price system is represented by Equations (9.9)–(9.11), as follows:

$$P_x^*(1+t) = \overline{W}_S a_{Sx} + r a_{Kx}, \tag{9.9}$$

$$P_y = w a_{Ly} + r a_{Ky}, \tag{9.10}$$

$$P_z^* = w a_{Lz} + R a_{Tz}. \tag{9.11}$$

All factor coefficients other than a_{ly} and a_{ky} are constant.

Full employment conditions for skilled labour, unskilled labour, capital and land are given by Equations (9.12),–(9.15), respectively.

$$\bar{S} = a_{Sx} X + V, \tag{9.12}$$

$$e\bar{L} = a_{Ly} Y + a_{Lz} Z, 0 < e \leq 1, \tag{9.13}$$

$$\bar{K} = a_{Kx} X + a_{Ky} Y, \tag{9.14}$$

$$\bar{T} = a_{Tz} Z. \tag{9.15}$$

Finally, the demand function for Y is given as follows:

$$Y = \frac{\alpha(w\bar{L})}{P_y} + G, 0 < \alpha \leq 1. \tag{9.16}$$

The working of this model is similar to that of the model developed in Section 9.2

9.4.1 *Comparative Static Exercises*

Now, we analyse the implications of a fall in the efficiency parameter, a decline in domestic capital formation and a reduction in the world price of the exportable product, as consequences of the COVID-19 pandemic. We then proceed to examine the effects of a rise in government expenditure as a measure of recovery from the pandemic.

9.4.1.1 *Fall in Efficiency of Workers or Labour Scarcity*

In this case, we consider a fall in the efficiency parameter of unskilled labour or a scarcity of labour, i.e., a decrease in e. Since the wage rate of skilled labour is institutionally given, the rental rate of capital remains unchanged. Under certain conditions, the unit labour requirement of sector Y, i.e.,a_{Ly}, falls. Hence, the wage rate of unskilled workers, w, increases. This in turn raises the price of commodity Y, i.e., P_y by a fraction, and also lowers the return on land, R.

On the other hand, there is no change in the production of Z. The production in sector Y expands since the real wage of unskilled labour in terms of P_y increases. Unaltered capital endowment implies a contraction in the production of X since the production of Y expands. Thus, the unemployment of skilled workers increases. An interesting feature that we can notice here is that the movements of Y and P_y are in the same direction.[14]

Proposition 9.5: A fall in the efficiency of unskilled labour or a scarcity of the same results in a decrease in the skilled–unskilled wage gap, but worsens the domestic economy by decreasing the production of the import-competing commodity, increasing unemployment of the skilled workers and reducing the return to land when $\left[\theta_{Ky}(Y-G) - S^{y}_{LK}Y\right] < 0$.

9.4.1.2 *Fall in Domestic Capital Formation*

In this case, we consider fall in domestic capital, i.e., a decrease in K_d. There is no change in the production of Y due to an unchanged production of Z, endowment of unskilled labour and its efficiency parameter. A fall in domestic investment implies a decrease in the total capital endowment, which is used only in sectors X and Y. Since the production of Y remains unaffected, sector X contracts to accommodate the decrease in capital endowment.

Consequently, the requirement for skilled workers who are intensively used in the production of commodity X decreases owing to the contraction in this sector. As a result, the unemployment of skilled labour increases when there is a decrease in domestic capital formation.

The rental rate of capital, r, remains unchanged since the wage rate of skilled labour ($\overline{W}_s$) is institutionally given and fixed, and there is no change in the protectionist policy or in the world price of commodity X. Since there is no expansion or contraction in the production of commodity Y, the domestically determined price of Y does not change. As a result, the wage rate of unskilled labour also remains unchanged leading to no change in R.

Proposition 9.6: A fall in the domestic capital formation does not affect the skilled–unskilled wage gap, rather it worsens the domestic economy by decreasing production of the import-competing commodity and an increase in unemployment of the skilled workers when $\left[\theta_{Ky}(Y-G)-S_{LK}^{y}Y\right]<0$.

9.4.1.3 Reduction in World Price of Exportable Commodity

In this case, we consider a reduction in the world price of commodity Z, i.e., fall in P_z^*. There is no change in the production of Y due to an unchanged production of Z, the endowment of unskilled labour and its efficiency parameter; and because capital endowment also remains unchanged, there is no change in the production of X. Consequently, the requirement for skilled workers who are intensively used in the production of commodity X remains unaffected, and hence the unemployment of skilled labour neither contracts nor expands.

The rental rate of capital, r, remains unchanged since the wage rate of skilled labour ($\overline{W}_s$) is institutionally given and fixed, and there is no change in the protectionist policy or in the world price of commodity X. Owing to no expansion or contraction in the production of commodity Y, the domestically determined price of Y does not change. As a result, the wage rate of unskilled labour also remains unchanged. Therefore, in order to accommodate the fall in P_z^*, R falls.[15]

Proposition 9.7: A fall in the world price of the exportable commodity does not affect the skilled–unskilled wage gap, unemployment or production of goods. Rather, the land owners are rendered worse-off following a fall in the return on their land holdings when

$\theta_{Ly}+S_{LK}^{y}>1$ and $\left[\theta_{Ky}(Y-G)-S_{LK}^{y}Y\right]<0$.

9.4.1.4 Increase in Real Government Expenditure

In this case, we consider an increase in real government expenditure, i.e., increase in G. An increase in government expenditure influences the skilled–unskilled wage gap, which is conditional upon the distribution of expenditure in different sectors. In our case, since the government expenditure is made on sector Y, the domestically produced commodity's production will increase due to the increased investment. Since the capital endowment in our model is fixed and considering that more investment is made in domestically produced sector, there is a reduction in the production of X, the import-competing commodity, and hence unemployment of skilled labour rises. There is no change in production of Z. Also, since the production of domestically produced good rises, the wage of unskilled labour rises due to an increased demand for unskilled labour, thereby reducing the skilled–unskilled wage gap. Hence, given our model, the return to land owners reduces.[16]

Proposition 9.8: An increase in real government expenditure will reduce the skilled–unskilled wage gap, decrease the production of import-competing commodity thereby increasing unemployment of skilled labour, reduce the return to land owners and increase the price and production of domestic good when $\left[\theta_{Ky}\left(Y-G\right)-S_{LK}^{y}Y\right]<0$.

9.5 Concluding Remarks and Policy Implications

Most developing countries have made a prominent move in the direction of a liberalised trade regime. However, the distribution of the gains from such economic reforms should be put under scanner since globalisation produces inequality of different types. The empirical evidence by and large suggests that increasing income inequality has been a sequel to trade liberalisation, barring a few exceptions like Argentina. In this chapter, we have developed a three-sector general equilibrium model, taking into consideration some specific features of a small developing economy, like diverse trade patterns, the existence of imperfection in the labour market and a non-traded non-farm sector producing goods for mass consumption. Using the model, we arrive at the conclusion that Tariff Liberalisation worsens the skilled–unskilled wage inequality scenario, without any significant effect on the unemployment of skilled labour. The capital owners are found to be better off while the land owners are worse-off. Agricultural trade liberalisation is found to improve the earnings of the rentier class. Capital-account liberalisation increases production in the import-competing sector and decreases unemployment of skilled labour. Land-augmenting technological progress decreases the wage gap and the rentier class is now worse-off. Following the outbreak of the COVID-19 pandemic, a fall in labour efficiency and a downturn in domestic capital formation have resulted in an increase in the unemployment of skilled labour. While a fall in the world price of the exportable commodity has rendered landowners worse-off following a decrease in the return on their land holdings. Government expenditure as a measure of recovery is observed to increase the unemployment of skilled workers under a particular condition.

The findings have a specific accent on policy-making for a developing country like India. The removal of protectionist policies and trade liberalisation is usually aimed at reducing commodity market distortion, which is an extremely common occurrence in developing countries. But these might have undesirable impacts on unskilled labour who belong to the most marginalised and vulnerable groups of the workforce. Thus, implementation of such liberalisation policies and reforms should be done only after proper planning and taking into account all possible outcomes, both desirable and undesirable. This chapter makes a humble attempt to address issues pertaining to the pandemic crisis as well. The pandemic crisis which is an eye-opener merits special attention and warrants a relook at policy-making.

Appendix A

A.1 Equations of Change

Totally differentiating Equations (9.1)–(9.8) and arranging them in a matrix form, we get

$$\begin{pmatrix} \theta_{Kx} & 0 & 0 & 0 & 0 & 0 & 0 & 0 \\ \theta_{Ky} & \theta_{Ly} & 0 & -1 & 0 & 0 & 0 & 0 \\ 0 & \theta_{Lz} & \theta_{Tz} & 0 & 0 & 0 & 0 & 0 \\ 0 & 0 & 0 & 0 & \lambda_{Sx} & 0 & 0 & V/\bar{S} \\ \lambda_{Ly}S^{y}_{LK} & -\lambda LyS^{y}_{LK} & 0 & 0 & 0 & \lambda_{Ly} & \lambda_{Lz} & 0 \\ -\lambda_{Ky}S^{y}_{KL} & \lambda_{Ky}S^{y}_{KL} & 0 & 0 & \lambda_{Kx} & \lambda_{Ky} & 0 & 0 \\ 0 & 0 & 0 & 0 & 0 & 0 & 1 & 0 \\ 0 & 1 & 0 & -1 & 0 & -1 & 0 & 0 \end{pmatrix} \begin{pmatrix} \hat{r} \\ \widehat{w} \\ \widehat{R} \\ \widehat{P}_y \\ \widehat{X} \\ \widehat{Y} \\ \widehat{Z} \\ \widehat{V} \end{pmatrix} = \begin{pmatrix} \hat{tt} \\ 0 \\ \widehat{P^*_Z} \\ 0 \\ \hat{\bar{L}} \\ \hat{\bar{K}} \\ \hat{\lambda} \\ \hat{\bar{L}} \end{pmatrix} \tag{A.1}$$

$$\text{Here}, \Delta = \theta_{Kx}\theta_{Tz}\frac{V}{\bar{S}}\lambda_{Ly}\lambda_{Kx}\left(\theta_{Ky} - S^{y}_{LK}\right). \tag{A.2}$$

Solving (A.1) by Cramer's rule, the following expressions are obtained:

$$\hat{r} = \frac{\hat{tt}}{\theta_{Kx}} \tag{A.3}$$

$$\hat{w} = \frac{\hat{tt}}{\theta_{Kx}} - \hat{\lambda}\frac{\frac{\lambda_{Lz}}{\lambda_{Ly}}}{\left(\theta_{Ky} - S^{y}_{LK}\right)} + \hat{\bar{L}}\frac{1-\lambda_{Ly}}{\lambda_{Ly}\left(\theta_{Ky} - S^{y}_{LK}\right)} \tag{A.4}$$

$$\hat{R} = \frac{\theta_{Kx}\widehat{P_z^*} - t\hat{t}\theta_{Lz}}{\theta_{Kz}\theta_{Tz}} + \hat{\lambda}\frac{\theta_{Lz}\lambda_{Lz}}{\theta_{Tz}\lambda_{Ly}\left(\theta_{Ky} - S_{LK}^y\right)} - \hat{\bar{L}}\frac{\left(1-\lambda_{Ly}\right)\theta_{Lz}}{\lambda_{Ly}\theta_{Tz}\left(\theta_{Ky} - S_{LK}^y\right)} \quad (A.5)$$

$$\widehat{P_y} = \frac{t\hat{t}}{\theta_{Kx}} - \hat{\lambda}\frac{\theta_{Ly}\lambda_{Lz}}{\lambda_{Ly}\left(\theta_{Ky} - S_{LK}^y\right)} + \hat{\bar{L}}\frac{\left(1-\lambda_{Ly}\right)\theta_{Ly}}{\lambda_{Ly}\left(\theta_{Ky} - S_{LK}^y\right)} \quad (A.6)$$

$$\hat{X} = \frac{\hat{\bar{K}}}{\lambda_{Kx}} + \hat{\lambda}\frac{\lambda_{Lz}\lambda_{Ky}\left(\theta_{Ky} + S_{KL}^y\right)}{\lambda_{Ly}\lambda_{Kx}\left(\theta_{Ky} - S_{LK}^y\right)} + \hat{\bar{L}}\frac{\lambda_{Ky}\left\{-\left(\theta_{Ky} - \lambda_{Ly}S_{LK}^y\right) + S_{KL}^y\left(1-\lambda_{Ly}\right)\right\}}{\lambda_{Ly}\lambda_{Kx}\left(\theta_{Ky} - S_{LK}^y\right)} \quad (A.7)$$

$$\hat{Y} = -\hat{\lambda}\frac{\lambda_{Lz}\theta_{Ky}}{\lambda_{Ly}\left(\theta_{Ky} - S_{LK}^y\right)} + \hat{\bar{L}}\frac{\theta_{Ky} - \lambda_{Ly}S_{LK}^y}{\lambda_{Ly}\left(\theta_{Ky} - S_{LK}^y\right)} \quad (A.8)$$

$$\widehat{Z} = \hat{\lambda} \quad (A.9)$$

$$\hat{V} = \frac{-\lambda_{Sx}}{\lambda_{Kx}\frac{V}{\bar{S}}}\hat{\bar{K}} - \hat{\lambda}\frac{\lambda_{Sx}\lambda_{Lz}\lambda_{Ky}\left(\theta_{Ky} + S_{KL}^y\right)}{\lambda_{Ly}\lambda_{Kx}\frac{V}{\bar{S}}\left(\theta_{Ky} - S_{LK}^y\right)} - \hat{\bar{L}}\frac{\lambda_{Sx}\lambda_{Ky}\left\{-\left(\theta_{Ky} - \lambda_{Ly}S_{LK}^y\right) + S_{KL}^y\left(1-\lambda_{Ly}\right)\right\}}{\frac{V}{\bar{S}}\lambda_{Ly}\lambda_{Kx}\left(\theta_{Ky} - S_{LK}^y\right)} \quad (A.10)$$

A.2 Comparative Static Exercises

Using Equations (A.3)–(A.10), the following results are obtained for the comparative statics exercise:

A.2.1 Tariff Liberalisation

When $\hat{t} < 0$,

$$\hat{r} = \frac{t\hat{t}}{\theta_{Kx}} < 0,$$

$$\hat{w} = \frac{t\hat{t}}{\theta_{Kx}} < 0,$$

$$\hat{R} = \frac{-t\hat{t}\theta_{Lz}}{\theta_{Kz}\theta_{Tz}} > 0,$$

$$\widehat{P_y} = \frac{t\hat{t}}{\theta_{Kx}} < 0,$$

$$\hat{X} = \hat{Y} = \hat{Z} = 0,$$

$$\hat{V} = 0.$$

A.2.2 Agricultural Trade Liberalisation

When $\widehat{P_z^*} > 0$,

$$\hat{r} = \hat{w} = 0,$$

$$\hat{R} = \frac{\theta_{Kx}\widehat{P_z^*}}{\theta_{Kz}\theta_{Tz}} > 0,$$

$$\widehat{P_y} = 0,$$

$$\hat{X} = \hat{Y} = \hat{Z} = 0,$$

$$\hat{V} = 0.$$

A.2.3 Capital-Account Liberalisation

When K_f increases, i.e., $\widehat{\overline{K}} > 0$,

$$\hat{r} = \hat{w} = \hat{R} = 0,$$

$$\widehat{P_y} = 0,$$

$$\hat{X} = \frac{\widehat{\overline{K}}}{\lambda_{Kx}} > 0,$$

$$\hat{Y} = \hat{Z} = 0,$$

$$\hat{V} = \frac{-\lambda_{Sx}\widehat{\overline{K}}}{\lambda_{Kx}\frac{V}{\overline{S}}} < 0.$$

A.2.4 Land-Augmenting Technological Progress

When $\hat{\lambda} > 0$, there are two possible sub-cases.

(i) $\theta_{Ky} > S^{y}_{LK}$,

$$\hat{r} = 0,$$

$$\hat{w} = -\hat{\lambda}\frac{\frac{\lambda_{Lz}}{\lambda_{Ly}}}{\left(\theta_{Ky} - S^{y}_{LK}\right)} < 0,$$

$$\hat{R} = \hat{\lambda}\frac{\theta_{Lz}\lambda_{Lz}}{\theta_{Tz}\lambda_{Ly}\left(\theta_{Ky} - S^{y}_{LK}\right)} > 0,$$

$$\widehat{P_y} = -\hat{\lambda}\frac{\theta_{Ly}\lambda_{Lz}}{\lambda_{Ly}\left(\theta_{Ky} - S^{y}_{LK}\right)} < 0,$$

$$\hat{X} = \hat{\lambda}\frac{\lambda_{Lz}\lambda_{Ky}\left(\theta_{Ky} + S^{y}_{KL}\right)}{\lambda_{Ly}\lambda_{Kx}\left(\theta_{Ky} - S^{y}_{LK}\right)} > 0,$$

$$\hat{Y} = -\hat{\lambda}\frac{\lambda_{Lz}\theta_{Ky}}{\lambda_{Ly}\left(\theta_{Ky} - S^{y}_{LK}\right)} < 0$$

$$\hat{Z} = \hat{\lambda} > 0,$$

$$\hat{V} = -\hat{\lambda}\frac{\lambda_{Sx}\lambda_{Lz}\lambda_{Ky}\left(\theta_{Ky} + S^{y}_{KL}\right)}{\lambda_{Ly}\lambda_{Kx}\frac{V}{S}\left(\theta_{Ky} - S^{y}_{LK}\right)} < 0.$$

(ii) $\theta_{Ky} < S^{y}_{LK}$,

$$\hat{r} = 0,$$

$$\hat{w} = -\hat{\lambda}\frac{\frac{\lambda_{Lz}}{\lambda_{Ly}}}{\left(\theta_{Ky} - S^{y}_{LK}\right)} > 0,$$

$$\widehat{P_y} = -\hat{\lambda}\frac{\theta_{Ly}\lambda_{Lz}}{\lambda_{Ly}\left(\theta_{Ky} - S^{y}_{LK}\right)} > 0,$$

$$\hat{R} = \hat{\lambda}\frac{\theta_{Lz}\lambda_{Lz}}{\theta_{Tz}\lambda_{Ly}\left(\theta_{Ky} - S^{y}_{LK}\right)} < 0,$$

$$\hat{X} = \hat{\lambda}\frac{\lambda_{Lz}\lambda_{Ky}\left(\theta_{Ky} + S_{KL}^{y}\right)}{\lambda_{Ly}\lambda_{Kx}\left(\theta_{Ky} - S_{LK}^{y}\right)} < 0,$$

$$\hat{Y} = -\hat{\lambda}\frac{\lambda_{Lz}\theta_{Ky}}{\lambda_{Ly}\left(\theta_{Ky} - S_{LK}^{y}\right)} > 0,$$

$$\hat{Z} = \hat{\lambda} > 0,$$

$$\hat{V} = -\hat{\lambda}\frac{\lambda_{Sx}\lambda_{Lz}\lambda_{Ky}\left(\theta_{Ky} + S_{KL}^{y}\right)}{\lambda_{Ly}\lambda_{Kx}\frac{V}{\overline{S}}\left(\theta_{Ky} - S_{LK}^{y}\right)} > 0.$$

Appendix B

B.1 Comparative Static Exercises for Model with Pandemic Crisis

Totally differentiating Equations (9.9)–(9.16) and arranging them in a matrix form:

$$\begin{pmatrix} \theta_{Kx} & 0 & 0 & 0 & 0 & 0 & 0 & 0 \\ \theta_{Ky} & \theta_{Ly} & 0 & -1 & 0 & 0 & 0 & 0 \\ 0 & \theta_{Lz} & \theta_{Tz} & 0 & 0 & 0 & 0 & 0 \\ 0 & 0 & 0 & 0 & \lambda_{Sx} & 0 & 0 & V/\overline{S} \\ \lambda_{Ly}S_{LK}^{y} & -\lambda_{Ly}S_{LK}^{y} & 0 & 0 & 0 & \lambda_{Ly} & \lambda_{Lz} & 0 \\ -\lambda_{Ky}S_{KL}^{y} & \lambda_{Ky}S_{KL}^{y} & 0 & 0 & \lambda_{Kx} & \lambda_{Ky} & 0 & 0 \\ 0 & 0 & 0 & 0 & 0 & 0 & 1 & 0 \\ 0 & 1 & 0 & -1 & 0 & -\frac{Y}{(Y-G)} & 0 & 0 \end{pmatrix} \begin{pmatrix} \hat{r} \\ \hat{w} \\ \hat{R} \\ \hat{P}_y \\ \hat{X} \\ \hat{Y} \\ \hat{Z} \\ \hat{V} \end{pmatrix} = \begin{pmatrix} 0 \\ 0 \\ \widehat{P_z^*} \\ 0 \\ e\hat{e} \\ \hat{\overline{K}} \\ \hat{\lambda} \\ \frac{-G\hat{G}}{(Y-G)} \end{pmatrix}. \quad (B.1)$$

$$\Delta = \theta_{Kx}\theta_{Tz}\frac{V}{\overline{S}}\lambda_{Ly}\lambda_{Kx}\left(\theta_{Ky} - \frac{Y}{(Y-G)}S_{LK}^{y}\right). \quad \text{Here, (B.2)}$$

Solving (A.1) by Cramer's rule the following expressions are obtained:

$$\hat{r} = 0. \quad (B.3)$$

$$\hat{w} = \frac{Ye\hat{e} - \lambda_{Ly}G\hat{G}}{\lambda_{Ly}\left[\theta_{Ky}(Y-G) - S_{LK}^{y}Y\right]}. \quad (B.4)$$

$$\hat{R} = -\frac{\left\{\lambda_{Ly}\widehat{P_z^*}(Y-G)\left(\theta_{Ly}+S_{LK}^y-1\right)+\theta_{Lz}Ye\hat{e}-\theta_{Lz}\lambda_{Ly}G\hat{G}\right\}}{\theta_{Tz}\lambda_{Ly}\left[\theta_{Ky}(Y-G)-S_{LK}^yY\right]}. \tag{B.5}$$

$$\widehat{P_y} = \frac{\theta_{Ly}\left\{Ye\hat{e}-\lambda_{Ly}G\hat{G}\right\}}{\lambda_{Ly}\left[\theta_{Ky}(Y-G)-S_{LK}^yY\right]}. \tag{B.6}$$

$$\hat{X} = \frac{\lambda_{Ky}e\hat{e}\left[(Y-G)\left(\theta_{Ly}-1\right)-S_{KL}^yY\right]+\lambda_{Ly}\lambda_{Ky}G\hat{G}\left(S_{LK}^y+S_{KL}^y\right)+\lambda_{Ly}\hat{\overline{K}}\left[(Y-G)\left(1-\theta_{Ly}\right)-S_{LK}^yY\right]}{\lambda_{Ly}\lambda_{Kx}\left[\theta_{Ky}(Y-G)-S_{LK}^yY\right]}. \tag{B.7}$$

$$\hat{Y} = \frac{-e\hat{e}(Y-G)\left(\theta_{Ly}-1\right)-\lambda_{Ly}S_{LK}^yG\hat{G}}{\lambda_{Ly}\left[\theta_{Ky}(Y-G)-S_{LK}^yY\right]}. \tag{B.8}$$

$$\hat{Z} = 0. \tag{B.9}$$

$$\hat{V} = -\lambda_{Sx}\frac{\lambda_{Ky}e\hat{e}\left[(Y-G)\left(\theta_{Ly}-1\right)-S_{KL}^yY\right]+\lambda_{Ly}\lambda_{Ky}G\hat{G}\left(S_{LK}^y+S_{KL}^y\right)+\lambda_{Ly}\hat{\overline{K}}\left[(Y-G)\left(1-\theta_{Ly}\right)-S_{LK}^yY\right]}{\frac{V}{\overline{S}}\lambda_{Ly}\lambda_{Kx}\left[\theta_{Ky}(Y-G)-S_{LK}^yY\right]}. \tag{B.10}$$

Using Equations (B.3)–(B.10), the following results are obtained for the comparative statics exercise:

B.1.1 Fall in Efficiency of Workers or Labour Scarcity

When $\hat{e} < 0$ and if $\left[\theta_{Ky}(Y-G)-S_{LK}^yY\right] < 0$, then we have:

$$\hat{r} = 0,$$

$$\hat{w} = \frac{Ye\hat{e}}{\lambda_{Ly}\left[\theta_{Ky}(Y-G)-S_{LK}^yY\right]} > 0,$$

$$\hat{R} = \frac{-\theta_{Lz}Ye\hat{e}}{\theta_{Tz}\lambda_{Ly}\left[\theta_{Ky}(Y-G)-S_{LK}^yY\right]} < 0,$$

$$\widehat{P}_y = \frac{\theta_{Ly} Y e \hat{e}}{\lambda_{Ly}\left[\theta_{Ky}\left(Y-G\right)-S_{LK}^{y}Y\right]} > 0,$$

$$\hat{X} = \frac{\lambda_{Ky} e \hat{e}\left[\left(Y-G\right)\left(\theta_{Ly}-1\right)-S_{KL}^{y}Y\right]}{\lambda_{Ly}\lambda_{Kx}\left[\theta_{Ky}\left(Y-G\right)-S_{LK}^{y}Y\right]} < 0,$$

$$\hat{Y} = \frac{-e\hat{e}\left(Y-G\right)\left(\theta_{Ly}-1\right)}{\lambda_{Ly}\left[\theta_{Ky}\left(Y-G\right)-S_{LK}^{y}Y\right]} > 0,$$

$$\hat{Z} = 0,$$

$$\hat{V} = \frac{-\lambda_{Sx}\lambda_{Ky} e \hat{e}\left[\left(Y-G\right)\left(\theta_{Ly}-1\right)-S_{KL}^{y}Y\right]}{\frac{V}{\overline{S}}\lambda_{Ly}\lambda_{Kx}\left[\theta_{Ky}\left(Y-G\right)-S_{LK}^{y}Y\right]} > 0.$$

B.1.2 Fall in Domestic Capital Formation

When $\hat{\overline{K}} < 0$ and if $\left[\theta_{Ky}\left(Y-G\right)-S_{LK}^{y}Y\right] < 0$, then we have

$$\hat{r} = 0,$$

$$\hat{w} = 0,$$

$$\hat{R} = 0,$$

$$\widehat{P}_y = 0,$$

$$\hat{X} = \frac{\hat{\overline{K}}\left[\left(Y-G\right)\left(1-\theta_{Ly}\right)-S_{LK}^{y}Y\right]}{\lambda_{Kx}\left[\theta_{Ky}\left(Y-G\right)-S_{LK}^{y}Y\right]} < 0,$$

$$\hat{Y} = 0,$$

$$\hat{Z} = 0,$$

$$\hat{V} = -\lambda_{Sx}\frac{\hat{\overline{K}}\left[\left(Y-G\right)\left(1-\theta_{Ly}\right)-S_{LK}^{y}Y\right]}{\frac{V}{\overline{S}}\lambda_{Kx}\left[\theta_{Ky}\left(Y-G\right)-S_{LK}^{y}Y\right]} > 0.$$

B.1.3 Reduction in the World Price of Exportable Commodity

When $\widehat{P_z^*} < 0$ and if $\theta_{Ly} + S_{LK}^y > 1$ and $\left[\theta_{Ky}(Y - G) - S_{LK}^y Y\right] < 0$, then we have

$$\hat{r} = \hat{w} = 0$$

$$\hat{R} = -\frac{\widehat{P_z^*}(Y - G)\left[\theta_{Ly} + S_{LK}^y - 1\right]}{\theta_{Tz}\left[\theta_{Ky}(Y - G) - S_{LK}^y Y\right]} < 0,$$

$$\widehat{P_y} = \hat{X} = \hat{Y} = \hat{Z} = \hat{V} = 0.$$

B.1.4 Increase in Real Government Expenditure

When $\hat{G} > 0$ and if $\left[\theta_{Ky}(Y - G) - S_{LK}^y Y\right] < 0$, then we have

$$\hat{r} = 0,$$

$$\hat{w} = \frac{-G\hat{G}}{\left[\theta_{Ky}(Y - G) - S_{LK}^y Y\right]} > 0,$$

$$\hat{R} = \frac{\theta_{Lz} G\hat{G}}{\theta_{Tz}\left[\theta_{Ky}(Y - G) - S_{LK}^y Y\right]} < 0,$$

$$\widehat{P_y} = \frac{-\theta_{Ly} G\hat{G}}{\left[\theta_{Ky}(Y - G) - S_{LK}^y Y\right]} > 0,$$

$$\hat{X} = \frac{\lambda_{Ky} G\hat{G}\left(S_{LK}^y + S_{KL}^y\right)}{\lambda_{Kx}\left[\theta_{Ky}(Y - G) - S_{LK}^y Y\right]} < 0,$$

$$\hat{Y} = \frac{-S_{LK}^y G\hat{G}}{\left[\theta_{Ky}(Y - G) - S_{LK}^y Y\right]} > 0,$$

$$\hat{Z} = 0,$$

$$\hat{V} = \frac{-\lambda_{Ky}\lambda_{Sx} G\hat{G}\left(S_{LK}^y + S_{KL}^y\right)}{\frac{V}{S}\lambda_{Kx}\left[\theta_{Ky}(Y - G) - S_{LK}^y Y\right]} > 0.$$

Notes

1 With globalisation, market reforms for economic liberalisation not only allowed developing countries to catch up to their developed counterparts, but they also created a new elite within developing countries, hence increasing income disparity within the country; see Bourguignon (2016).
2 See Round and Whalley (2009); Bhagwati (2004).
3 See Dhanani (2004).
4 See Dasgupta & Rajeev (2020); Dev & Sengupta (2020).
5 ETNOWNEWS (2020), https://www.timesnownews.com/business-economy/economy/article/how-the-covid-19-outbreak-has-affected-the-joblessness-rate-in-india-explained-in-4-charts/634284.
6 "Post-COVID conditions are a wide range of new, returning, or ongoing health problems people can experience four or more weeks after first being infected with the virus that causes COVID-19", Centers for Disease Control and Prevention.
7 According to the IMF, India's fiscal package until September 11, 2020, amounted to 7% of the GDP with above-the-line measures or actual spending amounting to 1.8% and an additional 5.2% from below-the-line measures.
8 https://www.indiaspend.com/governance/migrant-workers-no-reliable-data-or-policy-737499.
9 Skilled workers are assumed to be unemployed also when they are actively looking for jobs in a reference period, while unskilled workers who cannot afford these long periods of job search are fully employed at all times.
10 Refer to Appendix A.2.1.
11 Refer to Appendix A.2.2.
12 Refer to Appendix A.2.3.
13 Refer to Appendix A.2.4.
14 See Appendix B.1.1.
15 See Appendix B.1.3 for detailed derivation.
16 Refer to Appendix B.1.4.

References

Bhagwati, J. (2004). *In Defense of Globalization*, Oxford University Press, New York, NY.

Bourguignon, F. (2016). Inequality and Globalization: How the Rich Get Richer as the Poor Catch Up. *Foreign Affairs*, *95*, 11–16.

Chakrabarti, A. (2000, December). Does Trade Cause Inequality? *Journal of Economic Development*, *25*(2), 1–21. Retrieved August 2021, from https://core.ac.uk/download/pdf/6294609.pdf.

Chaudhuri, S., Mahata, S., & Chaudhuri, S. (2021). COVID-19 Disaster and Employment Generation Program in a Developing Economy. *Journal of Social and Economic Development*, *24*(2), 46–64.

Chaudhuri, S., & Yabuuchi, S. (2007). Foreign Capital and Skilled-Unskilled Wage Inequality in a Developing Economy with Non-traded Goods. *MPRA Paper from University Library of Munich*, Germany.

Dasgupta, D., & Rajeev, M. (2020, May 30). Paradox of a Supply Constrained Keynesian Equilibrium the COVID-19 Case. *Economics and Political Weekly*, *55*(22), 22–27.

Dasgupta, K., & Murali, S. (2020, May). Pandemic Containment and Inequality in a Developing Economy. IIM Bangalore, *Working Paper No: 613*.

Dev, S. M., & Sengupta, R. (2020). Covid-19: Impact on the Indian Economy. Indira Gandhi Institute of Development Research, *Working Papers 2020-013*.

Dhanani, S. (2004). *Unemployment and Underemployment in Indonesia, 1976–2000: Paradoxes and Issues*. International Labour Office, Geneva.

Marjit, S., & Ahuja, R. (2021, November 6). Liberalizing Trade and Capital Flows and the Wage Gap: Does Sequencing Matter? *Open Economies Review*.

Marjit, S., Beladi, H., & Chakrabarti, A. (2004). Trade and Wage Inequality in Developing Countries. *Economic Inquiry*, 42(2), 295–303. Retrieved August 2021.

Rojas-Vallejos, J., & Turnovsky, S. J. (2017, September). Tariff Reduction and Income Inequality: Some Empirical Evidence. *Open Economies Review*, *28*(4), 603–631.

Round, J., & John, W. (2009, February). Globalisation and Poverty: Implications of South Asian Experience for the Wider Debate. *IDS Bulletin*, *35*. https://doi.org/10.1111/j.1759-5436.2004.tb00104.x.

10 Trade Liberalisation and Environmental Regulation in Developing Economy

Dibyendu Banerjee and Purbasha Bhattacharyya

10.1 Introduction

Skilled–unskilled wage differential and unemployment have been two widely discussed issues over the last few decades. Most of the developing countries have been adopting liberalised policies to attract a substantial amount of foreign capital in the post-reform period. According to the United Nations Conference on Trade and Development (UNCTAD) (2013) report, there was a record 52% of global foreign direct investment (FDI) inflows in developing countries increasing from 637 billion dollars in 2010 to 703 billion dollars in 2012. This inflow of FDI in developing countries exceeded that in developed countries for the first time ever in 2012. According to the UNCTAD (2020) report, the inflow of FDI in India has increased by 16% during 2018–2019. Economic liberalism involves not only liberalised investment policy resulting in higher foreign direct investment but also removal of the protectionist policy like reduction in the import tariff.

There exist numerous works in the context of developing countries that attempt to determine the implications of economic reform on wage inequality. Empirical investigations demonstrating that skilled–unskilled wage gap accentuated in developing countries include studies of Feenstra and Hanson (1997), Robbins (1996), Wood (1998), Khan (1998) and Banga (2005). However, the experience of East Asian countries between the 1960s and 1970s is consistent with the view that a greater openness tends to reduce the skilled–unskilled wage gap in developing countries.[1] Esquivel and Lopez (2003) have also shown that trade liberalisation lowers wage inequality in Mexico. Considering the data of more than 100 countries for the period 1980–2002, Figini and Gorg (2011) analysed the relationship between the inflow of FDI and wage inequality. Their study produced different conclusions for different levels of development (i.e., for developed and developing countries).

The theoretical literature explaining the deteriorating wage inequality in developing countries as a result of international mobility of factors includes works of Marjit et al. (2004), Marjit and Kar (2005), Anwar (2006), Yabuuchi and Chaudhuri (2007), Oladi and Beladi (2007), Beladi et al.

DOI: 10.4324/9781003375050-10

(2008), Chaudhuri and Banerjee (2010), Gupta and Dutta (2010), Anwar and Sun (2015) and Pi and Zhou (2015). They have shown how trade liberalisation and inflows of foreign capital might produce unfavourable effects on wage inequality. In another paper, Das (2002) considered the impact of FDI on the relative wage for a developing economy and concluded that, as opposed to Feenstra and Hanson (1997), FDI would cause the relative wage to fall.

Persistence of urban unemployment is another major problem in the developing world. The Harris and Todaro (1970) type of model is one way to explain such unemployment of unskilled labour in a general equilibrium framework. Existing studies analyse the role that different development policies play in reducing urban unemployment. These include works of Yabuuchi and Beladi (2001), Marjit and Acharyya (2003), Chaudhuri (2007), Yabuuchi (2007), Chaudhuri (2008, 2004) and Chaudhuri and Banerjee (2010). But none of the above-referenced theoretical papers has examined the policy of environmental regulation in the determination of the skilled–unskilled wage inequality as well as urban unemployment in developing countries.

Pollution control in recent times is considered one of the most important policy measures facing the policy-makers of developing countries. Environmentalists are very much concerned about the state of the natural environment in developing countries. For sustainable development, it is necessary to adopt proper measures that can continue the production process without creating pollution at an extreme level. Most of the productions generate some sort of pollution which can be modelled either as an *input* or as an *output*. Modelling pollution as an output captures the idea that "good output" cannot be produced unless pollution (bad output) is generated. According to this view, pollution is a by-product of the production process. Pollution can also be viewed as a proxy for the use of environmental resources, and more use of which will lower environmental quality. Those who model pollution as an *input* argue that by reducing pollution, the output can be reduced and in this sense pollution can be treated as an input into the production process. It is often thought that any gains from different economic policies would be substantially outweighed by the damage it would do to the environment through pollution and loss of natural resources. Some theoretical studies have investigated the impact of different economic policies incorporating pollution control in terms of general equilibrium structure. Yohe (1979) examined the impacts of pollution control on the sizes of the polluting and non-polluting sectors and national income in a two-sector general-equilibrium model with full employment. Yu and Ingene (1982) analysed the effects of pollution control on unemployment and national income in a two-sector general-equilibrium model with rigid wages. Wang (1990) investigated the effects of pollution control on the wage rate, the rental rate and national income in a two-sector general-equilibrium model with unemployment and the sector-specific rigid wage. Beladi, Frasca and Chou (1999) constructed a three-sector general-equilibrium model and analysed how pollution control affects output, income and unemployment. Pan and Zhou (2013) developed a three-sector general-equilibrium model accommodating environmental pollution and investigated the impact of international migration of factors on wage inequality. In their model, the urban low-skill sector generates environmental pollution, which deteriorates the rural environment and thereby influences the production of agricultural sector. Pi and Zhang (2017) analysed how foreign capital and pollution control influence skilled–unskilled wage inequality in developing countries in terms of a three-sector general-equilibrium model. However, they emphasised the role of the quantity instrument in determining the skilled–unskilled wage inequality.

None of the above-mentioned studies have considered the impact of price instrument (as a means of pollution control) like changes in environmental tax in the context of developing economy, plagued by a significant degree of skilled–unskilled wage inequality and high levels of unemployment of unskilled labour. The present analysis is devoted to filling in the above vacuum in the theoretical literature using a three-sector, specific-factor general-equilibrium model incorporating environmental pollution. Our research focus here is to investigate how trade liberalisation, the inflow of FDI and pollution tax influence the skilled–unskilled wage inequality and unemployment in a developing country. Our study finds that foreign capital inflow produces a favourable impact on the average unskilled wage of the economy and improves relative wage inequality unequivocally although the unemployment situation of unskilled labour may worsen. Trade liberalisation, on the other hand, aggravates wage inequality but improves the urban unemployment problem unconditionally. Besides, the imposition of environmental tax by the government in an attempt to improve environmental quality may lower the magnitude of unemployment of unskilled labour and is also likely to affect the income of unskilled workers adversely and thereby aggravating wage inequality. A proper balance among various policies should thus be made keeping in mind the interests of the average unskilled workers of the economy.

The rest of this chapter is organised as follows: we establish the basic theoretical model featuring the Harris–Todaro (HT) type urban unemployment in Section 10.2; in Section 10.3, we conduct a comparative static analysis to investigate the impacts exerted by the foreign direct investment, import tariff and pollution tax on the skilled–unskilled wage inequality and urban unemployment. Concluding remarks are given in Section 10.4.

10.2 The Model

Let us now present a simple model that can be used to examine the determinants of skilled–unskilled wage inequality and urban unemployment in less developed countries (LDCs, henceforth). We assume a small, open, developing economy consists of two broad sectors: rural and urban. The urban sector is again sub-divided into two sub-sectors: high skilled and low skilled. Thus, as a whole, we have three sectors, a rural agricultural sector (sector 1), an urban low-skilled manufacturing sector (sector 2) and an urban high-skilled sector (sector 3). The rural sector, which is an export sector, produces the primary agricultural commodity, X_1, using specific input land (N) and unskilled labour (L).[2] Sector 2, which is an urban low-skilled sector, produces manufacturing product, X_2, by means of capital (K), unskilled labour (L) and environmental input (E). As this urban sector is an import-competing sector, it is assumed to be protected by an import tariff. The urban high-skilled sector uses capital (K) and sector-specific input-skilled labour (S) to produce export commodity, X_3. So, sectors 1 and 3 are two export sectors, whereas sector 2 is tariff-protected, import-competing sector. This type of structure is very appropriate for developing countries like India which exports both agricultural products and high-skilled products like computer software or IT-related services. Production functions of the three sectors can be expressed as follows: $X_1 = F^1(L_1, N)$, $X_2 = F^2(L_2, K_2, E)$ and $X_3 = F^3(S, K_3)$. The production function of each of the three sectors satisfies all the standard neo-classical properties including constant returns to scale (CRS).

Environmental input, E, can be viewed as the factor of production used by the urban unskilled sector that will lower environmental quality. Hence, it can be treated as the "dirty input" or "pollution". Following Yohe (1979) and Yu and Ingene (1982), we treat pollution as an input in the production process so that compensation is paid by the polluter (or pollution-emitting firm) for adversely affecting environmental quality. If pollution is a factor of production, then environmental tax, τ, can be treated as its price[3]. Our model assumes that the government imposes an environmental tax (τ) on the use of input E by the urban manufacturing sector. One justification for assuming this type of urban-polluting sector is that in many developing countries urban unskilled sectors are engaged in activities (like printing, chemical works, etc.) which are emission intensive. Likewise, the production of more X_2 generates more pollution here; although there is no essential difference analytically between treating E as an input and as a joint product.[4] For simplicity, we assume that the market for pollution does not exist. The degree of substitutability between pollution and other factors of production in urban low-skilled sector will thus play a crucial role in this model.

Capital is perfectly mobile between sectors 2 and 3; while unskilled labour is imperfectly mobile between 1 and 2. Land, skilled labour and environmental inputs are specific to rural, urban high-skilled and urban low-skilled sectors, respectively. Unskilled workers in the urban low-skilled sector receive institutionally given[5,6] wage rate ($\bar{W}$), while their counterpart in the rural sector earns competitive wage, W, which is market determined and $\bar{W} > W$. This wage differential leads to rural–urban migration. In the urban sector, unskilled workers either earn $\bar{W}$ (if employed) or no wage (if not employed). In this situation, rural workers have two alternatives – staying in the rural sector in order to secure a job at a low-wage rate or migrating to the urban low-skilled sector in order to seek a job at a high-wage rate at the risk of unemployment. The two wage rates $\bar{W}$ and W are connected by Harris and Todaro (1970) migration equilibrium condition such that expected urban wage (which is the product of the urban unskilled wage and the probability of securing a job in this sector) is equal to the rural sector wage when the economy is in equilibrium. The migration process comes to an end when this equilibrium is attained. Hence, there exists Harris–Todaro (HT) type unemployment of unskilled labour in this model. All other factors of production (except unskilled labour) are fully employed. Capital consists of both domestic and foreign counterparts, which are perfect substitutes. This assumption has widely been used in the theoretical literature on trade and development. All markets except the urban unskilled labour market are perfectly competitive. Input coefficients are of variable type. The representative firm maximises profit. Finally, commodity 1 is chosen as the numeraire. Our theoretical structure, thus, incorporates some of the salient features of the developing economy, e.g., factor market distortion, dual economy feature, urban unemployment and also environmental pollution.

Given the perfectly competitive commodity markets, zero-profit conditions relating to the three sectors are expressed as follows:

$$a_{L1}W + a_{N1}R = 1, \tag{10.1}$$

$$a_{L2}\bar{W} + a_{K2}r + a_{E2}\tau = P_2(1+t), \tag{10.2}$$

$$a_{S3}W_S + a_{K3}r = P_3. \tag{10.3}$$

As all the commodities are internationally traded, P_i's are exogenously given due to small open economy assumption. W_S, $\bar{W}$ and W represent wage rates of the skilled labour employed by the urban high-skill sector, the unskilled labour employed by the urban low-skill sector and the unskilled labour employed by the agricultural sector, respectively. R is the rate of return to land, r is the interest rate of the capital and τ represents the shadow price of pollution. a_{ji} denotes the per-unit requirement of the jth input in the ith sector, with i = 1, 2, 3 and j= L, K, E, N. Notation S_{ji}^k represents the degree of substitution between factors in sector k. For example, $S_{LL}^1 = \left(\frac{W}{a_{L1}}\right)\left(\frac{\partial a_{L1}}{\partial W}\right)$, $S_{LN}^1 = \left(\frac{R}{a_{L1}}\right)\left(\frac{\partial a_{L1}}{\partial R}\right)$, etc. $S_{ji}^k > 0$ for $j \neq k$; and $S_{jj}^k < 0$.

Besides, we define $\theta_{ji}\left(= \frac{w_j a_{ji}}{P_i}\right)$ and $\lambda_{ji}\left(= \frac{a_{ji}X_i}{J_i}\right)$ as the distributive and allocative shares of the jth input in the ith sector which would be used subsequently in stating the results. Notation '$\wedge$' represents the proportionate change. Finally, t denotes the ad-valorem rate of tariff imposed on the import of commodity 2. Thus, two types of distortion, labour market distortion in the form of unionised wage and commodity market distortion that takes the form of a tariff on import, have been introduced in the model.

The market-clearing conditions for skilled labour, unskilled labour, capital, land and environmental input are given as follows:

$$a_{S3}X_3 = \bar{S}, \tag{10.4}$$

$$a_{L2}X_2 + a_{L1}X_1 + L_U = \bar{L}, \tag{10.5}$$

$$a_{K2}X_2 + a_{K3}X_3 = \bar{K}_D + K_F, \tag{10.6}$$

$$a_{N1}X_1 = \bar{N}, \tag{10.7}$$

$$a_{E2}X_2 = E. \tag{10.8}$$

$\bar{S}, \bar{L}, \bar{K}_D$ and $\bar{N}$ represent endowments of skilled labour, unskilled labour, domestic capital and land, respectively. K_F represents the amount of foreign capital endowment. An inflow of foreign capital is captured by an increase in the endowment of K_F which is a perfect substitute for K_D.

In the unskilled labour endowment equation (10.5), L_U measures the extent of unemployment of unskilled labour. We know that in an HT framework, the unskilled labour allocation mechanism is such that in the labour market equilibrium, the rural wage rate (W) equals the expected wage income in the urban sector.[7] Since the probability of finding a job in the urban low-skill sector is $\left(\dfrac{a_{L2}X_2}{a_{L2}X_2 + L_U}\right)$, the expected unskilled wage in the urban low-skill sector is $\bar{W}\left(\dfrac{a_{L2}X_2}{a_{L2}X_2 + L_U}\right)$. Therefore, the rural–urban migration equilibrium condition of unskilled labour can be expressed as

$$\bar{W}\left(\frac{a_{L2}X_2}{a_{L2}X_2 + L_U}\right) = W \tag{10.9}$$

Using (10.5), (10.9) can be rewritten as

$$\frac{\bar{W}}{W} a_{L2}X_2 + a_{L1}X_1 = \bar{L} \tag{10.9a}$$

In this general equilibrium structure, there are nine endogenous variables, namely, W, r, R, W_S, E, L_U, X_1, X_2 and X_3; and the same number of independent equations, namely, (10.1)–(10.8) and (10.9a); so the system is determinate. The production structure does not possess the decomposition property; and so factor prices cannot be solved independent of factor endowments. The working of the general equilibrium model is as follows.

r is found from Equation (10.2) as the values of $\bar{W}$ and P_2 are exogenously given; and t and τ are the policy parameters of the government. Once r is determined, W_S is obtained from Equation (10.3). Given the endowment of skilled labour, X_3 can be solved from Equation (10.4). We can get X_2 from Equation (10.6), given the value of X_3 and the total endowment of capital. Equations (10.1), (10.7) and (10.9a) simultaneously solve for W, R and X_1, given the values of τ, t and K_F. L_U and E are then found from Equations (10.5) and (10.8), respectively.

10.3 The Comparative Static Analysis

In this section we shall examine the consequences of different economic policies, e.g., stringent environmental policy, liberalised investment and trade policies on skilled–unskilled wage inequality and urban unemployment. Investment and trade liberalisation are captured through the inflow of FDI and the reduction of protection of domestic industries, strict environmental regulation, on the other hand, takes the form of an increase in pollution tax by the government. Although different economic policies might be undertaken concurrently in a developing economy, to fix our ideas we may consider their effects one by one.

10.3.1 Impact on Wage Inequality

Following Chaudhuri et al. (2018), Pi and Zhang (2017), Pi-Zhou (2013, 2014), Pan and Zhou (2013), Chaudhuri and Banerjee (2010), Beladi et al. (2008) and Marjit and Kar (2005), the skilled–unskilled wage gap improves (worsens) in absolute terms if the gap between W_S and W falls (rises). On the other hand, wage inequality improves (deteriorates) in both absolute and relative terms if $\left(\hat{W}_S - \hat{W}\right) < (>) 0$, where $\hat{W}_S = \dfrac{dW_S}{W_S}$.

10.3.1.1 Impact of Reduction in Tariff Rate on Wage Inequality

Differentiating Equations (10.2) and (10.3) after substitution, we get

$$\hat{W}_S = \left(\frac{\theta_{K3}\theta_{E2}}{\theta_{K2}\theta_{S3}}\right)\hat{\tau} - \left(\frac{\theta_{K3}T}{\theta_{S3}\theta_{K2}}\right)\hat{t} \tag{10.10}$$

Here we assume $\hat{K}_F = \hat{\tau} = 0;\ \hat{t} < 0$.

Putting this condition in (10.10),

$$\frac{\hat{W}_S}{\hat{t}} = -\left(\frac{\theta_{K3}T}{\theta_{S3}\theta_{K2}}\right) < 0. \tag{10.10a}$$

From the land endowment equation (10.7), we have,

$$\hat{X}_1 + \frac{S^1_{NL}}{\theta_{N1}}\hat{W} = 0 \tag{10.11}$$

Differentiating Equations (10.9) and (10.6), after some minor adjustments the following equation can be obtained:

$$A\hat{W} = -B\hat{\tau} + \left(\frac{\lambda^*_{L2}k}{\lambda_{K2}}\right)\hat{K}_F + C\hat{t}, \tag{10.12}$$

where A > 0, C > 0 and B > 0 if $\left(\frac{S^2_{LK}}{\theta_{K2}} > \frac{S^2_{LE}}{\theta_{E2}}\right)$.

Exact expressions of constants A, B and C are given in Appendix A. Solving (10.11) and (10.12), it is easy to show

$$\frac{\hat{W}}{\hat{t}} = \frac{\frac{\lambda^*_{L2}T}{\theta_{K2}}\left[\left(S^2_{LK} - S^2_{KK}\right) + \frac{\lambda_{K3}}{\lambda_{K2}\theta_{S3}}\left(S^3_{KS} + S^3_{SK}\right)\right.}{\lambda^*_{L2} + \frac{\lambda_{L1}}{\theta_{N1}}\left(S^1_{NL} + S^1_{LN}\right)} > 0. \tag{10.13}$$

Using these expressions, the following proposition can be ascertained.

> **Proposition 10.1**: Removal of the protectionist policy accentuates skilled–unskilled wage inequality.

The above proposition can be explained in the following manner. A reduction in import tariff as a result of trade liberalisation lowers the domestic price ($P^*_2 = P_2(1+t)$) of import-competing product X_2. This leads to a contraction of sector 2. It reduces the demand for labour, as well as capital, in that sector. Sector 2 will thus release capital and unskilled labour. This released capital will go to urban high-skilled sector that lowers the return to capital and leads to an expansion of that sector. Demand for skilled labour, which is a specific factor in sector 3, will rise leading to an increase in the skilled wage rate. A lower return to capital, again, will encourage the producers of sector 2 to adopt relatively less labour-intensive technology that also adds to the excess supply of unskilled labour. As sector 2 contracts, employment opportunity in that sector gets reduced leading to a fall in the expected urban unskilled wage. Rural sector wage, which is equal to the expected unskilled wage according to HT envelope condition, will fall as a consequence. Trade liberalisation thus produces depressing effects on the average unskilled wage of the urban sector. Skilled–unskilled wage inequality worsens unequivocally. The result does not hinge on the capital intensity ranking between the two sectors.[8]

10.3.1.2 Impact of Pollution Tax on Wage Inequality

In this section, we discuss the impact on wage inequality of an increase in pollution tax or shadow price of pollution assuming $\hat{K}_F = \hat{t} = 0;\ \hat{\tau} > 0$. The result obtained can be summarised in terms of Proposition 10.2.

> **Proposition 10.2:** Stricter environmental regulation by the government in terms of an increase in pollution tax rate produces an ambiguous effect on skilled–unskilled wage inequality. Wage inequality worsens if $\frac{S_{LK}^2}{\theta_{K2}} > \frac{S_{LE}^2}{\theta_{E2}}$.

The above proposition can be explained as follows. An increase in pollution tax raises the cost of production of the urban unskilled polluting sector. Sector 2 will contract as a consequence. This will become evident from the following expression.[9]

$$\frac{\hat{X}_2}{\hat{\tau}} = -\left[\left(\frac{1-\theta_{L2}}{\theta_{K2}}\right)S_{KE}^2 + \frac{\theta_{E2}S_{KL}^2}{\theta_{K2}} + \frac{\lambda_{K3}\theta_{E2}}{\lambda_{K2}\theta_{K2}\theta_{S3}}\left(S_{KS}^3 + S_{SK}^3\right)\right] < 0. \tag{10.14}$$

Demand for unskilled labour employed by this sector will reduce (call it **force I**). Capital demand falls as well. As capital is perfectly mobile between sectors 2 and 3, this will lead to an excess supply of capital in sector 3. Sector 3 expands leading to an increased demand for sector-specific, factor-skilled labour. The skilled wage rate of the economy rises as a consequence, which is clear from the following expression which can easily be derived from Equation (10.3).

$$\frac{\hat{W}_S}{\hat{\tau}} = \left(\frac{\theta_{K3}\theta_{E2}}{\theta_{S3}\theta_{K2}}\right) > 0. \tag{10.15}$$

Again imposition of pollution tax makes environmental input, *E*, relatively costly. Producers of sector 2 will substitute *E* by relatively cheaper input and unskilled labour. Consequently, unit unskilled labour demand, a_{L2}, rises and unit demand of environmental input, a_{E2}, falls leading to an increase in the demand for unskilled labour in sector 2 (**force II**). So, the degree of substitutability between factors *L* and *E* in sector 2 (S_{LE}^2) plays a crucial role in determining the strength of force II. The higher the value of S_{LE}^2, the easier will be the substitution possibility between *L* and *E* in the urban low-skilled sector. Thus, the demand for unskilled labour in sector 2 will increase more as a result of an increase in τ.

Also, from Equation (10.2), it can be easily shown that the return to capital plummets as the pollution tax rises. This is evident from the following expression:

$$\frac{\hat{r}}{\hat{\tau}} = -\frac{\theta_{E2}}{\theta_{K2}} < 0. \tag{10.16}$$

Capital thus become relatively cheaper, which will impel the producers of sector 2 to save on capital input by adopting relatively more capital-intensive technology. Demand for unskilled labour falls as a consequence (call it **force III**). The value of degree of substitutability between factors L and K in sector 2, S_{LK}^2, also plays a vital role in determining the magnitude of reduction in unskilled labour demand. If the value of S_{LK}^2 is high, then the demand for unskilled labour will fall relatively more as a result of a fall in the rental price of capital. Hence, the impact on a_{L2} is uncertain as forces II and III are working on it in opposite direction.

Thus, three different forces are acting on overall unskilled labour employment in different ways. Forces I and III put contractionary pressure on employment; force II does the opposite. The net impact on the urban employment of unskilled labour is thus uncertain, as that will be determined by the relative strength of these effects. The probability of getting employed in sector 2, $\left(\frac{a_{L2}X_2}{a_{L2}X_2 + L_U}\right)$,, thus changes, as a_{L2}, X_2 and employment possibilities, all are changing. The expected urban wage for a prospective rural migrant for every unskilled worker also changes, but the direction of change is uncertain. Hence, W will change to satisfy the HT migration equilibrium condition given in Equation (10.9). The lower the degree of substitutability between labour and environmental input in sector 2 (S_{LE}^2), and/or the higher the degree of substitutability between labour and capital (S_{LK}^2), the higher will be the possibility of reduction of W as a result of an increase in pollution tax. Hence, the impact on unskilled wage and skilled–unskilled wage inequality is uncertain. Ultimately W will fall aggravating the wage inequality[10] if the sufficient condition as stated in the above proposition is satisfied.

10.3.1.3 Impact of FDI on Wage Inequality

In this subsection, we consider the impact of investment reform encapsulated through an inflow of foreign capital (FDI) on wage inequality. Hence, we assume $\hat{\tau} = \hat{t} = 0$; $\hat{K}_F > 0$. Though an inflow of foreign capital (K_F) increases the availability of capital endowment for the production of sectors 2 and 3, the return to capital and skilled labour will not be affected, as the equilibrium values of W_S and r are determined from Equations (10.2) and (10.3), given the exogenously determined unionised unskilled wage. Hence, $\frac{\hat{W}_S}{\hat{K}_F} = \frac{\hat{r}}{\hat{K}_F} = 0$. Once W_S and r are solved, a_{S3} is determined as a function of factor prices, W_S and r. Given the endowment of skilled labour, X_3 can be obtained from full employment condition (10.4). Clearly, the inflow of foreign capital will not affect the output of the high-skilled urban sector, i.e., $\frac{\hat{X}_3}{\hat{K}_F} = 0$. So the entire foreign capital will be absorbed by sector 2 and will expand as a result. This becomes clear from the expression $\frac{\hat{X}_2}{\hat{K}_F} = \left(\frac{k}{\lambda_{K2}}\right) > 0$.[11] $a_{L2}(\bar{W}, r, \tau)$ also remains unchanged as factor prices are not changing. The employment scenario of unskilled labour in sector 2 thus improves, leading to an increase in the probability of getting job $\left(\frac{a_{L2}X_2}{a_{L2}X_2 + L_U}\right)$, there. The average unskilled wage, which is also equal to the rural sector wage, accentuates. Hence, unskilled workers will be benefited as a result of this liberalised investment policy. The wage inequality unquestionably improves.[12] Factor intensity ranking condition between two capital using sectors is not required for predicting the outcomes of FDI inflow on wage inequality. The following proposition summarises the result.

> **Proposition 10.3:** The relative wage inequality unambiguously improves as a result of inflows of FDI.

10.3.2 Impact on Urban Unemployment of Unskilled Labour

Our next task is to analyse the outcomes of the aforementioned liberalisation policies on the level of urban unemployment. An increase in the environmental tax, imposed as a price instrument by the government, on the unemployment of unskilled labour in the urban area, will also be examined first. Subtraction of Equation (10.5) from Equation (10.9a) yields

$$L_U = a_{L2}X_2\left(\frac{\bar{W} - W}{W}\right) \tag{10.9b}$$

Differentiating Equation (10.9b) we can get Equation (10.17)

$$\hat{L}_U = \left[\left(\hat{X}_2 + \hat{a}_{L2}\right) - \left(\frac{\bar{W}}{\bar{W} - W}\right)\hat{W}\right] \tag{10.17}$$

From this equation, the following proposition can be established.[13]

> **Proposition 10.4:** Urban unemployment problem of unskilled labour may (i) improve following a reduction in tariff rate; (ii) aggravate due to the inflow of foreign capital; and (iii) reduce owing to an increase in pollution tax if $\left[\frac{\lambda_{L1}}{\theta_{N1}}\left(S_{LN}^1 + S_{NL}^1\right) > \left(\frac{\bar{W}\lambda_{L2}}{\bar{W} - W}\right)\right]$.

The proposition can be explained in the following manner.

Trade liberalisation in terms of a reduction in import tariff leads to a contraction of urban unskilled sector which has already been discussed in Proposition 10.1. The rate of return to capital also falls leading to a rise in $\left(\frac{\bar{W}}{r}\right)$. a_{L2}, unit labour demand coefficient in sector 2, decreases as a consequence. Employment of labour in that sector, $a_{L2}X_2$, shrinks. The probability of getting job is $\left(\frac{a_{L2}X_2}{a_{L2}X_2 + L_U}\right)$, and hence the expected urban wage of a job seeker falls which leads to a reverse migration from urban to rural sector. This is the centrifugal force which improves the extent of urban unemployment.[14] Again rural wage rate falls as a result of the reduction in tariff rate which will be clear if one looks at Equation (10.13). This drives the rural unskilled workers to move away from the rural sector to join the urban unemployment pool. This is centripetal force which worsens the urban unemployment situation. In Equation (10.17), the term $\left(\hat{X}_2 + \hat{a}_{L2}\right)$ represents centrifugal force, whereas $\left(\frac{W}{\bar{W} - W}\right)\hat{W}$ represents the magnitude of centripetal force. Clearly, centrifugal and centripetal forces work in the opposite direction to each other. If the magnitude of the centrifugal force is stronger, the economy will experience an improving unemployment situation in the urban sector after adopting this policy of tariff reform.

An increase in pollution tax rate as a measure of stricter environmental regulation leads to a contraction in the polluting urban low-skill sector and expansion in high-skill labour-intensive sector 3. The impact on unit labour demand in sector 2, $a_{L2}\left(\bar{W}, r, \tau\right)$, and rural unskilled wage are not certain as explained in Proposition 10.2. Both will fall under the sufficient condition $\left(\frac{S_{LK}^2}{\theta_{K2}} > \frac{S_{LE}^2}{\theta_{E2}}\right)$.[15] Thus, the direction of both the centrifugal force, indicated by the sign of $\left(\hat{X}_2 + \hat{a}_{L2}\right)$, and the centripetal force, indicated by the sign of $\hat{W}$, as a result of an increase in pollution tax, become uncertain. The impact on L_U is thus not definite. If $\left(\frac{S_{LK}^2}{\theta_{K2}} > \frac{S_{LE}^2}{\theta_{E2}}\right)$ holds, then X_2, a_{L2} and W will fall as a result of an increase in τ. The centrifugal force will reduce urban unemployment and centripetal force will do the reverse. The former effect will outweigh the latter, improving the urban unemployment situation, if the condition stated in the above proposition is satisfied.

Let us now discuss the impact of liberalised investment policy on the extent of urban unemployment. Skilled wage rate and return to capital, which are determined independent of factor endowments, will not change as a result of an *inflow of FDI*. The unit labour demand coefficient in sector 2, $a_{L2}\left(\bar{W}, r, \tau\right)$, will remain unaffected as both unskilled wage rate and return to capital are not changing. The output of high-skilled sector remains constant (which is also evident from Equation (D.2) given in Appendix D). This leads to an expansion of low-skill urban manufacturing sector as the entire excess supply of capital will be absorbed by this sector only. Thus, centrifugal force works in a negative direction, in this situation, which will be clear if one looks at Equation (10.17). The job availability in sector 2 expands as a consequence. The expected urban wage of a prospective rural migrant, $\left(\dfrac{\bar{W}}{1+\dfrac{L_U}{a_{L2}X_2}}\right)$, increases, as the probability of getting a job in this sector raises for every unskilled worker. This lures the rural workers to move into the urban sector, producing adverse impact on urban unemployment.

On the other hand, an inflow of foreign capital raises the rural sector wage.[16] This prevents rural workers from migrating into the urban sector. The centripetal force will thus produce a positive impact on urban unemployment. Clearly, these are two opposite effects that determine the size of the unemployed urban unskilled workforce. Hence, the impact of FDI inflow on urban unemployment is ambiguous. If the impact of an increase in the rural unskilled wage rate (centripetal force) is less strong than the expansionary impact of sector 2 (centrifugal force), then an exogenous increase (decrease) in FDI raises (lowers) the unemployment of unskilled labour.[17]

10.4 An Extension of the Model

In this section we replace the traditional rural sector by an advanced rural sector which uses capital instead of land along with unskilled labour. Thus, modern agricultural sector now produces export good X_1 using primary inputs capital and labour. The production function of this sector will be replaced by $X_1 = F^1(L_1, K_1)$. Capital is now perfectly mobile among all three sectors of the economy. This assumption is not new in this literature because many papers like Marjit and Kar (2005), Oladi and Beladi (2007), Yabuuchi and Chadhuri (2009), Gupta and Dutta (2010), Zhang (2013) and Pi and Chen (2016) have considered capital mobility in all the sectors of the economy.

Zero-profit condition of the rural sector will change in the following way,

$$a_{L1}W + a_{K1}r = 1 \tag{10.1a}$$

The system now becomes decomposable such that the values of factor prices will be determined from the price system alone, independent of the values of factor endowments. So any change in factor endowment will leave factor prices unaltered.

Equation (10.6), showing full employment of capital, will now be replaced by (10.6a),

$$a_{K1}X_1 + a_{K2}X_2 + a_{K3}X_3 = \bar{K}_D + K_F \tag{10.6a}$$

As capital is perfectly mobile between all three sectors, it is sensible to assume that the urban manufacturing sector (sector 2) is more capital-intensive relative to unskilled labour vis-à-vis rural sector (sector 1) in both physical and value sense. This implies $\left(\frac{a_{K2}}{a_{L2}W^*} > \frac{a_{K1}}{a_{L1}W}\right)$.

From (10.1a), we obtain

$$\hat{W} = -\left(\frac{\theta_{K1}}{\theta_{L1}}\right)\hat{r}. \tag{10.18}$$

Differentiating Equation (10.2) and using Equation (10.18), one can write

$$\hat{W} = -\frac{\theta_{K1}}{\theta_{L1}\theta_{K2}}\left[T\hat{t} - \theta_{E2}\hat{\tau}\right]. \tag{10.19}$$

Differentiating (10.3) and utilising (10.19), the following proposition can be readily established.

> **Proposition 10.5:** Skilled–unskilled wage inequality deteriorates following a reduction in import tariff or an increase in pollution tax, if the high-skill sector is relatively capital-intensive vis-à-vis rural sector (in a special sense). FDI inflow, on the other hand, will leave relative wage inequality unaltered.[18]

Given the value of $\overline{W}$, the return to capital will fall to maintain the zero-profit condition given by Equation (10.2) as a result of an increase in pollution tax rate. This will lead to an increase in both W and W_S, as is evident from Equations (10.1a) and (10.3), respectively. Unlike the basic model, poor unskilled workers become definitely better off as a result of an increase in τ. Two wage rates, W and W_S, increase because of saving on capital cost in the respective sectors. Capital cost saving will be higher in the sector that uses capital more intensively. The decrease in capital cost will be more in sector 3 than that in sector 1 if sector 3 is relatively capital intensive. In our case, a proportionate increase in skilled wage will be higher than that of rural wage if high-skill sector is capital intensive in a sense that $\left(\theta_{K3} > \theta_{K1}\right)$.[19,20] If the distributive shares of capital in these two sectors are equal, then both W and W_S will increase at the same rate leaving the wage inequality unaltered.

A reduction in tariff rate contracts the urban unskilled sector due to a fall in the domestic price of X_2. As in the case of pollution tax reduction, it also produces similar effects on r, W and W_S as is evident from the price system of the model. In complete contrast with the basic model here, we find that the situation of the unskilled workers improves as a result of trade liberalisation. This becomes clear if one looks at Equation (10.19). What happens to skilled–unskilled wage inequality once again depends on the relative increase in W and W_S. If sector 3 is relatively capital intensive than that of sector 1 (in Jones–Neary sense), then wage inequality will accentuate.[21]

An inflow of FDI, which expands the capital endowment of the economy, will not affect factor prices because of the decomposable structure of the system. Hence in this situation, $\hat{W}_S = \hat{W} = \hat{r} = 0$. The relative wage inequality will remain unaffected as a consequence.

Let us now investigate the impact of different policies on the urban unemployment of unskilled workers. Equation (10.17) can be used to explain the following proposition.

> **Proposition 10.6:** Urban unemployment problem (i) improves following a reduction in import tariff; (ii) aggravates due to the inflow of FDI and (iii) is likely to improve as a result of an increase in pollution tax.[22]

A fall in the domestic price of X_2 following a reduction in import tariff (t) leads to a contraction of this sector as before. Both capital and labour will be released from this sector. Other two capital using sectors, sectors 1 and 3, will expand as a consequence. From Equations (10.1a) and (10.2), it is also clear that return to capital will fall and rural unskilled wage (which is also the average unskilled wage of the economy following the "envelope property" of HT structure) will increase as a result of a cut in t. Due to a fall in return to capital, the producers of sector 2 will adopt relatively capital-intensive technology which will reduce the unit labour requirement (a_{L2}) in that sector. As both a_{L2} and X_2 fall, the centrifugal force produces a favourable impact on urban unemployment situation. An increase in W also generates a centripetal force that reduces the extent of urban unemployment. Thus, both the centripetal force and the centrifugal force work in the same direction and cause the urban unemployment of unskilled labour to decline unambiguously.

An inflow of FDI, which increases the capital endowment of the economy, will not have any impact on factor prices due to the decomposable structure of the system. Unit labour requirement in sector 2, $a_{L2}(\bar{W}, r, \tau)$, will not change either. High-skilled sector will remain unaffected because both $a_{S3}(W_S, r)$ and endowments of skilled labour (S) remain unaltered. This becomes clear if one looks at Equation (10.4). All the extra capital will thus be absorbed by the two unskilled labour-using sectors. Both sectors 1 and 2 use two common inputs capital and unskilled labour. Given the pollution tax rate, these two sectors can be conceived to form a Heckscher–Ohlin (HO) "nugget". As sector 2 is assumed to be relatively capital-intensive vis-à-vis sector 1, the former expands following an increase in the supply of capital as a result of the Rybczynski effect. Clearly, centrifugal force in this situation produces negative impact on the extent urban unemployment because X_2 is rising, a_{L2} remaining unchanged. The centripetal force is absent here because of the insensitivity of W with respect to a change in capital endowment. Thus, urban unemployment problem unquestionably deteriorates.

An increase in pollution tax will reduce r and X_2 but raise both W and W_S, as has already been explained in Proposition 10.5. Three forces will be generated[23] as a consequence, which will work differently on the extent of urban unemployment. Contraction of sector 2 and fall in r (force I and III together) produce positive impacts on urban employment of unskilled labour; force II, on the other hand, will act in the reverse direction. Unit labour demand in sector 2, $a_{L2}\left(\bar{W}, r, \tau\right)$, will fall if cumulative effect of force I and III outweighs that of II. If $\frac{S_{LK}^2}{\theta_{K2}} > \frac{S_{LE}^2}{\theta_{E2}}$ is satisfied, then both a_{L2} and X_2 will fall, and centrifugal force will act to reduce urban unemployment. An increase in W also generates a centripetal force that works in the same direction. Ultimately the unemployment situation of the average unskilled workers improves if $\frac{S_{LK}^2}{\theta_{K2}} > \frac{S_{LE}^2}{\theta_{E2}}$ is satisfied (without any additional condition as was needed in the basic model).

10.5 Concluding Remarks and Policy Implications

Increasing skilled–unskilled wage inequality and unemployment of unskilled labour are two major problems that affect developing countries during the liberalised economic regimes. This chapter tries to explore a simple tractable analytical framework, addressing the environmental aspects that can be useful in analysing how different economic policies affect the two serious issues with which most developing countries are plagued with. We have developed a basic general equilibrium structure with three sectors and specific factors with an eye to examine different policy effects on wage inequality and urban unemployment incorporating different types of distortions, dual economy features and urban unemployment, which are some of the essential characteristics of the developing countries. The entire analysis is divided into two parts. In the basic model, derived in the first part of the analysis, capital is perfectly mobile between the two urban sectors only, while land, skilled labour and environmental input (pollution) are specific to rural, urban high-skilled and low-skilled sectors, respectively. The second part of the analysis considers capital as being perfectly mobile among all three sectors of the economy. The unemployment problem of urban unskilled labour is tackled using the Harris–Todaro mechanism. Most importantly, the pollution tax implemented on the urban-polluting sector by the government is used as an instrument to control the quality of the environment. The study is an improvement over the existing literature because it investigates the impact of price instruments like environmental tax on wage inequality and unemployment.

The theoretical analysis developed here is useful for predicting how investment as well as trade liberalisation and environmental control affect the skilled–unskilled wage inequality and urban unemployment in a small open developing economy. Many interesting results have been derived from this model. Trade liberalisation captured by import tariff reduction worsens wage inequality but improves the urban unemployment problem unconditionally. On the contrary, the inflow of FDI, as a part of liberalised investment policy, exerts a favourable impact on the average low-skilled wage of the economy as well as on the relative wage inequality although the unemployment situation of urban unskilled workers may worsen. Stringent environmental regulation is also likely to produce an unfavourable impact on the average unskilled wage and on skilled–unskilled wage inequality but may improve the unemployment situation. In the second part of the analysis, the model assumes that the rural sector uses capital instead of land along with unskilled labour. The inflow of FDI has no impact on wage inequality though the unemployment problem definitely worsens. The extent of urban unemployment, however, improves following a reduction in import tariff and/or increase in pollution tax though relative wage inequality worsens if the high-skill sector is more capital intensive (in a special sense) than the rural sector. This capital intensity ranking condition was not at all required in the basic model. Although different economic policies can be adopted concurrently, a proper balance among various policies is utterly important in order to protect the interests of the average unskilled workers, from the perspective of income earning as well as employment opportunities, as they produce incongruent consequences. Also, that might be a solution to deteriorating skilled–unskilled wages in developing nations.

However, the study considers pollution as an input and hence is captured on the producer's side only. But pollution might affect consumer's efficiency adversely through negative externality. This issue can be captured by introducing consumer's disutility function. Also to keep the analytical structure simple, we have ignored the negative impact of pollution on the production capacity of other sectors of the economy. Future research should incorporate these issues and examine the role of various policies on different economic variables.

Appendices

Appendix A: Some Useful Expressions

Totally differentiating Equations (10.1)–(10.4), (10.6), (10.7) and (10.9), we get Equations (A.1)–(A.7).

$$\theta_{L1}\hat{W} + \theta_{N1}\hat{R} = 0, \tag{A.1}$$

$$\hat{r} = -\frac{\theta_{E2}}{\theta_{K2}}\hat{\tau} + \frac{T}{\theta_{K2}}\hat{t}, \text{where } T = \frac{t}{1+t} > 0. \tag{A.2}$$

From Equations (10.2) and (10.3), we have

$$\hat{W}_S = \left(\frac{\theta_{K3}\theta_{E2}}{\theta_{K2}\theta_{S3}}\right)\hat{\tau} - \left(\frac{\theta_{K3}T}{\theta_{S3}\theta_{K2}}\right)\hat{t}, \tag{10.10}$$

$$\hat{X}_3 = \left(\frac{\theta_{E2}S_{SK}^3}{\theta_{K2}\theta_{S3}}\right)\hat{\tau} - \left(\frac{TS_{SK}^3}{\theta_{K2}\theta_{S3}}\right)\hat{t}. \tag{A.3}$$

Here S_{ji}^k is the degree of substitution between factors in sector k. For example,

$$S_{LL}^1 = \left(\frac{W}{a_{L1}}\right)\left(\frac{\partial a_{L1}}{\partial W}\right),\ S_{LN}^1 = \left(\frac{R}{a_{L1}}\right)\left(\frac{\partial a_{L1}}{\partial R}\right),\ \text{etc., } S_{ji}^k > 0 \text{ for } j \neq k; \text{ and } S_{jj}^k < 0.$$

$$\hat{X}_2 = -\left[\left(\frac{1-\theta_{L2}}{\theta_{K2}}\right)S_{KE}^2 + \frac{\theta_{E2}S_{KL}^2}{\theta_{K2}} + \left(\frac{\lambda_{K3}\theta_{E2}}{\lambda_{K2}\theta_{K2}\theta_{S3}}\right)\left(S_{KS}^3 + S_{SK}^3\right)\right]\hat{\tau},$$
$$+\left(\frac{k}{\lambda_{K2}}\right)\hat{K}_F + \frac{T}{\theta_{K2}}\left[\frac{\lambda_{K3}\left(S_{KS}^3 + S_{SK}^3\right)}{\lambda_{K2}\theta_{S3}} - S_{KK}^2\right]\hat{t} \tag{A.4}$$

where $k = \frac{K_F}{\bar{K}_D + K_F}$.

Differentiating land endowment equation (10.7), we can derive Equation (10.11) given in the body of the text.

$$\hat{X}_1 + \frac{S_{NL}^1}{\theta_{N1}}\hat{W} = 0. \tag{10.11}$$

Also from Equation (10.2), we get $\hat{a}_{L2} = S_{LK}^2\hat{r} + S_{LE}^2\hat{\tau}$

$$\hat{a}_{L2} = \left(S_{LE}^2 - \frac{S_{LK}^2\theta_{E2}}{\theta_{K2}}\right)\hat{\tau} + \frac{S_{LK}^2 T}{\theta_{K2}}\hat{t} \tag{A.5}$$

Differentiating Equation (10.9a) and inserting the values of $\hat{a}_{L1}, \hat{a}_{N1}, \hat{a}_{L2}$ and $\hat{R}$, we obtain the following equation which is the same as Equation (10.12) in the body of the text.

$$A\hat{W} = -B\hat{\tau} + \left(\frac{\lambda_{L2}^* k}{\lambda_{K2}}\right)\hat{K}_F + C\hat{t} \tag{10.12}$$

where $A = \left[\lambda_{L2}^* + \frac{\lambda_{L1}\left(S_{NL}^1 + S_{LN}^1\right)}{\theta_{N1}}\right] > 0; \lambda_{L2}^* = \left(\frac{\bar{W}}{W}\right)\lambda_{L2} > 0.$

$$B = \lambda_{L2}^*\left[\left(\frac{\theta_{E2}S_{LK}^2}{\theta_{K2}} - S_{LE}^2\right) + \left(\frac{1-\theta_{L2}}{\theta_{K2}}\right)S_{KE}^2 + \frac{\theta_{E2}S_{KL}^2}{\theta_{K2}}\right.$$
$$\left. + \left(\frac{\lambda_{K3}\theta_{E2}}{\lambda_{K2}\theta_{K2}\theta_{S3}}\right)\left(S_{KS}^3 + S_{SK}^3\right)\right];$$

$$B > 0 \text{if} \left(\frac{S_{LK}^2}{\theta_{K2}} > \frac{S_{LE}^2}{\theta_{E2}} \right).$$

$$C = \frac{\lambda_{L2}^* T}{\theta_{K2}} \left[\left(S_{LK}^2 - S_{KK}^2 \right) + \frac{\lambda_{K3} \left(S_{KS}^3 + S_{SK}^3 \right)}{\lambda_{K2} \theta_{S3}} \right] > 0$$

(+)

Appendix B: Results Related to Tariff Reduction on Wage Inequality

Here we assume, $\hat{K}_F = \hat{\tau} = 0;\ \hat{t} \neq 0.$

Differentiating Equations (10.11) and (10.12), the following expression can be derived which is the same as Expression (10.13) given in the body of the chapter.

$$\frac{\hat{W}}{\hat{t}} = \frac{\frac{\lambda_{L2}^* T}{\theta_{K2}} \left[\left(S_{LK}^2 - S_{KK}^2 \right) + \frac{\lambda_{K3} \left(S_{KS}^3 + S_{SK}^3 \right)}{\lambda_{K2} \theta_{S3}} \right]}{\lambda_{L2}^* + \frac{\lambda_{L1} \left(S_{NL}^1 + S_{LN}^1 \right)}{\theta_{N1}}} > 0. \quad \text{(B.1)}$$

$$\frac{\hat{r}}{\hat{t}} = \left(\frac{T}{\theta_{K2}} \right) > 0;\ T = \left(\frac{t}{1+t} \right) > 0.$$

$$\frac{\hat{W}_S}{\hat{t}} = -\left(\frac{\theta_{K3} T}{\theta_{S3} \theta_{K2}} \right) < 0. \quad \text{(B.2)}$$

$$\frac{\hat{W}_S - \hat{W}}{\hat{t}} = -\left(\frac{\theta_{K3} T}{\theta_{S3} \theta_{K2}} + \frac{C}{A} \right) < 0. \quad \text{(B.3)}$$

$$C = \lambda_{L2}^* \frac{T}{\theta_{K2}} \left[\left(S_{LK}^2 - S_{KK}^2 \right) + \frac{\lambda_{K3} \left(S_{KS}^3 + S_{SK}^3 \right)}{\lambda_{K2} \theta_{S3}} \right] > 0;\ A = \left[\lambda_{L2}^* + \frac{\lambda_{L1} \left(S_{NL}^1 + S_{LN}^1 \right)}{\theta_{N1}} \right] > 0.$$

$$\frac{\hat{W}_S - \hat{r}}{\hat{t}} = -\left(\frac{T}{\theta_{S3} \theta_{K2}} \right) < 0,$$

$$\frac{\hat{X}_1}{\hat{t}} = -\left(\frac{S_{NL}^1 C}{\theta_{N1} A} \right) < 0. \quad \text{(B.4)}$$

$$\frac{\hat{X}_2}{\hat{t}} = \frac{T}{\theta_{K2}}\left[\frac{\lambda_{K3}\left(S_{KS}^3 + S_{SK}^3\right)}{\lambda_{K2}\theta_{S3}} - S_{KK}^2\right] > 0. \tag{B.5}$$

$$\frac{\hat{X}_3}{\hat{t}} = -\left(\frac{TS_{SK}^3}{\theta_{K2}\theta_{S3}}\right) < 0. \tag{B.6}$$

Appendix C: Results Related to Environmental Tax on Wage Inequality

Here we assume, $\hat{K}_F = \hat{t} = 0;\ \hat{\tau} > 0$

$$\frac{\hat{R}}{\hat{\tau}} = -\left(\frac{\theta_{L1}B}{\theta_{N1}\Delta}\right) > 0;\ \textit{if}\ B > 0, i.e. \left(\frac{S_{LK}^2}{\theta_{K2}} > \frac{S_{LE}^2}{\theta_{E2}}\right). \tag{C.1}$$

Differentiating Equation (10.6) and substituting the values of $\hat{a}_{K2}$ and $\hat{a}_{K3}$, we can obtain equation (10.14).

Similarly, from Equations (10.3) and (10.2), equations (10.15) and (10.16) can easily be derived.

$$\frac{\hat{a}_{L2}}{\hat{\tau}} = -\left(\frac{\theta_{E2}S_{LK}^2}{\theta_{K2}} - S_{LE}^2\right), \tag{C.2}$$

$$\frac{\hat{a}_{L2}}{\hat{\tau}} < 0, \text{if} \left(\frac{S_{LK}^2}{\theta_{K2}} > \frac{S_{LE}^2}{\theta_{E2}}\right),$$

$$\frac{\hat{X}_1}{\hat{\tau}} = -\left(\frac{S_{NL}^1}{\theta_{N1}}\right)$$

$$\frac{\lambda_{L2}^*\left[\left(\frac{\theta_{E2}S_{LK}^2}{\theta_{K2}} - S_{LE}^2\right) + \left(\frac{1-\theta_{L2}}{\theta_{K2}}\right)S_{KE}^2 + \frac{\theta_{E2}S_{KL}^2}{\theta_{K2}} + \left(\frac{\lambda_{K3}\theta_{E2}}{\lambda_{K2}\theta_{K2}\theta_{S3}}\right)\left(S_{KS}^3 + S_{SK}^3\right)\right]}{\Delta}$$

$$> 0;$$

$$\frac{\hat{X}_1}{\hat{\tau}} > 0, \textit{if} \left(\frac{S_{LK}^2}{\theta_{K2}} > \frac{S_{LE}^2}{\theta_{E2}}\right). \tag{C.3}$$

$$\frac{\hat{X}_3}{\hat{\tau}} = \left(\frac{\theta_{E2}S_{SK}^3}{\theta_{K2}\theta_{S3}}\right) > 0. \tag{C.4}$$

$$\frac{\hat{W}}{\hat{\tau}} = \frac{\lambda^*_{L2}\left[\left(\frac{\theta_{E2}S^2_{LK}}{\theta_{K2}} - S^2_{LE}\right) + \left(\frac{1-\theta_{L2}}{\theta_{K2}}\right)S^2_{KE} + \frac{\theta_{E2}S^2_{KL}}{\theta_{K2}} + \left(\frac{\lambda_{K3}\theta_{E2}}{\lambda_{K2}\theta_{K2}\theta_{S3}}\right)\left(S^3_{KS} + S^3_{SK}\right)\right]}{\Delta}. \tag{C.5}$$

Here, $\Delta = -\left[\lambda^*_{L2} + \frac{\lambda_{L1}\left(S^1_{NL} + S^1_{LN}\right)}{\theta_{N1}}\right] < 0;$

$$\frac{\hat{W}}{\hat{\tau}} < 0, \text{ if } \left(\frac{S^2_{LK}}{\theta_{K2}} > \frac{S^2_{LE}}{\theta_{E2}}\right).$$

$$\frac{\hat{W}_S - \hat{W}}{\hat{\tau}} = \frac{\theta_{K3}\theta_{E2}}{\theta_{K2}\theta_{S3}}.$$

$$+\frac{\lambda^*_{L2}\left[\left(\frac{\theta_{E2}S^2_{LK}}{\theta_{K2}} - S^2_{LE}\right) + \left(\frac{1-\theta_{L2}}{\theta_{K2}}\right)S^2_{KE} + \frac{\theta_{E2}S^2_{KL}}{\theta_{K2}} + \left(\frac{\lambda_{K3}\theta_{E2}}{\lambda_{K2}\theta_{K2}\theta_{S3}}\right)\left(S^3_{KS} + S^3_{SK}\right)\right]}{\lambda^*_{L2} + \frac{\lambda_{L1}\left(S^1_{NL} + S^1_{LN}\right)}{\theta_{N1}}} \tag{C.6}$$

$$\frac{\hat{W}_S - \hat{W}}{\hat{\tau}} > 0 \text{ ;if } \left(\frac{S^2_{LK}}{\theta_{K2}} > \frac{S^2_{LE}}{\theta_{E2}}\right).$$

Appendix D: Results Related to Foreign Capital Inflow on Wage Inequality

Here we assume $\hat{\tau} = \hat{t} = 0;\ \hat{K}_F > 0$.

From Equation (10.2) and (10.3), it is easy to check

$$\frac{\hat{W}_S}{\hat{K}_F} = \frac{\hat{r}}{\hat{K}_F} = 0. \tag{D.1}$$

From Equation (10.4) and (10.6), it is easy to establish

$$\frac{\hat{X}_3}{\hat{K}_F} = 0; \tag{D.2}$$

$$\frac{\hat{X}_2}{\hat{K}_F} = \left(\frac{k}{\lambda_{K2}}\right) > 0. \tag{D.3}$$

Equations (10.7) and (10.9) give

$$\frac{\hat{W}}{\hat{K}_F} = -\left(\frac{\lambda^*_{L2}k}{\Delta\lambda_{K2}}\right) > 0; \tag{D.4}$$

where $\Delta = -\left[\lambda^*_{L2} + \frac{\lambda_{L1}\left(S^1_{NL} + S^1_{LN}\right)}{\theta_{N1}}\right] < 0.$

$$\frac{\hat{X}_1}{\hat{K}_F} = \left(\frac{\lambda^*_{L2}S^1_{NL}k}{\lambda_{K2}\theta_{N1}\Delta}\right) < 0; \tag{D.5}$$

Using (10.1) and (D.4), one gets

$$\frac{\hat{R}}{\hat{K}_F} = \left(\frac{\theta_{L1}\lambda^*_{L2}k}{\theta_{N1}\lambda_{K2}\Delta}\right) < 0. \tag{D.6}$$

From (D.1) and (D.4), the following result can readily be established:

$$\frac{\hat{W}_S - \hat{W}}{\hat{K}_F} = \frac{1}{\Delta}\left(\frac{\lambda^*_{L2}k}{\lambda_{K2}}\right) < 0. \tag{D.7}$$

(-)

Appendix E: Impact on Urban Unemployment

Equation (10.9b) can be derived from (10.9a) through minor manipulation,

$$\frac{\bar{W}}{W}a_{L2}X_2 + a_{L1}X_1 = \bar{L}, \tag{10.9a}$$

$$L_U = a_{L2}X_2\left(\frac{\bar{W} - W}{W}\right). \tag{10.9b}$$

Differentiating Equation (10.9b), we obtain

$$\lambda_{LU}\hat{L}_U = \lambda_{L2}\left[\left(\frac{\bar{W}}{W} - 1\right)\left(\hat{a}_{L2} + \hat{X}_2\right) - \frac{\bar{W}}{W}\hat{W}\right.$$

From here it is easy to derive Equation (E.1) which is the same as Equation (10.17) in the body of the article.

$$\hat{L}_U = \left[\left(\hat{X}_2 + \hat{a}_{L2}\right) - \left(\frac{\bar{W}}{\bar{W} - W}\right)\hat{W}\right]. \tag{E.1}$$

Using (E.1), the following equations can easily be derived.

$$\frac{\hat{L}_U}{\hat{t}} = \left(\frac{T}{\theta_{K2}\Delta}\right)\left[\lambda_{L2}\left(\frac{\bar{W}}{\bar{W}-W}\right) - \frac{\lambda_{L1}\left(S^1_{LN}+S^1_{NL}\right)}{\theta_{N1}}\right]\left[S^2_{LK} - S^2_{KK} + \frac{\lambda_{K3}\left(S^3_{KS}+S^3_{SK}\right)}{\lambda_{K2}\theta_{S3}}\right]$$

(-)

(E.2)

$$\frac{\hat{L}_U}{\hat{t}} > 0 \text{ when } \left[\frac{\lambda_{L1}\left(S^1_{LN}+S^1_{NL}\right)}{\theta_{N1}} > \left(\frac{\bar{W}\lambda_{L2}}{\bar{W}-W}\right)\right],$$

$$\frac{\hat{L}_U}{\hat{\tau}} = \left(\frac{-B}{\lambda^*_{L2}\Delta}\right)\left[\lambda_{L2}\left(\frac{\bar{W}}{\bar{W}-W}\right) - \frac{\lambda_{L1}\left(S^1_{LN}+S^1_{NL}\right)}{\theta_{N1}}\right. \tag{E.3}$$

(+)

$$\frac{\hat{L}_U}{\hat{\tau}} < 0 \text{ when } \left[\frac{\lambda_{L1}\left(S^1_{LN}+S^1_{NL}\right)}{\theta_{N1}} > \left(\frac{\bar{W}\lambda_{L2}}{\bar{W}-W}\right)\right] \text{ and } \left(\frac{S^2_{LK}}{\theta_{K2}} > \frac{S^2_{LE}}{\theta_{E2}}\right).$$

$$\frac{\hat{L}_U}{\hat{K}_F} = \left(\frac{k}{\lambda_{K2}\Delta}\right)\left[\lambda_{L2}\left(\frac{\bar{W}}{\bar{W}-W}\right) - \frac{\lambda_{L1}\left(S^1_{LN}+S^1_{NL}\right)}{\theta_{N1}}\right] \tag{E.4}$$

(-)

$$\frac{\hat{L}_U}{\hat{K}_F} > 0 \text{ if } \left[\frac{\lambda_{L1}\left(S^1_{LN}+S^1_{NL}\right)}{\theta_{N1}} > \left(\frac{\bar{W}\lambda_{L2}}{\bar{W}-W}\right)\right]$$

Appendix F: Results Related to Extended Model

$$a_{L1}W + a_{K1}r = 1 \tag{10.1a}$$

$$a_{K1}X_1 + a_{K2}X_2 + a_{K3}X_3 = \bar{K}_D + K_F \tag{10.6a}$$

Differentiating (10.1a) and using (A.2), we get equation (10.19)
Equations (A.3) and (10.19) together give

$$\hat{W}_S - \hat{W} = \frac{\left(\theta_{K1}\theta_{S3} - \theta_{K3}\theta_{L1}\right)}{\theta_{S3}\theta_{L1}\theta_{K2}}\left[T\hat{t} - \theta_{E2}\hat{\tau}\right] \tag{F.1}$$

$$\frac{\hat{W}_S - \hat{W}}{\hat{t}} = \frac{\left(\theta_{K1}\theta_{S3} - \theta_{K3}\theta_{L1}\right)}{\theta_{S3}\theta_{L1}\theta_{K2}} T \tag{F.2}$$

$$\frac{\hat{W}_S - \hat{W}}{\hat{t}} < 0 \text{ when } \left(\theta_{K3}\theta_{L1} > \theta_{K1}\theta_{S3}\right) \Rightarrow \theta_{K3} > \theta_{K1}$$

$$\frac{\hat{W}_S - \hat{W}}{\hat{\tau}} = -\frac{\theta_{E2}\left(\theta_{K1}\theta_{S3} - \theta_{K3}\theta_{L1}\right)}{\theta_{S3}\theta_{L1}\theta_{K2}} \tag{F.3}$$

$$\frac{\hat{W}_S - \hat{W}}{\hat{\tau}} > 0 \text{ when } \left(\theta_{K3}\theta_{L1} > \theta_{K1}\theta_{S3}\right) \Rightarrow \theta_{K3} > \theta_{K}$$

$$\frac{\hat{X}_2}{\hat{K}_F} = \frac{\lambda_{L1}}{|\lambda|} k > 0. \tag{F.4}$$

If sector 2 is more capital-intensive vis-à-vis sector 1 in a value sense, then $|\lambda| = \left(\lambda_{L1}\lambda_{K2} - \lambda_{K1}\lambda^*_{L2}\right) > 0$.

$$\frac{\hat{X}_2}{\hat{t}} = \frac{1}{|\lambda|}\left(\lambda_{L1}D + \lambda_{K1}G\right) > 0. \tag{F.5}$$

$$G = \left[\lambda^*_{L2}\left(S^2_{LK} + \frac{\theta_{K1}}{\theta_{L1}}\right) + \frac{\lambda_{L1}S^1_{LK}}{\theta_{L1}}\right]\frac{T}{\theta_{K2}} > 0,$$

$$D = \frac{T}{\theta_{K2}}\left[\frac{\lambda_{K3}\left(S^3_{SK} + S^3_{KS}\right)}{\theta_{S3}} + \frac{\lambda_{K1}S^1_{KL}}{\theta_{K1}} - \frac{\lambda_{K2}S^2_{KK}}{\theta_{K2}}\right] > 0,$$

(-)

$$\frac{\hat{X}_2}{\hat{\tau}} = -\frac{1}{|\lambda|}\left(\lambda_{L1}F + \lambda_{K1}I\right). \tag{F.6}$$

$$F = \left[\left(\frac{\lambda_{K3}\theta_{E2}}{\theta_{S3}\theta_{K2}}\right)\left(S^3_{KS} + S^3_{SK}\right) + \frac{\lambda_{K1}\theta_{E2}S^1_{KL}}{\theta_{K1}\theta_{K2}} + \lambda_{K2}\left(S^2_{KE} - \frac{S^2_{KK}\theta_{E2}}{\theta_{K2}}\right)\right] > 0.$$

(+)

$$I = \left[\lambda^*_{L2}\left(\frac{\theta_{E2}S^2_{LK}}{\theta_{K2}} - S^2_{LE}\right) + \lambda^*_{L2}\frac{\theta_{K1}\theta_{E2}}{\theta_{L1}\theta_{K2}} + \frac{\lambda_{L1}S^1_{LK}}{\theta_{L1}\theta_{K2}}\right] > 0 \text{ when } \frac{S^2_{LK}}{\theta_{K2}} > \frac{S^2_{LE}}{\theta_{E2}},$$

$$\therefore \frac{\hat{X}_2}{\hat{\tau}} < 0 \text{ when } \frac{S_{LK}^2}{\theta_{K2}} > \frac{S_{LE}^2}{\theta_{E2}},$$

$$\frac{\hat{X}_1}{\hat{K}_F} = -\left(\frac{\lambda_{L2}^*}{|\lambda|}k\right) < 0. \tag{F.7}$$

$$(+)$$

$$\frac{\hat{X}_1}{\hat{t}} = -\frac{1}{|\lambda|}\left(\lambda_{K2}G + \lambda_{L2}^* D\right) < 0. \tag{F.8}$$

$$\frac{\hat{X}_1}{\hat{\tau}} = \frac{1}{|\lambda|}\left(\lambda_{K2}I + \lambda_{L2}^* F\right). \tag{F.9}$$

$$\frac{\hat{X}_1}{\hat{\tau}} > 0 \text{ when } \frac{S_{LK}^2}{\theta_{K2}} > \frac{S_{LE}^2}{\theta_{E2}}.$$

From Equation (10.17) or (E.1), it is easy to derive

$$\frac{\hat{L}_U}{\hat{t}} = \frac{T}{\theta_{K2}}\left[S_{LK}^2 + \left(\frac{\bar{W}}{\bar{W} - W}\right)\frac{\theta_{K1}}{\theta_{L1}}\right] + \frac{1}{|\lambda|}\left(\lambda_{L1}D + \lambda_{K1}G\right) > 0. \tag{F.10}$$

$$\frac{\hat{L}_U}{\hat{K}_F} = \left(\frac{\lambda_{L1}k}{|\lambda|}\right) > 0. \tag{F.11}$$

$$\frac{\hat{L}_U}{\hat{\tau}} = -\left[\left(\frac{S_{LK}^2\theta_{E2}}{\theta_{K2}} - S_{LE}^2\right) + \frac{1}{|\lambda|}\left(\lambda_{L1}F + \lambda_{K1}I\right) + \frac{\bar{W}}{\bar{W} - W}\frac{\theta_{K1}\theta_{E2}}{\theta_{L1}\theta_{K2}}\right]. \tag{F.12}$$

$$\frac{\hat{L}_U}{\hat{\tau}} < 0 \text{ when} \left(\frac{S_{LK}^2}{\theta_{K2}} > \frac{S_{LE}^2}{\theta_{E2}}\right).$$

Notes

1 See Wood (1997) in this context.
2 Several theoretical papers like Marjit (2003), Chaudhuri (2008), Chaudhury and Banerjee (2010) and Chaudhuri (2016), etc., have also used similar assumption.
3 SeeMcGuire (1982), Copeland and Taylor (1994), Daitoh (2003, 2008), Daitoh and Omote (2011) and Ko et al. (2017) in this context.
4 See Yohe (1979) and Yu and Ingene (1982).

5 The institutionally fixed wage could be due to strict implementation of the government's minimum wage legislation, collective bargaining of unskilled labour unions, etc. See Khan (1980, 1982) in this context.
6 In several theoretical papers the unionised wage in the urban sector has been assumed to be exogenously given. See for example, Corden and Findlay (1975), Chandra and Khan (1993), Grinols (1991), Chaudhuri (2007).
7 This is known as the "envelope property" of the HT structure.
8 See Appendix B for mathematical expressions.
9 See Appendix C in this respect
10 For details check Equation (C.6).
11 See Equation (D.3) in Appendix D.
12 This has been shown in Appendix D.
13 See Appendix E for details result.
14 The terms "centripetal" and "centrifugal" forces have been used in this context in Chaudhuri and Banerjee (2010), Chaudhuri and Mukhopadhyay (2014).
15 One can look at Equations (C.2) and (C.5) in this respect.
16 This becomes clear from Equation (D.4) in Appendix D.
17 For mathematical expression see Appendix E.
18 For mathematical expression see Appendix F.
19 Here sectors 1 and 3 use two different types of labour. But capital is intersectorally mobile. So, these two sectors cannot be classified in terms of factor intensities that are usually used in the HOS model. A special type of factor intensity classification in terms of the relative distributive shares of the mobile factor, capital, may be used for analytical purposes. The industry in which this share is higher relative to the other may be considered as capital intensive in a special sense. See Jones and Neary (1984) and Chaudhuri and Mukhopadhyay (2014) for details.
20 Note $(\theta_{K3}\theta_{L1} - \theta_{S3}\theta_{K1}) > 0$ implies $(\theta_{K3} > \theta_{K1})$.
21 See Appendix F for mathematical expression.
22 For details in mathematical results, see Appendix F.
23 For details in discussion, see Proposition 10.2.

References

Anwar, S. (2006): 'Factor mobility and wage inequality in the presence of specialisation-based external economies', *Economics Letters*, 93(1), 88–93.

Anwar, S. and Sun, S. (2015): 'Taxation of labour income and the skilled-unskilled wage inequality', *Economic Modelling*, 47, 18–22.

Banga, R. (2005): 'Impact of liberalisation on wages and employment in Indian manufacturing industries', *Working Paper, No. 153*, Indian Council for Research on International Economic Relations (ICRIER), New Delhi.

Beladi, H., Chaudhuri, S. and Yabuuchi, S. (2008): 'Can international factor mobility reduce wage inequality in a dual economy?', *Review of International Economics*, 16(5), 893–903.

Beladi, H., Frasca, R. and Chou, C. (1999): 'Foreign investment and environmental regulations in LDCs', *Resource and Energy Economics*, 21(2), 191–199.

Chandra, V. and Khan, M. A. (1993): 'Foreign investment in the presence of an informal sector', *Economica*, 60(237), 79–103.

Chaudhuri, S. (2004): 'International migration of skilled and unskilled labour, welfare and skilled-unskilled wage inequality: A simple model', *Journal of Economic Integration*, 19(4), 726–741.

Chaudhuri, S. (2007): 'Foreign capital, welfare and urban unemployment in the presence of agricultural dualism', *Japan and the World Economy*, 19(2), 149–165.

Chaudhuri, S. (2008): 'Wage inequality in a dual economy and international mobility of factors: do factor intensities always matter?', *Economic Modelling*, 25(6), 1155–1164.

Chaudhuri, S. (2016): 'Trade unionism and welfare consequences of trade and investment reforms in a developing economy', *Metroeconomica*, 67(1), 152–171.

Chaudhuri, S. and Banerjee, D. (2010): 'FDI in agricultural land, welfare and unemployment in a developing economy', *Research in Economics*, 64(4), 229–239.

Chaudhuri, S., Ghosh, A. and Banerjee, D. (2018): 'Can public subsidy on education necessarily improve wage inequality?', *International Review of Economics and Finance*, 54, 165–177.

Chaudhuri, S. and Mukhopadhyay, U. (2014): *FDI in Developing Countries: A Theoretical Evaluation*, Springer, New Delhi.

Copeland, B. R. and Taylor, S. M. (1994): 'North-south trade and the environment', *Quarterly Journal of Economics*, 109(3), 755–787.

Corden, W. M. and Findlay, R. (1975): 'Urban unemployment, intersectoral capital mobility, and development policy in a dual economy', *Economica*, 42(165), 59–78.

Daitoh, I. (2003): 'Environmental protection and urban unemployment: Environmental policy reform in a polluted dualistic economy', *Review of Development Economics*, 7(3), 496–509.

Daitoh, I. (2008): 'Environmental protection and trade liberalisation in a small open dual economy', *Review of Development Economics*, 12(4), 728–736.

Daitoh, I. and Omote, M. (2011): 'The optimal environmental tax and urban unemployment in an open economy', *Review of Development Economics*, 15(1), 168–179.

Das, P. (2002): 'Foreign direct investment and the relative wage in a developing economy', *Journal of Development Economics*, 67(1), 55–77.

Esquivel, G. and Lopez, A. (2003): 'Technology, trade, and wage inequality in Mexico before and after NAFTA', *Journal of Development Economics*, 72(2), 543–565.

Feenstra, R. and Hanson, G. (1997): 'Foreign investment and relative wages: Evidence from Mexico's maquiladoras', *Journal of International Economics*, 42(3–4), 371–393.

Figini, P. and Gorg, H. (2011): 'Does foreign direct investment affect wage inequality? An empirical investigation', *World Economy*, 34(9), 1455–1475.

Grinols, E. (1991): 'Unemployment and foreign capital: The relative opportunity costs of domestic labour and welfare', *Economica*, 58(229), 107–121.

Gupta, M. R. and Dutta, P. B. (2010): 'Skilled–unskilled wage inequality: A general equilibrium analysis', *Research in Economics*, 64(4), 247–263.

Harris, J. R. and Todao, M. P. (1970): 'Migration, unemployment and development: A two-sector analysis', *The American Economic Review*, 60(1), 126–142.

Jones, R. W. and Neary, J. P. (1984): 'Positive theory of international trade'. In: Jones, R. W. and Kenen, P. B. (eds.), *Handbook of Development Economics*, Vol. 1, North Holland, Amsterdam, 1–62.

Khan, A. R. (1998): 'The impact of globalization in South Asia'. In: A. S. Bhalla (ed.), *Globalization, Growth and Marginalization*, Macmillan, London, 103–124.

Khan, M. A. (1980): 'The Harris-Todaro hypothesis and the Heckscher-Ohlin-Samuelson trade model: A synthesis', *Journal of International Economics*, 10(4), 527–547.

Khan, M. A. (1982): 'Tariffs, foreign capital and immiserizing growth with urban unemployment and specific factors of production', *Journal of Development Economics*, 10(2), 245–256.

Ko, S. H., Kuo, K. H., Lee, C. T. and Fang, C. (2017): 'Environmental tax and return urban-rural migration', *Singapore Economic Review*, 62, 447–58.

Marjit, S. (2003): 'Economic reform and informal wage - A general equilibrium analysis', *Journal of Development Economics*, 72(1), 371–378.

Marjit, S. and Acharyya, R. (2003): *International Trade, Wage Inequality and the Developing Economy — A General Equilibrium Approach*, Springer-Verlag, Germany.

Marjit, S., Beladi, H. and Chakrabarti, A. (2004): 'Trade and wage inequality in developing countries', *Economic Inquiry*, 42(2), 295–303.

Marjit, S. and Kar, S. (2005): 'Emigration and wage inequality', *Economics Letters*, 88(1), 141–145.

McGuire, M. (1982): 'Regulation, factor rewards, and international trade', *Journal of Public Economics*, 17(3), 335–354.

Oladi, R. and Beladi, H. (2007): 'International migration and real wages', *Economics Bulletin*, 6(30), 1–8.

Pan, L. and Zhou, Y. (2013): 'International factor mobility, environmental pollution and skilled-unskilled wage inequality in developing countries', *Economic Modelling*, 33, 826–831.

Pi, J. and Chen, X. (2016): 'The impacts of capital market distortion on wage inequality, urban unemployment, and welfare in developing countries', *International Review of Economics and Finance*, 42, 103–115.

Pi, J. and Zhang, P. (2017): 'Foreign capital, pollution control, and wage inequality in developing countries', *International Review of Economics and Finance*, 48(C), 280–288.

Pi, J. and Zhou, Y. (2013): 'Institutional quality and skilled-unskilled wage inequality', *Economic Modelling*, 35, 356–363.

Pi, J. and Zhou, Y. (2014): 'Foreign capital, public infrastructure, and wage inequality in developing countries', *International Review of Economics and Finance*, 29(C), 195–207.

Pi, J. and Zhou, Y. (2015): 'International factor mobility, production cost components, and wage inequality', *B.E. Journal of Economic Analysis and Policy*, 15(2), 503–522.

Robbins, D. (1996): 'HOS hits facts: Facts win: Evidence on trade and wages in developing world', *Working Paper*, Harvard Institute for International Development, Kennedy school of Government, Cambridge, Massachusetts.

UNCTAD (2013): *World Investment Report. Global Value Chains: Investment and Trade for Development*, United Nations, New York and Geneva.

UNCTAD (2020): Investment Trends Monitor, *Global Investment Flows Flat in 2019, Moderate Increase Expected in 2020*, United Nations, New York and Geneva.

Wang, J. (1990): 'Growth, technology transfer, and the long-run theory of international capital movements', *Journal of International Economics*, 29(3–4), 255–271.

Wood, A. (1997): 'Openness and wage inequality in developing countries: The Latin American challenge to East Asian conventional wisdom', *World Bank Economic Review*, 11(1), 33–57.

Wood, A. (1998): 'Globalisation and the Rise in Labour Market inequalities', *The Economic Journal*, 108(450), 1463–1482.

Yabuuchi, S. (2007): 'Unemployment and international factor movement in the presence of skilled and unskilled labor', *Review of Development Economics*, 11(3), 437–449.

Yabuuchi, S. and Beladi, H. (2001): 'Urban unemployment, informal sector and development policies', *Journal of Economics*, 74(3), 301–314.

Yabuuchi, S. and Chaudhuri, S. (2007): 'International migration of labor and skilled–unskilled wage inequality in a developing economy', *Economic Modelling*, 24(1), 128–137.

Yabuuchi, S. and Chadhuri, S. (2009): 'Skill formation, capital adjustment cost and wage inequality', *Review of Urban and Regional Development Studies*, 21(1), 2–13.

Yohe, G. W. (1979): 'The backward incidence of pollution control-some comparative statics in general equilibrium', *Journal of Environmental Economics and Mangement*, 6(3), 187–198.

Yu, E. S. H. and Ingene, C. A. (1982): 'The backward incidence of pollution control in a rigid-wage economy', *Journal of Environmental Economics and Management*, 9(4), 304–310.

Zhang, J. (2013): 'Factor mobility and skilled-unskilled wage inequality in the presence of internationally traded product varieties', *Economic Modelling*, 30, 579–585.

11 Pollution Treaties, Bilateral Carbon Trade and Welfare[1]

Saibal Kar and Sarmistha Banerjee

11.1 Introduction

Participation in multilateral and multi-country pollution abatement treaties often suffers from standard problems of free-riding integral to all such issues in the domain of public economics, pertaining especially to environmental conservation.[2] The present study shows that the welfare implications of cross-country carbon trade could vary considerably across participating and non-participating countries through direct trade-related impacts. In fact, the strength of this argument lies in establishing that the justification for a country to be a party in multilateral negotiations can independently be motivated by selfish benefits associated with standard gains from international trade.

In this connection, we develop a model, reminiscent of Bhagwati et al. (1983), where two countries participate in a multilateral negotiation on environmental policies while one country chooses to stay out in a three-country world. The countries are linked via international trade with an opportunity to register as active players in efforts towards reducing global carbon emissions. Indeed, the recent developments associated with multilateral dialogues, namely the withdrawal of the United States from the Paris convention on the future of climate protection, allow one to explore important dimensions about the efficacy of bringing powerful nations to the negotiating table and ensuring strictly Pareto improving outcomes. Therefore, the present effort is a step towards investigating if standard trade-related outcomes in the presence of pollution treaties could provide sufficient motivation for large (and sometimes, environmentally rogue) countries to participate in such negotiations.

As briefly mentioned earlier, in appreciation of earlier efforts in understanding the scope of multilateral participation in global policies, such as policies on foreign aid or millennium development goals, we develop a model where trade in carbon-related pollution along with other tradable commodities could affect non-participating countries adversely.

The rest of the chapter is planned as follows. In Section 1.1, we discuss the scope of transboundary pollution as the chief reason for multilateral negotiations. In Section 11.2, we survey the related literature. In

DOI: 10.4324/9781003375050-11

Section 11.3, we develop a model, and in Section 11.4, we investigate the impact of policy changes with regard to the effects of carbon-related trade. Section 11.5 concludes.

11.1.1 Cross-Country Pollution and Treaties

Cross-country and cross-sector spillover of environmental pollution through the emission of greenhouse gases and water-borne effluents continue to be an important topic of research in environmental economics (see Bruvoll and Faehn, 2006; Dinar et al., 2011; Constantini et al., 2013, etc.). Environmental pollution, unambiguously accepted as a public "bad", requires intervention to ameliorate the negative externality associated with it. Policies ranging from carbon taxes to international treaties adorn the literature (see Nordhaus, 2006, 2007, etc.) and also measure projected implications for local activities (viz. Jackson, 2001).

The environmental treaties combined with trade treaties at the cross-country level have been specific to certain product types as well as plant and animal resources in the past. These include, for example, the North Sea Fur Seal Treaty of 1911, which did not allow non-signatories to trade in (non-authenticated) fur. Like many trade restrictions, it is easy to consider this as a version of protectionism practised by some developed countries, although in this case, it prevented the depletion of animal resources as an outcome. Similarly, harvesting and international trade in tunas require being a party to environmental treaties and therefore subjected to regulations, because it harms marine dolphins in the process. Yet, these were not coupled policies.

However, in 1997 the Kyoto Protocol was the first international treaty to attempt curbing greenhouse gas emissions, and since then a number of international summits have taken place. By virtue of the Kyoto negotiations, Barrett (1998) later comments that the projected reductions were unlikely to materialise, either because emission-intensive productions shall relocate to non-compliant countries (a phenomenon presently well-known as pollution haven hypothesis) or "because 'paper' trades will be promoted by the protocol's mechanisms" (p. 20). It was identified that the Kyoto Protocol did not deter non-compliance and only weakly dissuaded non-participation. The paper trade refers to trade in pollution permits as one of the well-known modes of addressing asymmetric pollution impact across countries (Copeland and Taylor, 1995; Hatzipanayotou et al., 2002; Tietenberg, 2003; McGinty, 2007; Harstad and Eskeland, 2010; Sawhney and Mitra, 2011).

Trade in pollution permits at the country level via cap-and-trade policy is based on participating countries agreeing to quotas negotiated via international arrangements. The price of per-unit pollution is determined by the excess demand conditions in the market. This was one of the routes that linked international pollution treaties to cross-country trade. In fact, a decade later (see, Barrett, 2008), discussions had already begun regarding the use of trade restrictions in order to make countries Kyoto compliant. Stiglitz (2011) suggests that tariff barriers be raised against countries that did not agree with the international mandates about reducing carbon and other harmful substances. But, despite clear acknowledgement of the fact that trade and efforts to lower greenhouse gas emissions were inextricably linked, it lacked formal connections (Barrett, 2011). While climate policies were largely ineffective, attempts to influence the reduction of chlorofluorocarbons (CFCs) via trade policies were few. The fear of trade wars and retaliation due to harsher measures, such as seeking pollution permits from international aircraft landing in Europe (as proposed for 2012; McCarthy, 2010), led to general avoidance of using trade policy to address climate change. Nevertheless, the Montreal Protocol of 1987 and later re-negotiations of 2007 actually led to a reduction in CFCs and hydrochlorofluorocarbons (HCFCs) by at least four times that was intended and achieved by the Kyoto Protocol. Even then the United States did not participate in the consorted effort partly because it did not agree with the international choice allowing developing countries lesser restrictions and partly due to the imprecise nature of the rules to follow and the cost to incur.

Against this backdrop, we re-assess the trade–environment connection. We develop a three-country two-commodity model, where one of the traded commodities generates transboundary pollution. Two countries are bound by environmental restrictions following environmental treaties, where the third nation is non-participating and thus the international treaty is not binding for the non-signatory nation. Given this structure, our approach follows the reaction of prices and factor returns when environmental policies are adopted. However, the effects are manifested via trade in commodities, rather than as independent events.[3] An authoritative discussion of various market-based pollution-trading policies is also available in Schmalensee and Stavins (2017).

11.2 The Pollution and Trade Literature in Brief

Some of the most compelling issues in transboundary pollution have already come up for seminal contributions and reviews. Between institutional approaches to the complexity of non-exclusion associated with transboundary pollution as a public good (or, bad) as in Livingston (1989) to recent survey articles on foreign direct investment (FDI) and environmental regulations in the host country (viz. Erdogan, 2014), the topic has been enriched by several domineering contributions. These include well-known studies by Copeland and Taylor (1995) considering global pollution under one umbrella and Antweiler, Copeland and Taylor (2001) showing that trade generally lowers pollution concentration and that large inflow of FDI raises pollution only by a minuscule amount.[4] Frankel and Rose (2005) offer further deposition on the relationship between trade and pollution albeit the impact on factor inputs is not dealt with. They show that while CO_2 is a global externality and one country's regulation is incapable of addressing it, at the cross-country level the effect of a rise in trade openness on suspended particulate matter (PM) is negative but insignificant statistically. The effect of trade on NO_2 is negative and significant at a 10% level, while for SO_2 trade openness significantly reduces pollution concentration. The upshot of these results is that the race-to-the-bottom effect is outweighed by the positive gains-from-trade effect (also see Ferrara et al., 2008, for effects of Most Favored Nations (MFN) tariff vis-à-vis discrimination on the choice of environmental standards with and without spillover; and, adoption and increase in MFN tariff for lowering emission as in Kar and Majumdar, 2016).

Notwithstanding, analytical results (Benarroch and Thille, 2001) do suggest that if international trade does not efficiently distribute production across countries, then the incidence of transboundary pollution exacerbates losses from opening up to trade.

On a related note, FDI as an indicator of openness for countries seems to have a negative relation with pollution. In Mexico (see Waldkirch and Gopinath, 2008), sectors that display lower emission intensities are the ones that receive up to 30% of total FDI and produce 30% of manufacturing output in the country. This type of results may dispel earlier ideas that FDI for "dirty goods" and "pollution havens"[5] leads to more pollution and that stronger regulation in the host country shall drive away potential investors carrying with it other possible gains from the capital inflow. Further, Dong, Gong and Zhao (2012) also show that contrary to the pollution haven hypothesis, if the market sizes of the two countries are small, FDI seems to raise the emission standard of the host country generating a "race-to-the-top" phenomenon. However, country sizes matter when non-cooperative policies at addressing spillovers are pursued simultaneously by two or more countries engaged in cross-border trade. The smaller country seems to get adversely affected if the large country undertakes environmental policies, essentially via the price effects of traded goods (Frankel, 2009).[6]

Note that these studies do not focus on how transboundary pollution may be addressed via trade in goods when trading countries do not abide by international treaties to curb emissions. It is useful to remind in this context that according to the United Nations Framework Convention on Climate Change (UNFCCC), *The Paris Agreement* is a legally binding international treaty on climate change. It was adopted by 196 Parties at COP 21 in Paris, on December 12, 2015, and entered into force on November 4, 2016. The treaty aims at limiting global warming to much less than 2°C as compared to pre-industrial levels. The main tenet of the agreement is that, in order to achieve this long-term temperature goal, countries must attain the global peaking of greenhouse gas emissions at the earliest, so that the emission rate should be falling subsequently in order to achieve a climate-neutral world by the mid-century. Indeed, the UNFCCC claims that the Paris Agreement is a landmark in the multilateral climate change process because, for the first time, a binding agreement brings all nations into a common cause to undertake ambitious efforts to combat climate change and adapt to its effects. Apparently, in 2017, the United States distanced itself from the Paris Agreement by claiming that it would undermine the economy. We show via a simple model that such a policy actually undermines gains from trade in the presence of opportunities to trade in both commodities and excess pollution, and therefore might be a factor in aggregate welfare loss.

11.3 Trade in Goods and Emissions

Consider a world economy consisting of three countries *A*, *B* and *C*. Country *i* produces and trades in one good and an (flow) amount of pollution, x^i and θ^i, respectively.[7] The commodity is akin to an intra-industry good and the empirical motivation of this theoretical work comes from trade in commodities and pollution quotas between advanced European countries. Production of the commodity x^i generates pollution θ^i in all countries, but given country-specific technologies $\theta^i \neq \theta^j\ \forall i, j = A, B, C$. However, these countries have independently instituted internal quotas on levels of pollution. Consequently, each of these countries has an excess or a reserve emission level measured by $\varepsilon^i = \left(\bar{\theta}^i - \theta^i\right)$. To identify the countries, let us assume that $\varepsilon^C > \varepsilon^B > 0 > \varepsilon^A$. Thus, the propensity to pollute is higher in country *A* than in country *C*.

Now, subject to a bilateral treaty, *A* transfers its excess pollution to *C* at a price $t < t^A$, where t^A is the price of abatement domestically in *A*. However, country *B* does not participate in the carbon trade. Let us denote q as the relative price of x^i depicting compensated import demand for x in country *i*; U^i is the welfare level in country *i*, such that $U^A = V^A(q,t); U^B = V^B(q);$ and $U^C = V^C(q,t)$. $\left(t\varepsilon^i\right)$ is the value of trade in pollution (the price of commodity *X* is treated as the *numeraire*). Further, $e^i\left(q,U^i,t\right)$ is the expenditure function and $r^i(q,t)$ is the revenue function, such that the overspending (S^i) function for country *i* at price q for achieving U^i is written as

$$S^i = e^i\left(q,U^i,t\right) - r^i(q,t). \tag{11.1}$$

The overspending function is the gap between the expenditure incurred to arrive at U^i given the revenue of the country at the relative price of *X*. Country *A* sells pollution ε to country *C* at a cost of $(t\varepsilon)$ as part of the environmental policy agreement. Unlike Bhagwati et al. (1983), where the transfer of aid naturally did not have a price (or cost) attached to it, the present chapter introduces a transaction that involves international prices. Using Equation (11.1),

$$S^A\left(q,U^A,t\right) - t\varepsilon = 0, \tag{11.2}$$

$$S^{B}\left(q,U^{B}\right)=0, \tag{11.3}$$

$$S^{C}(q,U^{C},t)+t\varepsilon=0. \tag{11.4}$$

Equilibrium for x^i (and overall, by Walras' law) is ensured by

$$x^{A}\left(q,U^{A},t\right)+x^{B}\left(q,U^{B}\right)+x^{C}\left(q,U^{C},t\right)=0. \tag{11.5}$$

Since $S^i = e^i\left(q,U^i,t\right)-r^i\left(q,t\right)$ meaning some country pollutes more while some country has cap space, we hold without loss of generality,

$$\frac{\delta S^i}{\delta U^i}=\frac{\delta e^i}{\delta U^i}-0=1. \tag{11.6}$$

Therefore, $e_U^A = e_U^B = e_U^C = 1$. Let us further denote the following:

$x_q^A + x_q^B + x_q^C = x_q$, $x_q < 0$, where a rise in the relative price of commodity x lowers its demand, and $x_t^A + x_t^B + x_t^C = x_t$, where non-participation by B leads to $x_t^B = 0$. Country A transfers excess pollution to C vide an international arrangement to collaborate with other countries for global reduction of pollution. Since country A has to spend for transferring pollution to C, the national income in A must fall owing to that and for a unit rise in the cost of transfer it should lower the demand for x in A and raise the same in B via income effects. Therefore, $x_t^A < 0$ and $x_t^C > 0$ by income effect. Let us assume that $x_t > 0$ following the environment treaty. The global production and consumption of x rises as an outcome of trade in pollution. Finally, by Shephard's lemma, $S_q^i = x^i \forall i = A,B,C$.

Further, we need the following assumption to establish the impact of environmental policy on consumption: $\left|x_U^A\right| > \left|x_U^B\right| = \left|x_U^C\right|$. Besides, as far as the consumption effects are concerned, assume $\Delta = \left[x_u^A x^A + x_u^B x^B + x_u^C x^C - x_q\right] > 0$, as the Marshall–Lerner stability condition derived from the determinant of the system of equations covering (11.2)–(11.5) mentioned earlier.

Note that global environmental policy is expected to control the flow of pollution. Therefore, we will consider that at any point in time, the overall effect is distributed between three countries.

$$d\left[\varepsilon^{A}\left(q,t,U^{A}\right)+\varepsilon^{B}\left(q,t,U^{B}\right)+\varepsilon^{C}\left(q,t,U^{C}\right)\right]\neq 0. \tag{11.7}$$

Equation (11.7) suggests that if country B were a party to international climate negotiations, then total excess pollution would not only be mitigated but would be so at a lower price improving global consumption further. However, if one or more countries distance themselves from the international programme, then Equation (11.8) should result. As B is not a signatory to this treaty, we will drop ε^B from Equation (11.7), such that

$$d\left[\varepsilon^{A}\left(q,t,U^{A}\right)+\varepsilon^{C}\left(q,t,U^{C}\right)\right]=0 \tag{11.8}$$

Equation (11.8) is the source to argue that there might be a reason to consider possible changes in the cost of mitigation of environmental damages and its impact on the country-wise welfare levels, as well as the price of the commodity in trade. To set up this analysis, we first observe possible changes in the system of equations.

Presently, fully differentiating Equations (11.2)–(11.5), we get

$$1.dU^A + 0.dU^B + 0.dU^C + x^A dq = \varepsilon dt, \tag{11.9}$$

$$0.dU^A + 1.dU^B + 0.dU^C + x^B dq = 0.dt, \tag{11.10}$$

$$0.dU^A + 0.dU^B + 1.dU^C + x^C dq = -\varepsilon dt, \tag{11.11}$$

$$x_U^A.dU^A + x_U^B.dU^B + x_U^C.dU^C + x_q dq = -x_t dt. \tag{11.12}$$

We form a matrix by using Equations (11.9)–(11.12)

$$\begin{bmatrix} 1 & 0 & 0 & x^A \\ 0 & 1 & 0 & x^B \\ 0 & 0 & 1 & x^C \\ x_U^A & x_U^B & x_U^C & xq \end{bmatrix} \begin{bmatrix} dU^A \\ dU^B \\ dU^C \\ dq \end{bmatrix} = \begin{bmatrix} \varepsilon \\ 0 \\ -\varepsilon \\ -x_t \end{bmatrix}. \tag{11.13}$$

From (11.13), we get: $\Delta_M = \left(x^A x_U^A + x^B x_U^B + x^C x_U^C - x_q\right)$as the negative of the excess demand schedule for all goods in the system as assumed above already. The Marshall–Lerner stability condition is satisfied, such that $\Delta_M > 0$. We can now try to understand the impact of changes in emission mitigation prices or the level of permits on the key variables in this relation.

11.4 A Rise in Mitigation Price

The withdrawal of one country from the collaborative arrangement towards global pollution reduction implies that all the remaining countries shall now face a steeper challenge to mitigate the entire pollution. The main implication is a rise in the per-unit mitigation cost for the countries that are still committed to curbing global pollution. This is the source of change that we investigate.

We wish to find, $\frac{dU^A}{dt}, \frac{dU^B}{dt}, \frac{dU^C}{dt}$ and $\frac{dq}{dt}$. Note that a change in *t* could also result from a more stringent and pervasive environment policy (rise) or due to a technological improvement (fall). A common tendency among some countries to freeride on the efforts of the signatories may also result in per-unit burden being higher. It is instructive at this point to enquire if the introduction of any other commodity traded internationally and subjected to quotas generate similar results? Apparently, the answer is no, because the way the pollution market operates is based on a cap-and-trade policy set in individual countries or via international coordination which differs in spirit from trade in commodities and services. Further, the flow of pollution is unlike the characteristics displayed by traded commodities but is an unavoidable by-product which needs to be mitigated.

Using Cramer's rule on Equation (11.13), we get

$$\frac{dU^A}{dt} = \varepsilon - \frac{1}{\Delta_M} x^A . \left[\varepsilon \left(x_U^A - x_U^C \right) + x_t \right]$$

or

$$\frac{dU^A}{dt} = -\frac{1}{\Delta_M} x^A x_t + \varepsilon \left[1 - \frac{1}{\Delta_M} x^A . \left(x_U^A - x_U^C \right) \right]. \tag{11.14}$$

For $\left(x_U^A - x_U^C\right) > 0$ and $x_t > 0$ $\dfrac{dU^A}{dt} < 0$ if $\left[\dfrac{1}{\Delta_M} x^A . \left(x_U^A - x_U^C \right) > 1 \right]$.

However, this might not hold under many conditions. In fact, the most important observation with regard to this comparative static is the following:

$$\frac{dU^B}{dt} = \frac{1}{\Delta_M} \left[\varepsilon . x^B (x_U^C - x_U^A) - x_t . x^B \right]. \tag{11.15}$$

Substitute in Equation (11.15), $\dfrac{dq}{dt} = \dfrac{1}{\Delta_M} \left[x^B (x_U^C - x_U^A) \right] < 0$, such that $\dfrac{dU^B}{dt} = \dfrac{1}{\Delta_M} \left[q_t - x_t . x^B \right]$.

Or, using the same conditions as mentioned earlier, i.e., $\left(x_U^A - x_U^C\right) > 0$ and $x_t > 0$, $\dfrac{dU^B}{dt} < 0$ unambiguously. If country *A* reports a greater response in consumption of *x* when the overall utility rises as compared to country *C* and the global production and consumption of *x* also rises despite a rise in the unit cost of pollution mitigation, then country *B* suffers owing to non-participation in the distribution of gains from trade.

We also find the welfare condition for country *C*:

$$\frac{dU^C}{dt} = -\frac{1}{\Delta_M} x^C x_t + \varepsilon \left[1 + \frac{1}{\Delta_M} x^C . \left(x_U^A - x_U^C \right) \right] \tag{11.16}$$

Equation (11.16) suggests that given $\left(x_U^A - x_U^C\right) > 0$ and $x_t > 0$, $\dfrac{dU^C}{dt}$ can be positive or negative, or even zero.

In Equation (11.16) if x_t is small, a rise in *t* must improve the overall welfare in country *C*.

Note that for Equations (11.14) and (11.15) if homothetic preference holds across all countries, then despite a rise in the mitigation cost, country *A* as the exporter of pollution must enjoy greater welfare transferred through greater production and consumption of *x* if $x_t < 0$. Country *B* owing to non-participation does not suffer any longer because overall consumption went down due to the rise in mitigation cost. If $\left(x_U^A - x_U^C\right) = 0$ country C shall also benefit from the trade when $x_t < 0$. This implies that the country which passes on the pollution burden is likely to benefit from it while the one which mitigates it also benefits. There is no penalty for the non-compliant country either. The well-known result due to Bhagwati et al. (1983) tends to hold under the above situation at least for the exporter of pollution. The exporter of pollution is enriched but the recipient's welfare also rises.

11.5 Concluding Remarks

Trade in pollution permits is one of the well-known modes of addressing asymmetric pollution impact across countries. In most cases, countries via domestic authorities and agencies auction pollution quotas for firms to buy according to their polluting capacities. The largest bidder is assigned quotas under the assumption that this should allow the designated firms to continue production and make use of the permit. In cases where the designated firms do not use up the quota that they have paid for in the auction, it is possible that part of the permit is traded to other firms that overshoot their respective quotas. In addition, it is also possible that firms that buy permits sub-contract production and buy back the produce under the premise that the assigned quota is not violated. This stands as one of the most efficient means to lower the pollution generated in any country.

In recent times, the pollution quota can also be traded across countries when the pollution is no longer restricted to individual countries and spread to many contiguous locations via spillover. The main routes through which pollution spills over to neighbouring regions and countries include water-borne and air-borne modes. The cap-and-trade policy is a system designed to reduce pollution in the atmosphere as devised by various climate protection agencies and funds duly supported by multilateral efforts in negotiating limits. The cap on greenhouse gas emissions that drive global warming is a limit on pollution. The cap gets stricter over time and requires wider compliance to mitigate the full scale. In our case, this translates into price effects per participating country. The trade in such permits offers a market for companies and effectively for the country as a whole to buy and sell allowances that acquiesce them to emit a certain amount. The market price is often an outcome of supply and demand but also set by public choice in some cases.

The present chapter explored one possibility hitherto left out of the literature that attempts coupling of trade and environmental policies. Here, a country decides to pull out of its commitment to multilateral agencies and chooses to set no further restrictions on the level of emission internally. Consequently, the cooperative prospect of global pollution reduction gets jeopardised. We model this possibility in a multi-country framework and show that the non-participating country stands to lose in terms of welfare if trade in pollution helps to improve consumption of the other tradable commodity. The mechanism is based on the interaction between the two other countries wherein the trade in pollution allows the most polluting and the least polluting countries to adjust their individual levels of emissions given country-specific caps.

The treaty between participating countries allows firms to continue producing the commodity which the non-participating country typically exports in large quantities when pollution quotas would otherwise restrict production in such countries. Without the quota, there may be no trade in commodities among relatively inefficient countries; whereas with the quota and the cap-and-trade policy, trade in commodities is more between participating nations at the cost of lesser transactions with the non-participating country. We argued that this is one of the stronger reasons why non-participation in environmental treaties could be harmful for specific countries, even if non-adherence does not lower their welfare directly.

Despite early suggestions to use adverse trade policies against countries that do not comply with international environmental treaties, not much has been done individually or as a consortium to apply such for the greater environmental improvement. One common reason is the distortions that trade barriers create with some undesirable distributional impact. It is also true that direct trade barriers have become increasingly unpopular with multilateral agencies for the fear of retaliation and loss of internal consumer welfare. This chapter uses a simple trade model that does not require tariff and non-tariff barriers for restricting trade flows that are environmentally harmful, but studies the implications of higher per-unit burden on the compliant countries on their demand for other traded commodities. We have shown that countries that do not participate in trade in emission suffer due to lower demand for the commodities that they trade in the world market. This is the main source of welfare loss that acts as a penalty for the non-participant and might force it to abide by international emission reduction treaties. Extensions of this result to multi-country and multi-product cases with varying degrees of pollution may enrich the present formulation and results.

Notes

1 The paper has benefited from comments at the XI Biennial INSEE Conference in 2021 and excellent suggestions by Anindita Sen. The remaining errors are our own.
2 We discuss environmental treaties and the related literature in the following section.
3 Hitchens (1997) offers a comprehensive collection of policies prevalent in the EU and their impact on regional competition in production.
4 See Unteroberdoerster (2001), which extends Copeland and Taylor (1995) to show that transboundary pollution has an impact on trade pattern with a possibility of raising both exposure and pollution levels.
5 It is well known that the literature on dirty goods and pollution haven is enormous. At the risk of being ignorant and trite, we only refer to some studies that bring out the analytical and empirical tension between FDI and pollution haven hypothesis in recent times; see Ederington and Minier (2003), Eskeland and Harrison (2003), Cole, Elliott and Frederiksson (2006), Dean, Lovely and Hua (2009), etc.

6 A compendium of some of these analyses with additional inferences is available in Acharyya (2013).
7 Kar and Majumdar (2021) discuss the production functions and sources of emission for CO_2 and other harmful gases with cross-border impact.

References

Acharyya, R. (2013) *Trade and Environment*, Oxford University Press, New Delhi.

Antweiler, W., B. Copeland and M. S. Taylor (2001) "Is free trade good for the environment?", *American Economic Review*, 91(4), 877–908.

Barrett, S. (1998) "Political economy of the Kyoto protocol", *Oxford Review of Economic Policy*, 14(4), 20–39.

Barrett, S. (2008) "Climate treaties and the imperative of enforcement", *Oxford Review of Economic Policy*, 24(2), 239–258.

Barrett, S. (2011) "Rethinking climate change governance and its relationship to the world trading system", *The World Economy*, 34(11), 1863–1882.

Benarroch, M. and H. Thille (2001) "Transboundary pollution and the gains from trade", *Journal of International Economics*, 55(1), 139–159.

Bhagwati, J. N., Brecher, R. A., and Hatta T. (1983) The Generalized Theory of Transfers and Welfare: Bilateral Transfers in a Multilateral World. *The American Economic Review*, 73(4), 606–618.

Bruvoll, A. and T. Fæhn (2006) "Transboundary effects of environmental policy: Markets and emission leakages", *Ecological Economics*, 59(4), 499–510.

Cole, M., R. Elliott and P. Fredriksson (2006) "Endogenous pollution havens: Does FDI influence environmental regulations?", *Scandinavian Journal of Economics*, 108(1), 157–178.

Costantini, V., M. Mazzanti and A. Montini (2013) "Environmental performance, innovation and spillovers. Evidence from a regional NAMEA", *Ecological Economics*, 89, 101–114.

Copeland, B. (1996) "Pollution content tariff, environmental rent shifting and the control of cross border pollution", *Journal of International Economics*, 40(3–4), 459–476.

Copeland, B. and S. Taylor (1995) "Trade and transboundary pollution", *American Economic Review*, 85(4), 716–737.

Copeland, B. R. (1997) "Pollution content tariffs, environmental rent shifting, and the control of cross-border pollution", *Journal of International Economics*, 40(3–4), 459–476.

Dean, J. M., M. E. Lovely and H. Wang (2009) "Are foreign investors attracted to weak environmental regulations? Evaluating the evidence from China", *Journal of Development Economics*, 90(1), 1–13.

Dinar, A., B. Blankespoor, S. Dinar and P. Kurukulasuriya (2011) "Does precipitation and runoff variability affect treaty cooperation between states sharing international bilateral rivers?", *Ecological Economics*, 69(12), 2568–2581.

Dong, Baomin, Gong, Jiong and Zhao, Xin, (2012) FDI and environmental regulation: pollution haven or a race to the top?, *Journal of Regulatory Economics*, 41, issue 2, p. 216–237.

Ederington, J. and J. Minier (2003) "Is environmental policy a secondary trade barrier? An empirical analysis", *Canadian Journal of Economics/Revue Canadienne d`Economique*, 36(1), 137–154.

Erdogan, A. M. (2014) "Foreign direct investment and Environmental Regulation: A survey", *Journal of Economic Issues*, 28(5), 943–955.

Eskeland, G. and A. Harrison (2003) "Moving to greener pastures? Multinationals and the pollution-haven hypothesis", *Journal of Development Economics*, 70(1), 1–23.

Ferrara, I., P. Missios and H. Yildiz (2008) "Trading rules and the environment: Does equal treatment lead to a cleaner world?", *Journal of Environmental Economics and Management*, 58, 206–225.

Frankel, J. (2009) *Environmental Effects of International Trade*, Expert Report no. 31 to Sweden's Global Council, Stockholm.

Frankel, J. A. and A. K. Rose (2005) "Is trade good or bad for the environment? Sorting out the causality", *Review of Economics and Statistics*, 87(1), 85–91.

Greaker, M. and K. E. Rosendahl (2008) "Environmental policy with upstream pollution abatement technology firms", *Journal of Environmental Economics and Management*, 56(3), 246–259.

Harstad, Bard and Eskeland, Gunnar, (2010), Trading for the Future: Signaling in Permit Markets, No 2010/2, Discussion Papers, Norwegian School of Economics, Department of Business and Management Science, https://EconPapers.repec.org/RePEc:hhs:nhhfms:2010_002.

Hatzipanayotou, P., S. Lahiri and M. S. Michael (2002) "Can cross-border pollution reduce pollution?", *Canadian Journal of Economics/Revue Canadienne d'Economique*, 35(4), 805–818.

Hitchens, D. (1997) "Environmental policy and the implications for competitiveness in the regions of the EU", *Regional Studies*, 31(8), 813–819.

International Carbon Action Partnership (2015) *Emission Trading Worldwide - ICAP Status Report*, International Carbon Action Partnership, Berlin.

Jackson, T. (2001) "Environmental taxation: A new tool for local planning?", *Regional Studies*, 35(1), 80–85.

Kar, S. and D. Majumdar (2016) "MFN tariff rates and carbon emission: Evidence from lower-middle-income countries", *Environmental and Resource Economics*, 64(3), 493–510.

Kar, S. and D. Majumdar (2021) "Transboundary pollution, land use and abatement policy", *Economic Analysis and Policy*, 72, 169–175.

Kheder, S. B. and N. Zugravu (2008) "The pollution haven hypothesis: A geographic economy model in a comparative study", *Documents de travail du centre d'economie de la Sorbonne*, 2008.83.

McCarthy, J. E. (2010) *Aviation and Climate Change*, Congressional Research Service, Washington, DC.

McGinty, M. (2007) International Environmental Agreements among Asymmetric Nations, *Oxford Economic Papers*, 59(1), 45–62.

Livingston, M. L. (1989) Transboundary Environmental Degradation: Market Failure, Power, and Instrumental Justice. *Journal of Economic Issues*, 23(1), 79–91.

Nordhaus, W. (2006) "After Kyoto: Alternative mechanisms to control global warming", *American Economic Review*, 96(2), 31–34.

Nordhaus, W. (2007) "To tax or not to tax: The case for a carbon tax", *Review of Environmental Economics and Policy*, 1(1), 26–44.

Sawhney, A. and S. Mitra (2011) "Examining tradeable permits with market power, banking and non-compliance: A finite period model", *Economics Bulletin*, 31(2), 1265–1274.

Schmalensee, R. and R. Stavins (2017) "Lessons learned from three decades of experience with cap and trade", *Review of Environmental Economics and Policy*, 11(1), 59–79.
Stiglitz, J. E. (2011) Chapter 3: The economists' voice: Top economists take on today's problems. (Eds.) Stiglitz, Joseph E., Aaron S. Edlin, and J. Bradford DeLong. In *A New Agenda for Global Warming*, Columbia University Press, New York, pp. 22–27.
Tietenberg, TH (2003) Environmental and Natural Resource Economics. 6th ed. Addison Wesley, NY.
Unteroberdoerster, O. (2001) "Trade and transboundary pollution: Spatial separation reconsidered", *Journal of Environmental Economics and Management*, 41(3), 269–285.
Waldkirch, A. and M. Gopinath (2008) "Pollution control and foreign direct investment in Mexico: An industry-level analysis", *Environmental and Resource Economics*, 41(3), 289–313.

12 Inflow of Educational Capital, Intermediation and Informal Sector

Sangita Roy and Biswajit Mandal

12.1 Introduction

The developing economies of the world are characterised by the existence of a vast informal sector. This sector in particular not only chalks out a way to help economies to solve its unemployment problem but also contributes significantly to domestic savings and investments. In simple words, the informal economy or the grey economy refers to those income-earning activities that are outside government regulation, taxation and observation. However, illegal activities are typically excluded from its definition. There are several examples of informal economic activity including people who sell produce at a roadside stand or those who perform day labour at a construction site in exchange for cash payments. The informal forms of organisations are major players in manufacturing, construction, transport, trade, hotels and restaurant services. Some of the characteristic features of informal employment are lack of protection in the event of non-payment of wages, compulsory overtime or extra shifts, lay-offs without notice or compensation, unsafe working conditions and the absence of social benefits such as pensions, sick pay and health insurance. To suit the purpose of the chapter, we define the informal sector as one which does not have to pay the minimum wage. A lot of papers in literature of informal sector have used this interpretation such as Agenor and Montiel (1997), Carruth and Oswald (1981), Marjit (2003), Marjit and Kar (2009, 2009a), Marjit, Kar and Beladi (2007), Kar and Marjit (2001), Beladi and Chao (1993) and Beladi and Yabuuchi (2001).

Emerging markets tend to rank highly among nations that have the largest informal economies, whereas developed markets tend to have the least informal economic activity within them. In a recent study by Schneider (2012), 162 countries were ranked by the relative size of their informal economies and it is found that Bolivia, Georgia and Panama are having the largest concentration of informal economic activity followed by the others. The United States ranked at the bottom at 161 followed by Switzerland. Shadow economies may seem advantageous to certain workers because wages are received free of taxes. However, the social cost of these wages

DOI: 10.4324/9781003375050-12

manifests themselves in the form of lost tax revenues and social security payments. Informalisation of jobs has become a matter of concern with the initiation of liberalisation policies in the early 1990s. On an average, more than 70 percent of the working population in developing economies is employed in the informal sector (Agenor, 1996). This sector also accounts for a large share in the gross domestic product (GDP) of developed and developing countries. Women in Informal Employment: Globalizing and Organizing (WIEGO) (WIEGO) has worked closely with the International Labour Organization (ILO) in the development of statistics on informal economy that led to the publication of the first-ever global estimates on the size of informal employment in 2018. The study based on micro-data collected from more than hundred countries comprising near about 90 percent of the world's population estimated that 61 percent of all the workers are informally employed. This accounts for nearly two billion workers worldwide (WIEGO, 2018). Developing countries contribute to 90 percent of informal employment, whereas for emerging and developed countries the contribution is 67 percent and 18 percent, respectively. Among the emerging and developing economies, sub-Saharan Africa (excluding Southern Africa) has the highest percentage of its workers employed informally and the figure is 92 percent. In Southern Asia, 88 percent of the employment is informal. The proportion is 77 percent in East and South-eastern Asia (excluding China), 68 percent in the Middle East and North Africa, 54 percent in Latin America and the Caribbean, and 37 percent in Eastern Europe and Central Asia (ILO, 2018). There are 92.4 percent of informal workers in India with no written contract, paid leave and other benefits. There are also 9.8 percent of informal workers in the organised sectors indicating the level of outsourcing. The share of informal employment has increased by 3.6 percentage points over 2011–2012 to 2017–2018 (NSS 68th round).

A lot of literature suggests corruption that has its roots lie deep in bureaucratic and political institutions as one of the reasons for the existence of informal sector in developing economies (Kaufmann, 1997; Johnson et al., 1998). In other words, the survival of informal sector requires some sort of negotiations with the administration as it is extra illegal by nature. This is done by politically supported intermediaries, called the "extortionists", who take care of legal troubles and other hurdles for the informal producers and in turn extract some amount of rent from the informal producer (Mandal, Marjit and Beladi, 2018). Theoretically, corruption and informal economy can be either complements or substitutes. The negative link between corruption and the size of informal economy is studied by scholars like Johnson et al. (1998); Choi and Thum (2004); Dreher et al. (2005) to name a few. The full employment model of Johnson et al. (1998) depicts informal economy as a substitute for the official (formal) economy and exhibits a negative relationship between the two. An increase in informal economy results in a decrease in the official economy. Higher corruption in the official economy increases the size of informal economy which functions like a tax on firms in the official economy and drives them underground. Choi and Thum (2004) present a model where the option of entrepreneurs to get underground constrains a corrupt official's ability to ask for bribes. The shadow or informal economy mitigates distortions in the official economy and disables bureaucrats from realising personal gains. The existence of the informal economy thus reduces corruption. Johnson et al. (1998), Schneider and Enste (2000) and Friedman et al. (2000), on the contrary, model corruption and informal economy as complements. Dreher and Schneider (2006) suggest that corruption and the informal economy tend to be substitutes in high-income countries but complement in low-income countries. Bribes are one of the main tools of corruption which raises transaction costs and uncertainty in an economy. It impedes long-term foreign and domestic investment, misallocates talent to rent-seeking activities and distorts sectoral priorities and technology choices. It pushes firms underground, undercuts the state's liability to raise revenues and leads to ever-higher tax rates being levied on fewer and fewer taxpayers (Gray and Kaufmann, 1998). Bribes can be used to reduce the amount of taxes and other fees collected by the Government to set up a legal institution or firm. Corruption, however, tends to flourish when institutions are weak and government policies generate economic rents. Substantial corruption among the law enforcement authorities, financial agencies, bureaucrats, politicians and other regulators would essentially mean more bribery and greater rent-seeking in the formal sector (Saha, 2001). Thus, the cost of creating a new business and maintaining it in the formal sector rises in the presence of intermediation activities, and this crowds out some entrepreneurs in preference for informal entrepreneurship as they seek to avoid bureaucratic rigidities and high tax burden. Marjit, Mukherjee and Kolmer (2006) analysed the causes behind the emergence of an informal sector in a political economy framework. For economies characterised by high unemployment, high inequality and poverty, the government may choose a lower level of good governance to maximise income for a large informal sector and avoid social conflicts and political disturbances. Loayza (1996) in a study of Latin American economies shows that a robust and less burdensome institutional framework reduces the size of informal sector. Specifically, a standard deviation improvement in the strength and efficiency of the institutional framework is associated with a 0.42 standard deviation decrease in the size of informal sector. In a study of 49 countries of Latin America, the former Soviet Union and the Organisation for Economic Co-operation and Development (OECD), it is shown that a one-point improvement in Transparency International (TI) corruption index is associated with a 5.1 percent reduction in the informal economy. Further, using the Global Competitiveness Survey as a proxy for bribery, a one-point improvement in the index implies an 8 percent reduction in informal sector (Johnson et al., 1998). Friedman et al. (2000) show that irrespective of country's level of economic activity as proxied by GDP per capita, a one-point improvement in the corruption index is associated with 9.7 percent reduction in the size of informal sector. Thus, regardless of the economy's level of economic activity and the kind of corruption index used, it is clear that the size of informal sector increases with the level of corruption. Dutta, Kar and Roy (2011) made an empirical attempt to investigate the corruption–informality linkage in India based on a study of 20 Indian states. The result confirms the positive relationship between level of corruption and size of informal sector. Besides this, the study also points out that as state-level productivity rises the positive impact of corruption on the size of informal sector reverses itself. It is noteworthy to mention that in order to reduce extortion in the informal segment countries like Ghana, Senegal, Kenya and others have already attempted to facilitate and promote registration and license to informal units. This has resulted in a significant reduction in the degree of extortion (Fjeldstad, 2001).

For the purpose of this study, we adopt the general definition of corruption as the misuse or abuse of public power for private gains (World Bank, 1997; UNDP, 1999). The World Bank (2009) defines corruption as

> It distorts the rule of law, weakens a nation's institutional foundation, and severely affects the poor who are already the most disadvantaged members of our Society and is among the greatest obstacles to economic and social development.

In such an environment, we introduce educational capital as an indirect factor of production. This educational capital is used only to train the unskilled labours of the economy and let them secure a job in the highly paid skilled sector. This form of capital is not directly involved in the production process. Again, the unskilled labour forces are employed by both formal and informal entrepreneurs. Even after the satisfaction of demand of formal and informal producers, some unskilled labours are still left without a job. Now, this part of labour force cannot remain unemployed for a long time and ultimately they get involved in the extortion sector to earn a livelihood. On the other hand, developing economies generally face a great crisis of educational capital or training facilities. Thus, educational capital now-a-days moves from developed to developing countries as the demand for skilled labour, and hence educational capital naturally grows with the process of development. Therefore, educational capital mobility is an important ingredient of development process. The importance of educational capital has been studied in a number of papers like Lucas (2002), Barro (1991), Easterly (2001), Findlay (1995), Banerjee and Newman (1993), Galor and Zeira (1993), Mandal and Roy (2018), etc., to name a few. Educational capital mainly enriches the human capital of an economy through the process of training. A microeconomic model shows that education investment for workers significantly affects his or her productivity in workplace (Lucas, 1988). Empirical literature on the link between human capital and growth indicates that it contributes not only towards output growth but also improves a country's capacity to adopt new technologies. Countries with a larger stock of human capital experience faster growth. Technology fails to flow to the poor countries because of their poor endowment of human capital and a high level of initial endowment of human capital improves economy's ability to utilise new ideas (Nelson and Phelps, 1966). Trade models capturing the issue of time zone difference and communication technology show that although the wage inequality between skilled and unskilled workers is widened under reasonable condition, it attracts educational capital from abroad and eventually alter the sectoral composition of the economy in favour of more skill-based activities (Mandal, Marjit and Nakanishi, 2018). Moreover, a recent study shows that economic recession may actually benefit a large number of informal workers as some of the unionised unskilled workers lose formal sector employment and move onto informal sector. As capital moves from the formal to informal segment of the economy, both informal employment and wage may boost up (Mandal, 2016). Economic reforms lead to an increase in informal output and informal wage depending on the degree of capital mobility and factor intensity assumption. It may have an expansionary effect on the number of extortionists (Mandal, Marjit and Beladi, 2018). The size of intermediation activities expands both following a tax cut and a fall in the degree of corruption. But surprisingly, a fall in the degree of corruption increases the number of intermediators while tax change has no such effect (Mandal, 2018). In this particular chapter, we have tried to trace out the effect of inflow of such educational capital on the output of an economy which is plagued with activities like corruption, bribery, etc.

The remainder of the chapter is organised as follows. Section 12.2 presents a detailed discussion of the structure of economy and the model. Section 12.3 talks about the results obtained and their intuitive explanations. Finally, Section 12.4 concludes. A detailed mathematical calculation is provided in Appendix A.

12.2 The Basic Model and Solutions

One important feature of informal sector is the existence of harassment related to corruption. Since by definition informal sector is illegal or extra-legal, it is susceptible to bureaucratic and political harassment. Therefore, in order to get rid of the harassment, producers need to get hold of intermediation. Precisely speaking, this intermediation is done by unskilled labour and capital. Thus, a part of the value of informal produce is lost which is spent on labour and capital used in intermediation. In this background, we have considered a small open economy comprising three sectors producing three different goods X, Y and Z and one intermediation (corruptive) sector represented by N. Out of these three goods X and Y are produced in formal sectors that use either skilled labour or labourers get a unionised wage. On the other hand, Z is produced informally using unskilled labour who fails to get a job with unionised wage in the formal sector. Physical capital and labour are used for producing these three commodities. According to the tradition, labours are segregated into skilled labour and unskilled labour. Skilled labours are sector specific and are trained using a certain amount of educational capital. Educational capital is not directly involved in the production process, it is used only for training the unskilled labour force of the economy. Physical capital is a direct input and is freely mobile among these three sectors. Unskilled labour and physical capital are assumed to be freely mobile between the informal sector and the extortion sector. Prices of the goods are determined in the rest of the world as the country in consideration is a small open economy with a small contribution in world's trade volume.

Commodity X is produced in a skill-specific formal sector using skilled labour (S) and physical capital (K). The labours of sector X have attained some special training to secure a job here. Special training can easily encompass the issues such as vocational training, technical training, computer literacy, software knowledge, etc. A software-developing firm may be a good example of this type of sector. Since X is a skill-intensive formal sector, the labours are paid a wage at a rate W_s which is obviously greater than the wage of unskilled labour. Physical capital (K) gets a return "r" per unit. The per-unit price of commodity $X(P_X)$ is determined in the international market, and the country in assumption being a small participant in world trade is unable to influence the price. The competitive price equation for this sector is given as

$$W_S a_{SX} + r a_{KX} = P_X. \tag{12.1}$$

Commodity Y is also produced in a formal sector using unskilled labour (L) and physical capital (K). The formal sector is characterised by the presence of strong labour union, and the workers here get a pre-negotiated fixed wage $\left(\bar{W}\right)$. Physical capital (K) gets a return "r" per unit. Labours of this sector do not have any specified skill as the labours employed in sector X, but they are lucky enough to secure a job in this formal sector and earn an assured high and fixed wage $\left(\bar{W}\right)$. As discussed earlier, the price of commodity Y is again assumed to be given as the country in consideration is a small participant in world trade. The competitive price equation for this sector is written as

$$\bar{W} a_{LY} + r a_{KY} = P_Y. \tag{12.2}$$

After satisfying the demand for labour in these two formal sectors, some labour still remains unemployed. This unemployed section of the workforce has neither any specific training nor are they lucky enough to secure a job in the unskilled formal sector Y. But they cannot of course remain jobless for a long time. They have to get engaged somewhere to obtain their subsistence level of earnings. This leads to the existence of informal sector Z in our model. Sector Z uses unskilled labour (L) and physical capital (K) for its production. Z being an informal sector, there is an absence of trade union to protect the interest of the workers and hence there is no minimum wage legislation law. Workers are paid a market-based competitive wage (W) and the capital gets a return r. However, this sector is distorted by the intermediation of local "tolapickers", and thus a certain proportion (α) of the value of the good (P_Z) is appropriated by L_N as a fee of extortion. The competitive price equation for this sector is written as

$$Wa_{LZ} + ra_{LZ} = P_Z(1-\alpha). \tag{12.3}$$

We further assume that unskilled labour and some amount of physical capital are involved in the activities of intermediation. Labours involved in the intermediation activities (L_N) get a wage equal to the wage of the informal workers (W) and capital involved in intermediation activities (K_N) gets r. Now the expenditure involved in intermediation activities must be equal to the value of lost output of the informal sector. Suppose α is the fraction of output that is lost due to institutional complications related to intermediations. Thus, we may write

$$WL_N + rK_N = \alpha P_Z Z. \tag{12.4}$$

We also assume that the production function for intermediation exhibits a linear relationship represented by the following equation:

$$L_N = \gamma K_N. \tag{12.5}$$

The economy is endowed with certain amount of skilled labour (S), unskilled labour (L), physical capital (K) and educational capital (E). It is assumed that all the factors are fully utilised in the production process.

Informal workers have a chance to get trained and secure jobs in the skill-specific sector X. We assume that L_1 number of informal workers are trained and upgraded to skilled labour S_1 using a certain amount of educational capital (E). Such upgraded skilled labour then gets a job in the skill-specific formal sector X. S is the number of skilled labours that were already given in the economy and S_1 is the number of informal labours that are getting trained in the process and adding to the stock of skilled labours. Hence, the full employment condition for skilled labour in the economy can be written as

$$a_{SX}X = S + S_1. \tag{12.6}$$

The concerned economy is already endowed with L number of unskilled labour. Out of this stock, L_N is the number of unskilled labours who are engaged in corruption activities and S_1 is the number of labours that go out for training. Thus, the full employment condition for unskilled labour is given by the following equation:

$$a_{LY}Y + a_{LZ}Z = L - L_N - S_1. \tag{12.7}$$

Similarly, the full employment condition for physical capital is given by the following equation:

$$a_{KX}X + a_{KY}Y + a_{KZ}Z = K - K_N. \tag{12.8}$$

The economy concerned is also endowed with certain amount of educational capital (E) which is used only for the purpose of training the unskilled labour. In this model, we do not incorporate the time factor needed in acquiring skills. This is a static model. Another important point to be noted is that the educational training sector reflects fixed proportion technology μ_{ES}. The cost of acquiring skill has to be borne by the unskilled labour himself. The full employment condition for educational capital is given by

$$\mu_{ES}S_1 = E. \tag{12.9}$$

For simplicity, we assume that only unskilled labours will undergo training in lieu of getting a job in the highly skilled intensive sector X where they could get a higher wage premium. This wage must compensate his earnings from the informal sector $Z(W)$ and the return to the educational capital spent on training. This is shown in Equation (12.10):

$$W + \mu_{ES}R = W_S. \tag{12.10}$$

The variables of the model are $W_S, \bar{W}, W, r$ and R that are determined using the price equations. All markets are assumed to be perfectly competitive along with the market for corruption-related activities. A competitive corruption market implies that the lost output due to intermediation is fully exhausted in paying out extortionists. We also have the standard neo-classical assumption of constant returns to scale and diminishing return to factors. We determined r from Equation (12.2). Substituting the value of r in Equations (12.1) and (12.3), we obtain W_s and W, respectively. Finally, using the value of W in Equation (12.10), we obtain R. Further solving the endowment equations (12.6)–(12.9), we get the output effect of sectors X, Y and Z. The mathematical results are summarised in Appendix A and this will help us in exploring the effects of inflow of educational capital on price of factors and output of different sectors of the economy. The set of symbols used in representing the equations of the model are usual and used in different trade models.[1]

12.3 Effect of Inflow of Educational Capital in the Presence of Intermediation Activities

An inflow of educational capital in the economy helps to train a large chunk of unskilled labour force of the economy. Thus, it induces to upgrade the unskilled labours into skilled labour. But an inflow of educational capital (E) will essentially have no impact on the rate of return to physical capital (r) as it is already determined from Equation (12.2) of the basic model, given the wage of formal labour $(\bar{W})$ and price of the commodity Y. The wage of unskilled labour (W) should also remain unchanged for any given α and P_Z, and wage of skilled labour (W_s) also remains unchanged as there is no change in r. Hence, there will be no change in the rate of return to educational capital (R). However, an inflow of educational capital raises the output of the skilled formal sector X by increasing the supply of skilled labour (S_1) in the economy. Some members of unskilled labours get trained using educational capital and secure a job in the skilled formal sector. Educational capital has a two-way effect on the supply of labour. On the one hand, it raises the supply of skilled labours in the economy, and on the other, it reduces the amount of unskilled labours in the economy. The unskilled labours going out for training may come from either sector Y or sector Z, the intermediation sector represented by N or from both. The expansion of the skilled sector also requires some capital that has to be relocated to X from either Y, Z or corruption activity represented by N. In general, as the output of sector X expands, the combined output effect of sectors Y, Z and N falls unambiguously. The magnitude of the output effect on these sectors depends significantly on the factor intensity assumption. The mathematical solution to this general equilibrium model shows that there is no change in the output of the informal sector Z (as is evident from Equation (12.4)), but the output effect on formal sector Y and that of the corruption sector N depends on the factor intensity assumption.

Proposition 12.1 There is no change in factor earnings following an inflow of educational capital in the presence of corruption.

Explanation: The solutions for factor prices in the model are obtained by solving the price equations of the model represented through Equations (12.1) to (12.4) and Equation (12.10) (see Appendix A). Using the simple solution method for the general equilibrium model through the use of zero-profit condition and envelope theorem, we first derive the solution for the rate of change in return to physical capital (r) from Equation (12.2). With the given wage rate $\left(\bar{W}\right)$ for unskilled labour and the given price of informal commodity Y, we find that there is no change in the rate of return to physical capital. Substituting the value of $\hat{r} = 0$. in Equation (12.1), we have $\widehat{W_s} = 0$. as the price of formal good (X) is considered to be given exogenously. Further substituting $\hat{r} = 0$ in Equation (12.3), we have $\hat{W} = 0$ with the given price of commodity Z. Then using $\hat{W} = 0$ in Equation (12.10), we obtain $\hat{R} = 0$ as μ_{ES} is constant.

Proposition 12.2 An inflow of educational capital increases the output of the skilled sector independent of any factor intensity assumption, whereas the output of the formal sector increases under specific factor intensity assumption even in the presence of intermediation activities.

Explanation: Differentiating Equation (12.7), we derive an expression for change in the output of skilled sector X as $\hat{X} = \hat{E}\lambda_{S_1T}$ (see Equation (12.16) of Appendix A). From the expression, it is evident that the change in the output of sector X is dependent on the change in educational capital used for training unskilled labours. Thus, $\hat{X} > 0$ when $\hat{E} > 0$. Again, on solving Equations (12.8) and (12.9) and manipulating it, we derive an expression for the change in output of formal sector Y as $\hat{Y} = \frac{\hat{E}}{|\lambda|}(\lambda_{KX}\lambda_{S_1T}\lambda_{LN} - \lambda_{S_1L}\lambda_{KN})$ (see Equation (12.20) of Appendix A).

Now, $\hat{Y} > 0$ if $\lambda_{KX}\lambda_{S_1T}\lambda_{LN} > \lambda_{S_1L}\lambda_{KN}$ as $\lambda > 0$. This is quite reasonable as $\lambda_{S_1T} > \lambda_{S_1L}$ and the intermediation sector may be assumed to be labour intensive in absolute term.

The model assumes that sector X is a skill-intensive technical sector that uses skilled labour (S) and a common type of physical capital (K) in its production process. Labours employed in this particular sector have gone through a certain specific training programme to secure a job here. As more and more unskilled labours from other sectors of the economy get trained using a certain amount of educational capital and are absorbed by the skill-intensive sector, their output gets a boost. On the other hand, sector Y is a formal traded sector of the economy that uses unskilled labour hired at a fixed higher pre-negotiated wage and physical capital in its production process. If we assume corruption sector to be more labour intensive in an absolute sense, then an inflow of educational capital in the economy will boost up the output of formal sector Y. Thus, the formal sector would expand.

Proposition 12.3 An inflow of educational capital leads to a reduction in the degree of pursuing intermediation activities.

Explanation: Differentiating Equation (12.9) and manipulating it, we derive the expression for the rate of change of amount of labour employed in the intermediation sector represented by N in our model. This is given by $\widehat{L_N} = \frac{\hat{E}}{|\lambda|}(\lambda_{KY}\lambda_{S_1L} - \lambda_{KX}\lambda_{LY}\lambda_{S_1T})$ (see Equation (12.21) of Appendix A). Now, λ_{KX} is significant as sector X is a skilled-intensive technical sector. Moreover, $\lambda_{S_1T} > \lambda_{S_1L}$ and thus $\widehat{L_N} < 0$.

The economy in consideration is characterised by the existence of intermediation activities which requires unskilled labour and physical capital. People enter the intermediation sector not by choice, but out of the need to survive. A secured highly paid job is always preferred over an uncertain illegal remuneration. Thus, an inflow of educational capital in the economy motivates the labours engaged in intermediation activities to get trained and secure a job in the formal sector. Thus, labour forces are driven out of the intermediation sector and its output falls unambiguously.

12.4 Conclusion

In this chapter, we have tried to trace out the effects of an inflow of educational capital on factor prices and output of different sectors of the economy. The economy comprises two formal and one informal sector along with a corruptive sector. It is found that an inflow of educational capital has no effect on factor prices used in the model. But, the output of skilled intensive formal sector gets a boost due to the inflow of educational capital independent of any factor intensity assumption. This is due to the fact that as educational capital flows in, more and more labour gets trained and secures a job in the skill-intensive formal sector thereby raising its output. On the other hand, the output of formal sector using unskilled labour in its production process may expand if the intermediation sector is assumed to be labour intensive in an absolute sense. This is quite a reasonable assumption. One most important and positive effect of the inflow of educational capital is that it drives out labour from the corruptive sector, motivates them for training and these labours secure a job in the highest paid skill-intensive formal sector of the economy. Thus, interestingly, an inflow of educational capital leads to a fall in intermediation activities in an economy.

Appendix A

Differentiating Equation (12.2) and using zero-profit condition and envelope condition, we get

$$\hat{r} = 0. \tag{12.11}$$

Similarly differentiating (12.1) and (12.3), we get

$$\widehat{W_S} = 0, \tag{12.12}$$

$$\hat{W} = 0. \tag{12.13}$$

Solving Equation (12.10), we obtain

$$\hat{R} = 0. \tag{12.14}$$

Differentiating Equation (12.9), we get

$$\widehat{S_1} = \hat{E}, \tag{12.15}$$

as educational capital has no other alternative use except for training the informal workers.

Differentiating Equations (12.6)–(12.8) and then manipulating them, we arrive at the following equations

$$\hat{X} = \hat{E}\lambda_{S_1T} > 0, \tag{12.16}$$

$$\lambda_{LY}\hat{Y} + \widehat{L_N}\lambda_{LN} = -\hat{E}\lambda_{S_1L}, \tag{12.17}$$

$$\lambda_{KX}\hat{X} + \lambda_{KY}\hat{Y} + \lambda_{KZ}\hat{Z} = -\widehat{K_N}\lambda_{KN}. \tag{12.18}$$

Using Equation (12.4), we have $\hat{Z} = 0$.

Substituting this value and manipulating Equation (12.18), we can write

$$\lambda_{KY}\hat{Y} + \widehat{L_N}\lambda_{KN} = -\lambda_{KX}\hat{E}\lambda_{S_1T}. \tag{12.19}$$

Solving Equations (12.17) and (12.19), we obtain

$$\hat{Y} = \frac{\hat{E}}{|\lambda|}\left(\lambda_{KX}\lambda_{S_1T}\lambda_{LN} - \lambda_{S_1L}\lambda_{KN}\right), \tag{12.20}$$

$\hat{Y} > 0$ if $\lambda_{KX}\lambda_{S_1T}\lambda_{LN} > \lambda_{S_1L}\lambda_{KN}$ as $|\lambda| > 0$,

$$\widehat{L_N} = \frac{\hat{E}}{|\lambda|}\left(\lambda_{KY}\lambda_{S_1L} - \lambda_{KX}\lambda_{LY}\lambda_{S_1T}\right). \tag{12.21}$$

$\widehat{L_N} < 0$ if $\lambda_{KY}\lambda_{S_1L} > \lambda_{KX}\lambda_{LY}\lambda_{S_1T}$.

Note

1 W_s = Wage of skilled labour, $\bar{W}$ = Wage of unskilled labour employed in formal sector, W = Wage of informal workers, r = rate of return to physical capital, R = rate of return to educational capital, X = output of skilled intensive formal sector, Y = output of formal sector, Z = output of informal sector, P_X, P_Y, P_Z = exogenous prices of commodities, E, L, S, K= Total supply of educational capital, unskilled labour, skilled labour and physical capital in the economy, S_1 = amount of unskilled labour upgraded to skilled labour. a_{ij} = input coefficients, θ_{ij} = relative share of the *i*th input in the total value of the *j*th commodity where $i = S, L, K$ and $j = X, Y, Z$, ^ = represents percentage changes for particular variables.

References

Agenor, P. 1996. "The labour market and economic adjustment". *IMF Staff Papers*, 32:261–355.

Agenor, R. and P. Montiel. 1997. "The determination of union and non-union wage-rates". *European Economic Review*, 16(2):285–302.

Banerjee, A.V. and A.F. Newman. 1993. "Occupational choice and the process of development". *Journal of Political Economy*, 101(2):274–298.

Barro, R.J. 1991. "Economic growth in a cross-section of countries". *Quarterly Journal of Economics*, 106(2):407–473.

Beladi, H. and C. Chao. 1993. "Non-traded goods, urban unemployment and welfare in LDCs". *European Journal of Political Economy*, 9(2):281–292.

Beladi, H. and S. Yabuuchi. 2001. "Tariff induced capital inflow and welfare in the presence of unemployment and informal sector". *Japan and the World Economy*, 13(1):51–60.

Carruth, A. and A. Oswald. 1981. "Non-traded goods, urban unemployment and welfare in LDCs". *European Journal of Political Economy*, 9(2):281–292.

Choi, J. and M. Thum. 2004. "Corruption and the shadow economy". *International Economic Review*, 12/4:308–342.

Dreher, A., C. Kotsogiannis and S. McCorriston. 2005. "How do institutions affect corruption and the shadow economy?" *University of Exeter, Devon. Discussion Paper 0505, Department of Economics*.

Dreher, A. and F. Schneider. 2006. "Corruption and shadow economy: An empirical analysis". *Discussion Paper*, Department of Economics, University of Linz,Linz

Dutta, N., S. Kar and S. Roy. 2011. "Informal sector and corruption: An empirical investigation for India". *IZA Discussion Paper No. 5576*. Institute for the Study of Labour, Bonn, Germany.

Easterly, W. 2001. *The Elusive Quest for Growth: Economists' Adventures and Misadventures in the Tropics*. MIT Press, Cambridge.

Findlay, R. 1995. "Factor proportions, trade and growth". *Ohlin Lectures*, Vol. 5. MIT Press, Cambridge.

Fjeldstad, O. 2001. "Donors turn blind eye to extortion in tax collection in Africa". *Development Today*, 11(8): 1–2.

Friedman, E., S. Johnson, D. Kaufmann and P. Zoido-Lobaton. 2000. "Dodging the grabbing hand: The determinants of unofficial activity in 69 countries". *Journal of Public Economics*, 76(3):459–493.

Galor, O. and J. Zeira. 1993. "Income distribution and macroeconomics". *Review of Economic Studies*, 60(1):35–52.

Gray, C.W. and D. Kaufmann. 1998. "Corruption and development". *Finance and Development*, *35*(1): 7–10.

ILO. 2018. *Women and Men in the Informal Economy: A Statistical Picture* (3rd edition). International Labour Office, Geneva.

Johnson, S., D. Kaufmann and P. Zoido-Lobaton. 1998. "Regulatory discretion and the unofficial economy". *American Economic Review*, 88(2):387–392.

Kar, S. and S. Marjit. 2001. "Informal sector in general equilibrium: Welfare effects of trade policy reforms". *International Review of Economics and Finance*, 10(3):289–300.

Kaufmann, D. 1997. "Corruption: The facts". *Foreign Policy*, 107:114–131.

Loayza, V.N. 1996. "The economics of informal sector: A simple model and some empirical evidence from Latin America". *Carnegie-Rochester Conference Series on Public Policy*, 45:129–162.

Lucas, R.E. 1988. "On the mechanics of development planning". *Journal of Monetary Economics*, 22(1):3–42.

Lucas, R.E. 2002. Lectures on Economic Growth. Havard University Press, Cambridge.

Mandal, B. 2016. "Recessionary shock, capital mobility and the informal sector". *South Asia Economic Journal*, 17(1):149–162.

Mandal, B. 2018. "Tax on traded goods, and corrupt non-traded goods sector: Implications for intermediation activities". *Review of Economics*, 69(1):27–41.

Mandal, B.S., S. Marjit and H. Beladi. 2018. "Reform, informal sector and extortion". *Economics and Politics*, 30(1):106–123.

Mandal, B. and S. Roy. 2018. “Inflow of educational capital, trade liberalization, skill formation and informal sector”. *Eurasian Economic Review*, 8(1):115–129.

Marjit, S. 2003. “Economic reform and informal wage: A general equilibrium analysis”. *Journal of Development Economics*, 72(1):371–378.

Marjit, S. and S. Kar. 2009. “A contemporary perspective on the informal labour market: Theory, policy and the Indian experience”. *Economic and Political Weekly*, 44(14): 371–378.

Marjit, S. and S. Kar. 2009a. “Urban informal sector and poverty”. *International Review of Economics and Finance*, 18(4):631–642.

Marjit, S.S., S. Kar and H. Beladi. 2007. “Trade reform and informal wages”. *Review of Development Economics*, 11(2):313–320.

Marjit, S., V. Mukherjee and M. Kolmer. 2006. “Poverty, Taxation and Governance”. *The Journal of International Trade and Economic Development*, 15(3):325–333.

National Sample Survey Organization. 2011–12. *(68th Round), Employment and Unemployment*, New Delhi.

Nelson, R.R. and E.S. Phelps. 1966. “Investments in humans, technological diffusion and economic growth”. *American Economic Review*, 56:69–75.

Saha, B. 2001. “Red tape, incentive bribe and provision of subsidy”. *Journal of Development Economics*, 65(1):113–133.

Schneider, F. 2012. “The shadow economy and work in the shadow: What do we (not) know?” *IZA Discussion Paper*, 6423.

Schneider F. and Enste D.H. 2000. “Shadow Economies: Size, Causes and Consequences”. *Journal of Economic Literature*, 38: 77–114.

UNDP (United Nations Development Programme). 1999. *Human Development Report 1999*. Oxford University Press, New York.

WEIGO. (Women and Men in Informal Economy). 2018. A Statistical Brief

World Bank. 1997. *Helping Countries Combat Corruption, a Report of the Poverty Reduction and Economic Management Network*, Washington, D.C.

World Bank (2009). The *World Bank Annual Report 2009: Year in Review*, Volume 1. Washington, DC.

13 Exportable Product Quality and International Fragmentation in a Small Open Economy

Sudeshna Mitra[1]

13.1 Introduction

From the experience of many economies, it has been traditionally experienced that volume of exports acts as an engine of growth. But recent research on trade and development indicates that composition as well as quality of export is more important than volume of export for the growth performance of any developing economy. For example, India is an exporter of rice as well as software. The export of software requires skilled personnel. Moreover, it is the quality of software that matters in the export market. Hence, the quality of export is an important issue for developing countries in the world market.

It is found that countries promoting exports of more sophisticated goods grow faster (Rodrik, 2006; Hausmann, Hwang and Rodrik, 2007) compared to countries which fail to promote such exports. The policy-makers of developing countries, therefore, search for measures that would contribute to the improvement of export quality. Accordingly, upgradation of exportable products by an economy has become an important policy issue nowadays. It has been empirically found by Harding and Javorcik (2012) that there exists a positive relation between foreign direct investment (FDI) and export quality. The process of economic development of a developing economy leads to the reallocation of resources towards more productive production units, diversification of products and improvement in the quality of the goods produced. Production of higher varieties of existing exportable products can raise the levels of export revenue and productivity. It has been found that the potential for improving quality is different for different products – it is higher for manufacturing goods and lower for primary products. Empirically it is observed that developed countries export higher quality products, whereas developing countries export lower quality ones in general. It has been possible to produce a commodity in a wide range of qualities and varieties with the advent of new technologies in the present era. By diversifying into higher quality varieties, developing countries can reap large benefits from trade.

The issue of the quality of exports is also important from the point of view of environment-friendly products. The conventional belief is that

DOI: 10.4324/9781003375050-13

developing countries export relatively pollution-intensive products compared to developed countries. So enhancement of environmental quality of exportable product of developing countries provides a scope for the developing countries to market their products in developed countries in the presence of stringent environmental regulations. In the literature on trade and environment, there are two opposite views regarding the impact of FDI on environmental quality. One view is that FDI causes dirty industries to migrate to developing countries leading to deterioration of environmental quality in these countries. The other view is that FDI causes transfer of environmentally sound technology (EST) from developed to developing countries which help to enhance the environmental quality of products in these countries. So the impact of liberalisation on product quality (not necessarily just environmental quality) is an important topic of research in the context of developing countries.

There are various faces of trade liberalisation in a developing country, and of all these faces, two faces deserve special attention. One of these two faces is trade liberalisation in terms of tariff cut and the other is trade liberalisation in terms of FDI. The impact of both these aspects on exportable product quality has been examined in this model, and additionally the impact of increased endowment of skilled labour has also been considered on exportable product quality.

A study becomes interesting and innovative when any issue is considered which is important and is relatively new in the context of contemporary policy-making in developing countries though it has been neglected earlier by the researchers. One such aspect is the issue of international fragmentation from the point of view of use of intermediate input by the final producers. The issue is more important when exportable product quality is linked with international fragmentation. International fragmentation implies that the production process is divided into two parts in terms of intermediate inputs where one part is produced domestically and the other part is produced internationally. The concept of international fragmentation has been first introduced in the seminal works of Jones and Marjit (2001) and Deardroff (2001). In the context of general equilibrium models these seminal works are followed by the works of Marjit, Beladi and Chakrabarti (2004), Jones and Kierzkowski (2005), Chatterjee and Gupta (2014a, 2014b) and Mitra and Gupta (2017). The present chapter attempts to consider the concept of international fragmentation in the context of exportable product quality and thus can be considered an important value addition in the context of the literature.

The motivation behind the study has been generated from the fact that liberalisation along with international fragmentation is an important area of research for developing countries. The issue becomes really relevant for developing countries when international fragmentation gets mixed with various tools of trade liberalisation. There is a dearth of research on this particular aspect, and research on the impact of trade liberalisation on exportable product quality in the presence of international fragmentation is totally missing in the literature. The present study not only attempts to fill up this lacuna from the point of view of academic research but also attempts to provide a guideline to the policy-makers who are associated with framing the export policies of developing economies.

The present chapter shows how tariff cut, FDI and increase in endowment of skilled labour force affects exportable product quality both in the presence and in the absence of international fragmentation. The study first develops a model without international fragmentation and then develops a model in the presence of international fragmentation. The chapter is thus organised in the following manner. Section 13.2 has considered the model without international fragmentation. Section 13.3 has been confined to an analysis of comparative static results in the absence of international fragmentation. Section 13.4 has developed the extended version of the model in the presence of international fragmentation and has examined the same comparative static exercises in the presence of such international fragmentation. Finally, the concluding remarks are made in Section 13.5 of this chapter.

13.2 The Model without International Fragmentation

To illustrate the issue of exportable product quality in the context of liberalisation, a four-sector model of a small open developing economy has been assumed here consisting of a traditional agricultural good exportable sector (x), traditional import-competing (manufacturing) sector (y), a non-traditional, highly skilled, good-producing exportable sector (z) like the software sector and an intermediate good-producing sector (v) to help the sophisticated skilled exportable sector. First, the model has been considered without international fragmentation as far as the supply of intermediate products is concerned. It is assumed that there exists a domestic intermediate goods sector which is able to provide the intermediate inputs to the final exportable sector (as for example the software sector). There are four domestic factors of production in the economy – land, unskilled labour, skilled labour and capital. Sector x requires unskilled labour (L) and land (T) to produce its product. Sector y and sector v produce their products with the help of unskilled labour (L) and capital (K). The non-traditional exportable good-producing sector, z, produces its product with the help of skilled labour (S), capital (K) along with the intermediate goods produced by sector v. Here, land is specific to sector x, whereas skilled labour is specific to sector z. On the other hand, unskilled labour is mobile among sectors x, y and v, whereas capital is mobile among sectors y, z and v. It is further assumed that all sectors, other than sector z, use variable coefficient technology. It is only in sector z it is found that the production method is based on fixed coefficient technology.[2] Next, we have one of the most important assumptions of the model. Here it is assumed that the intermediate goods sector is more capital intensive than the traditional manufacturing (tariff-protected) sector. The intermediate goods sector provides intermediate goods to the sophisticated quality-differentiated exportable final goods sector. Hence, the intermediate goods sector uses more capital-intensive method of production than the traditional manufacturing sector to provide specialised intermediate products to the exportable sector. The intermediate inputs in the final goods sector are handled by the skilled workforce. So in the intermediate goods sector, though we have unskilled workforce, capital plays a more important role than unskilled labour for production. This is true even in the absence of any threat from foreign intermediate supplier. However, in the presence of international fragmentation, this capital-intensity assumption obviously holds.

It is to be noted here that sector z produces an exportable commodity of different quality, and hence quality differentiation is considered for this sector. The quality (Q) of the produce of this sector can be indexed in a closed interval ranging from zero to one. For a particular quality level, competitive equilibrium condition holds well in the product market of sector z. However, producers of this sector enjoy market power to some extent with respect to quality differentiation. When we have quality differentiation, the buyers are willing to pay a higher price, for any given quantity that they buy, if the quality of the product is higher than what they would be willing to pay if the quality is lower. Therefore, sector z experiences an increasing price schedule with respect to quality[3], i.e.

$$P_Z^* = P_Z^*(Q) \text{ where } P_Z^{*'}(Q) > 0.$$

This provides incentives to the firms to raise the quality of the product. Thus, there is some element of an imperfectly competitive market structure when we have quality differentiation. Here we find marginal willingness-to-pay by the buyers and the cost of quality are the two basic forces underlying the choice of product quality. From the point of view of the producers, the firms will vary product quality in a manner such that the optimum quality is obtained from the profit-maximising condition (with respect to quality) which is given by marginal revenue from quality equal to the marginal cost of quality. The production technology in sector z is such that higher quality level requires more capital compared to lower quality levels with increasing rate of capital per unit of output for a higher level of quality. This implies that the higher quality varieties are more capital intensive relative to the lower varieties which are summarised in terms of input–output coefficients as follows:

$$a_{KZ} = a_{KZ}(Q), \text{ where } a'_{KZ}(Q) > 0 \text{ and } a''_{KZ} > 0.$$

The unit requirement levels of labour and intermediate goods are invariant to different quality levels. Thus in sector z, although all the input–output coefficients are fixed, it is only the capital coefficient which is sensitive to changes in quality (and not factor prices).

Due to the small open economy assumption, prices of the final good-producing sectors (sectors x, y and z) are internationally given. Production function in each sector exhibits constant returns to scale (CRS) with diminishing marginal productivity to each variable input. There is no open unemployment in the economy as workers cannot survive without jobs and hence the labour market always clears.

The following notations are used to describe the equational structure of the model.

P_i^* = world price of commodity i ($\forall i = x, y, z$)
P_i = domestic price of commodity i($\forall i = x, y, z, v$)
X = output level of sector x
Y = output level of sector y
Z = output level of sector z
V = output level of sector v
L = unskilled labour endowment
T = stock of land in the economy
S = skilled labour endowment
K = capital endowment
w = wage rate of the unskilled workers
w_S = wage rate of the skilled workers
r = rate of return on capital
R = rent on land
Q = quality level of the product of sector z
$\bar{t}$ = rate of ad-valorem tariff on the import-competing sector y
a_{ij} = quantity of the jth factor for producing one unit of output in the ith sector; $j = L, T, S, K, v$ and $i = x, y, z, v$.

By assumption, the product of the traditional agricultural sector is considered as the numeraire and its price has been set equal to unity, i.e., $P_X = 1$.

The competitive equilibrium conditions for sectors x, y, z (for a particular level of Q) and v are given by the following equations:

$$a_{LX}w + a_{TX}R = 1, \tag{13.1}$$

$$a_{LY}w + a_{KY}r = P_Y^*(1+\bar{t}) = P_Y, \tag{13.2}$$

$$a_{SZ}w_S + a_{VZ}P_V + a_{KZ}(Q)r = P_Z(Q), \tag{13.3}$$

$$a_{LV}w + a_{KV}r = P_V. \tag{13.4}$$

The full employment conditions are given by

$$a_{LX}X + a_{LY}Y + a_{LV}V = L, \tag{13.5}$$

$$a_{SZ}Z = S, \tag{13.6}$$

$$a_{TX}X = T, \tag{13.7}$$

$$a_{KY}Y + a_{KZ}(Q)Z + a_{KV}V = K, \tag{13.8}$$

$$a_{VZ}Z = V. \tag{13.9}$$

We now consider change in quality in the form of quality differentiation in the non-traditional quality-differentiated goods exporting sector, i.e., sector z. In case of quality differentiation, the profit-maximising behaviour of the producers of quality-differentiated sector gives us

$$ra'_{KZ}(Q) = P'_Z\,(Q). \tag{13.10}$$

Equation (13.10) implies the marginal cost of quality is equal to the marginal revenue from quality. Here we assume $ra''_{KZ}(Q) > P''_Z\,(Q)$ which implies that quality enhancement raises costs further and faster than the price of the product.[4]

In this structure, we have ten equations with ten unknowns: w, R, w_S, r, P_V, Q, X, Y, Z and V. Thus, the system is determinable. The model can be analysed in the following manner:

From Equations (13.2) and (13.4), we can express w and r as functions of P_V. Thus, $w = w\,(P_V)$ and $r = r\,(P_V)$, where given the assumption that the intermediate goods sector is more capital intensive than the import-competing sector, we have by Stolper–Samuelson effect $w' < 0$ and $r' > 0$.

Putting the value of r in Equation (13.3), we get that w_s can be expressed in terms of P_V and they are inversely related. Again, from Equation (13.1), we find that R can be expressed as a function of P_V and they are positively related. Thus, all factor prices are expressed in terms of P_V and hence all the input–output ratios (variable coefficients) can be expressed as function of P_V. From Equation (13.6), we find that a_{SZ} is given. Hence, we can determine z from Equation (13.6) for a given value of S. Thus, Z is determined independently of P_V. Once z is known, from Equation (13.9), with given a_{VZ}, we can determine V. Thus V is determined independently of P_V. In Equation (13.7), we find that a_{TX} is a function of P_V. As an increase in P_V increases R, it reduces a_{TX} and hence X increases, for given T. Thus, $X = X(P_V)$, where $X' > 0$.

From Equation (13.5), we find that a_{LX} and a_{LZ} are both positively related to P_V as an increase in P_V reduces w. Again, an increase in P_V raises the value of X. Thus, Y must fall as a result of an increase in P_V. In other words, $Y = Y(P_V)$, where $Y' < 0$.

The next step is to determine P_V and Q. Using Equations (13.6) and (13.9), from Equation (13.8) we get

$$a_{KY}(P_V)Y(P_V) + [a_{KZ}(Q) + a_{KV}(P_V)a_{VZ}]a_{SZ}S = K. \tag{13.8a}$$

From Equation (13.8a) we find that as P_V increases there is an increase in r and hence the levels of a_{KY} and a_{KV} fall. Again, an increase in P_V causes a decrease in

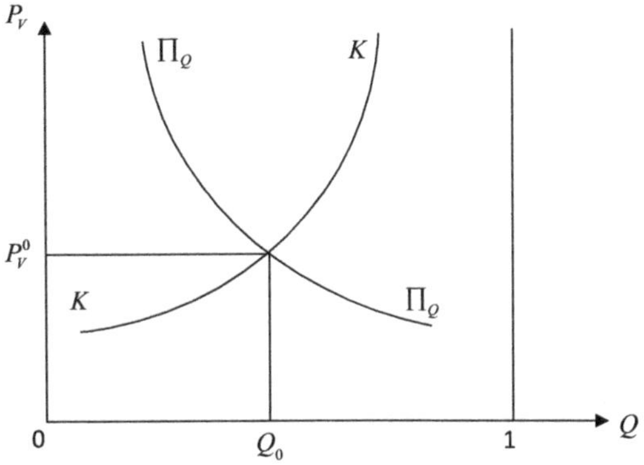

Figure 13.1 Determination of equilibrium values of the price of intermediate product and the quality of exportable product

the level of Y. Hence to maintain capital market equilibrium the level of Q must increase. In other words, the locus of P_V and Q such that the capital market is in equilibrium is positively sloped. It is shown by *KK* locus in Figure 13.1.

Profit-maximising behaviour of the producers of quality-differentiated sector gives us

$$r(P_V)a'_{KZ}(Q) = P'_Z(Q). \tag{13.10a}$$

An increase in Q leads to an increase in both $ra'_{KZ}(Q)$ and $P'_Z(Q)$, but increase in $a'_{KZ}(Q)$will be higher compared to an increase in $P'_Z(Q)$since we assume $ra''_{KZ}(Q) > P''_Z(Q)$. Therefore, r declines to maintain the equality condition of Equation (13.10a). It implies a decrease in the level of P_V. Hence, we can derive a negative locus of P_V and Q to maintain the profit-maximising condition with respect to the quality of sector z. This locus may be named as the $\Pi_Q\Pi_Q$schedule which is shown in Figure 13.1. The point of intersection of *KK* locus and $\Pi_Q\Pi_Q$ locus gives us the equilibrium values of P_V and Q as P_V^0 and Q_0. Once P_V is known, all other factor prices can also be known as all of them are functions of P_V. When all factor prices are known, the input–output coefficients of sectors x and y can be determined and X and Y can also be determined.

13.3 Comparative Static Analysis without Fragmentation

13.3.1 Trade liberalisation and quality of exportable product

One very common policy of liberalising trade is to reduce the rate of ad-valorem tariff on the import-competing sector. Equation (13.2) shows that sector y is protected by a given rate of tariff, $\bar{t}$. Let us assume that as a part

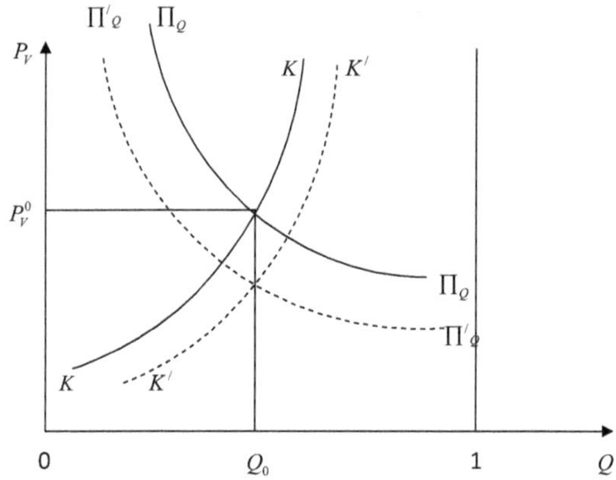

Figure 13.2 Impact of tariff reduction on the quality of exportable product

of liberalisation, this $\bar{t}$ is reduced by the government. Therefore, the domestic price of the product of sector y would fall in the economy and then, with unchanged P_V, there is a fall in the level of w and an increase in the level of r. This follows from the Stolper–Samuelson effect. Fall in w again causes an increase in R and it follows from Equation (13.1). We thus have fall in the levels of a_{KY}, a_{KV} and a_{TX} and increase in the levels of a_{LX}, a_{LY} and a_{LV}.

From Equation (13.7), we find that fall in a_{TX} causes an increase in the level of X which in turn, along with increase in the levels of a_{LX}, a_{LY} and a_{LV}, causes a fall in the level of Y, for a given level of P_V. Hence, the level of Q must increase to maintain balance as we find from Equation (13.8a), implying a rightward shift of the *KK* locus. Again a fall in $\bar{t}$ causes an increase in r, and hence to maintain balance in Equation (13.10a) the level of Q must fall implying a leftward shift of the $\Pi_Q \Pi_Q$ locus.[5] This is shown in Figure 13.2.

The following proposition is immediate from Figure 13.2.

> **Proposition 13.1** Trade liberalisation in the form of a reduction in the tariff rate on the import-competing sector reduces the price of the intermediate product, but the impact on the quality of the exportable product of a developing country is ambiguous.

13.3.2 FDI and Quality of Exportable Product

In this section, the impact of investment liberalisation policy of the government by allowing FDI within our assumed small economy has been examined. In the present structure, we find that FDI, in the form of an inflow of foreign capital, leads to an increase in the capital endowment of the economy.[6] Hence, the *KK* locus shifts to the right. However, there will be no movement of the $\Pi_Q \Pi_Q$ locus as a result of FDI.

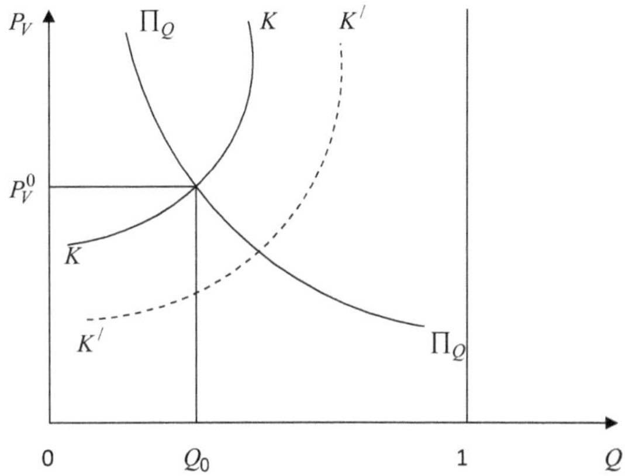

Figure 13.3 Impact of an inflow of foreign capital on the quality of exportable product

A new equilibrium is obtained at the intersection of the new KK locus and the $\Pi_Q \Pi_Q$ locus, where Q would rise and P_V would fall compared to their previous equilibrium levels. This is shown in Figure 13.3.

As argued earlier, a fall in P_V causes an increase in the level of Y though a fall in P_V causes no change in the level of Z. Thus, as a result of FDI, there is an increase in the level of exportable quality though there is no change in the level of output of the exportable sector.

We have thus the following proposition.

> **Proposition 13.2** FDI in the form of an inflow of foreign capital raises the quality of exportable product of our developing economy.

13.3.3 Skilled Labour and Quality of Exportable Product

In the present structure, we have assumed that the skilled labour endowment level of the economy is exogenously given. We shall now examine the impact of an increase in the endowment level of this factor[7] on the quality level of the quality-differentiated exportable commodity. Since skilled labour is specific to the exportable sector (z) of the economy in this model, the level of output of sector z would increase for a rise in the supply of skilled labour within the economy. This can be checked from Equation (13.6) of the model. Then from Equation (13.9), we find that an increase in Z leads to an increase in the output level of sector v, i.e. increase in V. Hence, for given P_V, from Equation (8.1), we find that Q must fall. It implies that the KK locus shifts to the left. In this case, there is no shift of the $\Pi_Q \Pi_Q$ locus. Hence, as shown in Figure 13.4, the equilibrium level of Q falls along with a rise in the equilibrium level of P_V.

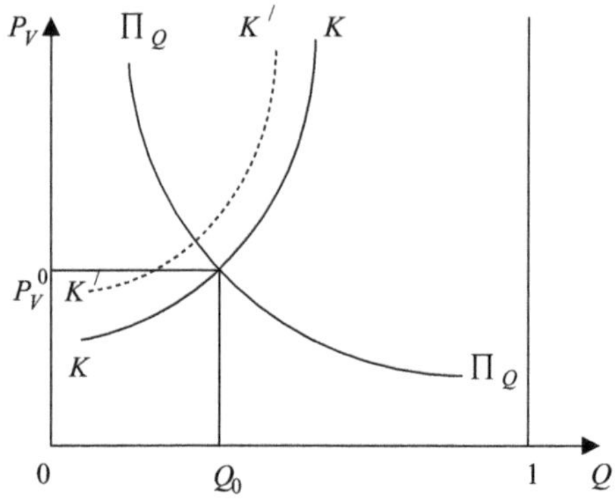

Figure 13.4 Impact of an increase in skilled labour endowment of the economy on the quality of exportable product

Interestingly we find that when skilled labour endowment increases, Z, the output level of the skilled exportable sector increases, though its quality falls. Hence, we find that increase in skilled labour endowment causes a trade-off between exportable quality and quantity. Thus, we have the following proposition.

Proposition 13.3 An increase in the skilled labour endowment of the economy lowers the quality of exportable product of a developing economy and creates a trade-off between the quality and quantity of exportable product.

13.4 The Extended Model with International Fragmentation

The basic model can be extended by introducing international fragmentation in the production process in the presence of quality differentiation. We have already mentioned in Section 13.1 that the concept of international fragmentation has originated from the seminal works of Jones and Marjit (2001) and Deardroff (2001). The idea of international fragmentation has been subsequently used in the context of general equilibrium models by Marjit, Beladi and Chakrabarti (2004) and Jones and Kierzkowski (2005). Recently authors like Chatterjee and Gupta (2014a, 2014b) and Mitra and Gupta (2017) have used this concept in the context of the general equilibrium model. However, none of the authors have analysed this concept in the presence of quality differentiation. In the present chapter, an attempt has been made to explore this untouched issue.

One can define international fragmentation as splitting up the production process into two phases. One is the foreign phase and the other is the domestic phase. Here we have considered the foreign part in terms of supplier of intermediate input, whereas the domestic part in terms of both supplier of intermediate input and producer of the final product. This partial break-up of the production process is usually referred to as *international fragmentation*. As an extreme case, we may have a situation when the intermediate product is produced only by the foreign country and the final product is produced by the domestic economy. We refer to this situation as *full international fragmentation.*

We first develop the concept of international fragmentation and then mix it with quality differentiation. It has been already mentioned earlier that in the absence of international fragmentation, the quality-differentiated sector (i.e. sector "z") is fully dependent on the domestic non-traded intermediate goods sector. The price of the intermediate goods sector P_V is determined endogenously on the basis of equality of demand and supply of intermediate products. The intermediate good can also be imported by the final good sector from abroad, but in this case, the final good sector will have to incur a fixed cost given by F. This fixed cost is basically the cost of transportation and is referred to as *iceberg cost* in the literature.

Suppose due to some exogenous factors there has been an increase in the demand for the product of the intermediate sector. It causes a rightward shift of the demand curve for the domestic intermediate product resulting in upward movement of the price of the domestic intermediate product. If the international price of the intermediate product, P_V^*, is fixed at a much lower level, then it causes downward pressure on the domestic price of the intermediate product, P_V. This is because the domestic intermediate good suppliers in this case face strong competition with that of international intermediate good suppliers. Thus, P_V falls and it continues to fall until it reaches the level P_V^*. There may be various levels at which P_V^* is fixed. Let P_V^+ be one such value of P_V^* so that P_V falls to P_V^+. We can refer to P_V^+ as the critical value of P_V^* (and hence of P_V) such that when the value of P_V^* is fixed at a level lower than P_V^+ (and hence P_V takes a value lower than P_V^+), the producers find it cheaper to import the intermediate products rather than domestically producing them. Actually when P_V becomes very low (may be lower than P_V^+), the final goods sector that uses intermediate input faces a trade-off. This sector may think of buying the intermediate input domestically or from abroad. From the competitive equilibrium condition of sector "z", i.e. Equation (13.3), we find that for given quality of the product of sector "z", a decrease in P_V (and hence a decrease in $r(P_V)$, $r' > 0$) raises the cost of hiring skilled workforce in this sector. In other words, lower cost of purchasing domestically produced product gets reflected in terms of higher cost of employing skilled labour force. So the owners of sector "z" will compare this cost with that of the fixed cost or *iceberg cost* of transportation of importing intermediate products from abroad.[8] If the iceberg cost is less than the additional cost of employing unskilled labour force due to a fall in P_V, then the producers will import the intermediate product from abroad and we have a situation of international fragmentation. If the reverse happens, then there will be no international fragmentation. If the two costs are the same, the owners of sector "z" will be indifferent between fragmentation and no fragmentation.

The whole analysis of fragmentation in the context of our model is contingent for a given level of quality for the product of sector "z".

When we have a situation of international fragmentation, P_V is no longer an endogenous variable, rather it is fixed at the level of international price of the imported intermediaries. In fact, we lose one variable but we add another variable, V^*, which is the level of imported intermediary. Other equations of the model remain the same. Hence, we modify Equation (13.9) as

$$a_{VZ}Z = V + V^* \tag{13.9a}$$

Equation (13.9) is thus replaced by Equation (13.9a). International fragmentation in terms of this equation implies an increase in V^*.

If we focus on working of the model, we find that as P_V is now given, from Equations (13.2) and (13.4), we can solve for w and r. Once r is known, from Equation (13.10) we can determine Q. As Q is known, we can determine w_S from Equation (13.3). Again as w is known, from Equation (13.1), we can determine R. Thus, factor prices and the quality level are determined independently of the output system. Given S, we can determine Z from Equation (13.6) and also given T, we can determine X from Equation (13.7). Knowing the values of Z and X, from Equations (13.5) and (13.8) we can determine Y and V. Finally, from Equation (13.9a), we can determine V^*.

When P_V is equal to the international price P_V^* which is fixed at the critical level P_V^+, we find r is at its equilibrium level r^+ and Q is at its equilibrium level Q^+ from Equation (13.10). Given Q at Q^+, we find that w_S is at the level w_S^+. This w_S^+ is contingent on the value of Q (here Q^+). Let w_S^0 be the initial equilibrium value of w_S when there was no fragmentation. It is to be noted that even when r falls as a result of a fall in P_V, Q increases but by Equation (13.10) ultimately $ra'_{KZ}(Q) = P'_Z(Q)$ as $ra''_{KZ}(Q) > P''_Z(Q)$.

Thus, w_S varies inversely with P_V, and hence $[w_S - w_S^0]$ also varies inversely with P_V and this is true even if the quality level increases. This is shown in Figure 13.5.

In Figure 13.5, $(w_S - w_S^0)$ can be interpreted as the additional cost per unit of skilled labour force incurred by the final goods sector "z" as a result of a fall in P_V.[9] Thus, $(w_S - w_S^0)S$ is the total additional cost of skilled labour incurred by the final goods sector as a result of a fall in P_V. For international fragmentation, this cost is to be compared with the iceberg cost, F.

Thus, formally we write (i) fragmentation is preferable on part of the final goods sector iff$(w_S - w_S^0) > \frac{F}{S}$, (ii) fragmentation is not preferable on part of the final goods sector iff$(w_S - w_S^0) < \frac{F}{S}$ and (iii) the final goods sector is indifferent iff$(w_S - w_S^0) = \frac{F}{S}$. The point of indifference is shown in Figure 13.5 by the point P_V^+ when the quality level is Q^+. From the figure we find

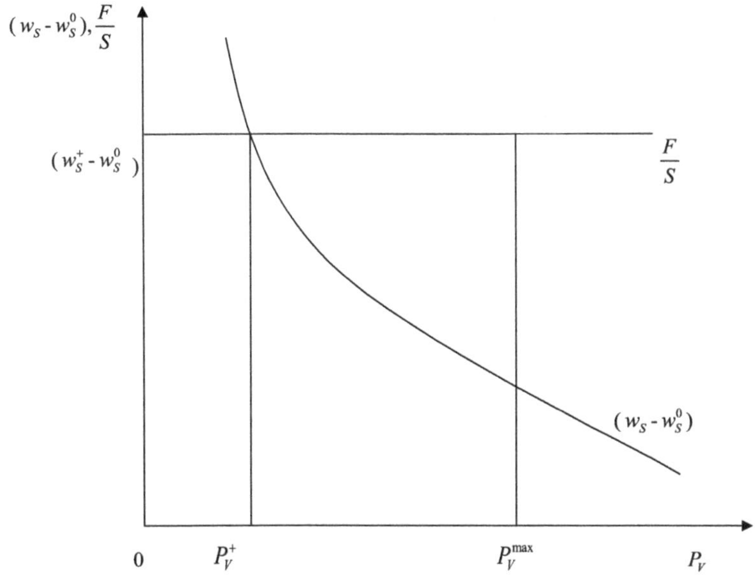

Figure 13.5 Description of International Fragmentation

that $\forall P_V \in [0, P_V^+)$ we have international fragmentation as from the figure we have $(w_S^+ - w_S^0) > \frac{F}{S}$; whereas $\forall P_V \in (P_V^+, P_V^{max}]$ we find that there is no international fragmentation as we have the reverse inequality, P_V^{max} is the maximum value of P_V. At $P_V = P_V^+$, we have $(w_S^+ - w_S^0) = \frac{F}{S}$, implying indifference on part of the owners of the final goods sector. Hence in summary, we can say that a fall in P_V is an indicator of international fragmentation.[10]

When P_V falls from P_V^+ to P_V^{++} (not shown in Figure 13.5), the level of r further falls from r^+ to r^{++} and as $ra''_{KZ}(Q) > P''_Z(Q)$, we find from Equation (13.10) that the level of quality further increases from Q^+ to Q^{++} though ultimately the fall in r and the increase in a_{KZ} along with an increase in P_z are balanced as ultimately $ra'_{KZ}(Q) = P'_Z(Q)$. Thus, the negative relation between fall in P_V and $(w_S - w_S^0)$ prevails irrespective of the fact that there has been an increase in the level of exportable product quality. We thus find in Figure 13.5 that when $P_V < P_V^+$, we have the possibility of fragmentation and in this situation, the product quality of final goods sector increases. The following proposition thus follows from the analysis of international fragmentation.

Proposition 13.4 In the presence of quality differentiation for the final goods sector, the possibility of international fragmentation enhances the product quality of the exportable final goods sector.

We next consider the same comparative static analysis that we have considered in the absence of international fragmentation. We start with a fall in the tariff rate of the import-competing sector. A fall in the tariff rate, $\bar{t}$, causes a fall in the domestic price of the product of the import-competing sector in Equation (13.2), and by *Stolper–Samuelson effect* (considering Equations (13.2) and (13.4)) we find that there is a fall in the unskilled wage rate, w, and a rise in the rate of return on capital, r. Hence from Equation (13.10), we find that there is a fall in Q. Thus, trade liberalisation in the form of tariff cut reduces exportable product quality in the presence of international fragmentation. As $a'_{KZ}(Q) > 0, P'_Z(Q) > 0$ along with $ra'_{KZ}(Q) = P'_Z(Q)$ and as there is no change in P_V, there will be no change in the level of w_S. Fall in the level of w causes from Equation (13.1) an increase in the level of rate of return on land, R, for given P_X. Thus, a_{TX} falls and a_{LX}, a_{LY} and a_{LV} rise. From Equation (13.7) we find that, given $\bar{T}$, a fall in a_{TX} raises the level of output, X, and hence $a_{LX}X$ rises implying a fall in the effective supply of unskilled labour for sectors y and v. Moreover, we find as r rises, the levels of a_{KY} and a_{KV} fall. Apart from this, a fall in Q reduces the level of a_{KZ}. Thus, the total demand for capital falls. Hence, effectively there is an excess supply of capital and a shortage of unskilled labour. This creates a *Rybczynski-type* effect as a result of which V expands and Y contracts.[11] Again, from Equation (13.6), we find that Z remains unaffected due to tariff cut and the demand for the intermediate product for sector "z" remains unchanged (see Equation (13.9a)).[12] Hence, an increase in V causes a reduction in the level of V^*. In other words, there is less possibility of international fragmentation along with reduction in exportable product quality as a result of tariff cut.

When there is an inflow of foreign capital in the economy, it leads to an increase in total capital stock, as a result of which the output level of the capital-intensive sector, V, expands and the output level of the labour-intensive sector, Y, contracts (according to *Rybczynski effect*). It is to be noted in this connection that the level of Q remains unchanged as a result of FDI. In fact, Z and X are not affected as a result of FDI.[13] Thus, the demand for the intermediate product for sector "z" remains unchanged due to FDI. It implies that an increase in V causes a reduction in the level of V^*. In other words, there is less possibility of international fragmentation as a result of FDI.

Finally, we consider the effects of an increase in skilled labour endowment, S. In terms of Figure 13.5, it implies a downward shift of the horizontal line, $\frac{F}{S}$, and thus increases the range for international fragmentation. An increase in S causes no change in factor prices and product quality of sector "z". However, from Equation (13.6) it leads to an increase in the level of output of sector "z", given by Z. Thus, from Equation (13.8), we find that there is an increase in the demand for capital which causes effective shortage of availability of capital for sectors y and v. Hence by *Rybszynski-type* effect, there is an increase in Y and a reduction in V. An increase in Z increases the demand for intermediate product by the final good-producing exportable sector so that a reduction in V increases the import of intermediate inputs and hence raises the possibility of international fragmentation. We have, thus, the following proposition to summarise our results.

> **Proposition 13.5** Trade liberalisation in the form of tariff cut reduces the quality of the exportable final product and also reduces the possibility of international fragmentation. Trade liberalisation in the form of FDI causes no change in the level of quality of the exportable final product and again reduces the possibility of international fragmentation. Finally, an increase in skilled labour endowment increases the possibility of international fragmentation.

The results stated in Proposition 13.5 are highly interesting in the context of a developing economy. First, we find there is a wide difference in the results obtained in with and without the presence of international fragmentation. Again, in the context of liberalisation, the impact of tariff cut and FDI on product quality and international fragmentation is contrary to the conventional belief. Finally, an increase in skilled labour endowment in the presence of international fragmentation creates no trade-off between quality and quantity of quality-differentiated exportable final product. In fact, in the absence of fragmentation, such an increase in skilled endowment reduces quality, whereas in the presence of international fragmentation, there is no effect on product quality though the level of output of the sector that uses skilled labour increases.

13.5 Concluding Remarks

In the present study, an attempt has been made towards examining the impact of trade liberalisation – in terms of tariff cut and FDI – on exportable product quality. Additionally, the impact of increased endowment of skilled labour on exportable product quality has also been examined here. In this chapter, two regimes have been considered: one is the absence of international fragmentation and the other is the presence of international fragmentation. The issue of international fragmentation deserves more attention especially when it is linked with exportable product quality. The present chapter shows how tariff cut, FDI and an increase in the endowment of skilled labour force affects exportable product quality both in the presence and in the absence of international fragmentation. In this study, international fragmentation plays a crucial role in achieving results related to the impact of trade liberalisation on exportable product quality as the results in the absence of international fragmentation are widely different from the results in the presence of international fragmentation.

In the absence of international fragmentation, we have two different impacts of trade liberalisation on the quality level of the exportable product.

First, tariff liberalisation, in terms of tariff cut of the importable sector, cannot definitely predict the movement of quality of exportable product. Second investment liberalisation in terms of FDI in the absence of international fragmentation, contrary to the conventional wisdom, reduces the quality of the exportable product. Liberalisation causes an inflow of knowledge in a globalised world and hence enhances the level of skill in developing countries. Interestingly, in the absence of international fragmentation, an increase in skilled labour endowment causes a trade-off between the quality and quantity of skilled exportable product. It increases the output of the skilled exportable product at the cost of reduction in its quality.

In the presence of international fragmentation, we find that there has been an enhancement in the quality of the exportable final goods sector. This result has strong implications for policy-makers because interlinkage between international fragmentation and exportable product quality is something new in the context of research on international trade and development. The issue is more interesting as there i a positive relationship between the two. Surprisingly, in terms of our model, trade liberalisation in the form of tariff cut or FDI reduces the possibility of international fragmentation and reduces the quality of the exportable product in case of tariff cut and makes the movement of quality of exportable product ambiguous in case of FDI. Unlike the no-fragmentation case, in the presence of international fragmentation increase in skilled labour endowment causes no trade-off between quality and quantity, rather the level of quality of exportable product remains unchanged though there is an increase in the level of output of the skilled exportable product.

The present analysis thus shows that international fragmentation plays a crucial role in framing policies related to the quality of exportable product in a developing economy. This study can be considered as a guideline to the policy-makers to achieve results which are opposite to that of the conventional wisdom and are very much relevant in a globalised world.

Notes

1 The author is extremely indebted to Prof. Kausik Gupta for his valuable comments on the chapter. However, the author is solely responsible for any error that may remain in the chapter. The usual disclaimer applies.

2 This is just a simplifying assumption which is widely used in the literature. See the works of Acharyya and Jones (2001), Marjit, Beladi and Chakrabarti (2004) and also Chatterjee and Gupta (2014a, 2014b). In fact, it can be argued that the skilled personnel of the quality differentiated exportable sector are frequently appointed on the basis of output targeted to be produced by that sector. Hence, per-unit skilled labour requirement is assumed to be fixed. In fact, per-unit intermediate good requirement of the final exportable sector is also assumed to be fixed as we find in the literature. Of course this appears to be a very simplifying assumption, but it is not at all unrealistic when we assume that the final exportable sector subcontracts the intermediate goods sector to produce its product. This assumption is widely used in the literature. See the works

of Gupta (1994), Chaudhuri (2003), Gupta and Basu (2004) and of course the works of Chatterjee and Gupta (2014a and 2014b). See also Chaudhuri and Mukhopadhyay (2009). Thus, the unit requirement of capital (the remaining input) is bound to be fixed and it precludes the possibility of any elasticity of substitution. Hence, all the input–output requirements are fixed. As already mentioned in the literature, this simplifying assumption is followed. One may relax this assumption and can consider variable coefficient technology. That will not add any new insight in the analysis; rather it will make the algebra cumbersome as partial elasticities of substitution are to be calculated. Hence, the assumption of fixed coefficient technology for this exportable sector is very much justified.

3 See the works of Mitra, Chatterjee and Gupta (2017) and also Acharyya and Jones (2001) for more details. See also Acharyya (2005) for a more elaborate treatment.

4 This assumption has been borrowed from the work by Acharyya and Jones (2001). See Acharyya and Jones (2001) for interpretation in detail of Equation (13.10). It is to be noted here that though competitive equilibrium condition has been assumed for sector *z* for a given quality (as shown by Equation (13.3)), for quality differentiation some elements of imperfect competition are found in that sector and the profit-maximising condition is then represented by the equality between marginal cost of quality and marginal revenue from quality. The choice of product qualities by a single firm and a perfectly competitive industry were first analysed independently by Mussa and Rosen (1978) and Gabszweicz and Thisse (1979). The subsequent literature grew out of these two seminal works. The assumption regarding the R&D sector in this study is close to that of the works of Mussa and Rosen (1978) and Gabszweicz and Thisse (1979). See the seminal works of Krugman (1979, 1980). In the context of small open economy, general equilibrium trade models the flavours of Krugman (1979 and 1980) type monopolistic competition model was first introduced by Sen, Ghosh and Barman (1997) and then it was followed by Acharyya and Jones (2001). Acharyya (2005) has considered a detailed analysis of product standard and product quality. Recently, Mitra, Chatterjee and Gupta (2017) have considered monopolistic competition in an otherwise small open economy general equilibrium set-up and their work is a follow up of the works of Sen, Ghosh and Barman (1997) and Acharyya and Jones (2001).

5 It is to be noted that we need to rewrite Equations (13.8a) and (13.10a) to analyse these comparative statics in the following manner. Equation (13.8a) can be written as $a_{KY}(P_V,\bar{t})Y(P_V,\bar{t})+[a_{KZ}(Q)+a_{KV}(P_V,\bar{t})a_{VZ}]a_{SZ}S=K$, whereas Equation (13.10a) can be written as $r(P_V,\bar{t})a'_{KZ}(Q)=P'_Z\,(Q)$.

6 Here, domestic capital and foreign capital are assumed as perfect substitutes. This is a standard assumption borrowed from the literature and can be considered as a reasonable assumption in the context of a globalized world. See the works of Chaudhuri and Mukhopadhyay (2002), Chaudhuri (2014), Chaudhuri and Mukhopadhyay (2014), Chatterjee and Gupta (2014a, 2014b).

7 We can assume that due to restriction on emigration imposed by the government, skilled labour endowment increases in the domestic economy. One can also analyse the impact of supply of skilled labour on the quality of exportable product by considering a sector which produces skill in a small open economy and thereby endogenising the skilled labour endowment of the economy.

8 One can refer to the works of Marjit, Beladi and Chakrabarti (2004), Chatterjee and Gupta (2014a and 2014b), Mitra and Gupta (2017).

9 It may appear confusing to the readers that if P_V is fixed, then how can it be measured along the horizontal axis? Actually, there is no point of confusion as

it explains the fact that we have various levels of P_V^* at which $P_V = P_V^*$. In fact, instead of P_V, one can measure P_V^* along the horizontal axis. P_V^+ is a particular level of P_V^* at which it is fixed (and hence P_V is fixed).

10 It is to be noted that fall in P_V is not the only indicator of fragmentation. It is one of the many indicators.

11 Here Equation (13.9) is replaced by Equation (13.9a) so V is not fixed when Z is fixed.

12 It is to be noted that a_{SZ} and a_{VZ} are fixed.

13 Here P_V is given internationally, so w and r are determined uniquely from Equations (13.2) and (13.4). Hence, R is uniquely determined from Equation (13.1). Hence, a_{TX} is known and Equation (13.7) helps us to determine X. Thus, X is determined independently of K. As a_{SZ} is fixed, Z is also known from Equation (13.6) and hence is independent of changes in K.

References and Notes

Acharyya, R. (2005): *Product Standards, Employment and Exports: An Analytical Study*, Physica/Springer Verlag, Heidelberg.

Acharyya, R. and R. W. Jones (2001): "Export Quality and Income Distribution in a Small Dependent Economy", *International Review of Economics and Finance*, 10(4): 337–351.

Chatterjee, T. and K. Gupta (2014a): "International Fragmentation in the Presence of Alternative Health Sector Scenario: A Theoretical Analysis", in S. K. Datta and A. Sengupta (eds), *Development, Environment and Sustainable Livelihood*, Cambridge Scholars Lady Stephenson Library, Newcastle upon Tyne UK, 233–253.

Chatterjee, T. and K. Gupta (2014b): "Trade Liberalization, Health Care and International Fragmentation: The Role of Health Capital Mobility", *The Pakistan Development Review*, 53(1): 57–65.

Chaudhuri, S. (2003): "How and How Far to Liberalize a Developing Economy with Informal Sector and Factor Market Distortions", *Journal of International Trade and Economic Development*, 12(4): 403–428.c

Chaudhuri, S. (2014): "Foreign Capital, Non-traded Goods and Welfare in a Developing Economy in the Presence of Externalities", *International Review of Economics and Finance*, 31: 249–262.

Chaudhuri, S. and U. Mukhopadhyay (2002): "Economic liberalization and welfare in a model with an informal sector," The Economics of Transition", *The European Bank for Reconstruction and Development*, 10(1): 143–172.

Chaudhuri, S. and U. Mukhopadhyay (2009): *Revisiting the Informal Sector: A General Equilibrium Approach*, Springer, New York.

Chaudhuri, S. and U. Mukhopadhyay (2014): *Foreign Direct Investment in Developing Countries: A Theoretical Evaluation*, Springer, New York.

Deardorff, A. V. (2001): "Fragmentation in Simple Trade Models", *The North American Journal of Economics and Finance*, 12(2): 121–137.

Gabszweicz, J. J. and J. F. Thisse (1979): "Price Competition, Quality and Income Disparities", *Journal of Economic Theory*, 20(3): 340–359.

Gupta, K. and T. Basu (2004): "Foreign Capital Inflow, Skilled-Unskilled Wage Gap and Welfare in the Presence of the Informal Sector", *The Pakistan Development Review*, 43(2): 125–147.

Gupta, M. R. (1994): "Duty Free Zone, Unemployment and Welfare: A Note", *Journal of Economics*, 59(2): 217–236.

Harding, T. and B. S. Javorcik (2012): "Foreign Direct Investment and Export Upgrading", *Review of Economics and Statistics*, 94(4): 964–980.

Hausmann, R., J. Hwang and D. Rodrik (2007): "What You Export Matters", *Journal of Economic Growth*, 12(1): 1–25.

Jones, R. W. and H. Kierzkowski (2005): "International Fragmentation and the New Economic Geography", *The North American Journal of Economics and Finance*, 16(1): 1–10.

Jones, R. W. and S. Marjit (2001): "The Role of International Fragmentation in the Development Process", *American Economic Review*, 91(2): 363–366.

Krugman, P. (1979): "Increasing Returns, Monopolistic Competition and International Trade", *Journal of International Economics*, 9(4): 469–479.

Krugman, P. R. (1980): "Scale Economies, Product Differentiation, and the Pattern of Trade", *American Economic Review*, 70(5): 950–959.

Marjit, S., H. Beladi and A. Chakrabarti (2004): "Trade and Wage Inequality in Developing Countries", *Economic Enquiry*, 42(2): 295–303.

Mitra, S., T. Chatterjee and K. Gupta (2017): "Product Differentiation, Quality of Innovation and Capital Mobility: A General Equilibrium Analysis", in S. Marjit and S. Kar (eds), *International Trade, Welfare and the Theory of General Equilibrium*, Cambridge University Press, Cambridge, UK, 149–162.

Mitra, S. and K. Gupta (2017): Fragmentation, Skill Formation and International Capital Mobility", *The Singapore Economic Review*, 63(1): 1–16.

Mussa, M. and S. Rosen (1978): "Monopoly and Product Quality", *Journal of Economic Theory*, 18(2): 301–317.

Rodrik, D. (2006): "Industrial Development: Stylized Facts and Policies", *Kennedy School of GovernmentMimeograph*, Cambridge.

Sen, P., A. Ghosh and A. Barman (1997): "The Possibility of Welfare Gains with Capital Inflows in a Small Tariff-Ridden Economy", *Economica*, 64(254): 345–352.

Index

For Product Safety Concerns and Information please contact our EU
representative GPSR@taylorandfrancis.com
Taylor & Francis Verlag GmbH, Kaufingerstraße 24, 80331 München, Germany

www.ingramcontent.com/pod-product-compliance
Ingram Content Group UK Ltd.
Pitfield, Milton Keynes, MK11 3LW, UK
UKHW020142200926
475702UK00005B/875
* 9 7 8 1 0 3 2 3 0 9 5 0 7 *